LOCAL CHURCH, GLOBAL CHURCH

LOCAL CHURCH,

STEPHEN J. C. ANDES & JULIA G. YOUNG, EDITORS

Catholic Activism in Latin America from
Rerum Novarum to Vatican II

GLOBAL CHURCH

 The Catholic University of America Press | Washington, D.C.

Image on title page reproduced with the permission of the Archives of the Museu
da Imagem e do Som, Rio de Janeiro.

Library of Congress Cataloging-in-Publication Data
Names: Andes, Stephen J. C. (Stephen Joseph Carl), editor.
Title: Local church, global church : Catholic activism in Latin America from Rerum
Novarum To Vatican II / Stephen J.C. Andes and Julia G. Young, editors.
Description: Washington, D.C. : Catholic University of America Press, 2016. |
Includes bibliographical references and index.
Identifiers: LCCN 2015024729 | ISBN 9780813227917 (cloth : alk. paper)
Subjects: LCSH: Catholic Church—Latin America—History—20th century. |
Catholics—Political activity—Latin America—History—20th century.
Classification: LCC BX1426.3 .L63 2016 | DDC 261.8/0882828—dc23 LC record
available at http://lccn.loc.gov/2015024729

❖ In memory of Peter D'Agostino, whose pioneering work on transnational Catholicism has not been forgotten

Contents

Part III ❖ Fighting for the Soul of the University

Part IV ❖ Development or Liberation?

Acknowledgments

This book originated in late October 2010, in the graceful colonial town of Querétaro, Mexico, when we, Stephen Andes and Julia Young, attended a conference panel about transnational Catholic activists and the Mexican Revolution. More than a year later, in January 2012, we met again in a vastly different setting, the lobby of an enormous corporate hotel in downtown Chicago. There, with fond memories of Querétaro and hopes of collaborating further, we came up with an idea for an international conference on transnational Catholic activism in Latin America. On the back of an envelope, we made a tentative list of participants and plowed ahead with the planning. The conference that would eventually result was titled "Catholic Activism in the Americas, 1891–1962: New Comparative and Transnational Perspectives," and took place at the Catholic University of America on October 17 and 18, 2013. This book is the end result of that conference.

In retrospect, the path from Querétaro to publication seems remarkably smooth. This is only because, from the beginning, we were lucky to receive the enthusiastic support of a number of people and institutions. At the Catholic University of America, the first two people to hear about this conference and express enthusiasm were Jerry Muller, chair of the Department of History, and Lawrence Poos, dean of the School of Arts and Sciences. Both were instrumental in providing initial support. CUA president John Garvey and his staff offered invaluable encouragement and resources for the project. Peter Gribbin in the dean's office and Ramon Sola in the Department of History facilitated the process of organizing the conference. Joanna Newman in the CUA Office of Development kindly and skillfully gave advice about applying for grants. The Office of the Vice Provost and Dean of Graduate Studies at CUA also provided generous funding to support the publication of this volume. At Louisiana State University, the Office of Research and Economic Development (Council on Research Summer Stipend) and the Manship Summer Research Fellowship provided support for the planning and research of the volume. The Robert Benson Meyer Jr. Foundation awarded additional funds for the conference.

The participation, enthusiasm, and contributions of a coterie of individuals during the conference made the event a success and made the revision of the papers for publication a smooth and pleasurable process. From CUA, panel commentators William D. Dinges and Thomas M. Cohen gave their time and timely critiques. From Brandeis University, Silvia Arrom offered wise counsel and provoked lively and productive debate on the subject of Catholic activism. As keynote speaker, John McGreevy, dean of the College of Arts and Letters at the University of Notre Dame, both challenged and encouraged the panelists to think about transatlantic connections in the Catholic Church. Each of the contributors of this volume makes clear the diversity and depth of Catholic activism in Latin America. We hope their hard work, skilled research, and prompt revisions will be well served in the book that has emerged. Additionally, the two anonymous readers provided suggestions that sharpened the arguments and deepened the analysis of the manuscript. Vanessa Corcoran provided invaluable assistance by compiling the bibliography. Finally, we are very grateful to Trevor Lipscombe, director of CUA Press, who believed in this project from the beginning and ably shepherded its revision and publication.

Toward a New History of Catholic Activism in Latin America

❖ Stephen J. C. Andes and Julia G. Young

Habemus Papam (We have a pope!). The Latin phrase provided the much-anticipated announcement that the College of Cardinals had elected a new pontiff to guide the world's 1.2 billion Catholics. As the announcement rang out from the central balcony of St. Peter's Basilica on the night of March 13, 2013, the world watched. Who would it be? Another European? An Italian native? Perhaps the 115 cardinal electors had chosen to place hopes in a Vatican insider, one who knew where all the bodies were buried, so to speak, and so to right the teetering barque of St. Peter, which most commentators agreed had veered off course during the pontificate of Benedict XVI (2005–2013) after a series of public relations fiascos, a faltering administration, and the fallout from priestly sex abuse and financial corruption in the Vatican Bank.

Then, it happened: the balcony doors opened and into the spotlight stepped Cardinal Jorge Mario Bergoglio. Not a Vatican insider, not an Italian native, but an Argentine—and a Jesuit, to boot. Shouts of "*¡Tenemos un papa latinoamericano!*" (We have a Latin American pope!) came from St. Peter's square. Bergoglio smiled at the crowd behind owlish rounded spectacles: "You know that the work of the conclave is to give a bishop to Rome," he began. "It seems as if my brother cardinals went to find him from the end of the earth, but here we are."

The new pope's comments articulated the distance, both spatial and symbolic, between Rome and the Catholic world in Latin America. Until this election, there had never been a pontiff from the Western Hemisphere, despite the fact that approximately half the world's Catholics live in Latin America. Here, then, embodied in one person, the "ends of the earth" had come to Rome to govern.

Immediately following the election of Pope Francis, the global media sought information about the Catholic Church in Latin America. Reporters peppered scholars and Catholic insiders with questions, trying to understand the religious context that had produced the new pontiff. In particular, the media focused on the past five decades: a time span that overlapped not only with Bergoglio's adult life but also with a series of watershed moments and profound challenges for the Catholic Church in Latin America.[1] This focus on the post-1965 period was understandable. After all, the era saw a remarkable amount of Catholic activism: political and social organizing by laypeople and clergy alike. This organizing centered around three main developments. First, the Second Vatican Council (1962–1965) introduced widespread reforms—endorsed and promoted by many within the Latin American episcopate—that promised to take the church and its faithful in a new, more liberal, and lay-oriented direction. Then, this period also saw the birth (and, later, the condemnation) of Liberation theology, which challenged established social structures and promoted grassroots organizing by calling for the "preferential option for the poor." Finally, from the 1970s onward, the Latin American church has continuously struggled to respond adequately to human rights abuses in the region, at times serving as a conservative ally for dictatorial governments while, in other times and places, aligning with and protecting victims of state-led violence.

The fervent media interest in the history of post-1965 Latin American Catholic activism is perhaps ephemeral, driven mainly by the need to understand Pope Francis and the context in which his career developed. And within the scholarly literature on Catholic activism in modern Latin America, there is a similar emphasis on the recent past. Indeed, a vast array of studies, while rich, layered, and illuminating, focuses heavily on the post–Vatican II period.[2] Yet such a fixed spotlight

---

1. In particular, commentators focused on the new pope's relationship to Liberation theology and his actions as provincial Jesuit superior during Argentina's "Dirty War," or the period of military dictatorship (1976–1983) in Argentina, when thousands of dissidents, including many priests, were kidnapped, tortured, and murdered. Several books, previously published while then-Cardinal Bergoglio was archbishop of Buenos Aires, quickly received renewed exposure: see Horacio Verbitsky, *El silencio: De Paulo VI a Bergoglio: Las relaciones secretas de la Iglesia con la ESMA*, 3rd ed. (Buenos Aires: Editorial Sudamericana, 2005); Sergio Rubin and Francesca Ambrogetti, *El papa Francesco: Conversaciones con Jorge Bergoglio* (Barcelona: Ediciones B, S. A., 2013).

2. A large portion of the literature is concerned with explaining the social and political

has left the rest of the stage in shadows. By concentrating on the most recent five decades, historians and social scientists have only partially explained why Latin America has developed as such an important region for the global church—and why it has produced a pope that is so oriented toward social questions, particularly economic inequality.[3] Indeed, for a fuller understanding of the context that formed the contemporary Latin American church in all its complexity, we must look farther back into history. If we do so, we discover that the changes that seemed to have originated with the Second Vatican Council—an increased focus on social justice, lay organizing, and clerical activism—were actually well underway by the late nineteenth century.[4] Furthermore, this earlier period of Catholic activism in Latin America was remarkably transnational.

NEW RESEARCH DIRECTIONS

This book investigates the many forms of Catholic activism in Latin America between the 1890s and 1962 (from the publication of the papal encyclical *Rerum novarum* to the years just prior to the Second Vati-

changes developing within the Latin American church after the Second Vatican Council and the Latin American Bishops Conference held in Medellín, Colombia (1968), which sought to apply the reforms of Vatican II to a Latin American context. Among the numerous studies mainly written from the perspective of political science, sociology, and religious studies, see, for example, Enrique Dussel, *A History of the Church in Latin America: Colonialism to Liberation (1492–1979)* (Grand Rapids, Mich.: Eerdmans, 1981); Brian H. Smith, *The Church and Politics in Chile: Challenges to Modern Catholicism* (Princeton, N.J.: Princeton University Press, 1982); Edward L. Cleary, *Crisis and Change: The Church in Latin America Today* (Maryknoll, N.Y.: Orbis Books, 1985); Paul E. Sigmund, *Liberation Theology at the Crossroads: Democracy or Revolution?* (Oxford: Oxford University Press, 1990); Dermot Keogh, ed., *Church and Politics in Latin America* (New York: St. Martin's Press, 1990); John Burdick, *Looking for God in Brazil: The Progressive Catholic Church in Urban Brazil's Religious Arena* (Berkeley: University of California Press, 1993); Anthony Gill, *Rendering unto Caesar: The Catholic Church and the State in Latin America* (Chicago: The University of Chicago Press, 1998).

3. An important exception to this trend is the work by Ana María Bidegain. See, for example, Ana María Bidegain, "From Catholic Action to Liberation Theology: The Historical Process of the Laity in Latin America in the Twentieth Century," The Helen Kellogg Institute for International Studies, University of Notre Dame, Working Paper 48, November 1985.

4. Three recent surveys of the Catholic Church in Latin America take note of this point. See Lee M. Penyak and Walter J. Petry, eds., *Religion and Society in Latin America: Interpretive Essays from Conquest to Present* (Maryknoll, N.Y.: Orbis Books, 2009); John Frederick Schwaller, *The History of the Catholic Church in Latin America: From Conquest to Revolution and Beyond* (New York: New York University Press, 2011); and John Lynch, *New Worlds: A Religious History of Latin America* (New Haven, Conn.: Yale University Press, 2012).

can Council). It argues that this period saw a variety of lay and clerical responses to the social changes wrought by industrialization, political shifts, and increasing secularization. Spurred by these local developments as well as by initiatives from the Vatican, and galvanized by national projects of secular state building, Catholic activists across Latin America developed new ways of organizing in order to effect social and political change within their communities. These forms of Catholic activism developed not uniformly but, rather, as a multitude of streams—sometimes diverging, sometimes converging. Thus, it was not a single river that led naturally to Vatican II but, rather, an alluvial floodplain from whose fertile soils the variety of Catholic activism grew in the 1960s and beyond. Indeed, Catholic activism in Latin America was always plural.

Catholic responses to the nation-state during this period, as well as producing profound social ferment within local and national communities, gave rise to a multitude of transnational movements that connected Latin American actors to counterparts in North America and Europe. The Catholic Church presents a particularly cohesive example of a transnational religious network. In this framework, churches at the local and national level were linked via pastoral initiatives to the papacy, while maintaining "a good deal of autonomy at the local level."[5] Transnational religious networks in Latin America served to "broaden, deepen, and customize a global religious system that [was] already legitimate, powerful, and well organized."[6] Whereas the study of international history emphasizes the interactions between and among nation-states, transnational history examines "units both greater and smaller than the nation-state."[7] The Catholic activists studied in this book were certainly embedded within a national context, remaining influential on the character and makeup of Catholic activism in Latin America. However, a transnational perspective decenters statist and elite narratives of Catholic activism, revealing that national loyalties were but one of many "potent forces" that motivated action.[8] The study of transnational Catholicism, then, emphasizes the interconnections,

5. Manuel A. Vásquez and Marie Friedmann Marquardt, *Globalizing the Sacred: Religion across the Americas* (New Brunswick, N.J.: Rutgers University Press, 2003), 56.

6. Levitt quoted in Vásquez and Marquardt, *Globalizing the Sacred*, 56.

7. Micol Seigel, "Beyond Compare: Comparative Method after the Transnational Turn," *Radical History Review* 91 (Winter 2005): 63.

8. Ibid.

shared symbols, and intertwined mobilization that characterized the Catholic activist movements of Latin America, even before Vatican II. Global Catholicism and local practice have a long history of interaction: a story that certainly predates the Second Vatican Council. Susanne Hoeber Rudolph adroitly states that "religious communities are among the oldest of transnationals: Sufi orders, Catholic missionaries, and Buddhist monks carried word and praxis across vast spaces before those places became nation-states or even states."[9] Indeed, the Catholic Church has been doing its work across borders for some time now. Peter Brown long ago wrote about the cult of saints, especially relics, as a kind of "global" currency uniting the local and the universal in the early Christian centuries.[10] Yet, in studies of the nineteenth- and twentieth-century Catholic renewal in Europe and the Americas, scholars have not given ample analysis to the translocal and transnational interconnections within the Catholic Church, which became critical to the energy, plurality, and endurance of Latin American Catholic activism leading up to, and moving through, the Second Vatican Council.[11] Moreover, by studying Latin America as a whole—"zooming out," so to speak—beyond regional and national varieties of Catholic thought and praxis, the emerging "map" assumes a larger degree of transnational and translocal complexity, connected across regional, hemispheric, transatlantic, and international borders.[12]

This book's focus on the pre–Vatican II period reveals that Latin American Catholicism was already firmly linked to global currents before the 1960s. In the area of politics, young lay activists in Latin America looked to European models of Christian Democracy for direction in forming their own opposition parties in the 1940s.[13] In the social and religious spheres, a hierarchically led lay apostolate called Catholic Ac-

9. Susanne Hoeber Rudolph, "Introduction: Religion, States, and Transnational Civil Society," in *Transnational Religion and Fading States*, ed. Susanne Hoeber Rudolph and P. Piscatori (Boulder, Colo.: Westview Press, 1997), 1.

10. Peter Brown, *The Cult of the Saints: Its Rise and Function in Latin Christianity*, The Haskell Lectures on History of Religions. (Chicago: The University of Chicago Press, 1982), chapter 5.

11. For a recent exception, see Austen Ivereigh, ed., *The Politics of Religion in an Age of Revival* (London: Institute for the Study of the Americas, 2000).

12. On the value of a transnational perspective applied to Latin American Catholicism, see Stephen J. C. Andes, *The Vatican and Catholic Activism in Mexico and Chile: The Politics of Transnational Catholicism, 1920–1940* (Oxford: Oxford University Press, 2014), 1–8.

13. Scott Mainwaring and Timothy Scully, eds., *Christian Democracy in Latin America: Electoral Competition and Regime Conflicts* (Palo Alto, Calif.: Stanford University Press, 2003).

tion dominated the activities of many Catholics worldwide from 1930 to 1960.[14] Jesuits trained in European social Catholicism directed the formation of many Catholic activists in the period. Catholic women participated in international youth organizations, traveled abroad on fundraising tours, and helped construct global networks focused on moralization, Eucharistic piety, and religious education. Thus, even while local religious practices provided a dynamic source for Catholicism in Latin America between the late nineteenth century and the 1960s, Latin American Catholics also fueled—and were fueled by—a global Catholic culture with common symbols, values, and methods.[15] Each of the eleven chapters of this volume, therefore, investigates Latin American Catholic activism during the 1891–1962 period, and highlights its transnational character.[16] Taken together, these chapters help explain not only the deeper roots of Catholic activism in Latin America but also the long-standing transnational bonds that kept Latin American Catholics firmly connected to the global church and ensured that the region would become ever more prominent in the global Catholic landscape through the twentieth century and beyond. Therefore, the give-and-take relationship between the local church and the global church gave rise to the variety of Catholic activism in Latin America before Vatican II.

14. For a recent collection of essays on Catholic Action in the United States, see Jeremy Bonner, Christopher D. Denny, and Mary Beth Fraser Connolly, eds., *Empowering the People of God: Catholic Action before and after Vatican II* (New York: Fordham University Press, 2014).

15. Historians have produced a vast literature on Latin American Catholicism in the late-nineteenth and early-twentieth centuries, but it mainly focuses on local and national stories. For some representative examples, see Jeffrey L. Klaiber, *The Catholic Church in Peru, 1821–1985: A Social History* (Washington, D.C.: The Catholic University of America Press, 1992); Edward Wright-Rios, *Revolutions in Mexican Catholicism: Reform and Revelation in Oaxaca, 1887–1934* (Durham, N.C.: Duke University Press, 2009); Ben Fallaw, *Religion and State Formation in Postrevolutionary Mexico* (Durham, N.C.: Duke University Press, 2013); Kenneth P. Serbin, *Needs of the Heart: A Social and Cultural History of Brazil's Clergy and Seminaries* (Notre Dame, Ind.: University of Notre Dame Press, 2006); Michael A. Burdick, *For God and the Fatherland: Religion and Politics in Argentina* (Albany: State University of New York Press, 1996); Patricia Londoño-Vega, *Religion, Society, and Culture in Colombia: Antioquia and Medellín, 1850–1930* (Oxford: Oxford University Press, 2002).

16. A new historical literature has begun to emerge, linking currents within global Catholicism to the United States and Latin America. See Peter D'Agostino, *Rome in America: Transnational Catholic Ideology from the Risorgimento to Fascism* (Chapel Hill: University of North Carolina Press, 2003); Federico Finchelstein, *Transatlantic Fascism: Ideology, Violence, and the Sacred in Argentina, 1919–1945* (Durham, N.C.: Duke University Press, 2010); Emelio Betances, *The Catholic Church and Power Politics in Latin America: The Dominican Case in Comparative Perspective* (Lanham, Md.: Rowman & Littlefield, 2007); and Susan Fitzpatrick-Behrens, *The Maryknoll Catholic Mission in Peru, 1943–1989: Transnational Faith and Transformations* (Notre Dame, Ind.: University of Notre Dame Press, 2011).

PART I: CATHOLIC SOCIAL ENCYCLICALS
ACROSS BORDERS

For the first quarter century after the wars of independence (ca. 1810–1820), the newly formed republics in Latin America were plagued by debt, economic insolvency, and the colonial legacy of regionalism, which acted as an obstacle to state formation. Throughout Latin America, conservatives dominated the political and economic landscape, seeking stability through continuity with the colonial past. But by approximately 1850, the political scene began to shift. New governments throughout Latin America were led by liberals bent on change: in economics, they built important infrastructure necessary for an export-led development model; in the political sphere, liberals touted electoral democracy and broadened citizenship rights; and in society, they endeavored to limit the power of the Catholic Church. As the bureaucratic muscle of the liberal state began to grow, the church became an important competitor for resources as well as for the allegiance of citizens: in other words, the church entered a battle for hearts and minds.[17]

Liberals repeatedly attempted to limit and check church privilege and power, placing civil registers under their own domain, fighting to control education, abolishing colonial *fueros* (privileges), and expropriating ecclesiastical properties. The historical process whereby the state endeavored to shift the boundaries of control over these functions away from the church and into the realm of state auspices can be defined as one aspect of secularization.[18] The perceived threat of secularization would become a major factor in rallying Catholics to fight the state to maintain its traditional powers and privileges. This battle became increasingly important in the early twentieth century, and lay Catholics began to mobilize in response. The church, and many lay activists, did not intend to loosen their grasp on the national soul, which they felt was rooted in Catholicism.

In the late nineteenth and early twentieth centuries, then, Latin American Catholic activists mobilized against state-led disestablishment. In fact, the battle over secularization was often embedded with-

17. John Lynch, "The Catholic Church in Latin America, 1830–1930," in *The Cambridge History of Latin America, Vol. IV, c. 1870–1930*, ed. Leslie Bethell (Cambridge: Cambridge University Press, 1986), 528–29.

18. Sol Serrano, *¿Qué hacer con Dios en la República?: Política y secularización en Chile (1845–1885)* (Santiago, Chile: Fondo de Cultura Económica, 2008), 22.

in the larger issue of state sponsorship of the Roman Catholic Church. In practical terms, separation of church and state represented a huge blow to ecclesiastical revenues: in many cases the postcolonial state inherited the role of patron after independence.[19] Moreover, church property continued to be a major source of income for the institutional church. Anticlerical governments threatened church wealth with nationalization, succeeding in Mexico in the 1850s. Education also became a major area of conflict. The Catholic Church had been the sole provider of education during the colonial era, and this continued after independence. Liberal governments endeavored to remove the education system from church control and, with it, church influence over the religious and moral training of Latin American citizens.

Processes of disestablishment in the region developed unevenly and followed different timelines. Mexico's separation of church and state occurred with the promulgation of a new constitution in 1857; Chile, on the other hand, separated church and state much later, in 1925.[20] Vatican officials in the Secretariat of State recognized the growing trend toward disestablishment, developing institutional mechanisms to deal with the threat. A cadre of papal representatives (apostolic nuncios, internuncios, and apostolic delegates) was trained to help oversee negotiations with Latin American governments. In the best scenario, papal nuncios would negotiate an official treaty, called a concordat, with secular powers, protecting church wealth, education, and the right of the Vatican to appoint new bishops. In practice, however, Vatican officials allowed compromise on disestablishment, especially when the state showed signs of moderation.[21]

In the Vatican, the turn toward negotiated compromise developed in relationship to the Holy See's historic encounter with Italian nationalism. The loss of the Papal States—and finally Rome in 1870—to Italy required subsequent popes to work toward a settlement via diplomacy and pragmatic conciliation. Pope Pius IX (1846–1878) failed to gain

19. For the classic work on church–state conflict in Latin America, see J. Lloyd Mecham, *Church and State in Latin America: A History of Politicoecclesiastical Relations* (Chapel Hill: University of North Carolina Press, 1966).

20. Ibid.

21. In Chile, for example, Vatican officials felt that the 1925 Constitution, which disestablished the church, represented a net gain for Catholic interests in the country, especially in terms of state compensation paid to the church after separation. See Máximo Pacheco Gómez, *La separación de la Iglesia y el Estado en Chile y la diplomacia vaticana* (Santiago, Chile: Editorial Andrés Bello, 2004).

traction through a policy of intransigence, or the wholesale rejection of the Italian nation. Beginning with his successor, Leo XIII (1878–1903), the Vatican began to pursue legitimacy through legal means.[22]

The fight against secularization and state power translated into a global call for Catholic renewal through organized Catholic activism. If the papacy could not win back its lost patrimony, which implied sovereignty over its own affairs, the popes employed a strategy of consolidating spiritual control over the Catholic world. Pollard notes that "after 1870, the popes took upon themselves more and more the task of laying down to the Catholic hierarchy, clergy and laity of the world rules and regulations regarding not only matters of spirituality, religious doctrine and discipline, but political, economic and social issues as well."[23] The teaching authority of the papacy grew considerably in the late nineteenth and early twentieth centuries, exemplified by a sharp increase in the publication of decrees, apostolic exhortations, encyclicals, and similar documents. Most notably, the 1870 declaration of Papal Infallibility underscored the move toward increased control over Catholic doctrine, belief, and practice. Concomitant with papal centralization, was a pronounced "Romanization" effort, often referred to as ultramontanism, in which European religious orders began to flood Latin America, papal nuncios sought to enforce Rome's line among Catholic bishops, and in 1899, the Latin American Plenary Council laid down new mandates for the region in terms of church discipline. The Pontificio Colegio Pío Latino Americano, a seminary in Rome, educated several generations of Latin American bishops.[24] Papal documents addressed the state and Catholic participation in public life (*Immortale Dei*, 1885) as well as Catholic participation in combating the "social question," or the problems brought on by increased industrialization and urbanization.

Many scholars assert that Pope Leo XIII's encyclical *Rerum novarum* (1891) heralded a crucial watershed moment in the development of "social Catholicism."[25] And indeed, the encyclical was a crucial "call

22. Frank J. Coppa, *The Modern Papacy since 1789*, Longman History of the Papacy, ed. A. D. Wright (London: Longman, 1998), 122–27.

23. John F. Pollard, *Money and the Rise of the Modern Papacy: Financing the Vatican, 1850–1950* (Cambridge: Cambridge University Press, 2008), 7.

24. Lisa M. Edwards, *Roman Virtues: The Education of Latin American Clergy in Rome, 1858–1962* (New York: Peter Lang, 2011).

25. See, for example, Paul Misner, *Social Catholicism in Europe: From the Onset of Industrialization to the First World War* (New York: Crossroad Publishing Company, 1991).

to arms" that prompted profound and widespread changes to Catholic life in Latin America. *Rerum novarum* offered an assessment of the condition of the working class in the capitalist age, stating that "some opportune remedy must be found quickly for the misery and wretchedness pressing so unjustly on the majority of the working class."[26] This remedy was not to overturn the capitalist system, but to revitalize civil society through *Christian* associations, organizations, and institutions. As the encyclical stated, citing the book of Ecclesiastes 4:9–10, "[i]t is better that two should be together than one; for they have the advantage of their society. If one fall he shall be supported by the other. Woe to him that is alone, for when he falleth he hath none to lift him up." The pope's encyclical further elucidated that "it is this natural impulse which binds men together in civil society; and it is likewise this which leads them to join together in associations," concluding "it will be easy for Christian working men to solve [the problem of the working classes] aright if they will form associations, choose wise guides, and follow on the path which with so much advantage to themselves and the common weal was trodden by their fathers before them."[27]

Certainly, Catholic activists across the Americas took the directives of *Rerum novarum* very seriously. But as the two chapters in part one of this volume reveal, grassroots Catholic associations preceded the publication of the encyclical, sometimes taking strength and sustenance from the pope's words, while at other times showing very little influence from the papal document. First, Lisa M. Edwards examines the unique dilemmas facing the papacy and national bishops in Latin America. Her chapter explores how the papacy's priorities in Italy (to carve out a political, religious, and symbolic space for itself after the *Risorgimento*) did not always correspond to the national vision of Latin American hierarchies, parish priests, or lay activists. Nevertheless, Edwards shows that pioneering bishops and entrepreneurial priests often successfully channeled grassroots Catholic activism into lay associations directed by the hierarchy. Within this framework, papal policy remained flexible enough to allow local, regional, and national differences, even while attempting to set boundaries around acceptable forms of social and political activism. Therefore, although *Rerum novarum*

26. Leo XIII, *Rerum novarum*, in Claudia Carlen, ed., *The Papal Encyclicals, 1878–1903* [hereafter vol. II] (Ann Arbor, Mich.: The Pierian Press, 1990), 241–57.
27. Ibid.

provided both an invitation and a framework for Catholics worldwide to undertake new forms of collective political action, the encyclical coincided with several ongoing historical developments and processes that affected Catholics—particularly urbanization, industrialization, and migration. These events, and their local and national particularities, were the important spark for a global wave of Catholic political and social activism in Latin America, and allowed Catholics in the region to interact in new ways with the Vatican and its representatives.

Narrowing in from a pan–Latin American framework, we turn to the fascinating case of Brazil in Dain Borges's chapter. Here, Borges argues that Catholic social activism in Brazil developed sporadically and unevenly since the 1870s. Even before the separation of church and state in the Republican revolution of 1889–1891, the religious field in Brazil had diversified from a monopoly into a semi-monopoly that was much more plural and contentious. Catholic doctrine and Catholic practice faced polemical challenges from freethinking anticlerical intellectuals and Masons, proselytizing Protestant missionaries, and Spiritists. After disestablishment in 1891, the upper clergy was forced to respond to a new landscape. Bishops emphasized organizational rebuilding through the recruitment of European religious orders and secular priests. Some of those European friars and nuns, and a handful of Brazilian clerical and lay activists and intellectuals, experimented with Catholic education, labor circles, mass media, and the new devotional associations. The most interesting—although perhaps not the most effective and influential—Catholic intellectual among them was the volatile polemicist Padre Júlio Maria (Júlio César Moraes Carneiro). Borges shows that Padre Júlio Maria was among the few to respond to Pope Leo XIII's *Rerum novarum*. Throughout the period, diversity aided the movements of Catholic activism in Brazil, allowing for a variety of forms and styles of lay associations and religious congregations, which provided Catholic organizations greater flexibility in responding to Brazil's national situation after disestablishment.

PART II: MARTYRDOM AND CATHOLIC RENEWAL IN THE MEXICAN REVOLUTION

In the first few decades of the twentieth century, new forms of Catholic activism included the formation of Catholic labor unions, political organizations and associations, militant lay associations, and numerous other new social groups, all of which attracted growing numbers of younger Catholics. These organizations and activities presented novel challenges to national governments, as political leaders in the late nineteenth and early twentieth centuries sought to create and consolidate national identities. As a result of this renewed Catholic activism, church–state conflicts and confrontations in Latin America surged in the early decades of the twentieth century and would continue into the 1960s.

One of the most significant instances of church–state tension took place in Mexico and resonated throughout the Americas. This was the Cristero War (1926–1929), a violent uprising that occurred after Mexican political leaders imposed new limits on the Catholic Church in the wake of the Mexican Revolution (1910–1940). This conflict would capture the attention of Catholic activist groups in numerous Latin American countries as well as in the United States, and Catholics interacted on a transnational level to confront the Mexican government. Matthew Butler's chapter describes the activities of a men's organization, the Mexican Nocturnal Adoration (Adoración Nocturna Mexicana, or ANM), which brought together a variety of diverse participants—from sophisticated city slickers to ranch hands on horseback—to worship the Eucharist during the bloody church–state conflict in Mexico. Butler provides an important corrective to the "feminization-of-religion" thesis, which contends that Catholicism in Europe, North America, and Latin America underwent a demographic and discursive shift in the late nineteenth century; in essence, church organizations and the sacramental life of the church were led primarily by women, accompanied by a more sentimental and affective religious practice. In contrast, Butler shows that groups such as the ANM recoded certain Eucharistic activities as "male" and created a paradigm of sacrificial religiosity for men. This "masculinization of religion" to Butler does not represent a "counterfeminization: checking or reversing the growing predominance of women, and women's religion, in the church" but, rather, "an overall reinvigoration of Catholicism that involved both men and women, whose declared aim was a religious restoration."

As Catholic activism created overlapping gendered categories, Revolutionary upheaval in Mexico produced increasingly gendered violence. Robert Curley explores how American priest (and later bishop)

Francis Kelley collected graphic witness testimonies from victims of religious violence—many of them female—in Mexico during the most violent phase of the revolution (1910–1917), and awoke an American Catholic audience to the growing tension between church and state in Mexico. The chapter focuses on Kelley's original foray into Mexican politics in 1914 and 1915, beginning when he learned of the refugee problem in Texas, in the fall of 1914, and ending with the U.S. recognition of Carrancista revolutionaries as the legitimate ruling party in October 1915.[28] Curley provides a careful reading and source critique of Kelley's diatribe, *The Book of Red and Yellow* (1915), which most historians have viewed as a fanciful and overembellished piece of propaganda. As Curley concedes, it may be impossible to decide whether Kelley's claims are true, but it might also be unnecessary. Curley's use of Kelley's personal archive shows that his assertions of Carrancista anticlerical violence against Catholics, and in particular the alleged rape of female religious, was backed up by affidavits of witness testimony of the events he describes in *The Book of Red and Yellow*. Thus, Curley's chapter considers the construction of Catholic memory, the historiographic uses of the body, and the question of whether, and to what extent, the book played a role in representing subaltern identities—giving a voice to the victims of war rape.

Because of the anticlerical violence of the revolution and the Cristero War, Catholic activists in Mexico conducted a variety of clandestine political activities between 1910 and 1920. Yves Solis investigates one such Catholic organization using fascinating new sources from both Vatican and Mexican archives. He traces the development and activities of the Union of Mexican Catholics (Unión de Católicos Mexicanos, or the U) from its foundation in 1915 by Mexican bishop (and future archbishop and apostolic delegate) Luis María Martínez to its survival as an exclusive Catholic organization during the Cristero War. In examining the activities and practices of the U, Solis describes an organization whose central goal was no less than the destruction of the Mexican revolutionary state. Furthermore, Solis demonstrates the importance of family networks to Catholic political activism in Latin America. He

---

28. The "Carrancistas" were so named for Venustiano Carranza, a northern revolutionary from the Mexican State of Coahuila, whose stated goal was to write a new national charter. This goal was realized in the writing of the 1917 Constitution. Carranza served as president of Mexico from 1917 to 1920.

also underscores that Mexican Catholic organizations sometimes competed for influence and power, even as they purportedly fought the same enemy. These tensions tested—and contested—the power of the Vatican, which tried and failed to close the secret society. Solis's chapter also illuminates the multidimensional character of the Roman Catholic Church. Far from monolithic, papal policy reflected the European bias of career Vatican bureaucrats, often at odds, yet sometimes converging, with national episcopacies, parish priests, and lay activists in Latin America.[29]

During Mexico's revolutionary upheaval, Catholic women played a leading role in reconstructing the organizational life of the church in the aftermath of 1910, as well as after the Cristero War. Important groups such as the Association of Catholic Ladies (founded in 1912 and renamed the Mexican Catholic Women's Union in 1922) and the Mexican Young Women's Catholic Association (f. 1926) mobilized thousands of Catholic women, formed occupational societies, and assisted in resistance to the Revolutionary state. Stephen J. C. Andes's chapter charts the life of an elite, educated Mexican woman who—deeply devoted to the newly canonized Saint Thérèse of Lisieux, known as the Little Flower—established Mexican Catholic women's associations and Mexican women's labor unions, and traveled tirelessly to promote her vision of higher education for Catholic women. The efforts of Sofia del Valle moved in transnational directions, even while reflecting local and national Catholic concerns, devotions, and priorities. Just as war in Europe created new possibilities for female mobilization, revolution in Mexico facilitated a revitalized public role for women, whom the male

29. The government and organization of the Roman Catholic Church can cause some confusion to the uninitiated. At the church's helm stands the pope, assisted by the Roman Curia, a body of clergy composed of cardinals, bishops, and priests. The "papacy" is a term referring to the pope and the Roman Curia. The central administration of the church is divided into congregations, or departments, staffed by the Roman Curia. The Secretariat of State is the branch of the papacy tasked with foreign affairs, led by a cardinal appointed by the pope. It was this body that deliberated and set policy regarding matters of church–state importance for Latin America and the wider Catholic world. The "Vatican" is used as shorthand, parallel to the way in which "Washington" or "Downing Street" is used to signify the state administration of the United States or Great Britain. Pastoral care is divided into archdioceses, dioceses, and parishes, duly led by archbishops, bishops, priests, and deacons. The "hierarchy" refers most often to archbishops and bishops, while the clergy signifies ordained priests. The "laity" refers to the nonordained. See Andes, *The Vatican and Catholic Activism in Mexico and Chile*, xiii; and Thomas Reese, *Inside the Vatican: The Politics and Organization of the Catholic Church* (Cambridge, Mass.: Harvard University Press, 1998).

hierarchy viewed as an important vanguard of the Catholic revival. Del Valle was given the mission of fundraising in the United States for the newly established associations of Catholic Action. She traveled across the Catholic networks of North America and participated in the burgeoning Catholic women's movement in Europe. Andes argues that like many Catholic women in Europe and the Americas, Sofia del Valle "helped shape this new public role for female lay activists and, in the process, created remarkably durable organizations which came to dominate the Catholic Action movement."

PART III: FIGHTING FOR THE SOUL OF THE UNIVERSITY

A central focus in the scholarship on modern Latin America has been the role of university students, who, in the late 1960s, mobilized across the region to effect political change. Scholars of Catholic activism in Latin America, however, have noticed something new about student organizing: first, student movements started well before the 1960s, and second, they were much more politically diverse than many historians have assumed. Indeed, student movements included not only liberals but also conservatives, and—of most interest here—prominent Catholic groups. During the 1940s and 1950s, Catholic student groups assumed a pivotal role in political activism in many different arenas.

Jaime M. Pensado investigates a group of students who advocated for a middle position between capitalism and communism—one rooted in Catholic values, as well as the social teachings of the Catholic Church—in order to improve the lives of the poor and repressed in the developing world. In addition, these student activists saw themselves as "a new generation of spiritual leaders" who could offer a moral critique not only of global society, but also of the Mexican government. By hosting national conferences, generating numerous publications, and promoting cooperation with other youth organizations, the Corporation of Mexican Students (Corporación de Estudiantes Mexicanos, or CEM) became a vibrant and successful training ground for a new generation of Catholic political leaders. Through his analysis of the activities of the CEM, Pensado demonstrates how conservative members of Mexico's middle class, including female Catholic activists, were transformed into key political players. Partly as a result, the church in Mexico underwent a resurgence in political status during the 1950s, forging a new and productive relationship with the Institutional Revolutionary Party, and recovering much of the ground that had been lost after the church–state conflicts of the 1920s and 1930s.

The political activity of Catholic university students is likewise a central focus of Colin M. Snider's chapter. In Brazil in the 1950s, there were only four Catholic universities, all of which were relatively new. Catholic student activism in the 1950s, therefore, operated via the Catholic University Youth (Juventude Universidade Católica, or JUC), a lay organization that had its roots in the Catholic Action movement of the 1930s, when Rio de Janeiro's Cardinal Sebastião Leme began to reassert the church's presence in politics. In 1950 JUC became a national organization, attracting thousands of participants by sponsoring masses, pilgrimages, and other religious events. Soon, the organization developed a larger presence in politics at the national and local levels: its leaders, influenced by Catholic philosophers such as Jacques Maritain and Emanuel Mounier, promoted a move toward social activism, especially university reform. This transformation reflected part of a broader shift toward "a social Christianity that sought to apply Christian ideals to real-world problems in order to improve the standing of the economically and socially marginalized." As a result, by 1960, Catholic university students in Brazil were steeped in the language of Catholic activism—a language that they would put to use during a series of massive student strikes in the 1960s. Through their studies of Catholic student movements, both Pensado and Snider demonstrate how Latin American youth had established themselves as Catholic activists well before the tumultuous period of the late 1960s.

PART IV: DEVELOPMENT OR LIBERATION?

Youth groups were certainly not the only movements focusing on social justice. At mid-century, Latin American societies faced ever more urgent demographic challenges: populations across the region were growing rapidly, but so, too, was economic inequality. Citizens found that the state could not meet the needs of the burgeoning populations of rural and urban poor, and increasingly, social groups turned to development projects to address poverty and related problems such as lack of education, infrastructure, employment, and indigenous rights. During the 1940s, 1950s, and 1960s, Catholic activists in Latin America experimented with new development projects within their societies. In addition, they forged new connections with Catholic lay and religious organizations throughout Europe and the Americas, appealing for training and funding and importing successful techniques and adapting them as they saw fit within the Latin American context.

One of these development projects originated in a remote village in Nova Scotia and would eventually be exported to a variety of sites throughout Latin America. Catherine C. LeGrand presents a transnational study of a social and economic movement that took form in the Canadian Maritimes in the 1920s and 1930s and later spread into the Caribbean and Latin America. Spearheaded by local Canadian Catholic priests associated with St. Francis Xavier University, the Antigonish Movement (AM) used adult education to forge communities and community leaders among the farmers, fishermen, and miners of Nova Scotia; in the 1930s it stimulated the formation of hundreds of study groups, credit unions and, cooperatives throughout Atlantic Canada. Early on, the "Antigonish Way" attracted international attention as a model for grassroots mobilization of poor people to bring them together to solve their own economic problems through cooperation. In her chapter, LeGrand demonstrates how AM penetrated Latin America, eventually playing a leading role in a diversity of Catholic social action projects that developed in the region during the cold war. By doing so, she traces how "community development"—often presumed to be a facet of Liberation theology—was in fact an earlier type of Catholic social action. Indeed, the Antigonish Movement not only predated Liberation theology but prepared the way for it as well.

Mary Roldán describes the history of the Colombian Catholic organization Popular Cultural Action (Acción Cultural Popular, or ACPO), which grew from modest origins in 1947, when Father José Joaquín Salceda, a twenty-six-year-old priest in the small town of Sutatenza, built a crude radio transmitter and began promoting adult rural literacy and rural development. Over the next decade, the organization expanded into "a multimedia-based educational juggernaut with transnational influence, partners and funding lauded ... as the model for Catholic-directed, radio-based rural education and community development." In her chapter, Roldán traces the ways that ACPO connected to other Catholic groups and individuals beyond Colombia's borders. She argues that the organization's founders were influenced not only by papal encyclicals such as *Rerum novarum* and *Quadragesimo anno* (1931) but also by Franklin Delano Roosevelt's New Deal and the U.S. Catholic Church's rural ministry in the 1930s. In particular, she looks at connections between ACPO and the National Catholic Welfare Conference, the National Catholic Rural Life Conference, and the U.S. Catholic Bishops Department of Social Action. These collaborations—strengthened by the tensions of the cold war—"opened the door to the flow of missionaries and humanitarian assistance typical of South-North connections in the post–Vatican II era." By investigating these connections, Roldán opens a window into the multifarious political, religious, and social factors that shaped Catholic transnational development efforts during the cold war years.

Transnational development projects were often introduced by foreign missionaries, but they were maintained—and as a result, altered—by local actors. This was certainly true in Guatemala, as Susan Fitzpatrick-Behrens demonstrates in her chapter. There, American Maryknoll missionaries—many of whom had received training at Antigonish—established a rural cooperative movement for Maya peasants in the western highland department of Huehuetenango. This movement aimed to create opportunities for financial, educational, and religious growth within communities. Cooperative development did not happen smoothly, however. Fitzpatrick-Behrens vividly describes the challenges and frustrations faced by two such Maryknoll priests, who were forced to reconcile their ideas about Catholicism with local devotional practices that occasionally "offended both their religious sensibilities and their Catholic sense of social justice." Over time, however, both the missionaries and the Maya villagers adjusted their expectations and developed a successful catechetical system whereby villagers would introduce Catholic doctrine to their communities. At the same time, they started a successful credit union system that allowed villagers access to new economic opportunities. Eventually, the Huehuetenango credit union, as well as five others, created the National Federation of Savings and Credit Cooperatives of Guatemala, which would cooperate with the U.S. Agency of International Development and other U.S. government agencies. Although the cooperatives became subject to government surveillance and state-sponsored terror during and after 1966, they had proved instrumental in fostering a spirit of solidarity, economic justice, and cooperation among Maya villagers. The chapters by

LeGrand, Roldán, and Fitzpatrick-Behrens each reveal a nuanced and, indeed complex, relationship between Catholic activist movements and a variety of state and nonstate agencies alike. Their contributions showcase how social Catholicism was already grappling with how to answer pressing issues of inequality, poverty, and exclusion before the 1960s and the development of Liberation theology.

CATHOLIC ACTIVISM IN LATIN AMERICA
BEFORE VATICAN II

Chapters in this volume suggest that Latin American Catholicism operated in a global sphere long before Vatican II, and certainly prior to the election of a Latin American pope in 2013. In fact, the dynamism of Latin American Catholic activism gathered momentum, matured, and developed in a variety of directions during the century or so predating the Second Vatican Council. Catholic activists in the preconciliar period did not merely seek religious renewal and institutional stability, but worked within state structures, and with international agencies, to bring about a more faithful society based on Catholic social doctrine. Moreover, the contributors uncover the local, national, and transnational origins of social Catholicism in the region, which have been largely overlooked by scholars. Although the chapters included in this book do not exhaustively cover Latin America (the Andean countries—Ecuador, Peru, Colombia, and Venezuela—are less examined here, and certainly deserve further investigation) the following chapters explore transnational Catholic activism spanning from Canada to Chile and reveal an extremely robust shared culture of Catholic activism. Ordinary lay Catholics, both men and women, as well as clerical collaborators, bishops, and even Vatican officials, assisted in moving the church in Latin America from the margins of global Catholicism, thereby facilitating a new pastoral vision for the region focused on accompanying the "People of God" in their ongoing journey toward human development and liberation.

PART I ❖ CATHOLIC SOCIAL ENCYCLICALS ACROSS BORDERS

CHAPTER 1

Messages Sent, Messages Received?

The Papacy and the Latin American Church at the Turn of the Twentieth Century

❖ Lisa M. Edwards

By the middle of the nineteenth century, the Catholic Church faced serious challenges from competing ideologies, including Protestantism, liberalism, Marxism, and anarchism. These new ideas and actors posed a real threat to the Catholic Church's privileges and moral influence in Latin America. Throughout the region, these challenges often took the form of debates over freedom of religion, the role of religion in state educational systems, civil marriage, and secular cemeteries. They were exacerbated by the proliferation of secular, and sometimes even overtly anti-Catholic, political parties. As an institution, the church had to revise its previous strategy of either condemning or ignoring competing ideologies; lay and clerical leaders recognized that only new approaches could solve the challenges created by modernity.

As the Catholic Church was increasingly affected by secularization and governmental challenges to its traditional authority, the papacy, its hierarchy, and its clergy weighed in on politics, sometimes very publicly, and debated how Catholics should participate in social and political life. During the late nineteenth and early twentieth centuries, many of these comments revealed a cautious and contingent approach to Catholic political activism. This caution stemmed from ambivalence: on one hand, Catholic leaders were reluctant to encourage Catholic political participation lest it be taken as accepting liberals' secularization program. On the other hand, they also understood that nonparticipation would inevitably result in the loss of Catholic influence. Catholic leaders generally promoted social Catholicism with more enthusiasm, however. Social Catholicism attempted to address the social question, which was a catchphrase for changes in society brought about by industrialization and urbanization. Catholic activists hoped to draw more people into the church while simultaneously eliminating the appeal of secularism, socialism, or anarchism.

This chapter focuses on the ways that Vatican officials and Latin American Catholic leaders responded to the changing political and social environment of the late nineteenth and early twentieth centuries. Whereas other chapters in this volume examine lay activism more directly, this study explores how the papacy, the hierarchy, and the clergy engaged in political and social activism, both directly and by advising the laity. As we consider the role of Catholic leaders in Latin America, we can make a number of intersecting observations: that social and political Catholic activism predated *Rerum novarum* in many parts of Latin America; that this activism before and after 1891 was shaped by a combination of papal guidance, local initiative, and European models; that protecting society from the spread of socialism was often a rhetorical and strategic justification for Catholic activism in Latin America and by the papacy (in both the political and social realms); and that political activism to protect the institutional church included clerical participation and, at least sometimes, direction by the hierarchy. By reviewing these reactions over time, it is evident that the Catholic leadership's response to new challenges in Latin America did not follow a straight line from intransigence to engagement with modern life but, rather, a more winding road to finding some kind of productive peace with the church's place in the new society.

PAPAL RESPONSES TO NEW IDEOLOGIES

Throughout the nineteenth and twentieth centuries, the papacy issued frequent guidelines to help Catholics navigate social and political issues without straying from doctrine or losing their faith. Some of these papal statements were general and addressed to Catholics around the world. Others were addressed to the bishops, the clergy, or the faithful of a particular nation or region but were then cited in later Vatican documents or distributed more widely so their influence could extend beyond the original recipients. As other chapters in this volume note, the reception of papal encyclicals (and other instructions) was uneven across the Americas—some Latin American Catholic leaders ignored them, while others embraced Rome's recommendations. When it was convenient, the region's clerical leaders used papal instructions to explain or justify their own actions to Catholics and to society at large. Over time, both the papacy and local Catholic leaders in Latin America recommended a more engaged approach to address broader political and social changes and issued more prescriptive instructions to the clergy and faithful about how to deal with the changes of modernity.

Under Pius IX (1846–1878) and Leo XIII (1878–1903), the papacy began to address current social and political issues regularly, educating the faithful about new ideas and suggesting ways to protect the church's authority and retain followers. Pope Pius IX, whose papacy witnessed the loss of the Papal States and the revolutions of 1848, worried for the church's future in the face of growing liberalism, Marxism, and anarchism.[1] His 1864 encyclical *Quanta cura* expressed his concerns about the people's vulnerability to the church's foes, and its accompanying *Syllabus of Errors* clarified which ideas and principles were forbidden for Catholics.[2] Overall, Pius IX's instructions on political and social changes can be characterized as reactionary and inflexible, often focusing on the evils of the church's enemies. He repeatedly recommended religious education and better clerical discipline to resist the advance of secularism and associated ideologies. The tone and messages of Leo XIII's first encyclicals were similar to those of his predecessor. His *Quod Apostolici muneris* (1878) specifically condemned socialism, warning that "a wicked confederacy" sought "the overthrow of all civil society whatsoever."[3] Despite socialists' claims to promote equality, he asserted, the church provided for the poor "with much greater wisdom and good sense" than those who tried to destroy the right to private property.[4]

Although Leo XIII and his successors continued to warn of many

1. For an overview of the papacy and papal encyclicals, see Eamon Duffy, *Saints and Sinners: A History of the Popes* (New Haven, Conn.: Yale University Press, 1997), or Owen Chadwick, *A History of the Popes 1830–1914* (Oxford: Oxford University Press, 2003).

2. Pius IX, *Quanta cura*, in Claudia Carlen, *The Papal Encyclicals 1740–1878* [hereafter vol. I] (Ann Arbor, Mich.: The Pierian Press, 1990), 381–86.

3. Leo XIII, *Quod Apostolici muneris*, in Claudia Carlen, *The Papal Encyclicals 1878–1903* [hereafter vol. II] (Ann Arbor, Mich.: The Pierian Press, 1990), 11.

4. Ibid., 14.

of the same dangers that Pius IX had, there was a shift in tone at the end of the nineteenth century. Rather than simply condemning the church's enemies, Leo XIII began to guide Catholics toward an acceptance of diverse political positions and engagement with modern society, sometimes with specific recommendations for action. One aspect of this was competing with secular groups that appealed to the populace. In *Etsi Nos* (1882), he underlined the usefulness of Catholic associations and a benevolent press, noting that "[anti-Catholic] writings must be opposed by [Catholic] writings, so that the same art which can effect most for the destruction, may in turn be applied to the salvation and benefit of mankind."[5] In *Humanum genus* (1884), on masonry, he recommended the reestablishment of Catholic guilds, noting that workers should "be invited to join associations that are good, lest they be drawn away to others that are evil."[6] Throughout his papacy, Leo XIII emphasized Catholic unity but noted that it could be compatible with a diversity of political opinions and party affiliations among Catholics.[7] The message was increasingly linked with an acknowledgment that Catholics could, and indeed should, be politically active. As early as 1885, *Immortale Dei* urged active citizenship, while *Libertas* (1888) and *Sapientiae christianae* (1890) acknowledged Catholics' political participation and roles as citizens, albeit with warnings to remain mindful of doctrine.[8]

As part of this general trend of increasing engagement with new political and social realities, Leo XIII issued *Rerum novarum* in 1891. It has often been considered his most important accomplishment because it signaled a turning point in church history, sanctioning new strategies to ameliorate the social question and even encouraging direct competition with secular groups to address workers' needs. Although, as we have seen, neither papal concerns about the welfare of the working class nor the idea of competing with secular activists was completely new, the level of commitment that *Rerum novarum* demonstrated was novel and remarkable. The pope condemned both socialism and exploitative capitalism; he noted that socialists' rejection of private property was against natural law and that workers needed to

5. Leo XIII, *Etsi Nos*, in Carlen, II: 66.
6. Leo XIII, *Humanum genus*, in Carlen, II: 100.
7. See, for example, *Cum multa* (1882), in Carlen, II: 76–78.
8. Leo XIII, *Immortale Dei*, in Carlen, II: 116–17; Leo XIII, *Libertas*, in Carlen, II: 180, and Leo XIII, *Sapientiae christianae*, in Carlen, II: 211–23.

be protected from the exploitation capitalism could so easily engender. He asserted that socialists' attempts to resolve this conflict would cause even greater problems for society and that both Catholics and the state had responsibilities to ensure the welfare of all, including by preventing conflicts between workers and employers.[9] The reception of *Rerum novarum* was mixed; many on the left believed it to be inadequate, whereas conservatives felt it was too radical.[10] Overall, however, and over time, this landmark encyclical, sometimes known as the "Magna Carta of Social Catholicism,"[11] infused the social Catholic movement with inspiration and energy.

EARLY CATHOLIC ACTIVISM IN LATIN AMERICA

Papal attention to social and political issues in the late nineteenth and early twentieth centuries intersected with national debates in Latin America about the roles of the church and devout Catholics in the modernization process. By the 1850s and 1860s, industrialization and urbanization were underway; migrants from rural areas and European immigrants poured into the cities to construct infrastructure, to work in factories, and to seek their fortunes. The instability of the independence era had settled into more orderly discussions about how to build new nations and how to ensure order and progress in most of the region.

Although they usually avoided physical violence, proponents of different views argued vehemently for their visions of what modern independent nationhood should look like. For many, both these political debates and the emergence of the social question required redefining the role of the Catholic Church. The clergy, the ecclesiastical hierarchy, and the activist laity began to rethink how to best protect the institution from direct political attacks and the loss of followers

9. Leo XIII, *Rerum novarum*, in Carlen, II: 242, 245, 246–49.

10. In Chile, for example, much of the hierarchy and political conservatives did not view *Rerum novarum* favorably. Rosa Bruno-Jofré, "The Catholic Church in Chile and the Social Question in the 1930s: The Political Pedagogical Discourse of Fernando Vives de Solar, S.J.," *The Catholic Historical Review* 99, no. 4 (October 2013): 704. On the European reception of the encyclical, see Nicholas Atkin and Frank Tallett, *Priests, Prelates, and People: A History of European Catholicism since 1750* (New York: Oxford University Press, 2003), 173–76.

11. Atkin and Tallett, *Priests, Prelates, and People*, 174; Pius XI called it the "Magna Carta of the Social Order" in his encyclical *Quadragesimo anno* commemorating the fortieth anniversary of *Rerum novarum*, in Claudia Carlen, *The Papal Encyclicals 1903–1939* [hereafter vol. III] (Ann Arbor, Mich.: The Pierian Press, 1990), 421.

to secular ideologies. Their strategies included both political activism, which would protect the church through confessional political parties and encouraging Catholic political participation, and social Catholicism, especially through the creation of new associations to provide services, education, and resources to workers. Although it may seem at first glance that the social and political issues were separate, they were inextricably intertwined, and the stakes were high. The Catholic responses to both were largely centered on preventing the spread of secularism and socialism and protecting the church's traditional moral authority. Although they followed papal guidance, many Latin American expressions of social Catholicism and political activism in support of the church preceded, rather than followed, papal pronouncements and European trends. A notable trend toward Catholic dialogue and engagement with modern society in Latin America began in the decades before *Rerum novarum.*

During the latter half of the nineteenth century, most of Latin America's bishops were intensely worried about the advance of the church's enemies and about how to maintain the church's influence, especially because many Latin American intellectuals and politicians saw secularization as a necessary part of modernization. The bishops and other Catholic leaders, including some members of the clergy, political figures, and lay leaders, used a number of strategies to define the church's position in relation to the state and society. These tactics included making appeals to congress and political leaders, holding public meetings and demonstrations, creating associations to foster a stronger sense of Catholic identity, establishing periodicals to rally support, and reforming seminaries. All of them were intended to reinforce the institution while simultaneously defining the church's position on social, political, economic, and cultural issues for both the Catholic faithful and the general population.

Latin American bishops had a unique role in protecting the church from hostile forces and in promoting activism to strengthen the institution. As new laws affecting the church were proposed by liberals in several Latin American nations during this period, bishops condemned them for diminishing the church's moral and political influence. With some frequency, they noted papal teachings to support their positions. In 1856 the Chilean bishops presented the Senate with their objections to the new civil code, which would affect the church's property rights, taxation, and jurisdiction over marriage.[12] A collective pastoral letter in 1874 reflected their continuing engagement with the ever-changing political landscape. At the time, a proposed reform of the penal code would eliminate the ecclesiastical *fuero*, the clergy's legal privilege to be held accountable within the church but exempt from the state's judicial system. Liberals also were proposing to secularize education and separate church and state. Like other presentations they made in this vein, the bishops' letter was serious and detailed, using a careful reading of the constitution to make a reasoned argument about why proposed changes would be detrimental not only to the church, but also to the state and society at large. They cited Pius IX's 1852 speech condemning the separation of church and state and noted that the same pope had reiterated the point in the *Syllabus of Errors*.[13] They insisted that Catholics had the right to object strenuously to secularization, although they did not offer specific details of how to do it.[14] In 1889 the Venezuelan bishops sent a letter to the president hoping for a better relationship between church and state. They asked President Rojas for the reinstatement of seminaries' legal status and a reversal or a modification of the civil marriage law.[15] These were just a few examples of the many times that bishops objected to liberal policies. Typical of the period, however, they did not offer specific instructions on how the local clergy and faithful should participate in reversing or preventing secularization.

Church leaders in Latin America often spoke collectively but also made individual statements about political and social issues. Arch-

12. "Representación del episcopado chileno al Senado de la República en 1856," in *Boletín Eclesiástico del Arzobispado de Santiago de Chile: Tomo XII (1892–1894)* (Santiago: Imprenta de Emilio Pérez L., 1895), 950–78.

13. *Carta pastoral que el Ilmo. i Rmo. Señor Arzobispo de Santiago e Ilmos. Señores obispos sufragáneos de la provincia eclesiástica de Chile, dirijen a los sacerdotes i fieles de sus respectivas diócesis* (Santiago: Imprenta del Correo, 1874), 9. In fact, church and state in Chile were not separated until 1925.

14. Ibid.

15. One way that liberals diminished the church's influence in this period was to insist that only state-sponsored institutions could confer degrees; once this privilege was not allowed in ecclesiastical seminaries, the number of students, and therefore future clergy, tended to decline significantly. This seems to have been the case in the Venezuelan situation. "Exposición del episcopado de Venezuela al señor Presidente de la República, Dr. J. P. Rojas Paul 26-9-1889," in *Conferencia Episcopal Venezolana, Decretos y reglamentaciones 1889–1984*, with introduction, compilation, and notes by Monseñor Baltazar Porras Cardozo (Caracas: Ediciones de la Presidencia de la República, 1986), 7–22.

bishop of Santiago Mariano Casanova made several statements about current affairs in the 1880s, at the peak of Chilean debates over secularization. Some of these seemed at first glance to address only religious matters but, in fact, were about the effects of political changes on the church. Like other bishops during this period and into the twentieth century, Casanova seldom distinguished between liberals and socialists seeking reforms. He labeled the proponents of secularization "socialists," even when they were not, and condemned them for attempting to harm the church. In 1888 Casanova addressed a letter to the clergy of his archdiocese on priestly vocations. He asserted that the wealthy were obligated to support vocations because they were the ones who benefited from the priests' "[defense of] their assets and [protection of] their interests and properties against the barbaric invasion of socialism, and averting [socialism's] criminal aims especially in the pulpit and the confessional."[16] He continued by emphasizing the benefits of religion, writing that "religion stops social revolutions and is the first to condemn disobedience to legitimate authority and to defend property and the sanctity of work."[17] Although the letter on vocations addressed primarily religious and institutional matters, albeit with a political component, Casanova also made other statements that were about politics from beginning to end. In 1888, for example, his pastoral letter on the proposed constitutional reform that would separate church and state noted that disestablishing the church would cause only problems, because the union of church and state had benefited society in many ways.[18]

Although bishops alone had the authority to issue pastoral letters, the clergy and the laity worked too for the preservation of the institutional church and its influence in Latin America. Rallies were organized to discuss local political and social realities and focus the actions taken by the faithful in defense of the church and Catholic values. These could serve as the basis for creating institutional structures to serve the church's long-term needs. These were usually organized by cooperative efforts of the laity and clergy and often presided over by

16. Mariano Casanova, "Carta al clero sobre la escasez de vocaciones al sacerdocio," in *Obras pastorales del Ilmo. y Rmo. Señor Dr. don Mariano Casanova, Arzobispo de Santiago de Chile,* ed. Mariano Casanova (Friburgo de Brisgovia, Germany: B. Herder, 1901), 90.

17. Ibid.

18. Mariano Casanova, *Pastoral del Illmo. i Rmo. Sr. Arzobispo Dr. D. Mariano Casanova sobre la reforma constitucional* (Santiago: Imprenta Católica de Manuel Infante, 1888), 9–10.

bishops. The Catholic Assembly in Valparaíso, Chile, attracted more than three thousand lay and clerical participants from across the nation on June 3, 1877. The then vicar general of Valparaíso Mariano Casanova urged the clergy in his province to organize the meeting because, as he said, too many Catholics were afraid to demonstrate their faith and needed to "stand up and show that they can demand respect for their religious convictions" in an era when they were in desperate need of religious liberty.[19] While the Catholic Assembly was publicized primarily as a way to commemorate the fiftieth anniversary of Pius IX's elevation to the episcopate, it also served as a response to the local church's need to defend itself in the face of secularization. Recognizing the parallels between attacks on the papacy and on the local church contributed to a stronger defensive identity for Catholics who could rally for the local church and the papacy simultaneously.

A similar sense of a defensive and universal Catholic identity emerged at the Uruguayan Catholic Congress held in Montevideo over three days in April 1889. Participants, who included bishops, clergy, representatives of Catholic workers' circles and other associations, and the laity, lamented both their own situation and the difficulties faced by Pope Leo XIII. Bishop of Montevideo Inocencio Yeregui urged attendees "to work by all legitimate means" to improve the church's situation and save not just the church but also democracy and even civilization itself.[20] He and other organizers of meetings like these hoped that they would reinvigorate existing social and political organizations and lead to the establishment of new ones.

Confessional political parties emerged during the late nineteenth century in many Latin American nations to represent the church's interests. The Chilean Conservative Party, for example, formed in 1857 during a church–state dispute and remained closely tied to the Catholic hierarchy through family and social networks well into the twentieth century. In a few cities, especially during the party's first decades, priests played critical roles in organizing party support and even running as Conservative political candidates. With and without their bishops' approval, the clergy in Latin America expressed their concerns

19. "Los que tienen fé se pongan de pié i muestren que saben hacer respetar sus convicciones relijiosas," quoted in *La asamblea católica de Valparaíso* (Santiago: Imprenta de "El Independiente," 1877), 7.

20. *Congreso católico uruguayo celebrado en Montevideo en los días 28, 29 y 30 abril de 1889* (Montevideo: Imprenta de "El Telégrafo Marítimo," 1889), 19.

about the political future of their nations and the church at election time. They tended to support conservative politicians in conservative-liberal contests, but not always. In some cases, clerical support of candidates was as divided as the general population's support, as Edgar Solano Muñoz discovered for the Costa Rican elections of the 1880s and 1890s.[21] The hierarchy periodically issued guidelines under which Catholic political participation was appropriate and acceptable, especially after the turn of the twentieth century.

Other organizations were formed for political reasons but worked primarily outside the political party system. The Peruvian Catholic Society was created in 1867, for example, as a response to anticlerical liberals' attempts to separate church and state.[22] Similar secularization debates in Chile led to the foundation of the Catholic Union in 1883. Its leaders aimed to protect the church's rights by creating local associations, supporting the Catholic press, encouraging Catholic activism, and generally working for Catholics to be more unified against secularizing forces.[23] Although these were both lay organizations, they were not wholly independent of the clergy. The Chilean Catholic Union, for example, submitted its statutes to the archbishop for approval before finalizing them.[24] Workers' circles were created to counter the influence of socialist and anarchist workers' associations in Argentina, Uruguay, Chile, and elsewhere in the second half of the nineteenth century.

Latin American bishops also worked to strengthen the church by reforming existing seminaries and opening new ones in their own dioceses to better prepare the clergy to fight secularizing forces, as Dain Borges points out in his chapter on Brazil in this volume. The bishops also sent students to the Latin American College in Rome (Pontificio Colegio Pío Latino Americano, which opened in 1858), where they would learn not only the philosophy and theology necessary to their future clerical duties but also loyalty to the papacy, increasingly necessary to institutional strength and unity in a modern world hostile to Catholicism.[25] These

21. Edgar Solano Muñoz, "La participación del clero costarricense en las campañas políticas de 1889 y 1894," *Diálogos, Revista Electrónica de Historia* 11, no. 2 (September 2010/February 2011): 1–21.

22. Jeffrey L. Klaiber, "The Catholic Lay Movement in Peru: 1867–1959," *The Americas* 40, no. 2 (October 1983): 150.

23. Archivo del Arzobispado de Santiago (hereafter AAS), legajo 44, expediente 62.

24. "Estatutos provisorios de la 'Unión Católica de Chile,' [1883]" AAS, legajo 44, expediente 62.

25. On the Latin American College in Rome, see Lisa M. Edwards, *Roman Virtues*.

strategies emerged from a combination of local initiatives responding to local conditions and papal direction responding simultaneously to local and global trends. The papacy instructed Internuncio F. Spolverini that the Brazilian bishops should discuss clerical reform at their 1890 conference, because the "spiritual health of the population" depended on the clergy.[26] Both the papacy and the bishops hoped to form clergy who would strengthen the church overall through greater institutional unity and coordinated strategies, a closer relationship between the local church and the papacy, the promotion of the Catholic press, and new or improved Catholic schools and universities for the laity.

MODERN POLITICS AND THE SOCIAL QUESTION
AFTER 1891

Following *Rerum novarum*, Leo XIII and his successors periodically issued instructions and guidelines about how Catholics should interpret and address the rapid social and political changes that were affecting the institution's influence and security in Europe as well as in Latin America. In 1902, for example, papal secretary of state Cardinal Mariano Rampolla issued an Instruction on Christian Democracy. This instruction was not about the modern political parties labeled "Christian Democratic" as we think of them today but addressed wider participation in the political process and the activist press, acknowledging a diversity of opinions among Catholics. At the same time, it also emphasized the principle of obedience to the church hierarchy.[27]

Although the Instruction on Christian Democracy suggested that varying Catholic political opinions (and, by extension, political decisions and actions) were acceptable, Pope Pius X's (1903–1914) attitude was one of caution. His encyclical *Il fermo proposito* (1905), directed to Italian bishops but distributed widely, acknowledged the church's need to adapt: "The Church in its long history and on every occasion has wisely shown that she possesses the marvelous power of adapting herself to the changing conditions of civil society. Thus, while preserv-

26. Archivo Segreto Vaticano (hereafter ASV), Archivio della Nunziatura in Brasile, Busta 67, fasciculo 323, folio 49v.

27. Roger Aubert et al., *The Church in the Industrial Age*, trans. Peter Becker (New York: Crossroad Publishing Company, 1981), 215. The instruction referenced the encyclical *Nobilissima gallorum* (1884) and the papal letter to the archbishop of Tours of December 17, 1888.

ing the integrity and immutability of faith and morals and upholding her sacred rights, she easily bends and accommodates herself to all the unessential and accidental circumstances belonging to various stages of civilization and to the new requirements of civil society."[28] *Il fermo proposito* signaled a reluctant willingness for Catholics to engage politically. It recalled Leo XIII's circular forbidding Italian Catholics from participating in legislative politics but also acknowledged that exceptions could be necessary. Catholics needed, therefore, to be aware of political trends that could affect the church. Pius X reminded Catholics that "[t]his concession places a duty on all Catholics to prepare themselves prudently and seriously for political life in case they may be called to it."[29] At times, the bishops and clergy took actions that might be seen as extreme, such as during the anticlerical Mexican Revolution. During the 1910s, as Robert Curley discusses in another chapter in this volume, much of the Mexican episcopate and many priests were exiled. In the United States, they worked with the American Catholic bishops, clergy, and laity to maintain clerical education and an institutional structure until they could return home.

Socially oriented Catholic associations seemed safer, however, than overtly political ones and were more eagerly promoted by the hierarchy. As a strategy to protect the church, the twentieth-century papacy promoted the creation of Catholic organizations and periodically requested information from Latin American bishops about existing Catholic groups and activities and how these could be strengthened. At times, this seems to have been motivated by specific threats, some of which were international. In 1910, for example, after reports about anti-Catholic organizations based in Paris reached the Vatican, Latin American bishops were asked to report on whether there were any Catholic organizations engaged in activities that were "not strictly religious," suggesting a preference for nonpolitical Catholic activities. The same memo, however, also asked about Catholic influence on the government, simultaneously acknowledging that political involvement was necessary at some level.[30] This can be seen as a careful approach to political engagement, rather than as a contradiction.

Catholic social action was primarily directed at providing resources

28. Pius X, *Il fermo proposito*, in Carlen, III: 39.
29. Ibid., 42.
30. ASV, Archivio della Nunziatura in Cile, B. 19, fasc. 38, ff. 299–301.

and education to workers, especially through the creation of associations, including Catholic workers' circles. While in some parts of Latin
America these were created in the late nineteenth century—in Chile,
for example, Catholic workers' circles were created as early as 1878 for
"the moralization, education, and union of Catholic workers,"[31] and
there were several Catholic workers' circles in Uruguayan cities by the
late 1880s—they were promoted by the hierarchy well into the twentieth century, particularly after *Rerum novarum*. They were valued as an
important means of "protect[ing] the working class from the depravity
[*los estragos*] caused by socialism and anarchism" and served as an alternative to socialist or anarchist workers' organizations.[32]

Church leaders also thought about other ways to appeal to and accommodate workers to protect their Catholic faith, increase their understanding of doctrine, and improve their access to the sacraments.
The papacy was concerned about overall social decline. As apostolic
delegates were assigned to the region, the papal secretary of state
warned them to pay attention to persistent problems such as "the slow
but progressive corruption of principles and of habits," which were
caused by errors such as too much liberty, excessive freedom of the
press, and the spread of masonry and other pernicious ideas.[33]

Papal representatives in the region played an active role in suggesting strategies to improve the church's situation and strengthen the resolve of the faithful. In 1917 papal delegate Plácido Gobbini suggested
several possible strategies that the Venezuelan clergy could use to
counteract Protestant propaganda: scheduling masses at times when
workers would be more likely able to attend, establishing a newspaper
for distribution in churches and areas where Protestants were actively proselytizing, creating night schools for workers emphasizing the
catechism, and organizing catechism classes "in areas threatened by
the [Protestant] sect."[34] The danger of Catholics straying to Protestantism was ever-present throughout the twentieth century, but preventing

31. *Boletín Eclesiástico o sea colección de edictos, estatutos i decretos de los prelados del Arzobispado de Santiago de Chile. Tomo VI* (Santiago: Imprenta de "El Correo," 1880), 646 and 665.
32. "Tercera reunión trienial del episcopado argentino [1909]," in *Documentos del episcopado argentino, Tomo I: 1889–1909*, Néstor Tomás Auza, recopilador (Buenos Aires: Conferencia
Episcopal Argentina, 1993), 212.
33. ASV, Archivio della Nunziatura in Argentina, B. 61, fasc. 3, ff. 230, 231, 233 [1907].
34. Gobbini's letter is reprinted in Lucas Guillermo Castillo Lara, *Apuntes para una historia
documental de la iglesia venezolana en Archivo Secreto Vaticano* (Caracas: Academia Nacional de
Historia, 2000), IV: 252.

communism emerged as a central theme of the hierarchy's warnings during the 1920s and 1930s.

The papacy frequently had occasion to be disappointed about the status of Catholic activism in Latin America but persisted in recommending it. In 1920 apostolic nuncio Francesco Marchetti Selvaggiani was reminded to pay special attention in his report to Venezuela's "religious and social problems and the development of Catholic action, to publish them in *L'Osservatore Romano*."[35] The news was not always good; Nuncio Selvaggiani reported that, among other problems, "Catholic social action is unknown [and] the Catholic press is minimal and of [poor] quality."[36] Another report in 1921 noted that Venezuela lacked any sort of Catholic public opinion or social action.[37] The nation's bishops finally established both the Conferences of St. Vincent de Paul and Catholic Action in the 1920s.[38]

Echoing papal frustration with the church's situation in the region, Latin American bishops frequently lamented the state of the modern era and worked in concert nationally and regionally to protect the church, particularly after the Latin American Plenary Council was held in Rome in 1899. Although most of the plenary council's conclusions addressed religious matters—such as guidelines for administering sacraments, doctrinal issues, and clerical education—the bishops also discussed contemporary social and political concerns, particularly the dangers of anti-Catholic influences. They worried about protecting workers from "the enemies of the faith" and prescribed the creation of workers' circles under the bishops' oversight as a preventive measure.[39] For several decades, the plenary council's *Actas* served as guidelines to church policy in Latin America.

A few years later, in 1905, Argentina's bishops labeled their age one of "social dissolution."[40] All aspects of society were at risk, they feared: "Every day, impiety is more daring, extending its de-Christianizing ac-

35. ASV, Seg. di Stato, Año 1920, Rúbrica 251, fasc. 11, reprinted in Castillo Lara, IV: 444.
36. Ibid., 445.
37. ASV, Nunz. Venezuela, fasc. 59 (4), reprinted in Castillo Lara, IV: 489.
38. On the conferences of St. Vincent de Paul, see "Segunda conferencia episcopal ordinaria: Acuerdos," in Conferencia episcopal venezolana, 91. The Venezuelan establishment of Catholic Action is discussed in this essay.
39. *Actas y Decretos del Concilio Plenario de la América Latina (Edición fácsimil)* (Vatican City: Libreria Editrice Vaticana, 1999), nos. 765, 767, 769. This is also discussed by Eduardo Cárdenas in his introduction to the *Actas* in the same volume, 68.
40. *Documentos del episcopado argentino*, 185.

tions to all the social classes and with pretensions of infiltrating Jesus Christ and His Church with their satanic hatred, in all the institutions that affect individuals, the family, and society."[41]

In their triennial meetings at the beginning of the twentieth century, the Argentine bishops repeatedly included education as a critical means of strengthening the laity, because religiously neutral or secular education "seriously compromises the stability of the social order."[42] Their argument in 1909 noted not only Pius IX's *Syllabus of Errors* and Leo XIII's encyclical *Aeterni patris*, which suggested the foundation of Catholic universities, but also German and Italian Catholic congresses, which emphasized the importance of education to save the church.[43] Papal delegate Carlos Pietropaoli hoped to foster the formation of a Catholic laity in Venezuela in the early twentieth century through the establishment of Catholic schools.[44]

Despite the immensity of protecting the church from secularism and socialism, the Latin American bishops persisted, organizing and fostering projects and associations from local initiative, European models, and papal guidelines. The Argentine bishops acknowledged in their 1905 resolutions that by implementing "the new dispositions on this subject [specifically, of strengthening religious education but, by extension, all Catholics' familiarity with Christian doctrine], ordered by His Holiness Pius X, we make the work of the parish clergy more burdensome."[45] The papacy and Latin American bishops continually emphasized the importance of the clergy, and especially clerical education, as key to improving the church's situation. Pius X noted this in his 1903 encyclical *E supremi*, which noted that "as a general rule the faithful will be such as are those whom you call to the priesthood."[46] Seminary reform, including the creation of central national seminaries and the use of the Latin American College in Rome to form an elite group within the clergy, was an important theme of papal communications and episcopal conferences throughout the twentieth century.

In Rome at the Latin American College and in diocesan and central

41. Ibid., 187.
42. Ibid., 206.
43. Ibid.
44. Castillo Lara, *Apuntes*, IV: 225.
45. "Segunda reunión trienial del episcopado argentino," in *Documentos del episcopado argentino*, 187.
46. Pius X, *E Supremi*, in Carlen, III: 8.

seminaries in Latin America itself, the priest's role in guiding social and, to a lesser extent, political Catholic activism became important themes by the early twentieth century. As they resolved to create Catholic Action in the 1920s, for example, the Venezuelan bishops agreed that seminaries should introduce sociology course work so that young clergy would have a practical understanding of "the most up-to-date social Catholic institutions."[47] This would also "prevent that the communists and atheists easily take control of the population."[48] Three decades later, Ecuadoran bishop Leonidas E. Proaño noted in his first pastoral letter in 1954 "the special conditions of our time, the problems of the present hour, [which are] so complex, *require of [the priest] boundless activity in the area of Catholic Action, in the solutions to the social question, [and] in the orientation of cultural and educational labor.*"[49]

During the early decades of the twentieth century, Catholic Action became an important vehicle for social Catholicism. Beginning in the late nineteenth century, the term *Catholic action* was used generically to refer to Catholic lay activities. Pius X began to define its limits more clearly, however. In his 1905 encyclical *Il fermo proposito*, which expressed his wariness about Catholic political engagement, he defined and sanctioned Catholic Action.[50] The message in this encyclical and in other papal documents (and some bishops' statements on the matter) was that political problems could be addressed through social action. Later that year, the Argentine bishops decided that each diocese would organize Catholic Action.[51] As they promoted and discussed Catholic Action with the faithful, the church hierarchy, from the papacy to local bishops, emphasized the importance of clerical oversight.

Although Catholic Action was established in some Latin American nations during the earliest years of the twentieth century, it was not institutionalized in most of the region until the 1920s and 1930s. The Venezuelan bishops decided at their 1923 meeting to establish Catholic Action "in accordance with the norms and teachings of the Holy

47. "Donde los seminaristas teólogos puedan hasta aprender prácticamente el funcionamiento de las instituciones católico-sociales más corrientes," quoted in *Conferencia Episcopal Venezolana*, 93.
48. Ibid., 154.
49. *Primera carta pastoral que el Excmo. y Rdmo. Sr. Leonidas E. Proaño, Obispo de Bolívar, dirige al Vble. Clero y fieles de la Diócesis. Trata del Seminario* (Quito and Guayaquil, Ecuador: Editorial Colón, 1954), 6. Emphasis in original.
50. Pius X, *Il fermo proposito*, in Carlen, III: 37–44.
51. *Documentos del episcopado argentino*, 189.

See." They envisioned multiple associations at the diocesan or parish level that would assist workers and the poor, including workers' circles, popular libraries, *cajas* (savings and loan associations), temperance societies, and sports associations.[52] Pius XI (1922–1939) formally organized Catholic Action and urged Latin Americans to follow the centralized structure that was already in place in Italy—precisely because it allowed for close clerical supervision of the lay movement.[53] Many Latin American bishops agreed that the clergy should lead the movement; the Venezuelan bishops cited papal teachings and instructions in defining Catholic Action as "the laity's cooperation to the priest's action" when they planned to found it in 1923.[54]

While they hoped social action would prevent or resolve political problems, Catholic leaders also expressed wariness about social action crossing over into the political realm. When Pius XI spoke to a group of Mexican pilgrims in Rome on June 2, 1931, he reiterated that Catholic Action's purpose should not be political, but only religious.[55] Ironically, Catholic Action itself became an important means of preparing the laity for constructive political engagement in Latin America by the mid-twentieth century. Many political leaders in twentieth-century Latin America gained their leadership experience and social and political networks through the church—in Chile, turn-of-the-century social Catholicism formed the group of young Conservatives who would break away from the Conservative Party in the 1930s to form the Christian Democratic Party. And in Peru, Jeffrey Klaiber's research found that "[n]early all of the leaders of the Christian Democratic party, founded in 1955–1956, had been formed in Catholic Action ... [as were some progressive bishops before their entry into the priesthood]."[56] Indeed, social and political Catholic activism were intertwined, and could not be separated from their common goals of ridding society of secular and socialist influence.

As the twentieth century moved on, the challenges would only

52. *Conferencia Episcopal Venezolana*, vol. 2, 93.

53. Misner states that "Catholic Action" remained a generic term until the papacy of Pius XI, but Pius X's *Il fermo proposito* and other scholars' work on the movement suggest that it became more closely supervised by the hierarchy and that the term was becoming more specific earlier. Misner, *Social Catholicism in Europe*, 654.

54. *Conferencia Episcopal Venezolana*, vol. 2, 92–93.

55. Pius XI, "Ad un pellegrinaggio messicano: La preghiera per i persecutori," in *Discorsi di Pio XI* (Vatican City: Libreria Editrice Vaticana, 1985), II: 556–57.

56. Klaiber, "Catholic Lay Movement in Peru," 150.

grow bigger. Increasingly from the 1930s, anticommunism became an important focus of papal and episcopal writings and pronouncements on the state of modern society. But the earlier period, especially between 1870 and the 1940s, had given the church leadership a chance to test a variety of responses to changes in economic, political, and social life in Latin America. Catholic leaders from the papacy to the local level had a common set of strategies to fight the church's enemies. They rejected both socialism and secularism as morally, socially, and politically destructive to the ideal Christian society they were trying to restore (or, perhaps, construct for the first time). Although they were reluctant to embrace political activism too tightly, they also knew that they could not avoid it. Therefore, they proceeded with a great deal of caution, emphasizing clerical reform, Catholic education, and clerical oversight of lay organizations.

An important aspect of these efforts was that they were transnational, involving not only the papacy and local actors, but also cooperation and inspiration across national boundaries. As part of an international institution, Catholic leaders received material and moral support from their colleagues who had faced or were facing similar challenges. Many forms of Latin American social Catholicism, such as the Conferences of St. Vincent de Paul, followed European forms and even sought institutional connections with the European promoters of those programs. In other cases, including the way that Catholic Action was organized, the papacy instructed the Latin American bishops to follow the European model because it was deemed effective. During the Mexican Revolution, Catholics there sought support from their fellow Catholics in the United States, as Stephen Andes examines in his study in this volume. Although there were always local and national variations, the papacy and the Latin American bishops and clergy sought institutional strength in unified strategies to address the political and social challenges of modernity.

CHAPTER 2

Catholic Vanguards in Brazil

❖ Dain Borges

To understand the roots of lay Catholic activism in Brazil, it is helpful to look to the last years of the empire and the first decades of the
republic. From 1870 to 1916, a variety of Catholic organizations built
the repertory for dynamic Catholic revival and restoration, a repertory
of new ideologies and new forms of lay social action that were just as
"globalized" as they were simply Roman and "ultramontane." During
this period, the Brazilian church connected with Baltimore, Leiden,
and Lourdes, as well as with Rome itself.

Within the existing literature, two events at the end of this period—
Archbishop Sebastião Leme's pastoral letter to Olinda of 1916 and the
foundation of the Centro Dom Vital think tank in 1922—are conventionally taken as the big-bang starting point both generally of modern
Catholic activism, and specifically of a partisan lobbying push that by
1934 won a compact of "neo-Christendom" between church and state,
in which a semiofficial church influenced society through state agencies.[1] While maintaining freedom of religion and prohibiting outright
establishment of any church, the 1934 constitution explicitly permitted
the government and churches to undertake "reciprocal collaboration
for the common good"—that is, in schools and through social services.[2] Thus, the Catholic Church accomplished a restoration as Brazil's

---

1. Riolando Azzi, "O início da Restauração Católica no Brasil: 1920–1930," *Síntese-Revista
de Filosofia* 4, no. 10 (1977): 61–89; on "neo-Christendom," see Thomas Bruneau, *The Political Transformation of the Brazilian Catholic Church* (Cambridge: Cambridge University Press,
1974); and Scott Mainwaring, *The Catholic Church and Politics in Brazil: 1916–1985* (Palo Alto,
Calif.: Stanford University Press, 1986), 26–27.

2. This article was omitted from the Estado Novo Constitution of 1937, though implicit
cooperation continued; it was restored in the 1946 Constitution. In 1934 the Catholic Electoral
League had also gotten the name of God at the head of the Constitution, secured the civil recognition of religious marriage, and inserted Catholic language about defense of the family.

civil religion. Social action associations were a key part of this; in 1922 Cardinal Leme organized a national Catholic Confederation to coordinate Catholic social action initiatives.[3]

Yet there was at least a half-century of less-centralized Catholic activisms and Catholic social doctrine before 1922. The following chapter offers a survey of these vital—albeit diverse and uneven—responses, movements, and discourses within the Brazilian church between 1870 and 1916. Before turning to the many strains of Catholic activism in Brazil, however, it is necessary to examine the challenges faced by the church in the late nineteenth century.

A CHURCH IN COMPETITION

After 1870, the Brazilian church faced real opposition and open competition—the kind that stimulates action. Anticlericalism and the republican revolution of 1889, which separated church and state, raised the stakes and goaded the Catholic clergy and laity into new forms of political and social organization. The most important challenge to Catholic hegemony, or the one most noticed and resented by priests, was the secularization of men in the upper class and the explicit anticlericalism of some upper-class politicians and middle-class and working-class radicals. Masonry became the vehicle for a non-Catholic deism or for freethinking, and for expression of those religious outlooks in philanthropic actions outside the church (although not necessarily against the church before the condemnations in Pius IX's *Syllabus of Errors*). It was ritualistic and fraternal, masculine and progressive. It could occupy the place of Catholic *irmandades* (confraternities) in a man's life.[4] A masonic lodge could even organize within an irmandade and take it over, as had happened in the city of Recife.[5] Masonic lodges were the focus of

3. São Paulo had organized a Catholic Confederation (*Confederação Católica*) as early as 1906 that held its Third Congress in 1916 (*Annaes Catholicos: Publicação Mensal sob os Auspicios da Confederação Catholica de São Paulo* 1, no. 1 [March 1917], 6–18). There were confederations in other cities, but Rio's 1922 Confederation is usually cited as the beginning of the unifying, umbrella function of the Catholic Confederations.

4. In Salvador, Bahia, 85 percent of adults mentioned *irmandades* in their will at the beginning of the nineteenth century, and only 15 percent mentioned it at the end. See Kátia Mattoso, *Bahia século XIX: Uma província no império* (Rio de Janeiro: Nova Frontiera, 1992), 400–401. See also João José Reis, *Death is a Festival: Funeral Rites and Rebellion in Nineteenth-Century Brazil* (Durham, N.C.: Duke University Press, 2003), 39–56, 305.

5. David Gueiros Vieira, "Protestantism and the Religious Question in Brazil: 1850–1875,"

anticlerical public action, but their anticlericalism waxed and waned; it peaked during the 1872–1875 Question of the Bishops (catalyzed by the Recife lodge merging with an irmandade), in which bishops were jailed for ignoring government orders to tolerate masonry, tapered off when the Question seemed settled, returned at the beginning of the republican revolution, and remained a small but constant challenge to the church.

Anticlericalism had many outlets in the press, though usually as a secondary satirical topic in reformist publications such as the popular weekly *Revista Illustrada* (1876–1898). In various admixtures with anarchism and other left ideologies, the weekly *A Lanterna: Folha Anticlerical e de Combate Social* sustained the most polemical, anticlerical line from 1909 through 1917. In 1910 *A Lanterna* and anticlerical organizations fanned the case of Idalina, an orphan allegedly "disappeared" by the Scalabrian Brothers in their orphanage.[6] Through the 1910s, the circulation of *A Lanterna*—at times unpaid circulation, at times perhaps sales—ranged between ten thousand and six thousand.[7] It might be reasonable to take that as an aggregate measure of the several Brazilian anticlericalisms: not massive but not miniscule, either, and swimming in the sea of everyday vulgar humor about backward priests, greedy priests, and priests' mistresses.[8] In Brazilian folktales, Jesus and Peter walk the world like Don Quixote and Sancho Panza, taking hospitality and insults from poor folk. Peter is always lecherous, gluttonous, and a little bit slow.[9]

The passive slippage of urban and rural masses from participation in Catholic institutions, even from the folkloric pageant religiosity of

---

unpublished PhD diss., American University, 1972; Alexandre Mansur Barata, *Luzes e sombras: A ação da Maçonaria brasileira (1870–1910)* (Campinas: Editora da UNICAMP and Centro da Memória-UNICAMP, 1999).

6. Riolando Azzi, *O estado leigo e o projeto ultramontano, vol. 4, História do pensamento católico no Brasil* (São Paulo: Paulus, 1994); Wlaumir Doniseti de Souza, *Anarquismo, estado e pastoral do imigrante: Das disputas ideológicas pelo imigrante aos limites da ordem: O caso Idalina* (São Paulo: Unesp, 2000); Eduardo Góes de Castro, *Os "quebra-santos": Anticlericalismo e repressão pelo DEOPS-SP* (São Paulo: Humanitas, 2007).

7. Azzi, *O estado leigo e o projeto ultramontano,* 118–131.

8. Thales de Azevedo, *A guerra aos párocos: Episódios anticlericais na Bahia* (Salvador: Empresa Gráfica da Bahia, 1991).

9. Oswaldo Elias Xidieh, *Narrativas pias populares* (São Paulo: Instituto de Estudos Brasileiros, 1962). Santos Barbosa, "Cristo na Terra, no século XX (Criticando um doido)," a series of columns in *A Lanterna,* nos. 227, 229 (January 1914), parodied the format of the Jesus and Peter stories.

patron saint festivals and processions in the street, was almost unde-
tectable. But it could be sensed by an attentive priest. People in some
cities and regions made little use of the sacrament of marriage (more
than 50 percent of the children were baptized illegitimate in cities such
as Salvador and provinces such as Maranhão), and although the omission is harder to register, many may not have troubled to find godpar-
ents and baptize their children at all.[10] Much as priests disliked the
autonomy and worldliness of lay brotherhoods, they must have been
troubled when irmandades merged and closed down in cities such as
Salvador. The conventional explanation of religious indifference was
the lack of religious instruction and lack of priests. Dozens of parishes
recorded no resident priest in the census of 1872, and perhaps a sixth
of the population lived in a county with a single priest or no priest at
all; however, neglect of baptism seems to have been just as prevalent in
the cities, where priests were available.[11]

The Roman Catholic Church also faced the competition of other
religions and other organized churches after 1860.[12] The Catholic
Church was used to coexisting with Afro-Brazilian *candomblé* houses
and other so-called witchcraft, with indigenous tobacco-using healing
shamans, and with improvised Catholic pilgrimages and quirky devotions. It was hard to draw a line between African pagan healing and the
superstitious blessings of *benzedeiras* (healers), who cured with special
versions of Christian prayer. But from the mid-nineteenth century on,
the Catholic hierarchy had to deal with organized counter churches.
Spiritualist séances, then Kardecist circles and doctrinal books came to
Brazil around 1861; by the 1880s Spiritism had organized circles and
small newspapers. The Brazilian Spiritist Federation of Rio de Janeiro
(Federação Espírita Brasileira), still undecided whether to define itself
as a scientific experimental association or as a church, was founded in
1884.[13] In the city of Rio, Spiritists reached a mass clientele through

10. My preliminary research on nineteenth-century parish registers suggests that published numbers of baptisms in the late nineteenth century must have been less than the number of births; see, for example, Johildo Lopes de Athayde, "La ville de Salvador au XIXe siécle:
Aspects démographiques (D'apres les registres paroissaux)," unpublished PhD diss., Université de Paris-X, 1975.

11. *Recensenseamento de 1872.*

12. "Relatório dos Reverendos Prelados Diocesanos," in Brazil, Ministério do Império,
Relatório do Ministro do Imperio José Joaquim Fernandes Torres ... 1867 (Rio de Janeiro: Typographia Nacional, 1868), Anexo C, 8–11.

13. David J. Hess, *Spirits and Scientists: Ideology, Spiritism and Brazilian Culture* (College

free clinics and pharmacies.[14] Followers of Auguste Comte established a new-age Positivist Church of Humanity in Rio de Janeiro in 1881, from which they exercised influence disproportionate to their small numbers by giving public lectures, publishing popular pamphlets, and converting military officers.[15]

Protestantism was the biggest threat of all. The 1824 constitution had tolerated other religions, as long as they were practiced discreetly. The English had built their Anglican chapels and had bought land for Anglican cemeteries, although the government instructed them courteously to build their Rio de Janeiro church with rectangular, rather than Gothic, windows. The government even paid the salary of Lutheran pastors for some of the officially sponsored settler colonies. Eventually, the needs of German Lutheran settlers encouraged liberals in the government to undermine the Catholic monopoly on marriage and birth registration. In the 1860s, the government created a civil registry of Protestant marriages. German colonies were not a grave threat. Many of the Germans were Catholic, the German pastors did not proselytize, and many nominally Lutheran settlers were eager to be unchurched and untithed in the Americas. German Lutheranism was a large but mostly inert challenge to the Catholic Church, an ethnic religion, confined to frontier enclaves. The threat was evangelical, proselytizing missions.

Organized missions, starting with the Presbyterians in 1859, had grown into a full-blown evangelical movement by 1880, with solid Presbyterian, Baptist, and Methodist churches, each of which had recruited at least one converted ex-priest as a spokesman on "why I left the Church of Rome." These missions by U.S. southern denominations were absolutely transnational, on the verge of being imperialistic; although Scottish and English Bible sellers and individual missionaries with strong personalities travelled and witnessed across Brazil

Station: Penn State Press, 2010); Emerson Giumbelli, *O cuidado dos mortos: Uma história da condenação e legitimação do espiritismo* (Rio de Janeiro: Ministério da Justicia, Arquivo Nacional, 1997).

14. Dain Borges, "Healing and Mischief: Witchcraft in Brazilian Law and Literature, 1890–1922," in *Crime and Punishment in Latin America: Law and Society since Late Colonial Times*, ed. Ricardo D. Salvatore, Carlos Aguirre, and Gilbert M. Joseph (Durham, N.C.: Duke University Press, 2001), 181–210.

15. Robert G. Nachman, "Positivism, Modernization, and the Middle Class in Brazil," *Hispanic American Historical Review* 57, no. 1 (1977): 1–23; José Murilo de Carvalho, "A ortodoxia positivista no Brasil: Um bolchevismo de classe média," *Revista Brasileira* 4, no. 8 (1989): 50–56.

(and although the Pentecostal churches would be founded by Swedish missionaries in Belem and take root first in an Italian congregation in the city of São Paulo), Protestant evangelization seemed solidly American.[16]

The resources that went into evangelization were significant. Mission boards budgeted frugally, and missionaries wrote home that the cost of living in Brazil was high. But the boards had enough money to finance militant newspapers such as *Imprensa Evangélica* (1864–1893) and to print or import thousands of tracts.[17] Catholic priests railed against the "falsified Bibles" of the Protestants, yet a Protestant Bible was often the only one a priest could obtain.[18] The Protestant missions quickly established Sunday schools and then day schools. At first they were modest: something for the missionary's unpaid wife to do as her mission and a place to improve the literacy of new converts. Quickly they became a service of appeal to convert families, one more reason to break social ties and join the Protestants. And not so long afterward, the schools earned a reputation for a high-quality American-style education in practical subjects such as business and engineering. They built a clientele of Brazilian upper- and middle-class families who were not (yet) converts but who preferred a Protestant American education.[19]

Although few in number (less than 1 percent of the population at that time), the Protestants represented a significant challenge to the Roman Catholic Church. And taken together, these changes in Brazilian society amounted to a new, competitive religious field. These challenges, as well as the legal separation of church and state, would spur initiatives in social action between 1870 and 1920.

---

16. James S. Dennis, Harlan P. Beach, and Charles H. Fahs, eds., *World Atlas of Christian Missions* (New York: Student Volunteer Movement for Foreign Missions, 1911), 97. For emphasis on the British mold, see Richard Graham, *Britain and the Onset of Modernization in Brazil 1850–1914* (Cambridge: Cambridge University Press, 1972), 277ff. On Pentecostal origins, see R. Andrew Chesnut, *Born Again in Brazil: The Pentecostal Boom and the Pathogens of Poverty* (New Brunswick, N.J.: Rutgers University Press, 1997).

17. Edwiges Rosa dos Santos, *O jornal Imprensa Evangelica: Diferentes fases no contexto brasileiro (1864–1892)* (São Paulo: Universidade Presbiteriana Mackenzie, 2009).

18. "Relatório dos Reverendos Prelados Diocesanos"; Z.C. [Zacharias Clay] Taylor, "The Rise and Progress of Baptist Missions in Brazil (An Autobiography)," typescript, n.d. [1916], 34, 133.

19. Paul Freston, *A carreira de Gilberto Freyre* (São Paulo: Instituto de Estudos Econômicos, Sociais e Políticos de São Paulo, 1987).

IMPERIAL GOVERNMENT RESPONSES

During the imperial period, the church and state were intricately intertwined. Under the terms of the state's patronage over the church, papal letters and appointments of bishops required ratification by the government, and priests were salaried government employees. With some justification, Catholic priests complained that the position of the church as "the official religion," "the religion of the state," under regalist Gallican supervision, had "enslaved" them and had done them more harm than good.[20] Certainly in many ways the regalist control of church doctrine, personnel, and finances by the Brazilian imperial government had inhibited response to even routine challenges. The Ministry of the Empire and the Council of State micromanaged jurisdictional disputes within the church, intervening in matters between priests and bishops (even though it might lean in favor of bishops' discretionary powers).[21] Yet, in two key ways, the imperial government launched the reconstruction of a Catholic Church that would be able to make an activist response to social questions, that is, a church that had the minimum capacity to react.

First, it backed the reform of seminaries and the training of a better-educated, professionalized clergy. At the time of independence, patriotic, politicized Brazilian priests were among the few lettered, mobilized men. They were natural local leaders. They led rebellions and served in parliament and in the government ministries. Over the course of the nineteenth century, however, priests' roles became more distinct and more professionalized.[22]

The foundation of better seminaries from 1830 to 1850 marked a watershed between generations of the clergy. Cândido da Costa e Silva has studied the chapter canons of the archdiocese of Bahia. In the early

20. Júlio Maria, "Memoria: A religião. Ordens religiosas. Instituições pias e beneficentes no Brasil," in Associação do Quarto Centenário do Descobrimento do Brasil, *Livro do Centenário (1500–1900)*, vol. 1 (Rio de Janeiro: Imprensa Oficial, 1900), chapter 2, 1–134; 86–89, 109. This had been the diagnosis of the Chilean Jesuit visitor José Ignacio Victor Eyzaguirre, *Los intereses católicos en América*, vol. 2 (Paris: Librería de Garnier Hermanos, 1859).

21. Manoel Francisco Correia, ed., *Consultas: Conselho de Estado sobre negócios ecclesiásticos, compiladas por ordem de S. Ex. O Sr. Ministro do Império*, 3 vol. (Rio de Janeiro: Typographia Nacional, 1869), for example, 2:127–143; C. F. G. de Groot, *Brazilian Catholicism and the Ultramontane Reform, 1850–1930* (Amsterdam: CEDLA, 1996), 48–50.

22. Cândido da Costa e Silva, *Os segadores e a messe: O clero oitocentista na Bahia* (Salvador: Secretaria da Cultura e do Turismo and EDUFBA, 2000).

nineteenth century, a first generation of canons was Brazilian-born but Coimbra-trained; they had graduated there in the late eighteenth century. Most of them left for Portugal after independence—a decimation of the top echelon of the clergy comparable to the expulsion of the Jesuits two generations earlier. The second generation included those left over: largely Brazilian-born priests from upper-class families who had been privately tutored at home; some of them had even been patriot leaders of the war of independence. If those in the second generation were parish priests or private chaplains, their lives were worldly. Until lawyers and career politicians elbowed them out, they filled many seats in the provincial assemblies and the national parliament. The graduates of the reformed Brazilian seminaries after 1830 constituted a third generation, more removed from lay people, more ideologically uniform, and more ultramontane. A further decisive change happened in Rome. The foundation of the Pontificio Colegio Pío Latino Americano seminary in 1858 allowed a few privileged students to get Roman training. They formed an elite group in the fourth generation. Not all of them became bishops and church leaders, but all were fast-tracked.[23] Some of them were aggressively ultramontane: Dom Vital de Oliveira, the youngest bishop in Brazil, picked a fight with the Masons in Olinda and precipitated the Question of the Bishops in 1872.

Both bishops and imperial politicians wanted "a wall of bronze" between the old clergy and the new and hoped that bringing boys up inside disciplined seminaries would accomplish this. By forbidding the admission of novices into Brazilian religious orders, the government tried to pinch off the old, conventual religious orders (Carmelites, Franciscans, Benedictines) that had accumulated property (urban real estate, plantations) and a reputation for murderous corruption. At the same time, it invited a few new educational congregations (feminine orders as well as masculine orders) and missionary congregations to enter Brazil. Even the Jesuits were permitted to reenter Brazil discreetly in the 1840s and were welcomed as professors in the new seminaries.

Second, the imperial government delegated social services and, in a sense, social policymaking to the church. Priests often taught prima-

23. Silva, *Os segadores;* the continuing importance of the Latin American seminary in Rome is chronicled in J. D Vital, *Como se faz um bispo: Segundo o alto e o baixo clero* (Rio de Janeiro: Civilização Brasileira, 2012), 69–103.

ry school, not just religion classes. Urban church agencies of all sorts, asylums, orphanages, hospices and hospitals, were funded as separate budget items in provincial budgets. Perhaps the imperial government could not have acted otherwise. It had feeble administrative capacity for social action: small budgets and inadequate personnel. It relied on rural parish priests to be the multipurpose agents of the government in country towns, collecting vital statistics, publicizing decrees, opening the parish church for elections, and organizing any sort of novel campaign, such as the attempt to establish parish land registries in the 1850s. The church depended on government funding, but the government depended on church personnel.

Indian affairs were basically delegated to the Catholic Church, mostly through a diminished continuation of the missionary village system of the colonial period. Then western campaigns during the Paraguayan War (1864–1870) introduced military officers to Indian scouts and to the lawlessness of the frontier. Officers wanted to set Indian policy and administer Indians' assimilation, and they revived a competition going back to the seventeenth and eighteenth centuries.[24] They won the big jurisdictional battle during the republic, with the creation of a secular Indian Protection Service (Serviço para a Protecção dos Índios, or SPI) in 1910. But both before and after the SPI, a parallel commissioning of the church continued. Religious congregations such as the Salesians were officially entrusted with frontier pacification and Indian assimilation.[25] Not only were Indian affairs, but also frontier and backlands affairs in general, understood to be the expertise of specialized Catholic religious orders. Italian priests were contracted to minister to Italian settler colonies. Vincentian-Lazarist and Claretian congregations ran a circuit of revival meetings throughout backlands counties that had few or no parish priests. When rebellions or riots loomed, the government would send revivalist missionaries in ahead of the police or alongside the police.[26] Rural state infrastructure relied markedly on Catholic clergy auxiliaries.

24. Thomas Cohen, *The Fire of Tongues: Antonio Vieira and the Missionary Church in Brazil and Portugal* (Palo Alto, Calif.: Stanford University Press, 1998).

25. Todd Diacon, *Stringing Together a Nation: Cândido Mariano da Silva Rondon and the Construction of a Modern Brazil, 1906–1930* (Durham, N.C.: Duke University Press, 2004). On the Salesians versus Rondon, see Sylvia Caiuby Novaes, *The Play of Mirrors: The Representation of Self Mirrored in the Other* (Austin: University of Texas Press, 1997).

26. The famous Capuchin missionary preacher Frei Caetano de Messina, asked to "pacify"

ABOLITIONISM: TOO LITTLE, TOO LATE?

The political crisis of the 1880s surrounding the emancipation of slavery offered the Catholic Church a Brazilian social question apparently made to order for charitable action. But the church missed the opportunity. With honorable exceptions, priests were not leaders in the early abolitionist movement, not even in the philanthropic emancipation societies for purchase of slaves' freedom. The gradual emancipationism implied by free-womb policy suited them best; after having declared all children born of their slaves free in the 1860s, the Benedictine order emancipated all their slaves in 1871. But other religious orders kept their slaves until the last minute. The Rio de Janeiro Catholic newspaper, *O Apóstolo*, praised the 1871 Free Womb Law, spoke out against the abuses of slavery, praised the charity of masters who voluntarily manumitted their slaves, and called both for defense of order and full abolition in late 1887. Unlike most of the abolitionist movement, which stopped cold at the end of slavery, *O Apóstolo* continued to advocate for the incorporation of freedmen as brothers.[27]

Whatever the complex reality, the simple image that stuck with the Catholic Church was that of a conservative supporter of slavery. Abolitionism was the sort of radical opposition movement that had elective affinities with anticlericalism. The anticlerical physician Luiz Anselmo da Fonseca, in *A escravidão, o clero, e a abolição* (1887), effectively mixed a chronicle of Bahian abolitionist efforts with a denunciation of the lack of action by Bahia's clergy.[28] Many prominent abolitionists, such as Luiz Gama, were Masons; Masonic lodges in some provinces were the seat of emancipation-fund clubs and abolitionist societies; as a young man, Rui Barbosa had taken a commission from the Masons to translate the anticlerical tract *O Papa e o Concílio* prefaced with his own essay.[29]

---

the 1852 Guerra dos Marimbondos rebellion in rural Pernambuco, got caught between the army and the rebels, preaching his mission. See Guillermo de Jesús Palacios y Olivares, "Revoltas camponesas no Brasil escravista: A 'Guerra dos Maribondos' (Pernambuco, 1851–1852)," *Almanack Braziliense* 3 (2006): 9–39, 17, 21–22, 27.

27. Martha Abreu, "Pensamento católico, abolicionismo e festas religiosas no Rio de Janeiro, 1870–1890," in Marco Antonio Villela Pamplona and Eduardo da Silva, eds., *Escravidão, exclusão e cidadania* (Rio de Janeiro: Access, 2001), 75–105; see also, "Abolição e moral: A formação da cidadania católica no Brasil, 1870–1890," MS.

28. Luiz Anselmo da Fonseca, *A escravidão, o clero, e a abolição* (Bahia: Imprensa Economica, 1887).

29. Rui Barbosa, "Prefácio," [Johann Joseph Ignaz von Dollinger], *O Papa e o Concílio:*

We know that some priests participated in clandestine direct-action abolitionist clubs and sheltered runaway slaves in the refugee camps organized by slave-stealing societies. In São Paulo, Antonio Bento organized the *Caiphazes*, a secret direct-action movement of slave stealers, in the chapel of the Brotherhood of the Rosary of the Black Men. He named his newspaper *A Redempção (Redemption)*, and he organized a famous, theatrical street procession in which the brotherhood of Our Lady of Remedios went out with their saints' images hung with chains and whips, led by a slave who had just been rescued from torture, under the banner of the crucified Christ.[30] This was unmistakably Christian but perhaps too radical to be lay "Catholic," in the way the word was understood at the time. Both at the time and in post-1888 memory, the religious dimension of the Caiphazes was virtually ignored, by Catholics and non-Catholics alike.

Joaquim Nabuco, one of the leading abolitionists, would not have a full religious "reconversion" until his exile in England in 1892, but he had already softened his anticlerical positions of the 1870s. Within the abolitionist movement, Nabuco's special role had been to recruit international support and pressure the Brazilian government. On losing his congressional seat along with the other abolitionist deputies in 1882, he had traveled to England and there had orchestrated support from the British abolitionists. After his return to Brazil, he maintained a quasi-consular role as liaison between the movement and its international sympathizers. In February 1888, Nabuco decided to visit the Vatican to ask Pope Leo XIII for an audience to discuss the issue of slavery. He obtained the promise of a letter. Before it was published, he was able to leak it to the Brazilian press. He had especially hoped to influence Princess Isabel, successor to the Brazilian throne, who was serving as regent during one of Dom Pedro II's ever-more-frequent leaves of absence for medical treatment. But *In plurimus* arrived too late. It was dated May 5, but in fact it did not arrive until after May 13, when abolition was a fait accompli, and the newspapers were distracted by celebrations and self-congratulation. The Catholic who received credit for Brazilian abolition was not the pope but Princess Isabel, who

---

A questão religiosa [1877], in *Obras*, vol. 1 (Rio de Janeiro: Ministério de Educação e Cultura, Fundação Casa de Rui Barbosa, 1977).

30. [António Manoel] Bueno de Andrada, "A abolição em São Paulo—Depoimento de uma testemunha," *O Estado de São Paulo*, May 13, 1918, 3.

had signed the law; the Brazilian bishops presented her with a golden rose in gratitude.

Still, *In plurimus* deserves more attention. The encyclical and some speeches by the American consul Hilliard were the only major interventions by a foreign power in Brazil's emancipation politics. It could have been a source of Brazilian pride. It was a major social encyclical, the first encyclical of the church against slavery, and it was primarily directed to Brazil, although its secondary objective was the continued slavery and slave trade within Africa. Or perhaps not so secondary: like the canonization of Saint Peter Claver in January 1888, it may have been aimed at maintaining the pope's role in post–Berlin Conference African partitions, and also to buttress the American bishops—in Baltimore and New Orleans—in their recruitment of African Americans.[31]

It could have backfired in Brazil. It was the most audacious and frontal intervention of the Vatican in Brazilian politics in years—for proslavery politicians, potentially a provocation that might have led to a confrontation like the Question of the Bishops. But the immense bandwagon of adherence to abolition in April and May 1888, and the desire of Brazilian elites to muffle all talk about slavery afterward, turned attention away from this papal intervention in Brazilian affairs. Eighteen months after abolition, the republican revolution of 1889 further narrowed the ideological parameters of Brazilian social discourse. For any Brazilian to have tried to read the message of *Rerum novarum* in light of the teachings of *In plurimus* would have been to imply that past slavery should be Brazilians' reference point for future labor questions, an insight that was extraordinarily inhibited at the time.[32] Indeed, it was not until 1922 that the collective pastoral letter of the Brazilian bishops in celebration of the Centenary of Independence became the first document to incorporate *In plurimus* into a postemancipation social discourse.[33]

31. Francis T. Furey, *Life of Leo XIII and History of his Pontificate: From Official and Approved Sources* (New York: Catholic Educational Company, 1903), 278ff. Stephen J. Ochs, *Desegregating the Altar: The Josephites and the Struggle for Black Priests, 1871–1960* (Baton Rouge: Louisiana State University Press, 1993). For a Josephite perspective, see Joseph Butsch, "Catholics and the Negro," *The Journal of Negro History* 2, no. 4 (October 1917): 393–410; compare the omission of slavery and imperialism in Misner, *Social Catholicism in Europe.*

32. Dain Borges, "Intellectuals and the Forgetting of Slavery in Brazil, 1888–1933," *Annals of Scholarship* 11, nos. 1–2 (1996): 37–60.

33. The letter foregrounds Brazilian bishops' pastoral letters of the late 1880s before praising *In plurimus.* See *Carta pastoral do Episcopado brasileiro ao clero e aos fieis de suas diócesis por ocasião do Centenário da Independência, 1922* (Rio de Janeiro: Papelaria e Typographia Marques, Araujo e Cia., 1922), 26–33, 117.

QUEBRA-QUILOS AND CANUDOS

Abolitionism and *In plurimus* were not the only missed opportunities to build a Brazilian lay Catholic action. In the northeast of Brazil, the romanizing bishops declined other opportunities and even squelched promising initiatives to cultivate a native, Brazilian style of social action, one aimed at the peasant majority.

The career of Padre José Antonio Maria Ibiapina (1806–1883) demonstrates the delicacy of any social initiative in the politically partisan and suspicious atmosphere of the rural northeast. Ibiapina lived between the politicized, revolutionary patriot clergy of the independence era and the politically militant clergy of the 1920s, without ever fully belonging to the ultramontane, seminary-raised generations between. His father and his brother had been executed for their participation in the 1825 Equator Confederation (Confederação do Ecuador) rebellion, called "the rebellion of the priests" because so many of its leaders were clerics. He had left the seminary for law school to support his family but eventually, at mid-career, returned to be ordained a priest.

As a priest, Ibiapina carried out an itinerant ministry to poor people in the small-farmer towns of the northeastern provinces. In dozens of towns he held revival missions and founded charity houses that were a mix of a workhouse for the poor, a house of retreat for women who wanted to live away from the world as *beatas*, a school for poor girls and boys, and an orphanage. A network of his houses still exists today in Paraíba and Pernambuco.[34] His charisma was unsettling; the bishop of Ceará mistrusted the fervor of Ibiapina's following and asked him to leave the diocese.[35] His anti-Masonry was subversive. During the Question of the Bishops, Ibiapina and priests linked to his charity house movement—some in the government said they were "Jesuits"— began to stir up the faithful to shun "Masons" in local government. Farmers had many grievances heavier than the plight of the bishops. Prices for cotton were bad, crops had failed, families were still feel-

---

34. Hugo Fragoso suggests that Ibiapina must have been aware of the Sisters of Charity of Saint Vincent de Paul but that the law then prohibited a Brazilian order with novitiates. See Hugo Fragoso, "As Beatas do Pe. Ibiapina: Uma forma de vida religiosa para os sertões do Nordeste," in *Padre Ibiapina e a igreja dos pobres*, ed. Georgette Desrochers and Eduardo Hoonaert (São Paulo: Edições Paulinas, 1984), 85ff; esp. 87–97.

35. Ralph Della Cava, *Miracle at Joaseiro* (New York: Columbia University Press, 1970), 21–23.

ing their losses from military recruitment for the Paraguayan War, and the government had introduced strange, new metric weights along with new, unadjusted market taxes. But priests would only go so far: once peasant protests against onerous market taxes turned violent and spread into the 1874 Quebra-Quilos revolt, the priests withdrew overt support of the rebels.[36]

Ibiapina's model remained strong through the 1890s, and again provoked confrontations with the church and with the state. It probably influenced the priest Padre Cícero, who became a folk saint after defending a local miracle in 1889: the miraculous transformation of the Host into blood in the mouth of one of the beatas in his town.[37] It inspired Antonio Conselheiro ("Counselor"), the wandering lay preacher who founded the Canudos religious community. He almost certainly fashioned himself after Padre Ibiapina, preaching from town to town and gathering volunteer brigades to repair shrines and cemeteries. Like Ibiapina, Conselheiro drew on the penitential devotional book *Missão Abreviada* by Manoel Gonçalves Couto, a nineteenth-century Portuguese missionary in Goa, that circulated through the north. Perhaps he had read or heard Ibiapina's apocalyptic prophecies.[38] But he also had some ideology of social justice. In 1893 Conselheiro supported a protest against draconian market taxes, and although he tried to hold the mob from violence, probably took fleeing members of the protest with him to found a new city, Belo Monte, on the Canudos ranch.

Padre Cícero was suspended by his bishop for stubbornly pursuing authentication of the miracle after a church commission had disapproved it. But the town of Juazeiro prospered as an unsanctioned pilgrimage center—today it is the largest pilgrimage in the north of Brazil—after suffering political ups and downs, including involvement in a regional rebellion against the state government. Conselheiro's Belo Monte, which had grown to thousands of residents, much larger in scale than Ibiapina's houses of charity, sparked a civil war. The government knew Conselheiro had been involved in tax protests, and

36. Roderick J. Barman, "The Brazilian Peasantry Reexamined: The Implications of the Quebra-Quilo Revolt, 1874–1875," *Hispanic American Historical Review* 57, no. 3 (1977): 401–424; Kim Richardson, *Quebra-Quilos and Peasant Resistance: Peasants, Religion and Politics in Nineteenth-Century Brazil* (Lanham, Md.: University Press of America, 2011), 49–52.

37. Della Cava, *Miracle at Joaseiro*.

38. "Documento no. 1: O padre Ibiapina em Picos, Piauí, em 1871," in *Padre Ibiapina e a igreja dos pobres*, 131–138.

his local political rivals made sure it also knew that he was preaching against civil marriage and the impious republic: worse than Masons, a "law of the satanic Dog."[39] In 1895 the interim bishop delegated two veteran missionaries to hold a revival mission in Canudos, try to talk with Conselheiro, and assess the character of the movement. Their report emphatically dissociated the church from Antonio Conselheiro and identified his preaching as antiliturgical, virtually authorizing the government to intervene.[40] Police raids escalated into an Army siege, and by 1897 into the massacre of thousands of residents of Canudos.

Not just the archbishop but all Catholics in Bahia also tried to distance themselves from the accusations that the Canudos community was a restorationist guerilla force with British and clerical backing. Lay Catholics made a great effort to show that they were loyal Brazilians, in favor of order. As the casualties began to pour into the capital city of Salvador, lay Catholics and priests organized the Patriotic Committee of Bahia, showing they were anything but monarchist subversives. Lellis Piedade, a journalist and state politician, organized the relief effort that took provisions, doctors, and medical students to the towns behind the front. Among them was a nineteen-year-old German-born Franciscan, Frei Pedro Sinzig, who was detached to the effort, camping in Queimadas, behind the lines, with a young, freethinking medical student; their quarrels over Zola, immoral novels, the dogma of the Trinity, and other matters shook Sinzig as much as the horrors of war and the massacre of prisoners.[41] He had come to Brazil as a missionary and had found echoes of the German *Kulturkampf* in the midst of a strange civil war.

RERUM NOVARUM

Leo XIII's encyclical *Rerum novarum*, of May 15, 1891, was an opportunity for the Brazilian Catholic Church and lay Catholics to take ultramontane cues for finding new paths of social action. Yet, as with

39. Ralph Della Cava, "Brazilian Messianism and National Institutions: A Reappraisal of Canudos and Joaseiro," *Hispanic American Historical Review* 48, no. 3 (August 1968): 402–420; Robert M. Levine, *Vale of Tears: Revisiting the Canudos Massacre in Northeastern Brazil, 1893–1897* (Berkeley: University of California Press, 1992).

40. João Evangelista Monte Marciano, *Relatório apresentado, em 1895, pelo Reverendo Frei João Evangelista de Monte Marciano, ao Arcebispado da Bahia sobre Antonio "Conselheiro" e seu sequito no Arraial de Canudos* (n.p., 1895).

41. "Diário de um frade," in Lélis Piedade, *Histórico e relatório do Comitê Patriótico da Bahia, 1897–1901*, ed. Antonio Olavo (Salvador: Portfolium Editora, 2002), 240–257.

earlier developments discussed in this chapter, the encyclical prompted uneven reactions. It was issued at a difficult time for the Brazilian
church, when questions of church and state, perhaps the formation of
a "Catholic party," held center stage. In February, the Constitution of
1891 had ratified the separation of church and state decreed by the pro-
visional government in January 1890. The Brazilian bishops had am-
bivalently welcomed the Republican disestablishment as an opportunity in their collective pastoral letter of 1890, saying that they preferred
republican indifference to the slow strangulation of regalist supervision. But they made clear that they preferred Catholicism to remain
the official religion.[42] The papal encyclical that mattered was *Immortale
Dei* (1885), "on the Christian Constitution of States." And during the
tremendous political turmoil of the 1890s—a military dictatorship,
press censorship, political imprisonment, and assassinations, a civil
war in the south in addition to the Canudos war, rebellion by the navy
in the Rio de Janeiro harbor—they had become more nostalgic about
the Empire and less sanguine about republican government. Their
collective pastoral of 1900, on the quadricentenary of the discovery of
Brazil, was far less sympathetic to republican government.[43]

As far as social action or defense of the family goes, bishops' early
republican years were marked by negotiating the practical terms of
civil marriage and securing the parish priests' begrudged cooperation
with civil marriage. As the constitution allowed, they tried to bring religious instruction back into state-level public schools. The concerns
highlighted in *Rerum novarum* (proletarian immiseration, familial disintegration, socialist subversion) were not at the forefront of the bishops' worries in the years after its release. Nevertheless, there were a
few mentions of the encyclical in letters by bishops, and invocation of
"the teachings of Pope Leo XIII on the working class" soon became a
rote refrain to any newspaper exchange about socialism.[44]

42. *O Episcopado brasileiro ao clero e aos fiéis da Egreja do Brazil* (São Paulo: Typografia Salesiana a Vapor do Lyceu do Sagrado Coração, 1890).
43. Azzi, *O estado leigo e o projeto ultramontano.*
44. For example: "Santa Sé," *A Cruzada* [São Luiz do Maranhão] no. 202, June 15, 1891, 3;
"Treze de Maio," *Gazeta de Noticias*, May 12, 1891, and July 8, 1891 (reporting lectures by Manuel
Francisco Correia on "irresponsible wealth"); José Augusto Vinhaes, "A questão social," *Gazeta
de Notícias*, May 29, 1891 (on "integralismo socialista"); "O tempo," *O Paiz*, June 21, 1892 (on
the Jubilee and "the wise encyclical").

ORGANIZATIONAL REBUILDING WITH EUROPEAN CLERGY

The Brazilian bishops, rather than fomenting new forms of social action intentionally, did so as an indirect outcome of institutional rebuilding and reorganization. Because the imperial government had deliberately restricted the growth of dioceses, and had discouraged the foundation of (expensive) new parishes in growing regions around the cities and on the rural frontiers, it was imperative that the church reorganize administratively. In 1889 there were twelve dioceses and archdioceses; by 1892, sixteen; in 1912, forty-three.[45] The creation of new dioceses was especially important in the southern states whose population was growing rapidly from European immigration. But it also mattered in the northeast, where inland frontiers finally got diocesan supervision. Parish creation probably should have gone even farther than it did. There were 1,440 parishes in 1872, 1,746 in 1890, 1,923 in 1912, and 2,845 in 1937. Brazilian parishes were much larger than in most of the Catholic world, perhaps unmanageably large; there were 6,700 Brazilians per parish, and 4,200 for each priest in 1872, and 15,000 per parish in 1937.[46] It was difficult to staff parishes. Although seminaries proliferated, boys dropped out before ordination; some seminaries were producing fewer priests than were retiring.[47]

Their solution was to bring in foreign religious and to appoint foreign priests as vicars, not only to immigrant parishes but also to Portuguese-speaking parishes. This had already begun under the Empire. In 1872 the census counted 404 foreign-born secular priests and 12 foreign-born men in orders. By 1920, there were 1,761 foreign-born male religious. In the south of Brazil, 66 percent of the male religious were foreign-born; in the north, 32 percent.[48] Most of the foreign priests

45. The count comprises archdioceses, dioceses, prelatures, and prefectures. See Maurício de Aquino, "Modernidade republicana e diocesanização do catolicismo no Brasil: As relações entre Estado e Igreja na Primeira República (1889–1930)," *Revista Brasileira de História* 32, no. 63 (2012): 143–70; Directoria Geral de Estatística, *Anuário Estatístico do Brasil (1908–1912), vol. 3, Cultos, Assistência, Repressão e Instrucção* (Rio de Janeiro: Typographia da Estatistica, 1927), 4–23.

46. See censuses of 1872, 1890; *Anuário Estatístico do Brasil, 1939–40*, 1163; de Groot, *Brazilian Catholicism*, 46–47, 73–74; Kenneth Serbin, *Needs of the Heart*, 114.

47. Serbin, *Needs of the Heart*, 93–99, 113–117; de Groot, *Brazilian Catholicism*, 74.

48. Across Brazil, 47 percent of male religious were foreign born. Brazil, *Recenseamento de 1872*; Brazil, *Recenseamento de 1920*, Volume IV, 5a parte, Tomo 2, *População segundo ... Estados e municipios ... profissões*.

arrived in groups establishing a branch of a European congregation. Europeans also revived the moribund traditional conventual orders, the Franciscans and the Benedictines, but ran them much more like a new congregation than like a cloistered order. Some of the Europeans came as political exiles expelled by anticlericalism in their home countries. French Trappists established a cloister at a plantation in Tremembé, in São Paulo, from which they taught peasant farmers household hygiene, farming techniques, and cooperative organization.[49] The most controversial exiles were the Portuguese Jesuits, a group of whom established leading secondary schools in Bahia in 1910. Understandably, at times there were sharp conflicts between the habits and outlook of native priests and the immigrant clergy.[50] The outcome of this migration into the hierarchy of the Brazilian church was rapid diversification of the styles of religious life and social action by clergy, a diversification that would not have happened in isolation.[51]

The biggest novelty—and one facilitating social action more than parochial assistance—was the importation of female religious congregations from Europe. A few cloistered orders came, but the vast majority of the nuns came in active congregations—such as the Sisters of Charity, who had been invited to enter by the imperial government—that ran schools, hospitals, and social services. There were 63 foreign-born nuns in Brazil in 1872 and 1,181 in 1920.[52] Because the separation of church and state had taken religious instruction out of public schools, and because the Protestant missionaries were doing too well at establishing American-style schools, the bishops were prodded to invest heavily and quickly in Catholic teacher-training academies, Catholic high schools,

49. Gilberto Freyre, *Order and Progress: Brazil from Monarchy to Republic* (Berkeley: University of California Press, 1986), 322–326. Freyre portrays the Trappists as exceptions, but the Trappists were by no means the only religious order providing social services in that municipality. Capuchins of the Convento de Santa Clara carried out missions and taught in Catholic schools; the Irmãs de São José ran a boarding school for two hundred girls, a day school for another three hundred, a hospital, and a poorhouse. See "Secção retrospectiva (Continuação): Taubaté," *Boletim Ecclesiástico de São Paulo* 1, no. 10 (Abril 1906): 319–20.
50. Eul-Soo Pang, "The Changing Roles of Priests in the Politics of Northeast Brazil, 1889–1964," *The Americas* 30, no. 3 (1974): 341–72.
51. Roger Finke and Patricia Wittberg, "Organizational Revival from Within: Explaining Revivalism and Reform in the Roman Catholic Church," *Journal for the Scientific Study of Religion* 39, no. 2 (June 2000): 154–70.
52. Total female religious in 1920 reached 2,942. See "População do Brazil por profissões segundo a nacionalidade e o sexo dos habitantes em 1872," in *Recenseamento de 1920*, v. 4, parte 5, viii–ix.

and even a few Catholic primary schools. French religious orders were notable for promoting women's education. Children of the upper and middle classes of Brazil were now much more likely to get a "Catholic education" than they had been in the nineteenth century, and by 1920 a generation had been formed in the new Catholic schools—which were also schools in a European, often French, mold.[53] Some of the orders would admit Brazilian girls as novices, and middle-class families were more accepting of girls' than boys' religious vocations. Thus by 1920, 60 percent of female religious were Brazilian-born.

NEW DEVOTIONS, NEW ASSOCIATIONS

During the first generation after *Rerum novarum*, there was relatively little explicitly Catholic action targeted at labor unions, factory discipline, or opposition to socialist parties. Instead, the key initiative of Catholic action, moving in the direction of the confederated Catholic Action of the 1920s, was to mobilize a Catholic-identified laity that was responsive to clerical leadership and that resonated with the global platform of the church.

Some of the initiative entailed subtle and unsubtle pressure to suppress older devotions. Bishops and parish priests did what they could to curtail autonomous *irmandades*, pilgrimages, processions, and festivals and, of course, to regulate purported miracles such as the bleeding Host in the mouth of Padre Cícero's *beata*. Traditional pilgrimage centers such as Bom Jesus da Lapa, the natural grotto on the banks of the São Francisco River in Bahia, were not shut down, but bishops tried to control them better. Typically, they sent in a European religious order to manage their finances, moderate the fairs and festivals around them, and channel devotions into a modern style. The bishops were most successful in upgrading regional devotions to the Virgin of Aparecida into a national pilgrimage. Perhaps they favored Aparecida because it was strategically located on the railway between São Paulo

53. On the Collège de Sion, founded in 1888 in Rio de Janeiro, see Jeffrey Needell, *A Tropical Belle Epoque: Elite Culture and Society in Turn-of-the-Century Rio de Janeiro* (Cambridge: Cambridge University Press, 1987), 58–62. When Brian Owensby argues that the idea of the middle class in Brazil (1920–1960) comprised an ethos of "social service as a nonpolitical vocation," he might recognize more emphatically that it was largely shaped in these Catholic normal schools. See Brian Owensby, *Intimate Ironies: Modernity and the Making of Middle-Class Lives in Brazil* (Palo Alto, Calif.: Stanford University Press, 1999), 217, 226–29.

and Rio de Janeiro, and perhaps because her image was a black Virgin. The bishop of São Paulo appointed Redemptorist fathers to administer the shrine at Aparecida and, in 1904, carried out a mass ceremony of coronation of the Virgin as a national civic and religious celebration.[54]

More of their initiative was creative and additive: to launch and favor the new associations and devotions, such as the Apostleship of Prayer (Apostolado da Oração) that had developed in Europe for mass evangelization in modernizing societies. A Jesuit, Father Bartolomeu Taddei, introduced the Apostolado, beginning in 1872 in São Paulo. He spread it rapidly. The apostleship had been founded by Jesuit seminarians in France to bring Jesuit practices of prayer and meditation to rural people. And in France, it defended a special devotion to the Sacred Heart of Jesus, the highly partisan symbol of rejection of the revolutionary, republican state and of allegiance to traditional Catholic patriotism. In Brazil, the Sacred Heart had less partisan connotation. But just as in France, color chromolithograph images of the Sacred Heart, distributed by the Apostolados, soon filled homes everywhere.

Two characteristics of the Apostolados were particularly innovative. It offered ascending degrees of spiritual commitment and local leadership; members in higher ranks took on greater commitments of prayer and of frequent communion. Chapter leaders, the *Zeladores* (promoters), had significant responsibilities of recruitment and fundraising. And it synchronized members in Brazil with those across the world; members were asked to pray on the pope's chosen "intention of prayer" theme for a month, a week, or a day. The *Messenger of the Sacred Heart of Jesus* bulletin, launched in Ireland in 1888, was imitated by apostleships around the world. Each issue of Brazil's monthly *Mensageiro do Coração de Jesus*, founded in 1896, opened by announcing the pope's intention for the coming month. For August 1898, it was devotion to the Holy Spirit, but for September 1898, it was to be "the question of workers"; members were primed to pray on this theme with an essay about Pope Leo's encyclical on the condition of the working classes and a discussion of the mutual obligations of employers and employees.[55] The Apostolados also promoted prayer on "special

54. De Groot, *Brazilian Catholicism*, 135–36.

55. "Intenção geral do mez de setembro: As classes operárias," *Mensageiro do Coração de Jesus* 3, no. 27 (August 1898): 121–127. There were concrete Brazilian initiatives to workers; the chaplain of the factory at Camaragibe, Pernambuco, wrote that devotion to the Sacred Heart had put an end to fighting among the workers. See *Mensageiro* 4, no. 39 (Agosto 1899): 189.

intentions" of national interest, such as the condition of the dioceses of Paraná, or "the revitalization of a parish." Addressing the Canudos war, the *Mensageiro* of October 1897 reminded its readers of the perspective of soldiers' mothers, who had perhaps tried to raise their sons with religion but found them at risk of dying "with a sentiment of vile hatred in their hearts."[56] Zeladores were asked to do more than pray; during the drought of 1899, the *Mensageiro* asked all to pray for relief of the horrors of hunger, disease, and drought in Bahia and asked Zeladores to collect alms.[57]

Like much of the rebuilt church, the Apostolados flourished as a women's organization, which diminished its potential as a lever of a coordinated Catholic political movement. In Rio de Janeiro and São Paulo around 1915, men were a fifth or less of its membership (they were usually at least half of the members of irmandades), and the Zeladores were almost always women (*Zeladoras*). This dismayed the editors of the *Mensageiro*; one contributor confided that "men's *scarecrow* is *confession!*"[58] Still, its membership was between 1 percent and 2 percent of the population—as large as any mobilized political group in Brazil, as large as the electorate. If women could not vote, they could write. It was probably the Apostolados who mobilized women for the Catholic petition drive of 1898 against a bill in Congress proposing liberalization of divorce. Within weeks, parish priests and activist women solicited 172,000 signatures against divorce.[59]

RELIGIOUS SOCIETIES AND CATHOLIC WORKERS' CIRCLES

Scores of new, differentiated societies were founded, including the Devotion of St. Joseph (Devoção de São José) aimed at working-class fathers and the Salesian Cooperators, dedicated to supporting vocational training for poor boys and girls. The Saint Vincent de Paul societies were probably the crucially activist lay association. The imperial government had invited French Vincentian fathers, the Congregation of the Mission, known in Brazil as the Lazaristas, to run seminaries

56. *Mensageiro* 2, no. 17 (October 1897): 236.
57. *Mensageiro* 3, no. 82 (Janeiro 1899): 426–27, 485.
58. *Mensageiro* 2, no. 17 (October 1897): 286.
59. De Groot, *Brazilian Catholicism*, 104–10.

and preach revival missions in the 1850s. It had also brought in the Vincentian Sisters of Charity. In Salvador, Bahia, a lay Sociedade de São Vicente de Paulo founded the Colégio Nossa Senhora dos Anjos, a school for poor girls, in 1854. They intended it to be run by the Filhas da Caridade de São Vicente de Paulo (Sisters of Charity) but because of a lack of funds had to close it and surrender it to the traditional, semi-official charitable brotherhood, the Santa Casa da Misericórdia (Holy House of Mercy), in 1862. The Bahian association seems to have dissolved then, but Vincentian Sisters of Charity returned a few years later. And associations calling themselves Sociedades de São Vicente de Paulo (Societies of Saint Vincent de Paul), apparently formed to raise funds for support of the male and female religious orders of Saint Vincent, appeared across Brazil in the 1850s and 1860s.[60]

The first lay Vincentian "conference" (a small group of no more than fifteen lay volunteers committing to visit the poor, and thus forming a Vincentian "family") was probably the one founded in 1872 in Rio de Janeiro, by Francisco Lemos Farias Coutinho (the Conde de Aljezur) and some Catholic physicians. Lazarist brothers in Rio may have prompted the 1872 founding. If so, then the Saint Vincent de Paul movement in Brazil grew less as a horizontal spread of activist lay volunteer associations, and more, like other pious associations, as an auxiliary organized vertically by priests.[61] Perhaps most "conferences" were like "societies," lay auxiliaries to the schools and charity houses run by the religious. Whatever the case, there were soon Conferences in Niterói (1873), Petrópolis (1873), Pernambuco (1874), and Ceará (1879).[62] There were at least fifty Saint Vincent associations in the state of Minas Gerais alone, in 1941.[63] In the 1950s, the Lazaristas claimed that there were more than 45,000 members of 2,907 Saint Vincent de Paul societies in Brazil. Today, the Brazilian web pages claim 20,000

60. Provincial budgets for São Paulo list subsidies to Saint Vincent de Paul Societies—not "conferences"—in the 1860s.

61. They may also have been less independent of the state than an ideal-type "voluntary association." Serbin points out that Vicentian organizations were the major recipients of state subsidies to social service works by Catholic lay and clerical organizations. See Kenneth Serbin, "State Subsidization of Catholic Institutions in Brazil, 1930–1964," Working Paper 181, Helen Kellogg Institute for International Studies, University of Notre Dame, 1992, 23.

62. Carlos Alberto de Menezes, *Ação social católica no Brasil: Corporativismo e sindicalismo*, edited by Padre Ferdinand Azevedo, SJ (São Paulo: CEPEHIB and Edições Loyola, 1986), 13.

63. Serbin, "State Subsidization of Catholic Institutions in Brazil, 1930–1964," table 4, [31], and [24–25].

conferences and 250,000 members of "the Vincentian Family" in Brazil; this would make Brazilians more than a third of the Vincentians in the world.[64] During the period in question, the Vincentian conferences were perhaps the most important site for the construction of an activist laity, rather than merely a partisan and ultramontane laity.[65]

The most publicized lay initiative toward industrial workers was Vincentian, the system established in Carlos Alberto de Menezes's textile factory in Camaragibe in 1891.[66] Menezes (1855–1904) brought the spirit and structure of the Vincentian Conferences to "the social question" of industrial workers' welfare and morale, organizing both managers and workers into welfare associations. He applied a disciplinary interpretation of the workers of the factory as a "family,"[67] echoing some of the invocations of *Rerum novarum*.[68] For some time, the suburban Camaragibe company town operated almost as an isolated utopian community, or at least as a special experiment in industrial paternalism. Later, "workers' circles" such as those of Camaragibe would become Brazil's preferred Catholic organizational response to the needs of workers.[69] By the 1920s and 1930s, not only through a succession of Brazilian experiments influencing one another but also by repeated reintroduction of French Catholic labor ideologies acquired in visits and study abroad, Catholic social teachings on labor paternalism had saturated the industrial ideology of military officers, engineers, and industrialists.[70] Menezes's early Catholic social experi-

64. Serbin, *Needs of the Heart*, 78; "A Sociedade de São Vicente de Paulo," www.ssvpbrasil .org.br/?pg=sobre_a_ssvp.

65. "Pelo Brazil," *Vozes de Petropolis* 3 (Julho 1909–Junho 1910): 222: "A worker writes in the *Bi-Hebdomario Catholico*: 'I can affirm with conviction that about the only Catholics in Brazil are the Vincentians (if we set aside the Ladies). Enter a church: we see just a few men approach the sacred supper of Communion; we call them aside … and barely a one of them is not a Vicentian. We go to the Catholic Circle, and we find that each of its members is a Vicentian. And if we went to all the other Catholic associations, their core is basically the same. The others, so-called Catholics, lack the ambition that dominates us: to all be practicing Catholics.'"

66. Menezes, *Ação social católica no Brasil*.

67. Sylvana Maria Brandão de Aguiar and Lúcio Renato Mota Lima, "A Fábrica de Tecidos de Camaragibe e sua organização cristã do trabalho (1891–1908)," *Revista de Teologia e Ciências da Religião da UNICAP* 1, no. 1 (December 2012): 160–95.

68. Nilo Pereira, "A encíclica Rerum Novarum em Pernambuco," *Ciência & Trópico* 19, no. 2 (Julho-Dezembro 1991): 287–94.

69. Jessie Jane Vieira de Souza, *Círculos Operários: A Igreja Católica e o mundo do trabalho no Brasil* (Rio de Janeiro: Editora UFRJ and FAPERJ, 2002).

70. Oliver Dinius, *Brazil's Steel City: Developmentalism, Strategic Power, and Industrial Relations in Volta Redonda, 1941–1964* (Palo Alto, Calif.: Stanford University Press, 2010), 28, 73.

ment was nearly forgotten, or it was dismissed as paternalism by historians influenced by liberation theology.[71] It is perhaps emblematic
of the lack of linear tradition in Brazil's Catholic social action that the
anthropologist Robin Nagle, writing about the famous showdown between liberation Catholics and conservative Catholics for control of the
parish of the Morro da Conceição in Recife, acknowledges but passes
over the dual role of Carlos Alberto de Menezes as both a precursor
of leftist social Catholicism ("a relevant Church") and as the patron of
the new, imported image of the Virgem da Conceição (Virgin of the
Conception) and the new, ultramontane-style mass procession to her
shrine in 1904.[72]

PADRE JÚLIO MARIA, CARDINAL LEME,
AND THE SOCIAL QUESTION

By 1910 a generic discourse on "the social question," the needs of
operários and *trabalhadores* (workers), as well as *pobres* (the poor), and
the dangers of anarchism and socialism had become routine and ubiq-
uitous across internal publications for clergy, devotional circulars for
pious families, and journals of opinion for sophisticated lay Catholics.
The *Boletim Interdiocesano do Rio de Janeiro*, for example, published a
series on the "social question" (titled *A questão social*), beginning in its
January 1921 issue. For a sick society, it stated, there were four dan-
gerous doctors: liberalism, anarchism, bolshevism, and socialism. The
true remedy, however, is Christianity, and Pope Leo XIII's encyclical
Rerum novarum, the guide.[73] Usually, this discourse seemed perfunc-
tory and superficial.

In Brazil, one of the few creative and heartfelt promoters of *Rerum
novarum* and a populist Christianity was the priest and polemicist Padre Júlio Maria. His idiosyncratic career may sum up the tentative ebb
and flow of a modern social Catholic intellectual identity before 1922.

He was born Júlio Cezar de Moraes Carneiro, in Angra dos Reis, in
1850; as a student at the São Paulo Law School, he spoke for a republic,
for European immigration, and for the abolition of slavery, and he brief-

71. Ralph Della Cava, "Catholicism and Society in Twentieth-Century Brazil," *Latin American Research Review* 11, no. 2 (1976): 7–50.
72. Robin Nagle, *Claiming the Virgin: The Broken Promise of Liberation Theology in Brazil*
(London: Routledge, 1997), 37–40.
73. *Boletim Interdiocesano do Rio de Janeiro* 3, no. 1 (Janeiro de 1921): 28–30.

ly joined a Masonic lodge—to learn to make speeches, he later claimed. After graduating, he tried political candidacies, switching from the Liberal to the Conservative Party, and obtained an appointment as judge in Mar de Espanha, Minas Gerais, where he married and, within a year, was widowed. He remarried and would be widowed again in 1889.[74]

Even then, a foreshadowing of the social question seemed to preoccupy him. In 1878 the planters of Mar de Espanha sent him as their representative to the Agrarian Congress (Congresso Agrícola) convened by the government to address a crisis of southern coffee planters: primarily, the need for agricultural credit and labor recruitment to replace slaves. There he spoke not only for the immediate implementation of relief credit, against railroads in favor of cart roads, and against Chinese contract labor in favor of European immigration ("civilized races") but also in favor of the training of "national" workers.[75] In the following years, he deepened his faith and began to attend church. After the death of his second wife and with his children grown, he entered the Mariana seminary at the age of thirty-nine, changing his name from Júlio Cezar to Júlio Maria; by 1891 he was ordained and appointed to the small industrial city of Juiz de Fora, Minas Gerais. He began to preach in towns across Minas.

In July 1894, Júlio Maria was invited to give lecture sermons in São Paulo, and the polemical series of lectures there made his national reputation. He spoke on faith and civilization; on faith, science, and reason; against positivism; and finally on liberalism and socialism. The lectures were transcribed and debated in the press. In 1895 he was given the title of Apostolic Missionary, which certified him to bishops as an itinerant preacher. From 1895 to 1903, he toured Brazil, delivering lectures on his favorite polemical topics, rarely failing to mention the church's commitment to the people. A series in Rio de Janeiro from March to May 1898, transcribed in the *Gazeta de Notícias*, hit hardest in citing European and American social Catholic teachings from the writings of Manning, Gibbons, and Ledeschi, promoting a populist, democratic church that would fight for social justice.[76]

74. Antonio Luiz Porto e Albuquerque, *Utopia e crise social no Brasil, 1871–1916: O pensamento de Padre Júlio Maria* (Rio de Janeiro: Fundação Casa de Rui Barbosa, 1994).

75. *Congresso Agrícola: Edição fac-similar dos anais do Congresso Agrícola, realizado no Rio de Janeiro, em 1878* (Rio de Janeiro: Fundacão Casa de Rui Barbosa, 1988).

76. Pe. Júlio Maria, C.S.S.R., *A igreja e o povo*, ed. João Fagundes Hauck (São Paulo: Edições Loyola and CEPEHIB, 1983).

These polemics begged opposition; a Positivist wrote a book rebutting his lectures in Belem do Pará. They provoked opposition within the clergy, too, from reactionary monarchists, knee-jerk antirepublicans, and those who feared any discussion of science. Theologians raised doubts about his arguments and came close to recommending that his works be placed on the Index. Bishops privately blackballed a proposal from the republican federal government that he be appointed bishop in Maranhão.[77] The lay intellectuals of the conservative Brazilian Historical and Geographical Institute (Instituto Histórico e Geográfico Brasileiro) admitted him to membership in 1899—although some of them, too, expressed reservations. Perhaps the height of his public life as spokesman for the progressive Catholic position was his publication of the article on "religion" in the official *Livro do Centenário* of 1900.[78] At the quadricentenary celebrations, he gave the sermon of the official Te Deum mass in Rio's Candelária Church.

In 1904 Júlio Maria entered the Redemptorist order after an abbreviated novitiate, not without reluctance on the part of the Dutch brothers who were happy to carry out missions in Brazil but not eager to integrate Brazilian recruits. Perhaps he was a poor fit, João Hauck suggests, because he preferred to preach to those outside the church, while the Redemptorists specialized in revivalism among Catholics. They saw little use for a brother who was a highbrow man of words. The Dutch brothers suspected that he was behind Cardinal Arcoverde's 1912 instruction requiring foreign religious to learn Portuguese before, not after, they began to preach and ordering them to schedule their revival missions at the convenience of parish priests. His late sermons turned to strident and apocalyptic jeremiads with a mystical tinge, warning that Brazil would soon be punished for its indifference and injustice.[79] Padre Júlio Maria died in 1916, leaving an ambivalent legacy and no direct successors.

Catholic Action in Brazil got its second wind—or for some, its first real breath—with the appointment of Dom Sebastião Leme to the archbishopric of Olinda and his 1916 pastoral letter on the need for a "rechristianization" of Brazil. Unlike Júlio Maria, Leme (1882–1942) was raised up in the church to become a leader: the son of a pious wid-

77. João Fagundes Hauck, "Esboço histórico," in *A igreja e o povo*, 21.
78. Maria, "Memoria: A religião."
79. Albuquerque, *Utopia e crise social no Brasil, 1871–1916.*

owed seamstress, he was placed in seminary at the age of twelve; was, at fourteen, sent to the Colegio Pío Latino Americano in Rome, where he finished at the top eight years later; was ordained in São Paulo at the age of twenty-two; and was called to be the auxiliary bishop to Cardinal Arcoverde of Rio at age twenty-nine. Leme was an inspiring organizer more than a polemicist. He responded to *A Lanterna* and the "case of Idalina" in 1910, not by writing rebuttals but by promoting a Catholic daily newspaper. He coordinated priests to regiment the Apostolados of São Paulo to march in a rally against the anticlerical lectures of Georges Clemenceau in 1910. His *Pastoral* of 1916 attracted notice because it argued confidently that Brazil already had a passive Catholic majority, passive because of religious ignorance, that could be turned into an effective majority by various forms of "education." His work in Rio de Janeiro and then in Recife showed a way: to commit priests and laypeople to catechism through the Congregation of Christian Doctrine (Congregação da Doutrina Cristã) and to coordinate existing Catholic associations into a strong Catholic action. When he was called back to Rio in 1921 as acting archbishop and then as cardinal, Leme spoke less himself directly than through the intellectuals he identified, inspired, and supported, such as Jackson de Figueiredo, who founded the journal *A Ordem* in 1921 and the Centro Dom Vital study group in 1922. In 1922 Cardinal Leme inaugurated a national Catholic Confederation (Confederação Católica) to unite, or at minimum coordinate, the various and diverse associations for occasional political and social action.[80] By 1937, he attempted to mandate that all Catholic lay associations join, and be subordinated to, an umbrella Catholic Action movement.[81]

Cardinal Leme is often credited with the rise of Brazilian lay Catholic social activism. Yet, as the examples discussed in this chapter demonstrate, his initiative was the culmination of movements to direct the clergy and laity toward social and political activism that began a generation earlier. True, they were sporadic, discontinuous, and diverse. But their diversity aided the growth of Catholic activism in Brazil, al-

80. Bruneau, *The Political Transformation of the Brazilian Catholic Church*, 44–47.

81. Irmã Maria Regina do Santo Rosário [Laurita Pessoa Raja Gabaglia], *O Cardeal Leme (1882–1942)* (Rio de Janeiro: J. Olympio, 1962); Euclides Marchi, "Igreja e povo: Católicos? Os olhares do Padre Júlio Maria e de Dom Sebastião Leme da Silveira Cintra sobre a catolicidade do brasileiro na passagem do século XIX para o XX," *História Questões & Debates* 55, no. 2 (July–December 2011): 83–110; Azzi, *O estado leigo e o projeto ultramontano.*

lowing for a variety of forms and styles of lay associations and religious congregations, which provided them greater flexibility in responding to Brazil's national situation after disestablishment.

By 1922, Catholic social actions—in the plural—had established a broad, internally inconsistent repertory of political stances and social initiatives. "Catholic" political positions were mostly conservative, but they could comprise the extremes of idealization of aristocracy or an equally idealized plebeian populist democracy. This latter Catholic populism required a casuistry by which to avoid endorsing the condemned "liberal" middle; the republican government could be accepted but not endorsed; all violence and disorder (anarchism, communism, even militant abolitionism) could only be condemned. Yet long before Leme's pastoral letter of 1916, lay and clerical leaders were insisting that Catholics could no longer be passive and "indifferent." Lay Catholics were demanded to support polarizing symbolic gestures of national Catholic identity and affiliation such as the placement of crucifixes in courtrooms (1892, 1906) and the coronation of the Virgin of Aparecida (1904). New associations, unlike the old confraternities, regimented and homogenized the vanguards of each parish; Catholics were now organized to subscribe to bulletins, to take cues, to pray on them, and to act on them. An early demonstration of their power showed in the petition campaign against divorce in 1898, and it would be confirmed by the mass rallies in Rio de Janeiro in the 1920s and 1930s.[82]

Catholic social interventions could extend deep into the lives of boys and girls in Catholic schools, including the working-class orphans sheltered in the Salesian vocational schools. Catholic missions were among the few initiatives that attempted to accelerate a nonviolent assimilation of Indians and to ease the adaptation of European immigrants to Brazilian life. Catholic associations provided about the only legitimate organizations through which women could participate in associational leadership and public life. The church sometimes defended the peasantry: priests undertook some pilot programs in rural cooperative organization, and a few populist lay preachers and priests supported peasant protests against heavy taxation and military recruitment. This support went far enough that the church hierarchy several times (Canudos in 1895, the Quebra-Quilos in 1874) had to publicly pull back and repudiate rebellions whose grievances had been nur-

82. De Groot, *Brazilian Catholicism*, 121–25.

tured by priests and lay preachers. And in a tentative way, Catholic businessmen and priests attempted to "moralize" the incipient organizations of factory workers and urban laborers.

None of this would have been possible without papal encouragement of the organizational reform of dioceses, a massive migration of European priests and religious to supplement the slow-growing Brazilian clergy, and a still-undocumented contribution of subsidies from Europe and from state governments that funded social services. That so many organizations, slogans, and symbols came ready-made from Europe, set for trimming to Brazilian circumstances, greatly facilitated the expansion and proliferation of Catholic organizations. It is notable that social questions not recognized in Europe, such as the appropriate manner in which to redress the many legacies of slavery, were much slower to be recognized by the Brazilian church. Homegrown Brazilian innovations such as Padre Ibiapina's houses of charity in small towns were downplayed and sometimes combated by bishops. And it is notable that the new forms of Catholic action flourished in the dynamic immigrant frontiers of the south and in the cities, not in the small towns of the north. Brazilian lay action was limited by the transnational content that gave it impetus.

PART II ❖ MARTYRDOM AND CATHOLIC RENEWAL IN THE MEXICAN REVOLUTION

CHAPTER 3

Eucharistic Angels
Mexico's Nocturnal Adoration and the Masculinization of Postrevolutionary Catholicism, 1910–1930

❖ Matthew Butler

On October 9, 1924, Catholic lawyer Miguel Palomar y Vizcarra addressed Mexico City's Eucharistic Congress on the topic of men and Holy Communion. Palomar's underlying theme was the affinity between Eucharistic participation and Catholic militancy, yet he described this relationship in masculine language: the Eucharist, Palomar stated, was an "ESSENTIALLY VIRILE SACRAMENT," an invigorating banquet of Christ's flesh that should fortify Catholics in the struggle to reconquer Mexican society. The Eucharist was also constitutive of Catholic manhood: "I have not come here to tell you that men should take communion because they are men," Palomar continued, "*but that they must be men because they take communion.*" Communion, in short, infused men with crusader strength, turning them into "real Catholics"; deprived of Eucharistic meat, they were weaklings.[1]

On one hand, Palomar recoded the practice of taking Communion as a masculine one, no doubt in an attempt to make Sunday Mass

My thanks to Julia Young and Steve Andes for their invitation to participate in the "Catholic Activism in the Americas" conference. Research was made possible by the generosity of the Mellon Foundation and Department of History at the University of Texas at Austin. In Mexico City, Father José Isaac, the ANM's spiritual director, kindly allowed me to consult issues of *La semilla eucarística*—the rare but essential source used here. I also thank Marco Pérez Iturbe of the Archivo Histórico del Arzobispado de México for his help.

1. Miguel Palomar y Vizcarra, *La comunión de los hombres: La Eucaristía es un sacramento esencialmente viril* (Mexico City: Editorial Ara, 1963), 1–9; emphasis original.

more appealing to men. His biblical citations, however, upheld a more inclusive notion of the Eucharist as the psalmist's "bread of angels," an idea powerfully expressed in the Spanish phrase "el pan de los fuertes" (the bread of the strong).[2] In addition, Palomar denounced the effete, pietistic church of the Porfiriato, whose sociopolitical "docility" he contrasted unfavorably with the Catholic militancy of the 1920s. In the final analysis, therefore, Palomar was not calling for a "defeminized" church but recasting the sociopolitical meekness of prerevolutionary Catholicism in gendered terms. The antidote was a normatively "masculine" church, one that incorporated men as well as women but that, fundamentally, had the courage of its Catholic convictions and defended those principles in the public sphere. Palomar's peroration was combative, yet also metaphorical: if Mexico were not to be decatholicized by revolutionaries then Catholics must fight to rechristianize the commonwealth, "in virile fashion, *like men.*"[3]

Palomar's speech vividly introduces a significant but neglected historiographical topic: the so-called "masculinization of religion," particularly in the early to mid-twentieth century.[4] At the same time, the ambiguities of his broadside—his conflation of agency and masculinity, the underlying tension between "discursive" and "demographic" variants of masculinization—forewarn us of the difficulties historians face when studying this phenomenon. What does the masculinization of religion *mean,* conceptually, and in any given historical setting?

This chapter hazards a preliminary answer to this question through a first study of the Mexican Nocturnal Adoration (Adoración Nocturna Mexicana, or ANM), a men's confraternity founded in 1900 mainly for the purpose of Eucharistic Adoration.[5] Along the way, I suggest

2. Psalm 78:25.

3. Palomar y Vizcarra, *La comunión de los hombres,* 13; emphasis added.

4. The existing historiography is Eurocentric. For useful overviews, see Patrick Pasture, Jan Art, and Thomas Buerman, eds., *Gender and Christianity in Modern Europe: Beyond the Feminization Thesis* (Leuven: University of Leuven Press, 2012); Yvonne Maria Werner, ed., *Christian Masculinity: Men and Religion in Northern Europe in the Nineteenth and Twentieth Centuries* (Leuven: University of Leuven Press, 2011). Elsewhere, I have argued that the reproachful Sacred Heart devotion was masculinized c. 1914 via a new and triumphalist devotional offshoot—the Mexican cult of Christ the King. Matthew Butler, "La coronación del Sagrado Corazón de Jesús en la Arquidiócesis de México, 1914," in *Revolución, cultura, y religión: Nuevas perspectivas regionales, siglo XX,* ed. Yolanda Padilla Rangel, Luciano Ramírez Hurtado, and Francisco Javier Delgado Aguilar (Aguascalientes: Universidad Autónoma de Aguascalientes, 2012), 24–68.

5. Studies of sacramental attitudes in Mexico are themselves rare. For a suggestive treatment focusing on women's Eucharistic Adoration, see Margaret Chowning, "The Catholic

that Catholic opposition to Mexico's postrevolutionary state cannot be understood without reference to organizations such as the ANM and the kind of Eucharistic fervor they inculcated in men. As we shall see, ANM branches ("sections") mushroomed after the revolution, becoming a feature of life in hundreds of parishes, especially in states associated with Cristero violence. As we shall also see, the ANM created a powerful Eucharistic identity for Catholic men, one that combined select aspects of hegemonic masculinity (quasi-military discipline, loyalty to authority, steadfastness) with a deeply emotive approach to the church's senior sacrament. Eucharistic Adoration also elevated laymen as religious mediators to an almost sacerdotal dignity. More than any other organization, the ANM created a link between men's Eucharistic and public selves. The significance of this becomes apparent when we recall that the strongest resistance offered by Mexican Catholics to the revolutionary state (or any other) originated in the impossibility, as of August 1926, of receiving the Eucharist in public. Henceforth, thousands of Catholic men, and as many women, risked their lives in a bloody and drawn-out confrontation with the Mexican government.

FROM FEMINIZATION TO MASCULINIZATION?

The question of men's everyday religiosity is thus an important, if neglected, one. Ultimately, however, my contention is that the history of Catholic action should embrace gender categories, including masculinity but not excluding others. Here we at once confront a conceptual, also an empirical, problem: how to reconcile an emphasis on Catholic men with the "feminization-of-religion" thesis.[6] If nothing else, this re-

---

Church and the Ladies of the Vela Perpetua: Gender and Devotional Change in Nineteenth-Century Mexico," *Past and Present* 221, no. 1 (2013): 197–237.

6. The "feminization-of-religion" thesis typically describes one of two things, or both. On the one hand, it is argued that women came to predominate in the religious sphere over the nineteenth century because men denied them outlets in the public sphere. Alternatively, it is claimed that devotion itself became "feminized," more given to affect and, in the case of Catholicism, to a sentimental, kitschy Marianism. Feminization thus denotes a demographic as well as a discursive shift. Barbara Welter, "The Feminization of American Religion: 1800–1860," in *Clio's Consciousness Raised: New Perspectives on the History of Women*, ed. Mary Hartman and Lois Banner (New York: Harper and Row, 1974), 137–57, is often cited as foundational. For Mexicanist examples, see Chowning, "The Catholic Church and the Ladies of the Vela Perpetua"; Silvia Arrom, "Mexican Laywomen Spearhead a Catholic Revival: The Ladies of Charity, 1863–1910," in *Religious Culture in Modern Mexico*, ed. Martin Austin Nesvig (Lanham, Md.: Rowman & Littlefield, 2007), 50–77; Edward Wright-Rios, *Revolutions in Mexican Catholicism*, and "La Madre Matiana: Prophetess and

quires us to clarify what we mean by "masculinization"—which I take to mean men's real and rhetorical participation in an increasingly gendered division of spiritual labor in the church, *not* the defenestration of Catholic women. Turning to our case study, the ANM recoded certain Eucharistic activities as "male" and created a paradigm of sacrificial religiosity for men. It also stressed the ties between worthy Eucharistic reception and Catholic social militancy. Yet it did so as part of an overall reinvigoration of Catholicism that involved both men and women, whose declared aim was a religious restoration.[7]

This is an important point, given that in some accounts, religious "masculinization" is seen as counterfeminization: checking or reversing the growing predominance of women, and women's religion, in the church. In this interpretation, moreover, religious masculinization is sometimes depicted as a cultural response to a secular crisis of masculinity, not a discrete or even a fundamentally religious phenomenon.[8]

Nation in Mexican Satire," *The Americas* 68, no. 2 (2011): 241–74, and *Searching for Madre Matiana: Prophecy and Popular Culture in Modern Mexico* (Albuquerque: University of New Mexico Press, 2014); Patience Schell, "An Honorable Avocation for Ladies: The Work of the Mexico City Unión de Damas Católicas Mexicanas, 1912–1926," *Journal of Women's History* 10, no. 4 (1999): 78–103; Laura O'Dogherty, "Restaurarlo Todo en Cristo: La Unión de Damas Católicas Mejicanas, 1920–1926," *Estudios de Historia Moderna y Contemporánea de México* 14 (1991): 129–58.

7. See José Alberto Moreno Chávez, *Devociones políticas: Cultura católica y politización en la Arquidiócesis de México, 1880–1920* (Mexico City: El Colegio de México, 2013); and, more generally, Matthew Butler, ed., *Faith and Impiety in Revolutionary Mexico* (New York: Palgrave, 2007).

8. In the United States, Gail Bederman argues that the "Men and Religion Forward" movement of the 1910s reacted against "effeminate" Victorian Protestantism in protest against the bland consumerism that had supplanted freewheeling nineteenth-century capitalism. As men's socioeconomic existences became less than heroic, they rejected the symbolic forms of emasculation that had been deployed to moralize the more virile capitalist order of the past and demanded churches governed by and for men. Meanwhile, in Wilhelmine Bavaria, or so argues Derek Hastings, so-called "Reform" Catholics saw growing feminization in the church as part of a *fin-de-siècle* crisis affecting German masculinity. Their response was to call for a hypermasculine Catholicism and reject Ultramontane piety as a "eunuch" religion. And in turn-of-the-century Ireland, says Joseph Nugent, Catholic nationalists feared that men would resubmit meekly to British hegemony following the collapse of Parnell's Home Rule movement. Once again, Catholicism—in the form of a patriotic cult to the Irish soldier saint Columba—was called upon to arrest a mundane crisis by providing a religious antidote to John Bull colonialism. See, respectively, Gail Bederman, "'The Women Have Had Charge of the Church Long Enough': The Men and Religion Forward Movement of 1911–1912 and the Masculinization of Middle Class Protestantism," in *A Mighty Baptism: Race, Gender, and the Creation of American Protestantism*, ed. Susan Juster and Lisa MacFarlane (Ithaca, N.Y.: Cornell University Press, 1996), 107–40; Derek Hastings, "Fears of a Feminized Church: Catholicism, Clerical Celibacy, and the Crisis of Masculinity in Wilhelmine Germany," *European History Quarterly* 38, no. 1 (2008): 34–65; Joseph Nugent, "The Sword and the Prayerbook: Ideals of Authentic Irish Manliness," *Victorian Studies* 50, no. 4 (2008): 587–613.

There are problems with such a reading. First, it rests on a notion of secular crisis affecting men in bourgeois societies that both transcends religion and the church yet is resolved through it. Likewise, it is too linear and presupposes a religious "reconquest" by men: a chronological shift from a femininized to a masculinized church occurs. For the same reason, it could be objected that this kind of interpretation is built on an inexact reading of the feminization thesis.[9] Some historians of European Catholicism, for instance, note that evidence for a demographic feminization of the nineteenth-century church is inconclusive; likewise, they show how discursively "feminine" elements, such as the Immaculate Conception, could be deployed in "masculine" ways, with Mary as warrior queen, not as eternal wallflower. As Stephen Andes argues in a subsequent chapter in this volume, for example, this masculinization of the feminine can be seen clearly in Mexican appropriations of the character of Thérèse de Lisieux.

Finally, it is arguable that the feminization thesis in some cases obscures ordinary men's religiosity by focusing on piety to the detriment of other spheres (politics, social action), where men were overrepresented. The point is not, of course, that the feminization idea is "wrong" but that it must not be used partially or as a kind of master narrative for the church.[10]

A more convincing interpretation, in my view, contends that masculinization was less a question of defeminizing religion than of rechurching men *as part of* a campaign to strengthen the church and broaden its base.[11] This has the advantage of placing religion center stage, rather than instrumentalizing it: it is the church that is in retreat, with men's mobilization viewed as a solution to a religious crisis, rather than the

9. See Patrick Pasture, "Beyond the Feminization Thesis: Gendering the History of Christianity in the Nineteenth and Twentieth Centuries," in *Gender and Christianity in Modern Europe: Beyond the Feminization Thesis*, ed. Patrick Pasture, Jan Art, and Thomas Buerman (Leuven: University of Leuven Press, 2012), 7–33; and Olaf Blaschke, "The Unrecognized Piety of Men: Strategies and Success of the Re-masculinisation Campaign around 1900," in *Christian Masculinity: Men and Religion in Northern Europe in the Nineteenth and Twentieth Centuries*, ed. Yvonne Maria Werner (Leuven: University of Leuven Press, 2011), 21–45.

10. Pasture, "Beyond the Feminization Thesis," 7.

11. Efforts to capture the souls of migrant Irish workers in nineteenth-century Boston and New York, for instance, were driven by the need to create a more inclusive, robust church, avers Colleen McDannell. The primary concern was religious, which is why masculinization meant adjusting Mass schedules to fit men's working lives and offering alternative sites of Catholic sociability to taverns and billiard halls. Colleen McDannell, "'True Men As We Need Them': Catholicism and the Irish-American Male," *American Studies* 27, no. 2 (1986): 19–36.

church coming to the aid of a floundering masculinity. This kind of interpretation also makes it easier to see feminization and masculinization as complementary, not contradictory. Tine Van Osselar's studies of Belgium's Sacred Heart League and Carol Harrison's fine study of papal *zouaves* (boy soldiers from nineteenth-century France who fought for Pius IX against Piedmontese nationalists) seem more persuasive in that they present a decidedly nonlinear, nuanced view of masculinization, both as practice and discourse. Belgian Catholic Action worked hard to enlist men in the 1930s, Van Osselar shows, because men were thought to influence the public sphere, not because women were running riot in the church. The idea that the church needed men to "save" it from women was unusual, she argues, the preserve of a few ecclesiastical eccentrics such as Father Mäder. League men were described as *milites Christi* (soldiers of Christ), yet they were also described as lamblike in submitting to ecclesiastical authority. Thus, a secular concept of masculinity was altered by the religious ideal of humility. Interestingly, Van Osselar argues, Belgian women were told to see themselves as home-front heroines. "Manliness" was an abstract virtue, in sum, that men were encouraged to show in one sphere and women in another.[12] The archetypal zouave, Harrison shows, was a courtly and saintly figure possessing "masculine" and "feminine" virtues, being both martial and chaste, courageous but seeking immolation on the field above victory. It was not that nineteenth-century French Catholicism deliberately subverted republican notions of gender, Harrison tells us, but that Catholic values—obedience, self-sacrifice—inflected zouave gender identities. The right question to ask, Harrison suggests, is what gender might mean to people whose worldview encompassed divine as well as social elements; the zouave experience makes no sense if we insist on a rigid division between masculine republicanism and a feminized Catholicism.[13] These insights are useful to understanding Mexico's Nocturnal Adoration as the purveyor of a Catholic form of masculinity and in clari-

12. Tine Van Osselar, "'From that Moment on, I Was a Man!' Images of the Catholic Male in the Sacred Heart Devotion," in *Gender and Christianity in Modern Europe*, ed. Patrick Pasture, Jan Art, and Thomas Buerman (Leuven: University of Leuven Press, 2012), 121–35; "Christening Masculinity? Catholic Action and Men in Interwar Belgium," *Gender and History* 21, no. 2 (2009): 380–401; and "'Heroes of the Heart': Ideal Men in the Sacred Heart Devotion," *Journal of Men, Masculinities, and Spirituality* 3, no. 1 (2009): 22–40.

13. Carol E. Harrison, "Zouave Stories: Gender, Catholic Spirituality, and French Responses to the Roman Question," *The Journal of Modern History* 79 (2007): 274–305, esp. 297, 304.

fying its primary purpose as a vehicle designed to involve men in the broad push to recatholicize Mexican society. In what follows, I try to bring these ideas out in discussions, first, of the theological bases of the ANM, and then of its modus operandi, structure, and history, most obviously within the Mexican Revolution.

THEOLOGICAL BASES OF NOCTURNAL ADORATION

Eucharistic Adoration as practiced by the ANM developed from two theological traditions, one more contemplative and medieval and one reparatory and modern. On one hand, Nocturnal Adoration—literally, gazing on the Blessed Sacrament in the quiet of night—was an act of private reflection, a meditation on Christ's Eucharistic sacrifice that was designed to inspire or intensify feelings of corresponding love in the adorer, ideally as a prelude to reception of the Eucharist. In this sense, the Nocturnal Adoration was similar to many other extraliturgical Eucharistic devotions, such as the Forty Hours or the Perpetual Vigil. In another sense, Nocturnal Adoration was distinctive, inasmuch as adorers were held to join actively with Christ in offering reparatory prayers to God, becoming co-participants in a kind of spiritual, even supernatural, agency. From an epistemological perspective, of course, any kind of expository, extraliturgical cult to the Blessed Sacrament only made sense in relation to the doctrine of transubstantiation, that is, the belief that the Eucharistic elements were transformed literally into Christ's flesh and blood through sacerdotal intervention in the Mass. The distant origins of all forms of Eucharistic Adoration were therefore found in the eleventh and twelfth centuries, when, as Miri Rubin shows, a "realist" doctrine of the Eucharist, premised on an Aristotelian distinction between the form and substance of matter, was introduced. This metaphysical division accepted, the Eucharistic elements were at once of divine substance, hence worthy of reverence, while retaining the appearance of their accidental forms, bread and wine. Initially, devotion centered on the transformative moment of the Mass, the elevation. Adoration of the Blessed Sacrament soon escaped the confines of the Mass, however, and was institutionalized in the feast of Corpus Christi, itself inspired by the visions of a female religious from thirteenth-century Lièges, then introduced to the thirteenth- and fourteenth-century church by Urban IV (*Transitorius*, 1264) and John XXII (*Clementines*,

1317). From here, it was a shorter step to early modern sodalities and modern canonical associations devoted to veneration of the Blessed Sacrament.[14]

Hence, Nocturnal Adoration was a relatively recent addition to the broad family of extraliturgical devotions that developed alongside the Catholic doctrine of the Eucharist and that ultimately rested on the theological identification of Eucharistic signifier and signified. Nocturnal Adoration's second precursor was the Holy Hour, a pious practice instigated by Margaret Mary Alacoque, the seventeenth-century French Visitandine most associated with her visions of the Sacred Heart.[15] The assimilation of the Holy Hour into the practice of Eucharistic Adoration made the Nocturnal Adoration distinctive, not only temporally (its vigils, such as the Holy Hour, were observed at night) but in terms of its own theology. Alacoque's ecstatic autobiography, written in her convent cell at Paray-Le-Monial from 1685 and published posthumously in Rome (1726), makes this clear. Alacoque vividly describes how Christ's Sacred Heart, wreathed in flames, instructed her to perform a Holy Hour lying prostrate before the Blessed Sacrament on Thursday nights from eleven to midnight. Thursday, it should be recalled, was the night in which Christ agonized in the garden, praying to God while the disciples disobeyed His command to keep watch and slept. As Alacoque recounted it, the purpose of the nocturnal vigil was therefore twofold. First, like some consoling angel, she was to comfort Christ as He submitted to God's will and accepted death on the cross. Second, she was to unite with Christ in praying to God for sinners, assuming an expiatory mantle and co-mediating between God and humankind.[16] This reparatory function brought the Holy Hour into similar devotion-

14. Miri Rubin, *Corpus Christi: The Eucharist in Late Medieval Culture* (Cambridge: Cambridge University Press, 1992), 14–30, 164–89.

15. Raymond Jonas, *France and the Cult of the Sacred Heart: An Epic Tale for Modern Times* (Berkeley: University of California Press, 2000).

16. Alacoque's citation is as follows: "'I will be thy strength,' He said to me, 'fear nothing, but be attentive to My voice and to what I shall require of thee that thou mayest be in the requisite dispositions for the accomplishment of My designs. In the first place thou shalt receive Me in Holy Communion as often as obedience will permit thee whatever mortification or humiliation it may cause thee, which thou must take as pledges of My love. Thou shalt, moreover, communicate on the First Friday of every month. Every night between Thursday and Friday I will make thee share in the mortal sadness which I was pleased to feel in the Garden of Olives, and this sadness, without thy being able to understand it, shall reduce thee to a kind of agony harder to endure than death itself. And in order to bear Me company in the humble prayer that I then offered to My Father, in the midst of My anguish, thou shalt rise between eleven o'clock

al territory to the Sacred Heart, with all that this implied in terms of redeeming a world beset by revolutionary convulsions and secular libertines. The difference was that reparation was to be achieved specifically through appeals to the Eucharistic Christ, not the Sacred Heart; devotion centered on the singular grace of Christ's self-sacrifice, not diffusely, on the sum total of His charity, as with the Sacred Heart. For this reason, however, adorers' prayers were held to be more efficacious. Indeed, theologians contended that the Holy Hour—as a memorial of Christ's agony in Gethsemane and preparation for the sacrifice of Mass—perfectly linked Christ's Eucharistic victimhood in the Last Supper and His physical victimhood on Calvary. The night hours thus provided the ideal window through which to contemplate, and so reciprocate, Christ's acts of sacrificial love, and to pray to God the Father in the presence of the dutiful, obedient Son.[17]

No matter how obscure or entangled these theological roots, adorers in 1920s Mexico must have been conscious of them, at least to a degree. "Adoration means ... to worship, and also to give thanks [to Christ] for the infinite love that He manifests for us in the Eucharist," the ANM's short manifesto ran.[18] Readers of the ANM's monthly periodical, *La Semilla Eucarística*, were reminded that the practice of adoration originated in the miracle of transubstantiation: just as it was indisputable that God had created laws to transubstantiate food into human flesh, ran a June 1926 article, "[r]eason tells me that God ... with His powerful Word can convert bread and wine into His flesh and blood."[19] These, evidently, were didactic devices, designed intellectually to interiorize the meaning of the Eucharist and its supporting doctrines. Beyond the more generic aspects of Eucharistic adoration, however, ANM publications cultivated an idea of lay priesthood based

---

and midnight, and remain prostrate with Me for an hour, not only to appease the divine anger by begging for mercy for sinners, but also to mitigate in some way the bitterness which I felt at that time on finding Myself abandoned by My apostles, which obliged Me to reproach them for not being able to watch for one hour with Me. During that hour thou shalt do what I shall teach thee.'" Margaret Mary Alacoque, *The Autobiography of St. Margaret Mary* (Rockford, Ill.: Tan Books and Publishers, 1986), 70–71.

17. See Joseph Dargaud, *Sainte-Marguerite Marie et l'Eucharistie* (Paray-Le-Monial, 1921), trans. and reprinted as *The Eucharist in the Life of St. Margaret Mary* (Kenasha, Wisc.: Prow/ Franciscan Marytown Press, 1979), 12, 146–50.

18. "Breves indicaciones sobre la Adoración Nocturna Mexicana," *La Semilla Eucarística*, March 15, 1914, 5.

19. *La Semilla Eucarística* XVIII, no. 12, June 1926, 1.

on reparation before, and with, the Eucharistic Christ. The preface of the 1924 *Ritual de la Adoración Nocturna Mexicana*, the office for adorers, was explicit about this: adorers were to imitate the priestly Christ in the Garden as He prayed to God the Father for humanity.[20] "So far as is possible," the preface ran, "[t]he Nocturnal Adorer of *Jesús Sacramentado* imitates his divine model, Jesus":

> He withdraws from the commotions of the night in order to accompany Jesus, who prays for sinners in the Blessed Sacrament. In the solitude of the night, the Nocturnal Adorer asks God to forgive his own sins, and endeavors to satisfy God on behalf of those who do not ask for forgiveness, those who offend Him, and those who curse Him. The Nocturnal Adorer pleads for all without exception; in imitation of Jesus in the Garden, he prays for those that do not pray, and asks for mercy and forgiveness of his own sins, for the sins of his brothers and enemies, as Jesus Christ shed His Blood for all; he pleads for the sins of the nation and of the whole world.[21]

Obviously, the *Ritual* represents this aspect of the devotion in its idealized form, leaving us with the tricky methodological problem of establishing a convincing rapport between pray*ers'* inner thoughts and their prayers as printed formulae rendered aloud. Formal Eucharistic iterations tell us only part of the story; what is also needed, as Rubin reminds us, is an appreciation of the enveloping cultural field—what Rubin calls a "framework of meaning"—in and against which paper formulae were received, understood, and reenacted.[22] Nonetheless, we are helped by *La Semilla Eucarística*, which regularly published devotional compositions from individual adorers. Perhaps unsurprisingly, given the general context of revolutionary persecution, these reveal that some 1920s adorers placed heavy emphasis on their mediatory function. In one text published in April 1927, for instance, "Prayer on the Lord's Agony," an anonymous adorer placed himself in the Garden of Olives as Christ's guardian angel and wished for His heroic fortitude in atoning for humanity's imperfections. "Why, my Divine Master, do I not learn from You where I must go to seek redress and consolation when I find myself tempted and afflicted?" this adorer asked,

---

20. *Ritual de la Adoración Nocturna Mexicana: Segunda parte del reglamento* (Mexico City: Imprenta J. I. Muñoz, 1924). Written in Latin with Spanish notes, and with outsize red and black print for easier reading in dark churches, the *Ritual de la Adoración Nocturna Mexicana*'s publication was timed to coincide with Mexico's 1924 Eucharistic Congress.

21. Ibid., vii–viii.

22. Rubin, *Corpus Christi*, 5–8.

You, my good Jesus, go to the Father who commands you to die for me, to the very hand that tries and falls heavily upon You, knowing that [God] will not dispense the suffering that is decreed for You … Oh, divine reflection of my soul, I see You sweating blood, clothed in sadness as You pray! At prayer I see you visited by an angel, and when You must feel the greatest despair, I watch You walk out and greet those who come to seize You … You reveal Yourself, love of my soul, as another: resolute in what You fear, strong in what You dread, resigned to what troubles You.[23]

If this was a very personal piece, another adorer's testimony published in July 1927 emphasized the adorer's role in co-mediating between God and a fallen world. "Our Lord is our Mediator, our Advocate," it began, "But how divinely does He carry out this office in the Holy Eucharist!":

That is where the attentive and vigilant soul who implores Him is truly present … Yet it would be too little to approach the Divine Mediator for our own benefit; let us embrace in our prayer all souls; let us offer them to the Father via Jesus. His Heart is all powerful in reconciling souls to God. If Jesus wishes to be honored, it is, above all, "so as to renew in our souls the effects of His Redemption" [the citation was attributed to Alacoque], becoming our Mediator … Next to the altar, at the sacred Table, we are, then, omnipotent. Let us eat there and rejoice in presenting to the God of all Holiness the Heart of the Redeemer, saying with the Prophet: "Listen, Oh God, to the prayers of your beloved Son and the pleadings of His Heart! Out of love for Him, show us your Face, incline, my God, your ear, and listen; open your eyes and gaze upon this Heart."[24]

A second text published in July 1927 shows how the devotion's expiatory ethos could be attuned to political matters and confirms, in passing, that an ad hoc form of public adoration continued in the absence of ordained priests and the Blessed Sacrament, which could not be displayed in churches during the Cristiada. In somewhat poetic fashion, lastly, this piece also highlights the rising vigor of lay devotion as a form of spiritual intermediation. In churches left "cold" by the departure of the Eucharistic Christ, adorers themselves now formed a kind of coronet of Sacred Hearts communing directly with God on behalf of sinners, Mexico, and the church: "Around the now empty Sacrarium, in the devout solitude of the sacred precinct, the faithful members of the [Nocturnal] Adoration form a beautiful crown of loving hearts …

23. *La Semilla Eucarística* XIX, no. 10, April 1927, 229.
24. *La Semilla Eucarística* XX, no. 1, July 1927, 5–8.

[T]he slowly intoned prayers of the Adoration's *socios* [associates] rise to the Lord's throne, in reparation for sins committed ... and to demand light and grace and forgiveness for the poor sinner. To demand, furthermore, comfort for the Church in her current tribulations; and strength and constancy for those who fight [*combaten*] for her; and [an end] to the countless calamities that afflict our unfortunate Fatherland."[25]

PRACTICE AND STRUCTURE OF NOCTURNAL ADORATION

As we have seen, the Nocturnal Adoration's association with Gethsemane placed adorers in an unusually privileged spiritual position as interlocutors before God with the Eucharistic Christ. The closing plea for strength in battle was not, however, merely one adorer's fantasy. Rather, it reflected the simultaneously ecclesiastical and militaristic language and structure of the ANM. On one hand, adorers acquired a sacerdotal dignity as a group of religious intermediaries; they were, at the same time, described as soldiers in Christ's household guard. The ANM's "military" dimension is obscure, but, like other aspects of the devotion, it probably originated in nineteenth-century France as an extension of the Sacred Heart devotion. Moreno Chávez, for instance, notes the arrival in early Porfirian Mexico of the archconfraternity of the Guard of Honor, a sodality founded in Bourg in 1863 whose members were symbolically described as a devout "army" dedicated to defending the Sacred Heart, but who, in reality, were charged with resacralizing the everyday by constant churchgoing and invocations of the *Sacré Cœur*.[26]

Thus, emblematic militarism was a feature of Porfirian Catholicism. It suggested, in part, the waging of a pious campaign against secularism, and recast everyday religious commitments such as attending Mass and publicly invoking the Sacred Heart in heroic terms. It also posited a standardized, military-style hierarchy linking pious "regiments" such as the ANM with episcopal colonels and a Roman generalcy. If familiar, however, this martial ethos penetrated the ANM to an unusual degree, shaping practice as well as rhetoric. As stated in a 1914 document, for example, the ANM's purpose was "to form an

---

25. Ibid., 1–3.
26. Moreno Chávez, *Devociones políticas*, 148–57.

army of Soldiers for Christ-in-the Sacrament," comparable to a palace
or republican guard, and protecting its chief at night, "when it would
seem that He is alone."[27] The way in which ANM vigils were performed also suggested a military as well as an ecclesiastical template:
some practices (issuing written orders, borrowing army-style nomen-
clature, identifying adorers by rank and number) were straight imports
from the barrack room, just as others were as distinctly ecclesiastical
in character.[28]

A programmatic review of the basic vigil bears out this interpene-
tration. For a start, ANM branches were called *secciones* (sections) while
adoration in sections fell to nightly *turnos* (watches); on-duty adorers,
likewise, had to report to a "guard room" (usually a church annex with
camp beds) at 9:30 p.m. sharp and produce written orders to attend.
Entry to the guardroom, furthermore, was by password—"Adored be
the Blessed Sacrament" (the ANM's motto)—only. Inside, the secretary
of the watch recorded attendance, assigned adorers a number indicating their hour in the vigil, and collected written intentions for placing
on the altar. Meanwhile, adorers recited prayers in Latin or spiritual
writings, most frequently *The Imitation of Christ*. At 9:45 p.m., adorers
formed lines and marched to church. The vigil began at 10 p.m. with
a procession up the nave. On arrival at the altar, four adorers knelt at
reclinatorios (prie-dieux) placed left and right before the altar so that
two "choirs," each with a "first" and a "second" adorer, were formed.
Three things happened before the vigil proper began. First, the priest
exposed the Blessed Sacrament and censed the church. Second, the
section flag was lowered before the altar then placed next to the Bible.
Third, the watch's intentions were presented to the Blessed Sacrament.
Again, the purpose of this was to stress adorers' solidarity with Jesus
as humanity's guardian angels. Each adorer's intention was a worldly
battle to be won through prayerful alliance with the Eucharistic Christ:
"Our duty is to adore You for those that do not adore You; bless You
for those that blaspheme and curse You; expiate our own sins, with
exquisite pain in our hearts, and seek forgiveness for all the sins committed in the world; unite our intentions and pleas with Yours, so as
to calm the wrath of vengeful God, and make His merciful blessings

27. "Breves indicaciones," 3–5.
28. Adorers were required to learn simple rules for the pronunciation of liturgical Latin
(*Ritual de la Adoración Nocturna Mexicana*, xv–xxiv).

descend upon the earth." After the presentation of the guard, the priest departed and all adorers retired to sleep except for the members of the first two choirs of the watch, who remained kneeling. Between them the watch secretary and chief would relieve the various choirs in hourly periods through the night. All would be awake for the 4:30 a.m. Mass, when most would also take communion. The Sacrament would then be reserved for the next night's vigil, and the previous night's vigil would end.[29]

In the hours from 10 p.m. to 4 a.m., successive pairs of adorers recited hour-long sections from the "Office of the Blessed Sacrament," using the *Ritual*. As already described, the office began with prayers of invitation and presentation of the guard. The first *nocturno* (night watch) then commenced, consisting of a series of lessons and psalms in Latin with the two choirs reading alternate verses. This exercise was interrupted by a prayer in Spanish on the half hour; afterwards came the second nocturno, beginning at 11. At midnight, a Trisagium to the Holy Trinity and other prayers were recited in Spanish. At 1 a.m., the *A Laudes* began, consisting of prayers, psalms, and various canticles; at 2 a.m. came the *A Prima*, at 3 a.m., the *A Sexta*; and at 4 a.m., the *A Visperas*. As this last segment was being completed, the watch chief would stir sleeping adorers with a handbell for prayers and a series of preparatory Eucharistic exercises before the Mass.[30] Given its pro-tracted, Latin format, to modern eyes the vigil might look arcane. It is worth stressing, however, that all of the prayers said *in Spanish* at intervals between the different Latin sections of the Office were repara-tions for modernity's classical sins: in the first nocturno, for example, the prayer was offered in atonement for religious persecution, for im-pious newspapers, and the ingratitude that secularized "Catholic" na-tions had shown to God; the midnight prayer sequence called for har-mony between church and state and the extirpation of heresy. The only exceptions to this reparatory pattern were the brief prayers said for souls in purgatory, which perhaps evidenced the Nocturnal Adoration's distant origins in confraternities of the Blessed Sacrament. The vigil's overall tenor, in sum, was that of a Eucharistic homage dotted with cosmic war cries against the revolutionary world's stereotypical evils. With a mixture of liturgical precision, military discipline, and private

29. Ibid., 1–14; "Breves indicaciones," 3–11.
30. *Ritual de la Adoración Nocturna Mexicana*, 15–234.

emotion, adorers turned their backs on the corruptions of the night and went to church to try to defeat them. By rote before the Blessed Sacrament, guards poured their hearts out *to* God and *through* God, heaping loving attention on the incarnate Son in the hope of unleashing the power of the Almighty Father against their foes.

As should by now be apparent, the ethos of the Nocturnal Adoration was Sacred Heart-style reparation rechanneled sacramentally through Christ's Eucharistic self, hence articulated through veneration and consumption of the Blessed Sacrament. Those who performed these spiritual duties were encouraged to see themselves as a kind of imperial guard fighting a war to save the church from new and terrible enemies, while holding irresistible reinforcements in reserve. The institutional bases of the Nocturnal Adoration, as well as its underlying principles and ritual methods, were designed to further these goals by mobilizing Catholic men within an ecclesiastically approved association, concentrating men's prayers with the single force of a spearhead and presenting God with a more compelling devotional imperative. The ANM's institutional history began, perhaps, with the colonial confraternity; fundamentally, however, the organization was an attempt to impose a nationwide structure, quasi-military/ecclesiastical esprit de corps, and militant politico-religious meaning on the once diffuse practice of Eucharistic Adoration. That the devotion was an old Eucharistic cult actualized in the name of Catholic restoration can best be seen, perhaps, in the ANM's 1918 *Reglamento*, which, with the 1924 *Ritual*, provided the organization with its essential theoretical and jurisdictional pillars.[31]

The ANM's "permanent intentions"—first among them to glorify God, ensure the church's triumph, advance the interests of the nation, restore Christianity, and consolidate Christ's social Kingdom—represented the conventional blueprint of a Catholic republic, albeit one achieved through Eucharistic means. Other permanent intentions—to promote diurnal and nocturnal Eucharistic Adoration everywhere, to increase the number of Holy Communions—had a tributary purpose, as spiritual capital for a modern Christendom. The last intention, which spoke of honoring defunct *adoradores* (adorers) and praying for souls in purgatory, had a vestigial feel.[32] In terms of means, article 1

31. *Reglamento de la Adoración Nocturna Mexicana: Parte primera, organización, La Semilla Eucarística*, May 1918.

32. Ibid., 13–14.

stated that all sections must obey the ANM's rules and (in capitals) its HIERARCHY. That hierarchy was both centralized, in the sense of being *capitalino* (based in Mexico City), and top down. Article 2 stated that the chain of command went from sections to the ANM's *consejo supremo* (supreme council) by way of intervening diocesan councils, although in fact these councils rarely feature in the literature and so seem like a device designed to ensure episcopal representation on the supreme council. In true Porfirian style, the supreme council was to be run by an elected lifetime president assisted by a spiritual direc-tor, a secretary, a treasurer, and various spokesmen, among them di-ocesan representatives. The supreme council ran the Mexico City sec-tion, whose adorers elected the national president—hence, power was permanently vested in the president and council, underwritten by the bishops. The organization's headquarters were located in the national expiatory church of San Felipe de Jesús, in central Mexico City.[33]

If the principle of central authority was carefully embedded in the ANM's *organigrama* (organizational chart), the standardization of Eu-charistic Adoration and the elimination of local religious variation was also stressed. Article 10 charged councils with extirpating "corruptions" as well as "practices, rules, or customs not included in the Regulations." To correct abuses, the supreme council had many powers of inspec-tion; the ANM's canonical incorporation into the archconfraternity at Rome, as a court of last appeal, was also emphasized (art. 13–22, 28).[34] Finally, there were important functional as well as jurisdictional divi-sions, especially in terms of gender. Articles 39 and 47 distinguished two "classes" of adorer: *activos* (or "active" male adorers), and *honorarios* ("honorary" adorers, meaning those who gave alms or performed home vigils). Women were only allowed to join the ANM as honorary mem-bers, a category that was also open to men who, for whatever reason, were unable to attend vigils in person. Women were prohibited from witnessing night vigils or entering guardrooms (art. 101).[35] Nonethe-less, the *Reglamento* said (art. 46), it was vital to recruit honorarios, es-pecially women, because they could contribute a great deal to the cause. Beneath these gendered categories, there were masculine subcategories for "veterans" (i.e., men who had notched up 144 vigils or twelve years

---

33. Ibid., 2–4. The administrative headquarters are now located in offices near the Basilica of Guadalupe.

34. Ibid., 6–11.   35. Ibid., 59.

of active service), and *tarcisios,* boy adorers named after Tarcisius, the Eucharistic martyr roasted on a griddle in ancient Rome.[36]

Even within sections, therefore, men were ranked by seniority and distinguished by medals and ribbons: veterans were at the top, followed by adorers on active service, then boys. This was not so unusual. Indeed, we might note that a similar ranking system was employed by other Catholic organizations and societies, such as the "U" studied in this volume by Yves Solis. At the same time, the ANM was not gender exclusive. Just as men were governed by women in the Vela Perpetua,[37] women were subordinate to men in the ANM but were not totally excluded. Only for men, however, was a career path set out, along which boys could see themselves maturing into active adorers at sixteen and battle-hardened veterans by the age of thirty. A central assumption was that men responded well to authority and another that men developed naturally into leaders. Two other principles, in particular—obedience and discipline—were repeated. "The nocturnal adorer must be a model of obedience and discipline," said the *Reglamento,* to give just one example, for "it is better to have a few, zealously observant, adorers, than many with no spirit of obedience and discipline." "Nominal" adorers were "good for nothing" and must be thrown out.[38] To be a man, therefore, was to be dependably pious, strong enough to run the gauntlet of anticlerical mockery and the temptations of the night. The preceding stern reprimand might suggest, however, that men's collective piety was seen as tepid in comparison to women's—which was sometimes true, although it is probably more accurate to say that the practice of Mexican masculinity was deemed insufficiently *Catholic.*

The modest ritual obligations required of adorers need to be seen in this light. After all that has been said, it might come as a surprise that adorers were obliged to perform only *one* vigil per month (art. 96).[39] Again, it is important not to misconstrue this, reading it as evidence that the ANM feared for men's religious partisanship so asked little of them.[40] First, the ANM's goals were that Christ be adored ubiquitously

36. Ibid., 22–26.
37. Chowning, "The Catholic Church and the Ladies of the Vela Perpetua."
38. Ibid., 60–61.
39. Ibid., 57.
40. Blaschke, "Unrecognized Piety of Men," 36–37, suggests that masculinizing European Catholicism meant recoding it as masculine, while keeping men's actual obligations at conservative, manageable levels.

and society rechristianized. This is why sections were told to institute new turnos whenever existing ones reached the maximum complement (thirty-four), the ideal being for each section to have thirty-one turnos so that vigils were celebrated every night (art. 51).[41] The aim, in sum, was to recruit adorers constantly and spread the organization. It was *not* for a small pool of adorers to lie prostrate in church, like an ascetic clerisy. The second, related point is that Eucharistic fervor was meant to drive other forms of religious action, especially social ones, not replace them. This was in keeping with the ANM's reparatory ethos. *La Semilla Eucarística*, too, stressed repeatedly that veneration of the Eucharist must stimulate a life of "Christian social action" outside church walls, and not remain an interior act.[42] In fact, adoration was meant to ground social action in theological Catholicism so that it was most pleasing to God. Overconfidence in social Catholics' mundane efforts, *La Semilla Eucarística* warned in 1926, could instill pride, "the heresy of charity."[43] An integral Catholicism was also the lesson in March 1927: "Becoming a good Christian ... is the first work of Catholic Social Action."[44] Here, then, was the precise link between adorers' Eucharistic fervor, imbued with notions of loving sacrifice, and a life of socially, even politically, militant Catholicism.

HISTORICAL DEVELOPMENT

As a reparatory Eucharistic crusade for men, it is not too surprising to find that the Nocturnal Adoration grew in relation to revolutionary processes, major developments in the so-called "Roman Question," and anticlerical campaigns against the church.[45] Mexico was no exception

41. *Reglamento de la Adoración Nocturna Mexicana*, 26–30.

42. *La Semilla Eucarística*, XIX, no. 1, July 1926, 15–19.

43. *La Semilla Eucarística*, XIX no. 2, August 1926, 41–45.

44. *La Semilla Eucarística* XIX, no. 9, March 1927, 271.

45. As a canonical institution, the Nocturnal Adoration began in Rome in 1809, when a canon of the church of Santa Maria in Via Lata, Giacomo Sinibaldi, adapted the Forty Hours devotion and organized the first confraternity. Its first vigil was held in 1810. In 1824 Leo XII elevated the sodality to archconfraternity, after which affiliates were founded abroad. The devotion first reached France, where it was instituted by Hermann Cohen (1820–1871), a German Jew and child prodigy who went to Paris to study piano under Liszt. Hermann's conversion to Catholicism was driven by intense, youthful fervor; yet his foundation of France's Nocturnal Adoration, whose first vigil was celebrated in December 1848, was also an act of reparation for Pius IX's flight from Rome. In 1863 Hermann (now a Discalced Carmelite whose name in religion was Augustin-Marie du Très-Saint-Sacrament) took the devotion to England. From

to this broad pattern. Nocturnal Adoration was established as a *devotion* in Mexico City by 1869,[46] but the founding of a national society devoted to the practice was a high Porfirian innovation. Furthermore, Nocturnal Adoration remained minoritarian and elitist until 1910, after which it suddenly flowered, partly in response to episcopal exhortation but also to the spiritual anxieties caused by the revolution. As we will see, the ANM's diffusion correlates strongly with several other phenomena: first, the territorial advance of intransigent "Roman" prelates, particularly into the prestigious archiepiscopal sees of the center-north and west; second, the upward curve of revolutionary anticlericalism under Presidents Obregón (1920–1924) and Calles (1924–1928); and, third, the political geography of the Cristero Rebellion (1926–1929), for which the Nocturnal Adoration provides a suggestive, if not infallible, kind of "Eucharistic ethnography."[47]

The movement was begun by a well-to-do Mexico City layman, Reynaldo Manero, whom we first encounter as confrère in the branch of the Confraternity of the Blessed Sacrament that was instituted in San Cosme in 1890 and canonically established two years later.[48] In 1894 Manero was instrumental in convening a new organization, the Central Eucharistic Council; Manero and his confrères were joined in this enterprise by fellow adorers in the parishes of San Sebastián, San José, Tacubaya, Regina Coeli, and Santa Ana. The express aim of the Council, which boasted an institutional membership of only six, was to unite Mexico's "diverse Sacramental Corporations" under lay leadership and the joint patronage of the Guadalupe and San Felipe de Jesús, Mexico's protomartyr and first (since 1862) saint.[49] Evidently, therefore, the ANM developed within, and reorganized, an existing group

France, it also spread to liberal Spain, where it was popularized by a lawyer, Luis de Trelles, hence to the Americas, to liberal Mexico and Colombia especially. See *Memoria de la Asamblea Eucarística celebrada en la ciudad de Puebla el 26 de octubre de 1930, a convocatoria del Consejo Supremo de la Adoración Nocturna Mexicana* (Mexico City: Imprenta de J. I. Muñoz, 1930), 1–10, for Mexico. For France, see Charles Sylvain's *Vie du R. P. Hermann, en religion Augustin-Marie du T.-S.-Sacrament, Carme Déchaussé* (Paris: Librairie H. Oudin, 1883). For Spain, see Francisco Puy Muñoz, *Luis de Trelles: Un laico testigo de la fe* (Madrid: CEU Ediciones, 2009).

46. Anon., *Obra de la exposición y adoración nocturna del Santísimo Sacramento en la Ciudad de México* (Mexico City: J. M. Lara, 1869 and later).

47. Perhaps cavalierly, I borrow the phrase from Rubin, *Corpus Christi*, 335.

48. AHAM, Fondo Alarcón y Sánchez, c. 65/exp. 57, memorandum signed by Reynaldo Manero, Mexico City, February 15, 1894.

49. AHAM, Fondo Alarcón y Sánchez, c. 65/exp. 57, "Reglamento del Consejo Central Sacramentario Discutido y Aprobado en la Sesión Celebrada el 26 de Agosto de 1894."

of Eucharistic Sodalities, not all of which were that old. This choice of divine patrons was also significant, for, as we shall see, the *meaning* of Eucharistic Adoration was also soon resignified and centralized, at least partly due to clerical influence. Two parish priests, one of whom would prove highly influential in Mexican Catholic history, presided over the 1894 junta: the *cura* (priest) of Manero's parish of San Cosme, Samuel Argüelles, later a leading light in the Mexico City curia; and the *párroco* (parish priest) of Tacubaya, Leopoldo Ruiz y Flores, in later years Archbishop of Monterrey, León, and Morelia, and, from 1929, apostolic delegate.[50]

In January 1900 it was Ruiz y Flores who, as the council's spiritual director and *encargado* (director) of San Felipe de Jesús, proposed that the movement relocate to his church. Here we should first recall that San Felipe de Jesús, a byzantine edifice that sits on today's Avenida Madero, had been designed by its clerical founder, José Antonio Plancarte y Labastida, as Mexico's Montmartre, its national monument of expiation. When Ruiz y Flores's proposal was accepted, the link between a nationally centralized form of Eucharistic Adoration and a sacrificial brand of expiatory piety, albeit one of modern, Franco-Roman inspiration, was complete, and it was finessed later that month when the Council decided to adopt the regulations and name of the Nocturnal Adoration, which it received, by chance, from Spain. The institution of Mexico's first Nocturnal Adoration *sección*, and the celebration of its first vigil, occurred on the night of February 4–5, 1900—which is to say on the eve and early morning of the feast of San Felipe de Jesús, whose day had been "profaned" since 1857 by the signing of Mexico's liberal constitution. The ANM's first act, then, was to atone for a national imposture (its secular regime) before the Blessed Sacrament. In 1904 the ANM was admitted into the archconfraternity in Rome; for years to come, however, it stubbornly refused to transcend its urbane confines.[51]

50. *Memoria de la Asamblea Eucarística*, 13–14.
51. A 1906 circular that required priests in the Archdiocese of Mexico to report whether the ANM was established in their parishes yielded six replies. The only functioning section was San Felipe's; every other parish gave excuses. The association did not exist in rural San Bartolomé Morelos "for want of personnel"; the cura of San José (Mexico City) wrote, "There exists only *Adoración diurna* [daytime adoration], which is carried out by the association of the Vela Perpetua." As late as 1910, there were only eleven turnos at San Felipe, which showed that nightly adoration was still way off. See AHAM, Fondo Alarcón y Sánchez, c. 127/exp. 33, *presbíteros* to the Mitre: José Santo, Mexico City, June 16, 1906; Antonio Martínez, San Bartolomé

To no small extent, Mexico's revolution—more specifically, its post-revolution—"made" the Nocturnal Adoration by revalorizing its ethic of altar-driven expiation in dramatic, if not traumatic, terms. Reparation requires damage, and that revolutionaries could produce in spades. The first section founded outside Mexico City (Silao's, in August 1910) was, admittedly, instituted three months shy of Madero's revolt, though again we might suspect the artful hand of Ruiz y Flores, who was transferred to the diocese of León in 1909. San Luis Potosí came next, and *en plena revolución*, in 1912. In June 1913, the ANM was raised to archconfraternity by Pius X, which meant it could add new sections without Rome's say-so. Reynaldo Manero was named president of the Supreme Council in the same year, a position that he still enjoyed in 1930.[52] The foundations were now there for fast growth, though the revolution's campaign against the church temporarily prevented this. The episcopate's return from exile in 1919, however, began a period of sustained growth. In 1919 the ANM founded its first sections in Michoacán, Durango, and Zacatecas; in 1920 it reached Jalisco, which in short order became its bastion.[53] The years between 1923 and 1926 were the best yet, in terms of growth.[54] The ANM could boast 84 sections in January 1923, but a further 121 had been added by the time the religious crisis broke in August 1926, making 205. Growth continued even during the Cristero revolt: by October 1930, there were 240 sections.[55] So prominent did the ANM become in Mexican Catholic circles, in fact, that Pius XI himself took note: in a 1925 audience granted to Reynaldo Manero, the pontiff is reported to have said that Mexico would be saved by prayer alone and that no prayers were more agreeable to God than those of the Nocturnal Adoration, because they were enveloped by sacrifice.[56] As it turned out, unhappily, that was a theory that would be put to the test.

By the mid-1920s, another, demographic, shift had also occurred: adoration had lost its bourgeois, Porfirian gloss and become *popular*. Diocesan sections now competed with one another, for instance, and with Mexico City. San Luis Potosí's section, one of the best organized,

---

Morelos, July 23, 1906; c. 160/exp. 44, Bonifacio Molina, Iztacalco, June 25, 1906; Romualdo Rodríguez, Mexico City (S. Pablo), June 26, 1906; Manuel Bedriñana y Martínez, Mexico City (S. José), June 25, 1906. *Memoria de la Asamblea Eucarística*, 16–22.

52. *Memoria de la Asamblea Eucarística*, 23–25.

53. Ibid., 27–34. 54. Ibid., 38–43.

55. Ibid., 103–12. 56. Ibid., 45.

invited the archbishop of Mexico, Mora y del Río, to its tenth anniversary vigil in 1922, an event that coincided with the "signal grace" of its "founding the 31 *turnos* that are necessary for adoration to be conducted on every night of the month." Now that this sección (the first in Mexico) could adore the Eucharist fittingly, an archiepiscopal visit was required: "We would lament it in the extreme," Mora was told, "were it not possible for you to attend."[57] Outside provincial capitals, rural people joined up. In places like Arandas (Jalisco), the ANM spread via the kinship networks on which *ranchero* (rural) society was built; shop-keeping families like the Sáinz Orozcos, intimates of the cura and with extensive outreach through clan and clientele, were the ANM's bedrock.[58] Even workers were becoming interested. In Mexico City, "various adorers" wrote to Mora y del Río in late 1924 to ask that he exempt them from a ten-peso levy, which was destined to refit the dormitory used by resting adorers at San Felipe de Jesús. The petitioners asked this because the *cuota* (fee) had been imposed "with harshness" by the better-off section at ANM headquarters, via the supreme council. The petitioners could not afford such a sum, moreover, because they were willingly paying another levy for the lavish monstrance unveiled at the Eucharistic Congress and because "we, like all the socios of the Adoración Nocturna, are in the main *obreros* [workers]."[59] Impressionistically, at least, we sense that Nocturnal Adoration had become entwined with local patriotism and organizational or individual self-respect to the point that highhandedness by the founders at San Felipe de Jesús met with criticism.

This was no more than a reflection of reality: as tables 3-1 and 3-2 show, the ANM had become a predominantly rural organization by the late 1920s. By 1930, it had reached twenty-seven states and the federal district (Baja California and Campeche being the two states with no sections), but the majority of sections existed in small, provincial towns. It is also clear that preeminently "Cristero" states (Jalisco, Guanajuato, Michoacán, Durango, Zacatecas, Aguascalientes, Nayarit, and Colima) were overrepresented. Jalisco alone had 41 of 219 sections (19 percent), Guanajuato 18 (8 percent), and Michoacán 12 (6 percent),

57. AHAM, Fondo Mora y del Río, c. 89/exp. 89, ANM president to Mora y del Río, San Luis Potosí, December 15, 1921.

58. Tiberio Munari, *Ramón Sáinz Orozco, primer presidente de la Adoración Nocturna en Arandas, sacrificado en 1937* (Guadalajara: Ediciones Xaverianas, 2007), 12–23.

59. AHAM, Fondo Mora y del Río, c. 89/exp. 89, "varios adoradores" to Mora, Mexico City, December 8, 1924.

Table 3-1. ANM Sections Established by 1930, by State

State	No. of *secciones*	State	No. of *secciones*
Jalisco	41	Sinaloa	4
Mexico	26	Colima	3
Guanajuato	18	Guerrero	3
San Luis Potosí	13	Oaxaca	3
Michoacán	12	Tlaxcala	3
Federal District	12	Tabasco	2
Puebla	11	Chiapas	1
Zacatecas	11	Morelos	1
Chihuahua	10	Nuevo León	1
Durango	10	Querétaro	1
Hidalgo	10	Sonora	1
Veracruz	7	Tamaulipas	1
Aguascalientes	4	Yucatán	1
Coahuila	4	Unknown	1
Nayarit	4	**TOTAL**	**219**

with Durango and Zacatecas having similar numbers. As a group, the eight unquestionably "Cristero" states, while comprising less than a third of the total, were home to 103 out of 219 sections, about half the total (47 percent), and this was despite the fact that two such states (Aguascalientes, Colima) were among Mexico's smallest. There were places (Chihuahua, San Luis Potosí, the federal district) where above-average ANM militancy did not go hand in hand with Cristero militancy, but more often than not, it did, at least as far as broad-brush statistics can tell us. In terms of sheer numbers, finally, by the mid-1920s the supreme council estimated that some thirteen thousand adorers celebrated four hundred vigils every month. This was from a total of 15,000 active adorers, 2,400 *aspirantes* (men awaiting full admission) and 7,000 honorary adorers, of which an unspecified number were women, making a grand total of 24,400 adult adorers. There were also 1,250 tarcisios. Unusually, then, this was a heavily male-dominated pious association: even if we assume that all *honorarios* were women, which they were not, it means that men were twice as numerous as women, and probably more, in the ANM. It is hard to tell, unfortunately, how many adorers were enrolled in each section, but what we know tends to corroborate the point about rurality: Mexico City's section had 924 activos in 1925, for example, with 711 honorarios, or 1,635

Table 3-2. ANM Sections Established by 1930

Branch (*sección*)	Location	Foundation	President
Acámbaro	Acámbaro, Gto.	1924	Pedro C. Sánchez
Acaponeta	Acaponeta, Nay.	1923	Gilberto Peña
Acolman	Acolman, Méx.	1926	Cipriano Aguilar
Adjuntas del Refugio	Valparaíso, Zac.	1923	Lucio Gamboa
Aguascalientes	Aguascalientes, Aguas.	1909	Sixto López
Ahuacatlán	Ahuacatlán, Nay.	1924	V. Banuet
Aldama	Aldama, Chih.	1922	Manuel Montaño
Allende	Allende, Chih.	1922	Paulino Villa
Ameca	Ameca, Jal.	1923	Román García
Amecameca	Amecameca, Méx.	1921	Crisanto Santamaría
Amozoc	Amozoc, Pue.	1926–1929	*Not known*
Angamacutiro	Angamacutiro, Mich.	1925	Carlos Cardona
Apam	Apam, Hgo.	1927	*Not known*
Apetatitlán	Apetatitlán, Tlax.	1923	Vicente Garaia
Arandas	Arandas, Jal.	1923	David Cardona
Aranzazú	Aranzazú, Méx.	1926	*Not known*
Asientos	Asientos, Aguas.	1924	Vicente Carrera
Atenco	Atenco, Méx.	1926	*Not known*
Atlacomulco	Atlacomulco, Méx.	1919	José M. Favila
Atlixco	Atlixco, Pue.	1923	Jesús Ponce
Atotonilco el Alto	Atotonilco el Alto, Jal.	1922	Manuel Valle
Atoyac	Atoyac, Jal.	1926	*Not known*
Autlán	Autlán, Jal.	1922	Daniel Valencia
Ayo el Chico	Ayo el Chico, Jal.	1921	Manuel Rivas Tejeda
Azcapatzalco	Azcapatzalco, DF	1921	Fidencio Zárate
Atzcapotzaltongo	Atzcapotzaltongo, Méx.	1929	*Not known*
Belem del Refugio	Belem del Refugio, Jal.	1923	Andrés Anda
Buenavista de Cuellar	Buenavista de Cuellar, Gro.	1925	Pastor López
Camargo	Camargo, Chih.	1923	Rafael M. Fernández
Canatlán	Canatlán, Dgo.	1925	Bernabé Valdés
Carbonera	Carbonera, SLP	1924	José Ruiz
Catorce	Catorce, SLP	1923	Juan Sánchez
Cedral	Cedral, SLP	1924	Nemesio Villanueva
Celaya	Celaya, Gto.	1924	Arturo J. Almeida
Charcas	Charcas, SLP	1919	Bartolomé Candía

Branch (*sección*)	Location	Foundation	President
Chalco	Chalco, Méx.	1924	Ángel R. Soto
Chietla	Chietla, Pue.	1926	*Not known*
Chilapa	Chilapa, Gro.	1926	*Not known*
Chimalhuacán	Chimalhuacán, Méx.	1926	*Not known*
Chihuahua	Chihuahua, Chih.	1922	Juan R. Serrano
Chipiltepec	Chipiltepec, Méx.	1924	Felipe Avila
Cholula	Cholula, Pue.	1924	José de Jesús Quiroz
Churubusco	Coyoacán, DF	1924	Rafael Farfán
Coatepec	Coatepec, Ver.	1925	Mauro Pomares
Cococitlán	Cococitlán, Méx.	1925	Marcelo Díaz
Cojumatlán	Cojumatlán, Mich.	1922	José Trinidad Orozco
Colima	Colima, Col.	1922	José M. Bazán
Colotlán	Colotlán, Jal.	1922	Aurelio M. González
Comala	Comala, Col.	1924	Miguel G. Contreras
Concepción del Oro	Concepción del Oro, Zac.	1926	*Not known*
Contreras	Contreras, DF	1924	Jesús Mendoza
Coronango	Coronango, Pue.	1926–1929	*Not known*
Cortázar	Cortázar, Gto.	1926	*Not known*
Coyoacán	Coyoacán, DF	1920	Manuel Velázquez
Cuernavaca	Cuernavaca, Mor.	1922	Ruperto Cruz Millán
Cuitzeo	Cuitzeo, Mich.	1920	Luis G. Murillo
Culiacán	Culiacán, Sin.	1922	José Echeverría
Charcas	Charcas, SLP	1919	Bartolomé Candía
Chalco	Chalco, Méx.	1924	Ángel R. Soto
Dolores Hidalgo	Dolores Hidalgo, Gto.	1919	Cirilo Flores
Durango	Durango, Dgo.	1919	Gerardo Rodríguez
Ébano	Ébano, SLP	1925	Elpidio Abrego
Encarnación de Díaz	Encarnación de Díaz, Jal.	1923	Librado Correa
Etzatlán	Etzatlán, Jal.	1930	*Not known*
Florencia	Florencia, Jal.	1923	Eulogio Arellano
Frontera	Frontera, Tab.	1921	Juan Boylán Gordillo
Guadalajara	Guadalajara, Jal.	1920	Luis Ugarte
Guadalupe Hidalgo	Guadalupe Hidalgo, DF	1914	Leopoldo Flores
Gómez Palacio	Gómez Palacio, Dgo.	1922	José M. Macías
Hacienda "El Rincón"	Zapoltitic, Jal.	1921	Agapito Munguía

Branch (sección)	Location	Foundation	President
Huamantla	Huamantla, Tlax.	1925	Vicente Meynet
Huejotzingo	Huejotzingo, Pue.	1926–1929	*Not known*
Iguala	Iguala, Gro.	1926	*Not known*
Irapuato	Irapuato, Gto.	1920	Patricio G. Rojas
Ixtlahuacán del Río	Ixtlahuacán del Río, Jal.	1924	J. M. Núñez
Ixtlán del Río	Ixtlán del Río, Nay.	1922	Hermenegildo Ballesteros
Jalapa	Jalapa, Ver.	1923	Juan Rojas (Prof.)
Jalostotitlán	Jalostotitlán, Jal.	1921	José del Rosario Álvarez Tostado
Jalpa de Cánovas	Jalpa de Cánovas, Gto.	1922	Agustín Gutiérrez y Vázquez
Jamay	Jamay, Jal.	1923	José S. Velazco
Jérez	Jérez, Zac.	1919	Hilario C. Llamas
Jesús María	Jesús María, Aguas.	1923	Antonio Borjas
Jiltopec	Jiltopec, Méx.	1923	Antonio Maldonado
Jilotzingo	Jilotzingo, Méx.	1925	Trinidad Torres
Jiménez	Ciudad Jiménez, Chih.	1922	Conrado Muñoz
Jocotitlán	Jocotitlán, Méx.	1926	Florencio González
Jiquilpan	Jiquilpan, Jal.	1924	Gumersindo López
Jungapeo	Jungapeo, Mich.	1923	Jesús Solís
Jurica, Hacienda de	Querétaro, Qro.	1917	Francisco J. Urquiza
La Barca	La Barca, Jal.	1925	V. A. Gutiérrez
Lagos	Lagos, Jal.	1922	Urbano Zamores
León	León, Gto.	1922	José Cruz Ríos
Maltrata	Maltrata, Ver.	1923	Pedro Peralta
Manzanillo	Manzanillo, Col.	1922	Crisóforo Jaramillo
Matehuala	Matehuala, SLP	1924	Vicente Calderón
Mazatlán	Mazatlán, Sin.	1922	Francisco Niebla
Mérida	Mérida, Yuc.	1925	Lugermillo Lara
México, Ciudad de	México, DF	1900	Guillermo Rodríguez
Mexticacán	Mexticacán, Jal.	1925	Teódulo Mendoza
Mezquital	Mezquital, Dgo.	1924	Narciso López
Mezquitic	Mezquitic, Jal.	1920	Demetrio Quintanilla
Mineral del Monte	Real del Monte, Hgo.	1924	Pedro L. Arriaga
Mixcoac	Mixcoac, DF	1926	*Not known*
Mocorito	Mocorito, Sin.	1923	Jesús F. Montoya
Monterrey	Monterrey, NL	1922	José María González

Branch (*sección*)	Location	Foundation	President
Morelia	Morelia, Mich.	1919	Franco Zavala
Moyahua	Moyahua, Zac.	1925	Ladislado Rodríguez
Naucalpan	Naucalpan, Méx.	1926	*Not known*
Navojoa	Navojoa, Son.	1924	Manuel Sálazar y Perrón
Nochistlán	Nochistlán, Zac.	1925	José María Ruiz
Nogales	Nogales, Ver.	1929	*Not known*
Nopala	Nopala, Hgo.	1925	Pablo García Quintanar
Noria de los Ángeles	Noria de los Ángeles, Zac.	1925	Bernardino Monreal
Oaxaca	Oaxaca, Oax.	1915	Rafael D. Torres (Pbro.)
Ocotlán	Ocotlán, Jal.	1922	Eudoxio Ruiz Velasco
Ojo Caliente	Ojo Caliente, Zac.	1923	José María Romo
Ojuelos	Ojuelos, Jal.	1920	Nicolás Mascorro
Orizaba	Orizaba, Ver.	1923	Manuel Gómez y Gómez
Pachuca	Pachuca, Hgo.	1924	Francisco Mendoza
Papantla	Papantla, Ver.	1924	Alberto Reyes Pérez
Papasquiaro	Papasquiaro, Dgo.	1923	Facundo López
Parral	Parral, Chih.	1922	Germán Sepúlveda
Parras	Parras, Coah.	1921	José Espinosa
Patambam	Patambam (Zamora), Mich.	1920	Agustín Hernández
Pénjamo	Pénjamo, Gto.	1924	Luis Navarro Origel
Peñón Blanco	Peñón Blanco, Dgo.	1923	Juan N. Moreno
Portezuelo	Portezuelo, Jal.	1925	Urbano Navarro
Puebla	Puebla, Pue.	1918	Carlos M. Abrego
Pueblo Nuevo	Pueblo Nuevo, Gto.	1922	Pedro Vela
Puruándiro	Puruándiro, Mich.	1923	*Not known*
Quemada, La	Estación Obregón, Gto.	1925	José Rangel
Resurrección	Parroquia Degollado, Jal.	1925	Ramón Amado
Río Verde	Río Verde, SLP	1921	Pedro Díaz de León
Rosario	Rosario, Sin.	1923	Modesto López
Sahuayo	Sahuayo, Mich.	1922	Carlos Tejeda
Salamanca	Salamanca, Gto.	1922	Prisciliano Arredondo
Saltillo	Saltillo, Coah.	1923	Melchor Rodríguez
Salvatierra	Salvatierra, Gto.	1926	Rosalío Lira
San Andrés Calpan	San Andrés Calpan, Pue.	1926	*Not known*
San Andrés Ixtayopa	San Andrés Ixtayopa, DF	1926–1929	*Not known*

Branch (*sección*)	Location	Foundation	President
San Ángel	San Ángel, DF	1917	Antonio del Collado
San Antonio de los Vázquez	Ixtlahuaca del Río, Jal.	1926	Sidronio Sandoval
San Ciro	San Ciro, SLP	1924	Secundino Rocha
Sandovales	Sandovales, Aguas.	1922	Taide Aguilar
San Diego de Alejandría	San Diego de Alejandría, Jal.	1929	*Not known*
San Francisco de los Adame	San Francisco de los Adame, Zac.	1926	*Not known*
San Francisco del Rincón	San Francisco del Rincón, Gto.	1924	Leonardo Serrano
San Gabriel	San Gabriel, Jal.	1923	José González de la Torre
San José Iturbide	San José Iturbide, Gto.	1920	Juan Salinas
San Juan Bautista	Villahermosa, Tab.	1922	Alejandro Martínez
San Juan del Mezquital	San Juan del Mezquital, Dgo.	1926	Manuel Moreno
San Julián	San Julián, Jal.	1925	José Carpio
San Lorenzo	San Lorenzo, Chih.	1926	*Not known*
San Luis de la Paz	San Luis de la Paz, Gto.	1920	Andrés Guardado
San Luis Potosí	San Luis Potosí, SLP	1912	Juan N. Ruelas (Lic.)
San Martín de los Pirámides	San Martín de los Pirámides, Méx.	1926	*Not known*
San Miguel del Mezquital	San Miguel del Mezquital, Zac.	1926	Gregorio Ruelas Padilla
San Pedro	San Pedro de las Colonias, Coah.	1923	Emilio Madero
San Pedro Tlaquepaque	San Pedro Tlaquepaque, Jal.	1925	Leopoldo Zúñiga
Santa Bárbara	Santa Bárbara, Chih.	1923	Santos Esparza
Santa Isabel	Santa Isabel, Chih.	1924	Manuel García
Santa María de los Ángeles	Santa María de los Ángeles (?)	1924	Antonio A. González
Santa María del Río	Santa María del Río, SLP	1922	Andrés R. Pacheco
Sauces de Salinas	Sauces de Salinas, Dgo.	1923	Juan Torres
Sayula	Sayula, Jal.	1923	Cesáreo Robles Contreras
Silao	Silao, Gto.	1910	Francisco Cadena
Soyaniquilpan	Soyaniquilpan, Méx.	1926	José Guadalupe Rebollar
Tacuba	Tacuba, DF	1919	Ángel R. Herrera
Tacubaya	Tacubaya, DF	1912	Hipólito Montero
Tamazula	Tamazula, Jal.	1922	Enrique García
Tampico	Tampico, Tamps.	1918	Jacobo Ostos
Tapachula	Tapachula, Chis.	1923	Pedro Q. Calcaneo
Tapalpa	Tapalpa, Jal.	1924	Encarnación Preciado
Taretan	Taretan, Mich.	1923	Antonio Zepeda León
Teacoalco	Teacoalco, Méx.	1922	Cornelio Domínguez

Branch (sección)	Location	Foundation	President
Tecamachalco	Tecamachalco, Pue.	1926	Alfredo Gómez Rosas
Tecolotlán	Tecolotlán, Jal.	1923	Julián Medina
Tecomaxtlahuaca	Tecomaxtlahuaca, Oax.	1917	Inés Mendoza
Tejamen	Tejamen, Dgo.	1925	Alfredo Nevarez
Temascalcingo	Temascalcingo, Méx.	1923	Florencio Quintana
Teotitlán	Teotitlán, Oax.	1925	Enrique López ("Sr. Cura")
Tepatitlán	Tepatitlán, Jal.	1923	Cristóbal Romero
Tepehuanes	Tepehuanes, Dgo.	1925	Domingo Alarcón
Tepejí del Río	Tepejí del Río, Hgo.	1921	José García
Tepexpan	Tepexpan, Méx.	1924	Mateo Urbina
Tepic	Tepic, Nay.	1922	José María Olague
Tesistán	Tesistán, Jal.	1923	Diego Quirarte
Tezontepec	Tezontepec, Hgo.	1920	Nabor Granado
Tezoyuca	Tezoyuca, Méx.	1923	Not known
Tlacopan	Tlacopan, Méx.	1926	Not known
Tlacotepec	Tlacotepec, Pue.	1923	Mateo Ramos
Tlalmanalco	Tlalmanalco, Méx.	1923	Joaquín Reyes
Tlalnepantla	Tlalnepantla, Méx.	1923	Agustín Barcés
Tlalpan	Tlalpan, DF	1922	Mariano Pineda
Tlaxcala	Tlaxcala, Tlax.	1926	Not known
Tlaxcalilla	Tlaxcalilla, SLP	1918	To San Luis Potosí, 1920
Tlaxcoapan	Tlaxcoapan, Hgo.	Not known	Francisco Ángeles
Toluca	Toluca, Méx.	1921	Ángel Arriaga Puente
Torreón	Torreón, Coah.	1924	Gregorio Ramírez
Tula	Tula, Hgo.	1925	José M. Arcia Godoy
Tulancingo	Tulancingo, Hgo.	1925	Roberto García Conde
Tuxcueaca	Tuxcueaca, Jal.	1924	Rafael Cuevas
Tuxpan	Tuxpan, Jal.	1925	Isabel Vargas
Tuxpan	Tuxpan, Mich.	1925	Arnulfo Arellano
Valle de Bravo	Valle de Bravo, Méx.	1924	Ramón Jiménez
Valle de Santiago	Valle de Santiago, Gto.	1923	Not known
Venado	Venado, SLP	1924	Isabel Teruel
Villa López	Villa López, Chih.	1922	Rosendo Marta
Villa del Refugio	Villa del Refugio, Zac.	1923	Juan J. Escobedo
Xico	Xico, Ver.	1923	Zacarías H. Razo

in total, which would have given it a 7 percent share of a national total of 24,400; "Catholic" Puebla, which in 1930 claimed 2,287 activos with 696 honorarios (2,983 in total), would have had a bigger share (12 percent), but that was probably inflated by the celebration in Puebla of the ANM's 1930 conference and a post-Cristiada surge in inscriptions.[60]

NOCTURNAL ADORATION IN THE CRISTIADA, 1926–1929

We have seen that Nocturnal Adoration promoted a kind of reparatory lay priesthood in an extended Eucharistic setting, as well as traditional adoration conceived as a reciprocal gift of love for the divine love of the Eucharist. At the same time, the ANM emphasized aspects of hegemonic masculinity (military discipline, obedience, loyalty, courage), while giving them a devoutly emotive inflection. Given the rapport that the ANM created between adorers and the Eucharist, to say nothing of the devotion's overtly sacrificial aspects, it is not surprising to find that it was from adorers' ranks that many well-known Cristero chiefs, militants, and martyrs, such as Luis Navarro Origel, Miguel Gómez Loza, and Luis Magaña Servín, all came.[61] This is less surprising still when we consider that Mexico's religious crisis climaxed, in July 1926, with the public withdrawal of all Catholic sacraments, including the Eucharist. *La Semilla Eucarística* was then among many Catholic voices clamoring that the Eucharist was a palpitating, warming presence, and that, without it, Mexico's churches turned "cold."[62] This calorific trope was less unusual than the central role adorers were told to play in keeping the embers of religion alive in the absence of both Christ and the clergy. Henceforth, the ANM proved an important rallying point for the church, in part because the rhetoric and the practice of the Adoration gave Catholic men a powerful religious idiom through which to interpret and respond to persecution.

We find right away, for example, a discursive distinction being made between manly, "amorous" adorers—men willing to sacrifice them-

60. *Memoria de la Asamblea Eucarística*, 103–12.
61. See Tiberio Munari, *Derramaron su sangre para Cristo: Los siervos de Dios Anacleto González Flores, Jorge Vargas González, Ramón Vargas González, Luis Padilla Gómez, Ezequiel Huerta Gutiérrez, Salvador Huerta Gutiérrez, Luis Magaña Servín, Miguel Gómez Loza* (Guadalajara: Ediciones Xaverianas, 1998).
62. *La Semilla Eucarística* XIX, no. 12, June 1927, 270.

selves for true love of Christ—and spiritually indifferent, tacitly "effeminate" Catholic men. This division, plainly, was designed to reinforce
adorers' religious commitments through appeals to a gender identity,
yet this was a Catholic masculinity premised not only on physical self-
control but spiritual—described as conventionally romantic—abandonment. A good example, one of many, appeared in *La Semilla Eucarística*
in December 1926. Adorers should recall with what stoicism the early
Christians endured pagan fury, the article said; hand-wringing, theater-
going Catholics—those "who wish to know nothing about their Religion, who 'resign' themselves easily to all the martyrdoms to which [the
church] is subjected, so long as their interests are not touched"—were
to be scorned. Here, interestingly, was a second distinction between
theatrical sentiment and deeper (religious) feeling: in their religious
lives, then, real men could express deeply felt emotion without compro-
mising their masculinity; fair-weather Catholics, religious ardor quelled
by "infernal prudence," were outside the "group of love," meaning men
who loved Christ enough to put Him before self.[63]

Accounts of Cristero-era vigils are filled with graphic accounts of
adorers' endurance, mixed with passion for Christ. The idiom was both
classical and modern: adorers were masters of their physical selves, like
early Christians or Roman stoics, yet were in the thrall of religious passions, like French zouaves or Saint Theresa.[64] The San Felipe de Jesús
section, maintained a 1930 report, kept up its vigil before an empty
Sacrarium throughout the persecution. Adoration stopped only for sev-
en nights, after one turno was arrested and thrown into the dungeons
of the Inspección de Policía. Here the brothers had kept up praying,
nonetheless, conquering "new soldiers for the armies of the Eucharistic
Jesus." To the "cruelty and sadism of the enemy," the section chief concluded, adorers had offered only "serene courage."[65] In the countryside
it was reported to be the same. Félix Sánchez, an adorer from Teacalco
(Méx.), spent the persecution walking the fields carrying the Viaticum
to the sick. "Wounded by love in the absence of our Eucharistic Lord,"
La Semilla Eucarística noted, Sánchez wept "abundant tears" and, when

63. *La Semilla Eucarística* XIX, no. 6, December 1926, 135.
64. For the modern comparison, see Harrison, "Zouave Stories"; for a study of the links
between Christian fortitude and Roman stoicism, see L. Stephanie Cobb, *Dying to Be Men: Gender and Language in Early Christian Martyr Texts* (New York: Columbia University Press, 2008),
esp. 60–91.
65. *Memoria de la Asamblea Eucarística*, 106–07.

he himself died in 1928, cried out "I die of love because I cannot live without my Jesus."[66]

Such reports, especially the latter, were clearly part of the ANM's material culture and designed to construct at least as much as to record a Catholic identity.[67] In similar spirit but with more practical problems in mind, the Supreme Council legislated for persecution. On April 24, 1926, the Council issued a circular (no. 106) ordering sections to continue their vigils no matter what, because suspending them "would be to betray our Divine Captain." Persecution justified extraordinary measures, never desertion: the *Miserere* and an exorcism were now to be recited, for instance, and vigils could be celebrated with the Tabernacle closed and finish with spiritual communion if there were no priest. If it was impossible to meet in church, adorers should gather in a private house.[68] In December, another circular (no. 115) told adorers to hold vigils "without the Real Presence of Our Divine Savior," viewing this privation as a sacrifice offered "to His Divine Majesty."[69] The "Recommendation" in March 1928 was to pray to the altar instead of the Blessed Sacrament: this was to offer Christ, *in absentia*, the cult that his enemies wished to deny Him; the altar—as a sepulcher for the apostles, not just a banqueting table—was also a fitting object of devotion, if not "impregnated with traces of the divine perfume of His Real Presence." The closing words were parable-like: a full-grained *mazorca* (cob) was strong, but the loss of a single grain destroyed its compactness and allowed all the fruit to be stripped, thus, with the church, which was why adorers, as exemplary Catholics, must keep the whole together.[70]

How well did adorers honor these norms? Because of the methodological problem cited above, this is not a simple question: though we have field reports from a good number of ANM sections during the 1920s persecution,[71] too many are mirror images of official ANM discourse with place names added. In the best reports, however, we see a division emerging between urban and rural accounts, one that

66. *La Semilla Eucarística* XX, no. 5, November 1928, 87.
67. Cobb, *Dying to Be Men*, 1–5.
68. *La Semilla Eucarística* XVIII, no. 12, June 1926, 7–10.
69. *La Semilla Eucarística* XIX, no. 7, January 1927, 149–51.
70. *La Semilla Eucarística* XX, no. 9, March 1928, 182–88.
71. Reports were requested for presentation at the ANM's 1930 congress in Puebla and publication in its *Memoria de la Asamblea Eucarística*.

revindicates the sources to the extent that it suggests that different reports genuinely reflected the political, religious, and even intellectual, contexts in which they were written.[72] In the big cities, for example, where the ANM took the lead in organizing public worship and played an overtly "vicarious" role in directing everyday religious activity, we find theological allegories on lay priesthood and spiritual communion written into reports of ANM activity. These allusions are usually absent from reports emanating from the perilous countryside, where it was often stressed that adorers had to overcome physical hardships to bear loving witness to Christ. The most finished martyrologies also emanated from city branches of the ANM, which in truth were less exposed to mortal danger than their rural counterparts but were more concerned to find a link between urban religious practice and Catholic heroism.

We see this in the account of the "Vigil of Christ the King" which was held by the Mexico City section in San Felipe de Jesús in October 1927, "despite the fury of Satan and his henchmen." For this festival, capitalino adorers knelt before the empty Sacrarium "in fervent penitence," while the church filled up with fellow adorers and "members of the public from outside our beloved Adoration." Adoration *was* the Eucharistic spectacle, in other words, and adorers the star players. The vigil itself consisted of a Rosary, then the Station of the Blessed Sacrament (a processional in which participants stood with arms outstretched in cruciform); then followed the exorcism and psalm, during which "many adorers performed acts of penitence," specifically an "act of flagellation" in the guardroom. At the end, the lucky few, essentially supreme council members in attendance, were led off to receive communion in an "improvised catacomb." The council apologized for this exclusivity and the "just reproaches" it occasioned.[73] It is obvious, nonetheless, that the reparatory, priestly aspects of ANM devotionalism were most prominent here, right down to adorers' public scourgings and symbolic crucifixions.

We see the same pattern in the "Minervas" celebrated by all the Mexico City sections in the Basilica of Guadalupe in January 1928 and 1929. Although the 1928 Minerva was kept simpler than usual, for want of the

---

72. Or, as Rubin (*Corpus Christi*, 83) puts it in another context, these sources convince because they "give us a picture of the horizon against which eucharistic teaching was received, understood, interpreted, and then put to work in the world."

73. *La Semilla Eucarística* XX, no. 6, December 1927, 111–13.

Blessed Sacrament (that "inestimable treasure of uncruel sacrifice"), an act of spiritual communion (inward, as opposed to symbolic reception of the Eucharist) was performed instead. What is noteworthy is the surprisingly deep identification of the adorers who directed these rituals with the Catholic clergy, who were absent. Two brothers from different turnos led the assembly through the ceremony and Mass. One in particular, Rafael Bustamante of the San Antonio de Padua turno, recited the prayers of the Mass before delivering a sermon in which he functioned as a kind of rhetorical celebrant of the Eucharist ("with the fervor for which he is well known, he brought us imaginatively before God's Minister in his holy functions as celebrant"). Another adorer then recited the Trisagium, making cherubim quiver with joy (or so said *La Semilla Eucarística*), and a fourth adorer recited the Rosary.[74] In 1929 the capital's adorers again marched to Tepeyac (the site of the appearance of the Virgin of Guadalupe). As before, an actual Eucharistic celebration was off limits politically, yet the adorers who led the ceremonies were again described as administering spiritual communions to the people, like honorary priests. The ANM's white flags, unfurled in lieu of the elevation, were likened to Eucharistic wafers, perhaps even the Holy Spirit:

Prayers and an intention to hear the Holy Sacrifice of the Mass were first recited. The brother Adorer commissioned to say these prayers grew more fervent with every passing moment as he read the culminating passages of the uncruel sacrifice [i.e., the liturgy of the Mass]; he transported us to the summit of the Mountain where we were redeemed, and at the moment in which we meditated upon the elevation of the Sacred Form, our beloved flags, their white folds unfurling, were lowered in a gesture of profound submission to, and veneration of, the God of Hosts, whom we also adored spiritually; to me [said *La Semilla Eucarística*'s observer] it seemed like a multitude of white doves which, tired of flight, sought rest on a calm plain.[75]

This was metaphorical language but not idly suggestive, given the sort of religious prerogatives with which lay people were equipped during the 1920s. It bears repeating, too, that this kind of description was largely absent from surviving reports from the countryside, where adorers faced violent treatment at the hands of soldiers, agrarians, and revolutionary unions.[76]

74. *La Semilla Eucarística* XX, no. 8, February 1928, 168–71.
75. *La Semilla Eucarística* XX, no. 9, March 1929, 196–98.
76. We have occasional reports. In Aguascalientes, military persecution of the *cristeros* was

The culmination of this first tendency, martyrdom, was conceived as absolute fidelity to Christ's Eucharistic sacrifice, supreme, not vicarious, reparation. The ANM was proud that it provided the first "martyr" of the *callista* persecution, José García Farfán, the ANM's wizened Puebla chief.[77] A "Consoling Report" written by his successor in April 1927 celebrated "the heroic and holy death of the *señor* adorer don José G. Farfán, who died acclaiming our King, Christ Our Lord." Farfán's "love of the Blessed Sacrament" was also stressed.[78] Boy martyrs were also lionized, none more so than the "martyr of Tlalpan," Juan Manuel Bonilla, an urban Cristero and adorer whose death was reworked in a 1927 hagiography inserted into *La Semilla Eucarística,* "Era of the Martyrs." Arrested in April 1927, on Good Friday, Bonilla was tortured, tied to a cross, and executed. While in prison, he styled himself as a human sacrifice ("I have offered my life to God and fight for His cause ... I hope that He accepts my sacrifice," a last letter to his sister stated). Bonilla was an ideal martyr, young, unblemished, and handsome, a vivid actualization of the crucified Christ.[79] It might seem counterintuitive that the deaths of young and old were most fêted in ANM discourse; yet this was a conventional, even ancient, narrative strategy that emphasized how specific masculinities were finished by, and incomplete without, Christian ardor. Youths such as Bonilla or frail old men such as Farfán became heroically, fully "masculine" in death as a result of virilizing Christianity.[80] The adulation of grizzled rural patriarchs who died for the cause was slower in coming, even if there were more of them. By 1928, for instance, ANM martyrs included Rosario de Álvarez Tostado, president of the ANM in Jalostotitlán (Jal.), "who died heroically," yet received only this three-word epitaph.[81]

---

so intense that vigils were completely abandoned. In San José Iturbide (Gto.), section members were at prayer in December 1926 when soldiers burst in and beat them. In Tepeji del Río (Hgo.) in May 1927, three adorers were tortured by "enemies of the Faith" who wished them to state that the clergy was stirring up a rebellion. *Memoria de la Asamblea Eucarística,* 115–40.

77. *La Semilla Eucarística* XIX, no. 3, September 1926, 53, and XIX, no. 10, Apr. 1927, 243–44.

78. *Memoria de la Asamblea Eucarística,* 113–14.

79. *La Semilla Eucarística* XX no. 2, August 1927, 32–33: "La Era de los Mártires" *fotograbado* insert.

80. This discursive strategy, Cobb notes (*Dying To Be Men,* 13), was as old as Christianity itself and often used by writers of early Christian martyrologies.

81. *La Semilla Eucarística* XX, no. 8, February 1928, 161. As late as 1937, rural adorers were being killed. That March, for instance, Ramón Sáinz Orozco, ANM president of Arandas (Jal.), was tied behind a horse, dragged from his pueblo, and executed in a thicket of *huizachales* by soldiers who accused him of being a Cristero diehard. Munari, *Ramón Sáinz Orozco,* 35–38.

Rural adoration was generally described differently, too. By way of transition, we might cite a report, "Siempre Adelante," which describes the experiences of a Mexico City adorer who, as Supreme Council inspector, was taken to a vigil held in rural Mexico State on the feast of San Pascual Bailón in May 1928. After greeting turno members at an agreed spot outside the capital, the inspector and his companions began walking up and down steep ravines and navigating by the light of the moon, which was frequently hidden from view by the forest canopy; after a long trek, the party was met by a car carrying "the Love of Loves" (the Blessed Sacrament) and driven to a hacienda where "soldiers of Christ" (adorers or *cristeros?*) were waiting to perform the Eucharistic vigil and receive communion.[82]

From war-torn Zacatecas came a touching report from a section that was "among those to have suffered religious persecution the most," with members kidnapped, assaulted, robbed, and threatened with death. But throughout 1927, adorers continued to convene in isolated parts of the countryside to hold secret vigils. "I recall with genuine tenderness," wrote one *socio*,

the night of 24 December 1927, in the worst days of the persecution, when, finding no safe place in which to celebrate the Vigil of Saint Anthony of Padua, we retreated into the mountains a few kilometers distant from [Zacatecas]. In a cave used by herders as a shelter, we spent the night celebrating our Vigil in the midst of the most profound silence, and in that mysterious night, we all recalled the higher scenes in the cave at Bethlehem, and with fervor and trust we begged for the liberty of the Church and for remedies to the many calamities that befall our unfortunate *Patria*.[83]

A predominant note here is empathy with Christ's human poverty, though the reparatory theme is not absent. Another Zacatecas report dated February 1928 bears out the first theme more. By this time, of course, Rome had granted Mexican Catholics the privilege of reserving the Blessed Sacrament in their own homes. Now it was the peasants' turn to visit favored urban Catholics in Zacatecas, whose homes had been converted into Eucharistic way stations. One such person reported a visit by three hundred rural adorers, "the majority of them working people of the countryside who, in order to attend their Vigils, [have] to walk 10, 20, 30, and even 50 kilometers, there being adorers who left

82. *La Semilla Eucarística* XXI, no. 1, July 1928, 6–11.
83. *Memoria de la Asamblea Eucarística*, 124–26.

their homes in the morning and arrived at the city at sundown." Performing the vigil thus took two whole days and a night, this informant wrote, "but they do it all with the greatest delight [*gusto*], delight which they communicate to the kind Jesus who is hidden there under the Sacramental Specie. All of them show genuine interest in being at the feet of the Blessed Sacrament, and they will leave only after receiving Him sacramentally." All in all, this informant wrote, the adoring peasants of Zacatecas showed "great love" for the Eucharistic Christ, "center of our loves, strength, sweetness, life, and salvation."[84] In Buenavista de Cuellar (Gro.), too, the dominant note of the vigils was intimate conversation with Christ. Buenavista's section chief, a *campesino* (peasant) who apologized for his lack of culture and rustic Spanish when making his report to the ANM, lamented that very few men had been interested in the Nocturnal Adoration at the start of the persecution (Christ had "wept" for these faint hearts); in May 1927, however, the government barred adorers from entering church, obliging them to meet in private. This decision seemed to have a vivifying effect on the ANM. In October 1928, the *jefe* wrote, "We received an interview with the Eucharistic Jesus [*Jesús Sacramentado*]. Do you know where? Out there, in the forest, in the middle of a creek that offered to Jesus the whisperings of the jungle and the humming of little birds. There in a thick forest, our song united with the murmuring cadences of a little stream, the keepers of the Watch offered their vassalage [to Christ], seconded by a great part of the Catholic people of Buenavista."[85] Another evocative report came from the small town of San Luis de la Paz (Gto.), whose "Christ the King" section had an astonishing 1,000 active and 354 honorary adorers. There were also four village turnos, whose members rode in on Saturday nights for their vigils. The section chief praised "the beautiful picture" of his vigil; rancheros on horseback, crowds "electrified by boundless and sincere love, acclaim[ing] Christ the King with delirious joy," and "pious field hands devoting themselves with all faith and determination to celebrate their Vigil." "To my mind," the chief finished, "it is fitting to compare our Eucharistic labor to that practiced in the Middle Ages by the pauper of Assisi." The modern world, like the medieval, was thought to be sinking into a quagmire, but outpourings of devotion like this could surely save it.[86]

84. Ibid., 125–26.   85. Ibid., 131–32.
86. Ibid., 151–55.

CONCLUSION

The meaning of Nocturnal Adoration thus varied depending on why and where it was practiced, although variation was seemingly within accepted parameters, fundamentally a question of emphasis. To theologically sophisticated Catholics in the Federal District or Puebla, Nocturnal Adoration was a chance to practice a special kind of ministry in reparation for the sins of the revolution, to live their lay status to the full in such a way that it became almost priestly. As purveyors, sometimes subjects, of Eucharistic sacrifices, adorers nonetheless helped the church survive persecution as a visible, public body. To rancheros and indigenes, Nocturnal Adoration more often provided continued evidence of a special bond with the Blessed Sacrament, proof that they loved Christ and were loved in return, that the community of their church was not lost. Adorers who wanted a good religious reason to move from symbolic to bloodier forms of sacrifice in the service of the church, even to Cristero militancy, could find it in the rituals and rhythms of the Nocturnal Adoration. Not all Cristeros were adorers, and not all adorers were Cristeros, but the link was a suggestive and sometimes powerful one. Either way, Mexico's Nocturnal Adoration involved ordinary lay*men*, in their thousands, from all across the country, in the spiritual life of the church, and did so in an intimately privileged way that historians have been slow to understand. The ANM reminds us that the stereotypical division between pious women and impious men is at best a simplification, and shows us that men, as well as women, have been the historic lifeblood of Mexican Catholicism.

CHAPTER 4

Transnational Subaltern Voices
Sexual Violence, Anticlericalism, and the Mexican Revolution

❖ Robert Curley

In 1914 Francis Kelley was an immigrant living in Chicago, a city with a large immigrant population. Born on Prince Edward Island, Kelley studied for the priesthood in Quebec, and was ordained in De-troit, Michigan. He came to Chicago in 1905 and founded the Catho-lic Church Extension Society with the support of the local archbishop, James Quigley.[1] Father Kelley would serve as president of the Exten-sion Society until his 1924 elevation as the second bishop of Oklahoma. The Extension Society was the official church office in charge of home mission, the effort to extend the church to areas where it was hitherto weak or absent. As president, Kelley published a monthly magazine that circulated nationally in the United States and boasted three million paid subscriptions. He was a devoted writer who published in most is-sues. Throughout his career, he authored hundreds of articles, as well as more than a dozen books, both fiction and nonfiction. Of these, the one that would be remembered longest was *The Book of Red and Yellow*.[2]

Research for this chapter was made possible by the generous support of Universidad de Guadalajara. I would also like to thank Lorena Cortés Manresa and Sylvia Arrom for their care-ful reading and scholarly solidarity.

1. In 1908 Kelley organized an international congress in Chicago to discuss the issue of Catholic mission. The first and second American Catholic Missionary Congresses were cele-brated in Chicago and Boston, respectively. See Francis C. Kelley, ed., *The First American Catho-lic Missionary Congress* (Chicago: J. S. Hyland & Company, 1909); *The Great American Catholic Missionary Congresses* (Chicago: J. S. Hyland & Company, n.d. [1913 or 14]).
2. Francis C. Kelley, *The Book of Red and Yellow: Being a Story of Blood and a Yellow Streak* (Chicago: The Catholic Church Extension Society of the United States of America, 1915). Kelley

In the fall of 1914, Kelley left Chicago and traveled to the southern United States at the request of Archbishop Quigley. His mission was to visit sites in south Texas, where a growing population of Mexican refugees challenged the resources of local institutions. His trip took him to Dallas, San Antonio, Laredo, Galveston, Houston, and Corpus Christi. From Texas he traveled to New Orleans, where he met with Archbishop James H. Blenk. From there Kelley and Blenk boarded a ship to Havana, Cuba, where they met with another contingent of religious refugees from Mexico. In south Texas and in Havana, Kelley took statements from men and women who had fled violence in Mexico. These statements became the cornerstone for a broad campaign with religious and political consequences in Mexico and the United States. They also set Kelley on a path that he would follow for much of the rest of his life, stretching well beyond the events of 1914, through the decades of the 1920s and 1930s.[3]

In south Texas Kelley found Archbishop José Mora y del Río, head of the Roman Catholic Church in Mexico, along with scores of Mexicans who had fled religious persecution and the violence of civil war at home. The Mexican clergy in Texas at that time included four archbishops, five bishops, and about forty priests living in the San Antonio area among the greater immigrant and refugee population.[4] The immediate problem Kelley confronted was that the Mexican clergy exiled in Texas had left home with little or no resources and needed everything from clothing and food to work. The Mexican hierarchy was intent on keeping their clergy together and feared that if they settled in other places, they would not return to Mexico. As a result, their concentrated presence placed a burden on the San Antonio diocese, the only local institution with an interest in providing for them.

From Havana, Kelley sailed to New York City on his way to Rome. There he made his case to Pope Benedict XV for a public Roman Catholic position in support of the Mexican church, and argued that the Vatican should pressure the Wilson administration in Washington against

founded the magazine *Extension* in 1906 as a quarterly. By 1907, it was published monthly; see Loyola University Chicago, *Archives and Special Collections, Catholic Church Extension Society*.

3. Francis Clement Kelley (1870–1948) was born on Prince Edward Island, Canada, and died in Oklahoma City. He was the second Roman Catholic bishop of Oklahoma, appointed in 1924 by Pope Pius XI. He held this office until his death.

4. James P. Gaffey, *Francis Clement Kelley and the American Catholic Dream*, vol. 2 (Bensenville, Ill.: The Heritage Foundation, 1980), 6–7.

recognizing the Constitutionalist rebels fighting under the direction of Venustiano Carranza. While in Rome, Kelley first met the archbishop of Guadalajara, Francisco Orozco y Jiménez, who spent many months between 1914 and 1916 advising the pope regarding the Mexican question. As a result of this initial meeting between Kelley and Orozco in Rome, the Guadalajara archbishop went directly to Chicago on his return, instead of heading for Texas. Only later did he continue on to San Antonio, where he stopped prior to returning, in disguise, to Mexico to rejoin his flock.

In this chapter, I focus on Kelley's original foray into Mexican politics in 1914 and 1915. The essay begins with his learning of the refugee problem in Texas, in the fall of 1914, and ends with the U.S. recognition of Carrancista revolutionaries as the legitimate ruling party in October 1915. The vehicle for the argument is a careful reading and source critique of Kelley's diatribe, *The Book of Red and Yellow*. By analyzing the claims made in the book, in this chapter I highlight the need to consider the construction of Catholic memory, the historiographic uses of the body, and the question of whether and to what extent the book played a significant role in representing subaltern identities.

The focus of this chapter is the construction of historical memory. This means it is important not to develop an argument that turns comfortably on the figure of Francis Kelley, as important as he is in the story. It is true that the central focus of the chapter is a book he wrote, along with the archive he built and left behind. But still, as or more important than Kelley are the sources that have been preserved in that archive, the way they were constructed, and what they can and cannot tell the historian. In this sense, I am taking Paul Ricoeur's cue and working through the construction of memory, source, and history.[5] So, in short, this is an inquiry into the making of historiographic narrative and the transnational context in which it was initially forged. The argument stretches from the geopolitics of American intervention in Mexico to the anticlerical violence of the Mexican revolution. But the ultimate focus is the material that Kelley collected in late 1914 and early 1915, with the idea of educating public opinion to the atrocities of the Mexican revolution and pressuring the Wilson administration to take a hard line against the revolutionaries.

5. Paul Ricoeur, *Memory, History, Forgetting*, trans. Kathleen Blamey and David Pellauer (Chicago: The University of Chicago Press, 2004).

A HUMANITARIAN CRISIS AND TESTIMONY AS A
METHOD OF DOCUMENTATION

When Kelley first traveled to south Texas, he was forced to confront issues that were related but not necessarily obvious. His stewardship at the Extension Society was focused on the theme of mission, the idea that the Catholic Church was unevenly represented, and that there were areas and populations that still required evangelization, in the broadest sense of the term. The American Catholic Missionary Congresses of 1908 and 1913 had addressed the problem of mission in the context of immigrant populations in the United States, but they had not thought much, if at all, about the Mexican immigrant population in the southern reaches of the nation. They were, perhaps not surprisingly, focused on the populations arriving from overseas, especially the Italians and the Irish. They had fairly extensive statistics on about forty nations or peoples that had been entering the United States as immigrants during the long nineteenth century. But the Mexicans were seemingly off the radar.[6]

So, the Mexican presence created a curious problem for Kelley and the Extension Society. They were an immigrant population but not necessarily similar to the other ones that hitherto demanded the attention of the Catholic Church policy on mission. First of all, they were a refugee population. And, second, although they were ensconced in a region that was ethnically, and to some extent linguistically, similar to their home region, they still clearly presented a humanitarian crisis of some proportion. Kelley traveled from town to town using the diocesan and parish networks that existed through south Texas and Louisiana, in order to command an institutional infrastructure that could get clothing, money, food, and jobs for these displaced Mexican clergymen and -women.

What he found was a population of Mexican clergy that were displaced from all across the vast Mexican Republic. They were not a particularly large group, but they represented, to a considerable degree, the institution of the Catholic Church in Mexico. For this same reason, Archbishop José Mora y del Río, the head of the Mexican church, was

6. R.A. McEachen, "Our Five Million Immigrants," in *The First American Catholic Missionary Congress*, 272–78; and P.J. Muldoon, "Immigration and the Immigrants in the United States," in *The Great American Catholic Missionary Congresses*, 132–47.

keen to maintain his flock of exiles united in one place. He feared that if they drifted apart in different directions, the clergy would settle in the United States and would not return to Mexico. Dispersion, therefore, presented Archbishop Mora with a potentially serious problem at a time when the Constitutionalist rebels in Mexico seemed to hold the decline of the church as a strategic objective. And in fact, some clergy did settle in the southern United States, as was the case with father Nicolás Corona, of La Piedad, Michoacán. His 1914 testimony ends with the statement that his superiors need not withhold his identity, as he did not plan to return to Mexico. Instead, he settled in the Galveston area and rebuilt his life.[7]

But most of the clergy stayed close to their pastor, Archbishop Mora, and this circumstance created both challenges and opportunities for Kelley. The main challenge was financial as well as logistical. The San Antonio and Galveston dioceses were not wealthy and would need financial support from the Extension Society for several years. But there was also the special challenge of housing a community of fifty to sixty or more people together. Kelley worked with Henry A. Constantineau, OMI, to find a building that might accommodate a large group of people; they were aided by the Sisters of the Divine Providence, who offered to lend them a building twenty-five miles outside of San Antonio, in Castroville, Texas.[8] The Castroville Seminary would become the center of Mexican Catholicism in the United States for the next four years, and the Extension Society would raise thousands of dollars for their welfare.[9]

The move to settle the Mexican clergy in one location offered Kelley a rare opportunity that would direct his activities during 1914 and 1915. Kelley felt that, alongside the task of providing basic material aid for the Mexican refugees, Extension must document the crisis. So, from the very beginning, he worked with U.S. and Mexican clergy in the south-

7. Archive of the Archdiocese of Oklahoma City (AAOC), Kelley Papers, Box 10, Folder Mexican Question, Document 49, N. Corona, Sworn Affidavit, Galveston, Texas, October 24, 1914, 2 pp.

8. Francis C. Kelley, *The Story of Extension* (Chicago: Extension Press, 1922), 179. A photograph of the Castroville Seminary follows (184); see also Gaffey, *Francis Clement Kelley and the American Catholic Dream*, 2:10. On Constantineau, see Texas State Historical Association, "Constantineau, Henry A.," http://www.tshaonline.org/handbook/online/articles/fcobl.

9. Kelley reported having raised upward of $75,000 through *Extension* for the Castroville Seminary between 1914 and 1917, a figure that would be close to $2 million today; Gaffey, *Francis Clement Kelley and the American Catholic Dream*, 2:11.

ern United States, Cuba, and Mexico, to collect the testimony of Mexican religious who had been obliged to flee violence at home. His basic method for collecting testimony and processing it as historical sources was to obtain letters sent from Mexico or from Mexicans in exile and to ask exiles to write down their experiences. He also went about collecting newspaper clippings and other assorted sources. But the written testimony of the exiles was the most direct and compelling aspect of this campaign, and Kelley had everything carefully translated into English, often with the help of a young, bilingual Mexican priest named Juan Navarrete, who assumed a key role as Kelley's secretary and interpreter and who would subsequently become the bishop of Sonora.[10] Kelley proceeded with the support of Archbishop Mora and the other Mexican bishops in Texas; he had several allies within the U.S. Catholic Church, including Father Constantineau; Galveston bishop Nicholas A. Gallagher; James H. Blenk, the archbishop of New Orleans; and Richard H. Tierney, the editor of the Washington-based Jesuit weekly *America*.

GEOPOLITICS AND TRANSNATIONAL CATHOLIC ACTIVISM

Following the collapse of Pancho Villa's rebels in the north, the Constitutionalist army of Venustiano Carranza consolidated its control over most strategic points across Mexico. Sensing the sea change, Catholics mobilized in the United States during September and October 1915 to sway President Wilson against recognition of Carranza. Many letters written by Catholics from across the United States argued, sometimes passionately, that Carranza would not uphold the basic freedom of religious expression and should not receive U.S. recognition. There were also letters to the opposite effect, arguing in favor of Carranza's faction, but they were the minority. As for the practical importance of recognition, the experience of the Huerta regime was a recent example of the difficulties a government might face without U.S. approval. The main external threat to Mexico was not another invasion but the possibility of being unable to borrow loans internationally.

10. Navarrete was only in his twenties at the time. At age thirty-two, he became the world's youngest Roman Catholic bishop at the time of his appointment in 1919; see Yolanda Padilla Rangel, *Los desterrados: Exiliados católicos de la Revolución Mexicana en Texas, 1914–1919* (Aguascalientes: Universidad Autónoma de Aguascalientes, 2009), 112–14; Arizona Archives Online, "Juan Navarrete y Guerrero Collection," http://www.azarchivesonline.org/xtf/view?docId=ead/uoa/UAMS423.xml;query=;brand=default.

The letter-writing campaign was waged mostly during the first three weeks of October.[11] In Robert Quirk's interpretation, the campaign was obviously organized by American clergy, a conclusion based on the observation that the letters were similarly worded.[12] There is no doubt that the campaign was organized, and that the U.S. clergy was involved. However, the laity sent most of the letters, and the variety is much richer than one might expect. Furthermore, because it was organized, it was explicitly political and should be considered as such. There is no scientific way to estimate the number of votes that the Catholic Church and its organizations could sway, nor can it be argued that people would necessarily vote based exclusively on the Mexican question. But it would be shortsighted to underestimate the extent to which Catholic identity was a unifying factor for many such groups in the United States. Catholics were a religious minority and generally an ethnic minority too, as is reflected in the names of several of the organizations.[13]

I found and examined sixty-one letters included among the State Department consular dispatches, of which fifty-two were against recognition and nine were in favor. Those in favor were often written after recognition and were of a congratulatory nature. These letters were generally written by people who identified themselves with Protestant churches. One came from a Los Angeles–based solidarity group called the Unión Constitucionalista de Obreros Mexicanos (Constitutionalist Union of Mexican Workers), a clear identification with the Carranza faction; in English they called themselves the Union Mexico Colony.[14] Some expressed explicit anti-Catholic sentiments, like the Rochester

11. Based on sixty-one letters included among the U.S. State Department Consular dispatches; see Records of the Department of State Relating to Internal Affairs of Mexico, 1910–1929 (SD), 812.00/16415, microfilm roll 49.

12. Robert E. Quirk, *The Mexican Revolution and the Catholic Church, 1910–1929* (Bloomington: Indiana University Press, 1973), 69. A similar opinion was also expressed by one correspondent who argued in support of recognition, saying that most Americans were in favor, even though they did not have a "regular letter-writing corps" to do their bidding. See SD, 812.00/16425, "Dodge to Lansing," Ruskin Tennessee, November 2, 1915.

13. Letters were sent by Irish, Lithuanian, German, Bohemian, and Slavic groups, who were careful to also identify themselves as "American citizens." Although the American Federation of Catholic Societies (AFCS) was not an ethnically specific organization, one of its main stated objectives was the destruction of bigotry. Like many such associations, the AFCS was founded in the period following *Rerum novarum*, in 1899.

14. SD, 812.00/16425, "Union Constitutionalists to President Wilson," Los Angeles, October 5, 1915.

man who reassured President Wilson that anti-Catholic voters out-
numbered Catholics five to one, and sent in press clippings declaring
that the "Romish prelates," despite their oaths of celibacy, and were
responsible for the vast numbers of illegitimate children in Rome and
Brussels and for the Philippine "old maids" with their large families.[15]
Another letter argued that 60 percent of Americans had no church at
all. E. W. Dodge, of *Riches Magazine*, offered the following read on the
Mexico question:

[The] trouble was commenced in Mexico at the instigation of the catholic hierarchy in return for a fund of $20,000,000, furnished by Standard Oil in
order to gain a foot-hold in the Tampico Oil fields and that the Christian Fathers knocked down the money, were unable to deliver the goods and have
finally been reduced to a point where they have had to murder American soldiers and citizens and organize raids into American territory for the purpose of
causing intervention to be followed by annexation and a subsequent looting of
the United States Treasury along the fruitful lines followed in the Philippines,
Cuba, and Porta Rica [*sic*].[16]

The pact with Standard Oil seems unlikely, as does a conspiracy
in which Christian fathers murdered American citizens; on the issue
of border raids, the author might be thinking of Villa's attack on Columbus, New Mexico, except that it was still about five months in the
future. However, it was not the first time rumors surfaced of a "Vil-
lista clerical party."[17] The final reference illustrates how race imbued
U.S.imperialism: in E. W. Dodge's view, poor, brown peoples take advantage of the white man's burden to leech the benefits of the affluent
society. This is the underlying message of the letter: recognize Carranza; do not get the United States involved in backward Mexico.

No Catholic wrote to endorse or congratulate the recognition of Carranza, and all fifty-two letters against recognition were sent by Catholics.
These came from all regions of the United States. Many were telegrams,
and because of the nature of that particular mode of correspondence,
they were similarly phrased. But many others were letters, and their
form often unique. Among the similarities, most of the correspondence
was written on letterhead from Catholic lay organizations, although

15. SD, 812.00/16425, "Dorethy to Lansing," Rochester, N.Y., October 18, 1915.
16. SD, 812.00/16425, "Dodge to Lansing," Ruskin, Tenn., November 2, 1915.
17. William B. Davis, *Experiences and Observations of an American Consular Officer during the Mexican Revolutions* (Whitefish, MT: Kessinger Publishing, LLC, 1920), 179.

bishops did send eleven letters. The secretary or president of the organization would begin by saying that he or she wrote on behalf of so many thousands of Catholic citizens. For example, the archbishop of Brooklyn represented 750,000 faithful; the Catholic Ladies of Columbia in Kenton, Ohio, represented 4,500 women; the Central Verein National Federation of German-American Catholics in New York represented 50,000 citizens; the Lithuanian Roman Catholic Alliance of America, located in Baltimore, represented 10,000 citizens; and the Ancient Order of Hibernians in America, located in Philadelphia, represented 175,000 citizens.[18] The Chicago-based Catholic Church Extension Society, Bishop Kelley's organization, simply warned that recognition would bring sorrow to sixteen million Catholics in the United States:

The Catholic Church Extension Society ... has more knowledge of [Mexico's] condition; has done more to alleviate its horrors than any single factor in America. In all its works it kept well within the spirit of true Americanism; it forestalled criticism against you, Mr. President, in well-founded conviction that you, as the champion of an ideal Democracy, would meet the tremendous obligation that has come to you in solving the problem of Mexico. It is our profound conviction that what you have done for the unfortunate people of Mexico would collapse entirely by the recognition of a man who is poles asunder in all that goes to make up the representative of a people who are striving to get to some plane of peace and security.[19]

Another letter, written by a priest from Jackson, Missouri, includes a composite of the press he had received on the Chautauqua circuit across Nebraska, Iowa, Illinois, Indiana, and Ohio. Father Michael Collins had lived for years in Mexico and, in 1915, had spent his time going from town to town and speaking on the problems of Catholic Mexico. One newspaper wrote, impressed, "Father Collins gave proof of his broad-mindedness, by saying that if he were not a Catholic and a Catholic priest, he would not mind being a Mason." No doubt such heterodoxy would not have been appreciated in Mexico, where the Masons were generally blamed for Catholic ills. Collins, for his part, made his opinion abundantly clear to President Wilson:

18. SD 812.00/16415, "Shields to President Wilson," Brooklyn, October 11, 1915; "Mathews to President Wilson," Kenton, October 6, 1915; "Frep to President Wilson," New York, October 6, 1915; "Vasiliauskas to President Wilson," October 5, 1915; "McLaughlin to President Wilson," October 11, 1915.
19. SD 812.00/16415, "Ledvina to Wilson," Chicago, October 5, 1915.

No priest can officiate at the graves of their deserted flocks, either at the time of sepulture or after; no priest is allowed to wear his clerical garb as the clergy of all denominations do here, when traveling or otherwise; no nun can wear the garb of her profession; were I to send a chalice, or other vessel or utensil, needed in the Church of a brother clergyman in Mexico, they would automatically and simultaneously become property of the State as soon as was brought into the church edifice [sic]; no donations or legacy can be willed to the Church; if attempted they become property of the State; the Church cannot and does not own so much as a splinter of wood, a grain of sand, or a piece of rock … [and] in the future, priests will not be allowed to hear confessions of their people, in health or dying … [R]ecognition of Carranza, at best, would be calamity to the Mexicans and the beginning of worse troubles …[20]

The campaign was ultimately unsuccessful, and recognition was extended on October 18, 1915. However, Catholic public opinion was mobilized. The State Department was concerned enough to send out something more than a mere acknowledgment in response to all the letters it received, and assured those who wrote that Carranza had promised to abide by his country's law.[21] No doubt this was cold comfort to the Catholic activists. Surely, despite anticlerical paranoia, the Catholic Church was far less powerful in the arena of the great powers than was Washington. And whether or not the five to one ratio of anti-Catholic to Catholic voters could be counted on domestically, Wilson went ahead and extended diplomatic recognition. What the church could do, however, that Washington could not was unify people under a faith across national borders. The campaigns certainly educated Catholics, and contributed in the formation of public opinion. However, the individual, local work, undertaken by Kelley and his collaborators in order to document the Catholic victims of revolutionary violence in Mexico, is the most compelling part of the story. I will turn to this in the final section of this chapter.

20. SD 812.00/16415, "Collins to Wilson," Jackson, Mo., October 9, 1915. It bears mentioning that Collins's commentary regarding funerals and cemeteries is not supported by law, which, in fact, characterized such circumstances as outside the public sphere. The key legislation was the November 27, 1874, circular that reformed a decree signed by Sebastián Lerdo de Tejada on May 13, 1873. The circular compared the separate plots of a cemetery to apartments in a large building, in which the particular religious customs of the inhabitants may be observed without harm to neighbors. It clearly stated that cemeteries were not to be considered public places; see Fernando A. Gallo Lozano, comp., *Compilación de leyes de reforma* (Guadalajara: Congreso del Estado de Jalisco, 1973), 152–54.

21. SD 812.00/16415, "Tumulty to Lansing," Washington, October 22, 1915.

VIOLENCE AND THE CATHOLIC BODY

The affidavits tell a story, or, more properly, they permitted Francis Kelley to tell a story. Nominally, it was the story of revolutionaries who were inspired by the anticlerical fervor of the nineteenth century and who marched down through Mexico, from north to south, meting out iconoclastic violence on a helpless Catholic Church. The local victims of such violence were men and women religious, high clergy and low, and the symbols of Catholicism, such as religious property and its furnishings. Buildings were damaged or destroyed, the saints were stripped, their wooden and plaster bodies were shot, confessionals were burned, chalices were defiled, and the Eucharist was cast to the floor and fed to the soldiers' horses. Kelley tells this story in stark terms, narrated variously through the eyes of victims and other witnesses, many of who fled the violence and, in the fall of 1914, lived as refugees outside of Mexico.

It is important to recognize the extent to which this is not the conventional story of 1914. Kelley was surely a partisan, a Catholic activist committed to telling the story of the Mexican revolution in terms that would serve as a defense for the Catholic Church. In his eyes the exiled clergy were the innocent victims of heinous crimes. Nevertheless, successive generations of historians tended to overlook much or all of this aspect of 1914. Historians have generally mentioned anticlericalism in passing and have implicitly dismissed it as unimportant. It has been foregrounded only occasionally, as in the work of Robert Quirk, who explained anticlericalism in terms of the revolutionary response to a reactionary clerical politics. It should be noted that this interpretation runs counter to the story told by Kelley, for if the clergy were involved in politics, they could no longer be the innocent victims of the fallout generated by those politics. As regards historiographic interpretation, it makes sense to view the work of Kelley and Quirk in terms of conventional state–church conflict. And yet, Kelley's sources put a human face on the Catholic Church, and challenged the idea that the religious got what they deserved. In turn, Quirk dismissed Kelley's history as unconvincing; Quirk saw Kelley as little more than an interloper, one more priest meddling in politics. But this is only one way of reading Kelley's work, and the letters and affidavits that he sought out, collected, and archived.

The letters and affidavits allude to subaltern pasts; to borrow from

Dipesh Chakrabarty, they constitute a window onto a sort of minority history.[22] Many of these subjects lived isolated from formal mechanisms of political representation during the late nineteenth and early twentieth century, and generally, their stories remained invisible in postrevolutionary historiography. A couple of letters that the Josephine priest, José María Troncoso, sent to Giovanni Bonzano, the apostolic delegate in Washington, will help to set out the general boundaries of this history. Troncoso was active in the social Catholic movement that flourished in Mexico between 1901 and 1914.[23] At the time he wrote these letters, he had ascended to secretary general of the Servants of St. Joseph in Mexico. Troncoso drew up both letters on October 19, 1914, apparently at the behest of a third party. Judging from the fact that Troncoso was then living in San Antonio, Texas, and given that Father Kelley kept copies of the letters, it is likely that Kelley was party to the petition that Troncoso write to the apostolic delegate. In Kelley's archive they are marked as documents 116 and 129.

Troncoso begins each letter in a testimonial mode, with the following statement: "Acceding to the request made upon me to relate the details that came under my notice of the persecuting to the Church in Mexico … I wish to make the following statements: …" Both letters include a signed Spanish version, as well as an English translation. Document 129 is countersigned by the bishop of Michoacán, Leopoldo Ruiz, and the bishop of Linares, Francisco Plancarte, who state that Troncoso is a person in whom they place confidence.[24] The longer of the two letters, document 116, is a list of events that were related to him by others. He relates the tribulations of priests who were insulted, beaten, imprisoned, or murdered during the Constitutionalist campaign against Victoriano Huerta. The bishop of Durango was thrown in jail on two separate occasions, once in his hometown and again in Morelia; the bishop of Tepic remained in prison serving an eight-year sentence when Troncoso wrote; Father Carrasco, with whom Troncoso

22. Dipesh Chakrabarty, *Provincializing Europe: Postcolonial Thought and Colonial Difference* (Princeton, N.J.: Princeton University Press, 2000), 97–113.

23. Manuel Ceballos Ramírez, *El catolicismo social: Un tercero en discordia. Rerum Novarum, la "cuestión social" y la movilización de los católicos mexicanos (1891–1911)* (Mexico City: El Colegio de México, 1991).

24. AAOC, Kelley Papers, Box 10, Folder Mexican Question, Document 116, "Troncoso to Bonzano," San Antonio, October 19, 1914, 9 pp.; ibid, Document 129, "Troncoso to Bonzano," San Antonio, October 19, 1914, 4 pp. I have used the original translation rather than offering a new one.

traveled in his flight from Mexico, was imprisoned, denied food for days, and forced to sleep on the cold, damp ground; a Zamora priest died of wounds to the head after he was pistol-whipped by General Joaquín Amaro; his crime was having shouted "Viva the Sacred Heart of Jesus"; General Cándido Aguilar banished the clergy in the state of Veracruz, and many found refuge by fleeing to the port, which was controlled by the U.S. Army; in Toluca, priests were subjected to forced labor, or recruited against their will as soldiers; in Monterrey, General Antionio Villareal made a bonfire in the city square using the confession booths, and profaned the saints.[25] In a similar vein, Troncoso references anticlerical violence in Puebla, Guadalajara, and Querétaro.[26]

One episode in particular stands out in this letter, and should be commented on in more detail. Troncoso relates the tribulations of a San Luis Potosí priest, Canon Jiménez, an older man, who was stripped of much of his clothing and dragged through the streets, reviled and insulted. "Un cojo" (a handicapped man) beat him so severely with his crutch so as to break his arm. Then he was thrown, nearly naked, into a cell with other priests, and eventually all were banished, and forcibly exiled. Along the road from San Luis to the border—a five-hundred-mile trek across the Sierra Madre Oriental—they were not fed. Troncoso adds that Canon Jiménez remained in exile in the United States at the time of writing. The episode is of special interest because it relates an act that feels much like a *jacquerie* (riot), in which the victim is publicly shamed. In this sense, it can be compared with ancient traditions from continental Europe.[27] This analogy suggests the basic commonality of anticlerical violence committed in revolutionary Mexico with older traditions in the Christian world.[28]

All of these examples rely, to a greater or lesser extent on Father Troncoso's relation of stories he received from others. Canon Jimé-

25. According to Eduardo J. Correa, writing at about the same time, Villareal's troops executed the statues of the saints by firing squad; see Eduardo J. Correa, *El Partido Católico Nacional y sus directores: Explicación de su fracaso y deslinde de responsabilidades* (Mexico City: Fondo de Cultura Económica, 1991).

26. AAOC, Kelley Papers, Box 10, Folder Mexican Question, Document 116, Troncoso to Bonzano, San Antonio, October 19, 1914, 9 pp.

27. For examples taken from Reformation-era France, see Natalie Zemon Davis, *Sociedad y cultura en la Francia moderna* (Barcelona: Editorial Crítica, 1993).

28. Compare this description, for example, with the testimony recorded by Jacob Megerich on Christmas Day of 1524 during the Lutheran Reformation. See Bob Scribner, "Anticlericalism and the Cities," in *Anticlericalism in Late Medieval and Early Modern Europe*, ed. Peter A. Dykema and Heiko A. Oberman (Leiden: E. J. Brill, 1993), 147–48.

nez and Father Carrasco, one may assume, were available to vouch for their respective misfortune, while other stories, such as the violence in Monterrey, Guadalajara, and Puebla, can be corroborated through other sources. General Aguilar's antics were of public record, as were, in all likelihood, the particular tribulations of the bishops. However, it is harder to corroborate the murder of the Zamora priest, and we may assume that Troncoso was not an eyewitness. It is often difficult to piece together supporting evidence for the many atrocities committed in the heat of war and territorial conquest. But this is an important issue, one that directly connects the historian's preparatory work, *source critique*, with the act of writing history, *historiography*. One example should make this point amply clear.

Troncoso, by all accounts an honest and respected man, tells a further story in document 116. He writes that, at Progreso, Yucatán, a man and his wife boarded the ship that carried him from Veracruz to the United States. As they continued on their voyage, the man told Troncoso and Father Carrasco that the bishop of Tabasco had been executed, along with other priests. Troncoso reported this news in the same matter of fact voice with which he related the rest of the stories. However, we know that Antonio Hernández y Rodríguez, appointed bishop of Tabasco in 1912, was not executed in 1914. In fact, he resigned in 1922, when he was appointed titular bishop of Tralles in Asia, near the Aegean Sea, in Prime Minister Mustafa Kemal Atatürk's nascent Republic of Turkey.[29] This example points to the difficulty involved in working from any sources, and particularly the body of texts that Kelley collected in 1914–1915, which consisted mainly of testimony that he himself went about transforming into historical source material. Such careful reading is imperative in the case of Troncoso's second letter, document 129.[30]

The second letter, also dated October 19, relates an incident that would have been proper to the specific knowledge Troncoso possessed as superior general of his order in Mexico. The letter was also of particular importance to Bishops Ruíz and Plancarte, who countersigned, "We know the Rev. Superior General.... He is a person of trust in whom every confidence may be placed." In it, Troncoso relates what he

29. Bishop Emeritus Antonio Hernández y Rodríguez died in 1926 at age sixty-one.

30. AAOC, Kelley Papers, Box 10, Folder Mexican Question, Document 129, "Troncoso to Bonzano," San Antonio, October 19, 1914, 4 pp.

knows regarding the outrages committed against *religiosas* (female religious) by the revolutionaries.[31] Again, his knowledge is secondhand:

The Superioress of the College for girls which the Josephine Sisters conduct in Vera Cruz was in Mexico in the month of June last year.[32] Having heard it said that a certain number of Sisters who had been outraged had arrived at the Capital, full of indignation and sorrow, she asked the permission of the Superioress General to find out where these poor sisters might be located in order to give them refuge. She at first turned her steps towards the Civil Maternity House in which she supposed they might be. There she was informed that the fact of these outrages was certain, but that they had been transferred to the House of the Good Shepherd. Satisfied that they were in a religious house she did nothing more. As the whole affair was painful and mortifying, she did not wish to do more.[33]

In a further paragraph Troncoso says he believes that the superioress would be willing to certify the story. This is the extent of the letter, and it stands in contrast to document 116, a longer missive with numbered paragraphs that separate the many stories contained within.

Taken together, the two letters speak to the violence inflicted on religious bodies during the Constitutionalist march against Huerta's army. The event played out like a reconquest of Mexican territory, begun in the far reaches of the north and northwest, and unfolded gradually over the period of a few months in the late spring and summer of 1914. Priests were reduced to the status of ordinary men; their bodies denied the devotion of spirit along with the material sustenance of food. They were beaten and humiliated. And, if we are to believe the charge made here, women living in religious community were also reduced to the status of ordinary women. In the context of territorial conquest, they were pillaged alongside the rest of the devotional landscape.

Gayatri Spivak has written of rape as a metonym for territorial conquest.[34] She argues that in war women are naturalized as a form of

31. The English translation reads "sisters," but Troncoso would have likely been referring to both sisters and nuns, as the term "religiosa" covered women of both groups, and from other sources we know that cloistered religious as well as sisters lost their convents during the Mexican revolution. See Rangel, *Los desterrados*, chapter 3.

32. Troncoso placed the incident in "June of last year"; however, I believe this is a *lapsus* and that he refers to the previous June—that is, 1914. I am not aware of any allegation of such incidents in mid-1913. As I will argue here, there are many traces of such events in 1914.

33. The House of the Good Shepherd is an English rendering of "casa de las religiosas del Buen Pastor"—in other words, the convent of a religious order.

34. Spivak was not the first to make this connection. Ernest Feder published his classic

property. This phenomenon may be understood in terms of a poetics of gender violence, that is, as a way of seeing and understanding its symbolic operations as opposed to its hermeneutics. She develops this idea in the context of a discussion on the practice of *Jauhar*, a Hindu ritual in which women took their own lives in advance of a conquering army, rather than be subjected to the inevitable violence/violation that would follow.[35] Her example is specific to India, but historians have long written on the topic of war rape, and examples abound from across time and the globe.[36] In the context of revolutionary Mexico, we may ask whether a practice akin to Jauhar ever materialized, whether war rape was an aspect of the Mexican revolution, and what consequences this topic holds for our understanding of contemporary historiography. However, first it will be necessary to tease out the implications of the statement Troncoso signed and sent off to the apostolic delegate in Washington. Is it plausible? If so, was rape common? How difficult is it to corroborate the use of rape in the revolution?

The news or testimony that remains after war is often partial or vague. This was the case with the following letters to which I now turn. Both were incomplete but offered hints regarding the violence committed by soldiers against women during the revolution. The letters were almost certainly written by the same person, judging by the paper and the handwriting. They would likely have found their way into Father Kelley's archive by way of one of his Mexican collaborators, perhaps an exiled priest. Neither was signed, but both were several pages long and quite detailed. The writer self-identifies as a woman. On October 3, she narrated the story of a wealthy matron who stopped at a Mexico City shop and left her chauffer and two daughters in an automobile out front. While she was inside, Carrancista soldiers chased off the driver and left with the car and the two daughters. When the woman's husband sought out First Chief Carranza's aid to rescue his daughters, the

---

study of Latin America's landholding system, *The Rape of the Peasantry*, nearly thirty years earlier. However, it must be pointed out that while Feder uses rape figuratively as a metaphor for violence in the form of land tenure, Spivak refers to rape literally, as a form of violence that reduces women's bodies to the equivalent of conquered territory. See Ernest Feder, *The Rape of the Peasantry: Latin America's Landholding System* (Garden City, N.Y.: Doubleday Anchor Books, 1971).

35. Gayatri Chakravorty Spivak, *A Critique of Postcolonial Reason: Towards a History of the Vanishing Present* (Cambridge, Mass.: Harvard University Press, 1999), 292–306.

36. In an early feminist classic, Susan Brownmiller argued that rape had a long historical connection with war. See *Against Our Will: Men, Women and Rape* (London: Secker & Warburg, 1975).

general told him that there was nothing he could do, that it was impossible to rein in an army.[37] In another letter, dated October 20, 1914, the writer offered that according to public gossip, Carranza was weak and lacked the energy to control his soldiers. She added that a soldier had recently cut a young woman's face because she ignored his advances. In a separate incident, a young woman was carried off to the Tacubaya barracks, and when her father protested, Carranza responded, "[T]hat's what women are for, relax!"[38]

These incidents seem plausible, and the prose in both letters is matter-of-fact, rough, and unrehearsed. Nevertheless, as is often the case, both documents cannot be authenticated because they are ultimately unidentifiable. Yet all the while, they are compelling. They add to Troncoso's statement by posing the possibility that gender violence was widespread, rather than an exceptional phenomenon tied to a small number of cases. They also raise the question of whether there is a meaningful difference between gender violence directed toward women in general and that which was directed toward women religious, women who had taken vows of chastity and lived their lives in the church.

Now I examine a series of affidavits taken mostly during late October and early November 1914. I consider them in three groups: the first signed by priests, the second by religiosas, and, the third, a solitary affidavit signed by a foreign-born layman. The affidavits lack the rough, spontaneous cadence of the letters; by contrast, they are more ordered and reflective. They reveal a context generated subsequent to the incidents they recall. They were made by petition of Kelley and his collaborators; often they are countersigned by at least two witnesses, including Kelley, Archbishop James Blenk, Henry Constantineau, and others. All the statements were made in the presence of a notary who signed and sealed the affidavits to render them legal documents. Those taken originally in Spanish were carefully translated, and Kelley archived the translation along with the original, sending a signed copy to the apostolic delegate. This was a well-organized, quickly executed campaign. Basically, the south Texas affidavits were made in late October, while the Havana affidavits were made in early November, a timeline that

37. AAOC, Kelley Papers, Box 10, Folder Mexican Question, Document 69, unsigned incomplete letter, Mexico City, October 3, no year; ibid., Document 68, unsigned incomplete letter, Mexico City, October 20, 1914.

38. Ibid., Document 68.

mirrors Kelley's initial trip south to study the refugee situation. In my
opinion, this is the center and very heart of the transnational network
constructed by Father Kelley and the Mexican bishops. From here, it
would develop and extend for many years, but affidavits made for the
most part in a two-week period during the fall of 1914 are at the center
of the effort. And the events they reveal are mostly invisible in Mexican
historiography.

On October 23 and 24, Francis Kelley interviewed several exiled
Mexican priests in Houston and Galveston. Father Enrique Servín had
been the pastor of Mexico City's second-oldest parish, San Miguel Ar-
cángel. He fled after the Carrancista army charged him for having permitted at his church the wedding of President Huerta's daughter, which
was officiated by Archbishop Mora y del Río. Father Manuel Díaz Santibáñez had been the Superior at San Felipe Neri, commonly known as
La Profesa, a famous church in downtown Mexico City.[39] Both Servín
and Díaz Santibáñez belonged to the religious elite that captained the
Catholic Church in Mexico City. Father Nicolás Corona, however, was
a provincial parish priest from the Bajío region of west-central Mexico
who fled La Piedad, Michoacán, fifty miles east of Lake Chapala. The
statements of all three men were bound together along with a couple
of simple identifying notes handwritten on stationary from St. Mary's
Cathedral in Galveston. Servín's statement seems to have been taken October 23 in Houston.[40]

According to Father Servín, the stories of outrages on sisters were
so common in Mexico City that they were believed by all. In his understanding, many sisters were pregnant, and others suffered loathsome
diseases as a result of the assaults on them by revolutionary soldiers.
He added that he had never heard a denial by those in whose interest it

39. Alfredo Taracena wrote that father Díaz Santibáñez, General Huerta, U.S. Ambassador Henry Lane Wilson, Archbishop Mora y del Río, and others met secretly at La Profesa in
November 1912 to plot the downfall of President Francisco Madero. See Alfredo Taracena, *Francisco I. Madero: Biografía* (Mexico City: Editorial Porrúa, 1973).

40. Statements 48, 49, and 50 were collected at the same time. They are bound with an archaic form of staple. There is a note on a separate piece of paper following statement 48, which
seems not to be considered as a document on its own. In it, Bishop N. A. Gallagher of Galveston
says he is sending two signed affidavits, one by a Rev. N. Corona and the other by Rev. E. Dies
Santivanez [*sic*]. He also recommends protecting the anonymity of the two in case they return
to Mexico. The two affidavits are documents 49 and 50 of the Kelley Archive. On Bishop Gallagher, see Mary H. Ogilvie, "Gallagher, Nicholas Aloysius," *Handbook of Texas Online*, http://
www.tshaonline.org/handbook/online/articles/fga07. Published by the Texas State Historical
Association.

would be to disprove them.[41] Díaz Santibáñez also stated that the stories of outrages on sisters were common in Mexico City and added that people were careful not to divulge the whereabouts of the Sisters as a means of protecting the victims. He also stated that, in late September 1914, there were sisters outraged by Revolutionists and in "pregnant condition" interned at the Casa de Cuna foundling asylum on Chapultepec Avenue in Mexico City, under the care of Miss Eliza Berruecos. He did not know how many but added that he also knew of six more that were currently being sheltered at a farmhouse near Mexico City.[42] For his part, Father Corona stated that "he had it on authority of Dr. Zarraga, a physician located on Calle de las Artes, Mexico City, that in his private house there were 17 Sisters who had been outraged by 'Revolutionists' and were in pregnant condition." He also testified that there were other Sisters in the same condition interned at the Mexico City Casa de Cuna.[43]

Kelley's 1915 book included a chapter on the violence committed against religious women. That chapter presented several different voices, although the central piece of testimony was that of a Discalced Carmelite nun who referred to herself as Elisa Maria del Santísimo Sacramento. I want to examine her testimony, but first I turn to a separate piece of evidence telling the story of a Capuchin nun.

The story of Sister María Eucaristía, abbess of the Capuchina Sacramentaria del Señor San José de México convent, offers an interesting perspective on the problem of representation in at least some cases regarding the experiences of religious women in the Catholic Church. Her story was recorded in Havana, where she was living in November 1914. As head of her convent, she was in charge of an unspecified number of sisters. She and her charges fled Mexico through Veracruz earlier that year. Her testimony is interesting because it seems to show

41. AAOC, Kelley Papers, Box 10, Mexican Question, Document 48, Signed Notarized Affidavit of Enrique Servín, October 23, 1914.

42. AAOC, Kelley Papers, Box 10, Mexican Question, Document 50, Signed Notarized Affidavit of Manuel Díaz Santivanez [sic], October 24, 1914.

43. AAOC, Kelley Papers, Box 10, Mexican Question, Document 49, Signed Notarized Affidavit of Nicolás Corona, October 24, 1914. The fact that Corona and Díaz Santibáñez both refer to the Casa de Cuna foundling asylum in Mexico City might be considered as corroborating evidence, but it is equally possible that they were interviewed together on October 24, 1914, in Galveston, Texas, and one repeated aspects of the statements made by the other. A further query might wonder why a provincial priest like Corona would have specific information regarding those aiding religious women in Mexico City, some 250 miles away. Such information is elusive, to say the least.

internal lines of communication. Sister María Eucaristía did not sit for the declaration but spoke with a priest who recorded her testimony. He was Father Manuel Reynoso, according to the signature at the end of the testimony, and he stated that he was authorized by the archbishop of Mexico City to speak for Sister María Eucaristía. She did sign the affidavit, but the entire testimony was recorded in the voice of Father Reynoso, a story told in the third-person point of view, as in "[s]he declared this to me to be true."

As for the content of the letter, Sister María Eucaristía recounted what she had seen and experienced and what she learned from others but had not witnessed personally. She recalled the story of a one young sister who was discovered by the Carrancistas, and who, having run, was able to escape them. She did not testify to rape or other extreme violence but did confirm the story of the Tacubaya sisters who were made to spend a night in the barracks. Her declaration on this point was that she did not know if they were forced to endure vexations or outrages other than the fact of having been made to spend the night in the barracks with the soldiers. That fact, in itself, constituted an outrage. In the eyes of a modern reader, and in light of other testimony regarding the rape of religious women that took place at the improvised barracks where the soldiers resided, the statement might seem naïve. What else, one might ask, would the soldiers use the hostage women for? And yet, this was all she declared, her testimony does not allow deeper scrutiny.[44]

The style and content of the letter merit discussion because of the particular limits they impose on historiographic interpretation. Her memory lays out the general context of the plight of religious women, and although it makes no pretense to speaking for the worst atrocities that were alleged at that time, it does suggest a basic honesty in the facts and experience that it reports. The series of filters revealed in this letter also suggest how and why the sisters could be seen as subalterns. Sister María Eucaristía never has a proper voice of her own, a choice she presumably made of her own free will when she took her vows. A male priest represents her, and he, according to the affidavit, is able to represent her by virtue of his archbishop's commission and because Kelley and his entourage had gone to Havana in search of such testi-

---

44. AAOC, Kelley Papers, Box 10, Mexican Question, Document 56, Signed Sworn Testimony of Sor Ma. De la Eucaristía Josefa, November 5, 1914.

mony. There is a clear, seemingly rigid, hierarchy and protocol to be seen here, alongside the circumstantial context of Kelley's campaign, and it imposes a formidable distance between the subject and the act of historiographic interpretation.

This circumstance invokes two different senses of subalternity. In the first sense, it recalls Gayatri Spivak's insight regarding subalternity as developed by Marx in "The Eighteenth Brumaire of Louis Napoleon Bonaparte." That is, the structure of political representation excludes the subject or makes her invisible. In the second sense, it recalls Dipesh Chakrabarty's observation regarding the nineteenth-century testimony of Santal rebels who insisted that they had not acted, that their god had acted in their place. Both notions of subalternity are meant to explain an irreducible space that separates the historian and her readers from their proposed subject. In an analogous manner, we are hopelessly at a distance from Sister María Eucaristía's agency as a historical subject.[45] In the end, we may decide that we have her voice, but it is tenuous, always already represented. This is not precisely the case in other testimony collected and notarized by Kelley. In fact, the document file he compiled in the making of *The Book of Red and Yellow* includes several sworn affidavits in which religious women identify themselves as such and directly offer their stories. It is to this testimony that I now turn.

María Elisa Thierry hand wrote a letter to James Cardinal Gibbons, archbishop of Baltimore and primate of the Catholic Church in the United States.[46] She wrote the letter on October 28, 1914 in Veracruz, but it seems likely that she arrived at Havana with letter in hand. There she met Father Kelley and Archbishop James Blenk of New Orleans. The header of the English translation repeats the date and place but is signed by Archbishop Blenk in Havana on November 5 at Sta. Therese,

45. According to Spivak, Marx identified the basic impediment to representation that local peasant farmers encountered. This was not, she stressed, an argument that they were prepolitical or somehow possessed of a false consciousness; it was simply a case of the particular political interests and arrangements of that time and place that made them invisible or silenced, and therefore lacking representation. See Spivak, *A Critique of Postcolonial Reason*, 259–60. Chakrabarty, for his part, deployed the Santals in order to explain how precisely the Marxist interpretation of his mentor, Ranajit Guha, failed to understand the displaced subjectivity of religious rebellion. In fact, he concluded, any modern (scientific) interpretation was bound to come up short in such circumstances: a historian simply cannot explain human subjectivity in terms of providence. See Chakrabarty, *Provincializing Europe*, 102–06.

46. It bears noting, as this is the only notarized letter or testimony that I found addressed to Cardinal Gibbons, that he and Kelley had a tense, somewhat adversarial relationship.

the cloistered convent run by the Discalced Carmelites at the island capital. María E. Thierry was the civil name of a Carmelite nun known by more than one religious name. Here she identified herself as Elisa María del Santísimo Sacramento and added that she had been told to use a false name in Spanish. So, the original letter has one signature, as does the translation, but there is a final page where she revealed this information and where Archbishop Blenk signed to the effect that she had made the statement under solemn religious oath. The statement is long and covers her experiences after being expelled from Aguascalientes and along the road on her way to Mexico City and then Veracruz. Here is a partial transcription:

All the communities of religious and nuns[47] in the Republic have been obliged to leave their homes and are scattered in private houses, being exposed to a thousand dangers from which they cannot save themselves. One half an hour has been allowed to most of us to leave the convents and many have been arrested and taken to the barracks where they run all kinds of risks in their vows to chastity. Many have been obliged to join the Red Cross and care for the wounded and under this pretext are held as slaves, being compelled to grind maze [sic] and wash the soldiers clothing, while others are forced to live with the soldiers as their wives. I have seen with my own eyes more than twenty religious of different orders in the city of Mexico, Hospital de Jesus, Casa del Buen Pastor, and maternity hospital, which are about to give birth and many others that in despair have been lost.[48]

Thierry starts with a sweeping statement that may be true but that really belongs more to an expository style dealing in grand generalizations. It is not likely something that she can really know, plausible although it may be. Then she explains the plight of the nuns in terms of slavery, a domestic slavery that combines the drudgery of marital subordination with sexual servitude. It is an explicit comment on the context of 1914, but there is a parallel between slave and wife that is probably not conscious, not inasmuch as the modern reader might see it. It is, however an explicit comment regarding the violence of subjugation to male power and desire, as seen by a woman who made vows of chastity and obedience to her God. This aspect of her statement can-

47. The original text reads: "*tanto de Religiosos como de monjas*" and thus refers to male religious as well as nuns. The capitalization of "Religiosos" is in the original text.
48. AAOC, Kelley Papers, Box 10, Mexican Question, Document 53, Signed Sworn Testimony of Sor Elisa Ma del Salvador, November 4, 1914.

not be overemphasized. She punctuates it with an explicit reference to
the pregnant sisters she has seen in several institutions, both civil and
religious. The passage ends with a passing reflection on those Sisters
who "de despecho se han perdido" (in despair have been lost). This is a
very loaded phrase. It is impossible to unpack, really, but it should not
go without consideration regarding the range of possible meanings,
all of which are barely beyond the historian's scrutiny. Who were these
"many others"? And how many were they? These questions are not
easily answered, and yet their loss is surely a reference to their vows of
chastity and obedience to a higher calling.

One further affidavit was signed by Leopold Blum.[49] He identified
himself as German by birth, a U.S. citizen, and a resident of Mexico for
thirty-six years. Mr. Blum had a business in Mexico City raising Thor-
oughbred horses. According to his testimony, recorded in New York
City on February 19, 1915, and certified by New York Co. notary public
Thos. M. Applegarth, Blum described going into hiding in San Pedro,
twenty minutes from Mexico City, following the battles of Zacatecas.
He remained under cover for three weeks at a brick factory owned by
a man called Olson. There was a very large hospital right opposite the
factory. Blum related speaking personally with a number of nuns living there who had escaped the north and had been outraged by revolutionists. According to Blum, there were eighty-one of these nuns at
the hospital. He heard there was another hospital, although he did not
know the name, with more nuns. However, he did attest to seeing the
nuns at this hospital and speaking with them. In fact, he claimed that
other neighbors, both foreign and "of the better class of Mexicans,"
would go over to the hospital to bring baby clothes and do other acts
of charity. According to Blum, three or four children were born of the
nuns while he was there in hiding.[50]

Reflection on these statements invites differentiation as to their
quality, as well as the aggregate information that they suggest. In the

49. AAOC, Kelley Papers, Box 10, Mexican Question, Document 55, Signed Notarized Affidavit, Leopold Blum, New York, February 19, 1915, 1p.

50. The Battle of Zacatecas ended on June 23, 1914, with a Constitutionalist victory under
the leadership of Francisco Villa. This indicates that Mr. Blum would likely have been in hiding
during July of that year. If he saw newborn infants during his visits to the hospital, they would
have been conceived as early as fall 1913, but it is also possible that they were not conventional
thirty-eight-week pregnancies, based on the hardships endured in flight. A premature birth
might indicate conception toward the end of the year.

most extreme case, these statements (and others archived in the Kelley papers) may allude to hundreds of women victims. Is this believable? Are we confronting the phenomenon of "war rape"? How might we distinguish between the violence committed generally against women, and the special case of sexual violence committed against religiosas? In returning to the idea of rape as an extension of territorial conquest, what does this mean in the context of anticlerical violence directed at the church? If war rape is inseparable from the act of humiliation that intends to intimidate women as well as send men the message that they cannot defend "their" women, how might this be read in the context of male priests, female religious, and the institutional church? Finally, what motives lay behind acts of violence and iconoclasm that sought to defile religious women alongside the sacred symbols of Catholicism? We may conclude here that the objectification of religious women reduced them to one more inanimate representation of religious devotion.

Moreover, we may return to Spivak's example of Hindu ritual suicide committed by women as a way of denying a conquering army the ultimate act of violence/violation. Revolutionary Mexico, to be sure, was a world away from the ancient Hindu traditions of patriarchy, conquest, and Jahuar. However, Spivak offers the historian a point of analogy that may serve as a final contextualization for the topic of sexual violence in revolution. Catholic Mexico had no tradition of self-immolation, pious or otherwise. Suicide of any sort was a sin against the true love of oneself implicit in the love of God. It was not unheard of but was not scripturally sanctioned. However, it merits asking whether such human behavior did not, in fact, accompany the violence of revolution.

In this context we may consider a final letter that a young woman from Toluca called Pilar sent to her pastor, who was living in exile. The letter is dated October 24, 1914, sent at the very same time that Francis Kelley was traveling through Texas collecting testimony on anticlerical violence. Pilar was not a religiosa, as far as can be gathered from her letter. She was probably the unmarried daughter of a well-to-do Toluca family, judging from her cleanly typed letter in blue ink, the handwriting of her signature, and her manner of expression. At the beginning of the letter she mused about the difficult times in which she lived: "everything is worse today than yesterday, and better today than tomorrow," she offered pessimistically in a turn of phrase that

Koselleck would have appreciated.[51] On the subject of the revolutionaries, she felt that Zapata need not be feared, but that his secretary—
Manuel Palafox—was a different story, and that the troops committed
many outrages. This is significant distinction, considering the times,
and begs the question of who Pilar really was, and how she developed
this interpretation. Unfortunately, Pilar is irreducibly beyond deeper
comprehension, and we can merely analyze the words she chose to
include in the letter. This makes her main statement all the more compelling. After exchanging local news, she wrote to her pastor, saying
that she must ask him a question and that she had never asked before
because it had not occurred to her that it was in any way pertinent. But
now she saw it as a real possibility. "Suppose someone falls into the
power of the Zapatistas, would it be better for her to take her own life
rather than allowing them to do their own will and what they are used
to do?"[52]

In the end, we do not know what became of Pilar, whether she fell
victim to, or managed to avoid the violence of revolutionary Mexico.
Or whether, in fact, she took her life in anticipation of impending
violence, real or perceived. Nor do we know what her pastor made
of all this. We may speculate that he frowned on the idea of suicide, but
even that minor speculation would be condescending. In the end, we
only have her words, a brief, hopelessly partial glimpse of her thought.

My interest here has been the nexus between big issues of transnational activism and geopolitics, on one hand, and the small tensions
between the historian's preparatory work in source critique and the
more formal stage of writing, or historiography, on the other. I have
tried to flush out the gendered subaltern stories that condition church-
state conflict and the early Constitutionalist phase of the Mexican revolution. I found them nestled in a peculiar tale of Catholic activism
that emerged in the U.S. church, wrapped in patriotism proper to that
moment of high imperialism. There is no question that Francis Kelley was a product of the period. He had volunteered as a war chaplain

---

51. There is an implicit nod here, *avant la lettre*, to Reinhart Koselleck's famous pairing of
"space of experience" and "horizon of expectation" as founding historical categories. See Reinhart Koselleck, *Futures Past: On the Semantics of Historical Time*, trans. and with an introduction
by Keith Tribe (New York: Columbia University Press, 2004).

52. AAOC, Kelley Papers, Box 10, Mexican Question, Document 47, "Pilar to Paul," October 24, 1914; ibid., Box 9, "Key to documents and names used and appearing in brief on outrages against clergy and religious in Mexico by Carranza forces," no date, 249pp.

in Theodore Roosevelt's army during the war against Spain in Cuba. He had traveled the Chautauqua circuit during the first decade of the twentieth century talking about the edifying role of the United States in its commitment to aid the Cubans in their quest for liberty. And he was moved by a similar call to duty in his effort to save the Mexican church. However, this is really a sort of backstory.

In my opinion, what makes Kelley a fascinating figure is a combination of meticulous attention to personal suffering and an understanding of the larger picture to which it belonged. This combination of abilities allowed Kelley to make his way through Texas and Cuba in the period of a few weeks during late 1914 and to marshal limited human resources toward the construction of an archive at the service of a very specific historical memory. The anticlerical component of the Constitutionalist revolution is often mentioned in the historiography; however, the lives of those affected by its violence have generally remained invisible, beyond historiography. One hundred years later, historians still know virtually nothing about the lives of men and women religious, and the tribulations they suffered during those critical months. So, in one sense, in this chapter, I have tried to make them visible, to fill lacunae in the historiography. One lacuna regards the lives of the Catholic religious in Mexico, while another has to do with Kelley's mission to create an archive that would preserve their voices, however tainted and tenuous. This act of power, the founding of an archive, was foundational, and without it, both lacunae would remain. Finally, in another sense, I have, in this chapter, tried to confront the historiography of revolution, cast as a fundamentally masculine event, and break down the ways historians render masculinity and femininity while teasing out the play between men and women, clergy and laity, and military and civilian, in a context of extraordinary violence.

CHAPTER 5

Secret Archives, Secret Societies

New Perspectives on Mexico's Cristero
Rebellion from the Vatican Secret Archives

❖ Yves Solis

Historians have used many archival sources to explore the vitriolic
relationship between church and state in Mexico during the first few
decades of the twentieth century (1910–1940). In 2006 the Vatican
opened its Secret Archives (Archivio Segreto Vaticano, or ASV), which
shed new light on the pontificate of Pius XI (1922–1939). Researchers
were able to learn more about the internal logic of the Holy See, papal
diplomacy, and the relationship between the Roman curia, apostolic
nuncios, the apostolic delegates, and the Catholic hierarchy of diverse
countries, including Mexico. Scholars have even been able to uncover
covert conspiracies developing within Vatican walls: Émile Poulat originally discovered a network of spies operating in the Vatican during the
pontificate of Benedict XV (1914–1922), and David Alvarez expanded
on the same topic in his recent survey of Vatican diplomacy, *Spies in
the Vatican*.[1]

Included among the files at the ASV are documents from the Vatican Secretariat of State (the Holy See's "Foreign Office"), which, even
today, deals with matters relating to politics and diplomacy, and is led
by a papal-appointed secretary of state. Before the reorganization of

I would like to thank Troy Swanstrom for the realization of this chapter. Without his help,
it would not have been possible to do this work in the language of Shakespeare.

1. Émile Poulat, *Intégrisme et catholicisme intégral: Un réseau secret international antimodern-
iste: La Sapinière, 1909–1921* (Paris: Casterman, 1969), 88, 104–05; David Alvarez, *Spies in the
Vatican: Espionage and Intrigue from Napoleon to the Holocaust* (Lawrence: University of Kansas
Press, 2002), 73–84.

the Secretariat of State in the 1960s, a special committee of cardinals advised the secretary of state on policy matters, who then made recommendations directly to the pope.[2] At the ASV, these special committee meetings are filed under the heading *"sessioni"* (sessions). It is in these files that historians of Mexico have begun to uncover intriguing new information.

Mexico was the subject of four of the sessioni during the pontificate of Pius XI. One meeting concerned Ernesto Eugenio Filippi, the apostolic delegate to Mexico who was expelled from the country in 1923; another was called to formulate a response to the scandal created among the faithful when the black-and-red banner of the anarcho-syndicalists was flown on the Cathedral building in Mexico City; there was also a session called in order to understand the complex meaning and consequence of socialist and sexual education in Mexico, implemented nationwide in 1934. Finally, one of these sessioni (in fact, among the first to be convoked by the recently elected Pius XI) was held to discuss strategies for dealing with a clandestine Mexican Catholic association: the Union of Mexican Catholics, known by its members and leaders either in an abbreviated form (UCM), or simply by its first initial, the U. The cardinals made a number of suggestions to the Mexican Catholic hierarchy based on their session in order to close the U, or at the very least, warn authorities of the dangers of these secret societies.[3] Ironically, the recommendations were not taken into account because of the expulsion of the apostolic delegate in 1923. The Holy See was forced to search for a diplomatic solution to the religious problem in Mexico, but the expulsion of the same apostolic delegate who tried to warn them, in fact, allowed more radical Catholic forces to carry out their projects. When the Mexican government increased its anticlerical position in 1926, it led to the Catholic hierarchy's decision to suspend masses and other sacraments, and later, resulted in the violent reaction of Catholics in the Cristero Rebellion (1926–1929), in which the U was actively involved.

This chapter makes use of the ASV's newly available documents to describe and analyze the role of the U, a secret Catholic society that was founded in Mexico in 1915. The exact characteristics and function

2. This special committee of Cardinals was known as the Sacred Congregation of Extraordinary Ecclesiastical Affairs.

3. Archivio Segreto Vaticano (ASV) Archivio Affari Ecclesiastici Straordinari (AES), Messico, "Circa una associazione segreta cattolica," June 1922, sessione 1252, stampa 1094; and ASV, AES, Raporti Sessioni, 1922, No. 75.

of the U remained obscure and relatively unknown for many years. Recent research by Stephen Andes, as well as my own work, represents
some of the first investigations into the history and development of the
U, making use of archives in both the Vatican and in Mexico.[4]

Based on Mexican and Vatican archives, this chapter offers a brief
and introductory description of the creation of the U, an analysis of
its significance, and a review of its organizational structure and activities. This chapter also aims to show how the case of the U presents a
compelling rationale for continued transnational research in archives
outside Latin America. The story of the U has been largely ignored by
historians of Mexico, most of whom have worked exclusively in local
and national archives, whether state or ecclesiastical. With the opening of the ASV, historians have been able to begin a reconstruction of
the U, providing a new window into the history of Catholic activism in
Mexico during the early twentieth century.

THE TRANSNATIONAL CONTEXT

The opening of new archives is not by itself a guarantee of relevant new
information. In this case, however, the files about the U clarify historiographical debates not only about Mexican Catholicism but also about
Mexico's place on the world stage. Indeed, the U was part of the complex
international reality of the first four decades of the twentieth century,
overshadowed by the dramatic events of World War I, the Mexican and
Russian Revolutions, and other complex international developments. Indeed, the Vatican's relationship to the U cannot be understood without
this international context in mind. For example, in 1921, just a year before papal officials met to discuss the U, a European Catholic exclusive
society operating within the Vatican was condemned by the Holy See.
The association, known as the Sodalitium Pianum (Sodality of St. Pius
V), was organized by Bishop Umberto Benigni during the pontificate of
Pius X (1903–1914) in order to gather information secretly about "mod-
ernist" bishops in the Vatican. Thus, when the special committee of cardinals gathered to discuss the U, this recent experience with clandestine
Catholic associations colored their view of the utility of such groups.

4. Andes, *The Vatican and Catholic Activism in Mexico and Chile*, chapter 2; Yves Solis, "El
orígen de la ultraderecha en México: La U," *El Cotidiano* 149 (2008): 25–38; and Yves Solis,
"Asociación espiritual o masonería católica: La U," *Istor* 33, no. IX (Summer 2008): 121–37.

During the 1910 Mexican Revolution (1910–1920) Catholic activism was incipient and sporadic, and its relationship to the revolutionary
process was complex, often displaying elements of both constructive cooperation and counterrevolutionary conspiracy towards the emergent
state.[5] Indeed, Catholic activism in Mexico never developed a single,
united strategy to confront the revolutionary chaos of 1910–1940. For
example, while supporters of President Francisco Madero (1911–1913),
known as *maderistas*, believed that they could maintain the loyalty of the
Catholic hierarchy as the Madero administration unraveled in a coup
d'état in February 1913, many high-profile Catholic politicians directly
participated in General Victoriano Huerta's counterrevolutionary government, including Eduardo Tamariz y Sánchez, the secretary of the
Department of Education.[6] Likewise, the majority of the Catholic hierarchy applauded General Huerta's coup, because they argued that it had
returned the nation to stability and order.

Another important charge levied against the church by revolutionaries regarded loans made by the Catholic Church to Huerta's government. Revolutionaries viewed these loans as a clear provocation, and
proof of the church's support for counterrevolution. Yet many Catholics alleged that Huerta forced the church to make the loans. And in the
areas controlled by maderista revolutionaries, the church was forced
to make similar loans to the maderista revolutionary "caudillos" who
fought the federal forces under General Huerta's command.[7] Indeed,
Catholic opinion remained divided on Huerta, especially after his administration dissolved the National Catholic Party in 1914. But these
nuances were lost, and to supporters of the various military factions,
the church appeared to be an enemy of the revolution.[8] By 1914, the
revolution had become more overtly anticlerical: various revolutionary

5. María Gabriela Aguirre Cristiani, *¿Una historia compartida? Revolución mexicana y catolicismo social, 1913–1924* (Mexico City: IMDOSOC, Xochimilco, 2009); Jean Meyer, *La crisitada:
Vol. 2, el conflicto entre la iglesia y el estado 1926–1929* (México City: Siglo XXI, 1989), 66–67.

6. Laura O'Dogherty Madrazo, *De urnas y sotanas: El Partido Católico Nacional en Jalisco*
(México City : Conaculta, 2001), 315.

7. Gloria Villegas Moreno, "Estado e Iglesia en los tiempos revolucionarios," in *Relaciones
Estado-Iglesia: Encuentros y desencuentros*, ed. Patricia Galeana (Mexico City: Archivo General de
la Nación-Secretaría de Relaciones Exteriores México, 1999).

8. Alan Knight offers a convincing argument for widespread Catholic support of Huerta,
while Robert Curley shows deeper divisions within the National Catholic Party over Huerta. See
Alan Knight, *The Mexican Revolution, Volume 2: Counter-revolution and Reconstruction* (Lincoln:
University of Nebraska Press, 1990), 203; and Robert Curley, "Political Catholicism in Revolutionary Mexico," Working Paper 349, Kellogg Institute, University of Notre Dame, 2008, 64.

armies had begun closing and dismantling churches, and many clergy members, as well as members of the Catholic hierarchy, were forced into exile. It was in this turbulent period that the U arose.

In 1915 Father Luis María Martínez was headmaster of the seminary in the west-central city of Morelia. At the time, the city was at the center of revolutionary upheaval. As Robert Curley's chapter in this volume indicates, after the defeat of Huerta's army during the revolution and the victory of Venustiano Carranza, a number of factions within the city hoped to ally with Carranza. These included revolutionary troops—the Red Battalions—and workers of the Casa del Obrero Mundial. Some of these factions tried to occupy Morelia's seminary.[9] This direct challenge to Catholic life in Morelia prompted Father Martínez to form a clandestine Catholic organization that would be able to defend the faith as well as promote its propagation.

It is important to pause the narrative here, in order to note that the existing published histories about the U and its founder have offered conflicting agendas and interpretations. Many publications have been memoirs and testimonies of members of the association who, depending on their rank within the organization, presented different visions of the group.[10] Enemies of the U also published their version of the history, as have defenders of the organization and its founder.[11] All of this enhances the mysterious aura surrounding the U while simultaneously placing a burden on historians who wish to recreate an unbiased narrative about its development and significance.

In his biography of Luis María Martínez, Pedro Fernández Rodríguez insisted on the fact that the U only sought social and religious welfare.[12] He concluded that Luis María Martínez represented an example of a true patriot and social apostle, arguing that Martínez founded the U with the single goal of forming a new generation of Catholic leaders.[13]

9. Andes, *The Vatican and Catholic Activism in Mexico and Chile*, 53.

10. For example, see Antonio Rius Facius, *México Cristero* (Mexico City: Editorial Patria, 1966), 291–93; and Jesús Degollado Guízar, *Memorias de Jesús Degollado Guízar: Último general en jefe del ejército cristero* (Mexico City: Editorial Jus, 1957).

11. Many of these writings, in both archival and published form, can be found in the Miguel Palomar y Vizcarra collection in Mexico City: Archivo Histórico, Instituto de Investigaciones sobre la Universidad y la Educación, Universidad Nacional Autónoma de México, Fondo Miguel Palomar y Vizcarra.

12. Pedro Fernández Rodríguez, *Biografía de un hombre providencial: Monseñor Luis María Martínez* (Mexico City: Editorial Seminario Conciliar de México, 2003), 82–84.

13. Ibid., chapter 6.

The mission of the U, he claimed was to extend "the presence of the Christian faith in society and establish the social Kingdom of Christ in Mexico."[14] As an advocate of Luis María Martínez's beatification, Fernández Rodríguez insisted on the political and social virtues of the founder of the U. For him, therefore, Martínez only took actions that were legal and legitimate.

In light of the newly available files at the ASV, however, a different view emerges. From the beginning, the aim of the U was no less than to destroy the postrevolutionary state. By studying the origin, organization, and goals of the U, we can better understand the counterrevolutionary forces of Catholic activism and its modus operandi.

NEW INFORMATION ABOUT THE U

In some ways, the U was similar to other secret societies. Hierarchically organized, the members were privy to limited information at first, and then more as they ascended through the ranks. Almost none of the members knew who the organization's leadership was. Yet the U also differed from traditional secret societies (such as the Freemasons) because of its relationship to the Catholic hierarchy in Mexico. Indeed, the hierarchy had full access to the society's constitution and the names of its members, and its members had to report directly to the hierarchy. The hierarchy, however, did not belong to the organization.[15]

The clandestine nature of the U was crucial to its survival, as the 1917 constitution had outlawed all religiopolitical organizations. During the presidencies of Álvaro Obregón (1920–1924) and Plutarco Elías Calles (1924–1928), this required the U to maneuver for space within the growing Catholic movement, while keeping its counterrevolutionary mission secret. As religious conflict increased in 1925–1926, leaders of the society had to be more cautious in order to avoid being discovered by the government. Members used coded language based on cryptographic writings. They also used false dates and places in order to create more confusion for the government in case their correspondence was intercepted.[16]

14. Ibid., 82.

15. Solis, "Asociación espiritual o masonería católica," 121–37.

16. Archivo Histórico del Arzobispado de México (AHAM), Base Luis María Martínez, Carpeta 79, Instituciones II, Letra "L, U-V," Caja 24. Exp. 6.

The U also developed a cellular organization to guard its members from providing evidence to authorities in case of arrest. This took the form of a pyramidal structure based on discrete cells, each of which consisted of five members and a spiritual advisor. In fact, the documentation provides a very precise map of the association, indicating each organization's structure and leadership, including the *Canciller* (chancellor), *Gerente* (supervisor), *Encargado* (manager), *Secretario* (secretary), *Tesorero* (treasurer), *Asistente Eclesiástico* (ecclesiastic assistant), and the *Comité Ejecutivo* (executive committee).[17]

The information that members of the U possessed correlated to their grade within the organization. Members of the U in the first grade were informed only that the purpose of the organization was to educate a society of Catholics seeking social action based on the triple principles of discretion, discipline, and charity. When they advanced to the second grade, they were allowed access to the procedures used for social action, and they also learned about the charitable organizations that depended on the U. By the third grade, the UCM was revealed as it really was: an organization for political and national action.[18] In the fourth grade of secrecy, members had access to precise points concerning organization and had a more perfect knowledge of the constitutions of the U.[19]

The fact that members operated with different levels of knowledge about the U has a direct impact on their value as historical witnesses. Four people in the same group could have four very different views of the association itself. In the archives, some documents also indicate that a fifth grade existed but was not revealed to most of the members. For researchers, this fact implies a greater need to question and criticize all testimonies or explanations in relation to the foundation of the U.

Through its cells, the U managed to gain a national presence. A document produced by Luis María Martínez reveals that the U was present

17. AHAM, Base Luis María Martínez, Carpeta 79, Instituciones II, Letra U y V, Caja 24, Exp. 6. These files contain several lists of members, one includes approximately forty individuals while another lists two hundred. Further research is needed to present a more precise understanding of the role these individuals played in the U.

18. The concept of "National Action" was used during the late 1930s when a political party was founded with the name National Action Party (PAN) in 1939 by Efraín González Luna and Manuel Gómez Morín. However, the PAN endeavored to distance itself from radical and clandestine Catholic activism and assumed a more secular political strategy, even while the principles of Catholic social action inspired many of its early leaders.

19. ASV, AES, Messico, "Circa una associazione segreta cattolica," June 1922, sessione 1252, stampa 1094; and ASV, AES, Raporti Sessioni, 1922, No. 75.

in at least fifty-two cities and towns, including the traditional Catholic bulwarks of Aguascalientes, Colima, Durango, Guadalajara, León, Monterrey, Puebla, Querétaro, and Mexico City, as well as many other smaller towns.[20] By 1925, the U still maintained a national presence, even as some centers were closed due to increased civil–religious hostilities.[21] It is clear that these centers predated the Cristero War, which enabled the U to exert a large amount of influence in zones controlled by Cristeros during the 1926–1929 period.

These cells endeavored to make an impact on political life and Catholic activism at local, regional, and national levels. One strategy employed by the group was to "infiltrate" other Catholic associations. As members of the U took up positions of leadership in a given Catholic organization, they were able to direct the group along lines laid out by the leadership of the organization. One interesting source reveals that Adalberto Abascal, who was officially in charge of the Caballeros de Colón (the Mexican Knights of Columbus), actually worked for the U throughout the country.[22] According to these files, the U leaders were able to know on whom they could count in order to realize more effective missions and fight against the state. For example, Adalberto Abascal's rating is described with high marks (3s) in coded language; for example, *Vino Celebrar* (Wine Celebration) referred to his level of efficiency.[23] By infiltrating key members, the U ensured that its members would respond more faithfully to the goals of the society, rather than to the other groups to which they belonged openly.

Given this interorganizational competition, it is perhaps unsurprising that the U became a factor of division in the episcopate.[24] Luis Tavares has examined the rupture between two rival factions within the Catholic activist movement. The first one included Catholic forces close to Guadalajara's Archbishop Francisco Orozco y Jiménez, the Young Men's Catholic Association (Asociación Católica de la Juventud Mexicana, or ACJM), the Mexican Social Secretariat and, for a time,

20. AHAM, Base Luis María Martínez, Carpeta 79, Instituciones II, Letra U y V, Caja 24, Exp. 6.

21. Ibid.

22. AHAM, Base Luis María Martínez, Carpeta 79, Instituciones II, Letra U y V, Caja 24, Exp. 7.

23. Information on Adalberto Abascal can be found in AHAM, Base Luis María Martínez, Carpeta 79, Instituciones II, Letra U y V, Caja 24, Exp. 7.

24. Luis Fernando Bernal Tavares, *Los católicos y la política en México* (Mexico City: Milestone, 2006), 167–70; 178–83; 236–47.

with the League for the Defense of Religious Liberty (Liga Nacional Defensora de la Libertad Religiosa, or LNDLR). The rival faction consisted of Catholic forces close to Leopoldo Ruíz y Flores and Luis María Martínez: the U, the Knights of Columbus, and the Feminine Brigades of St. Joan of Arc.[25] Thus, the clandestine strategy of infiltrating other associations produced conflict within the Catholic movement.

The most acute conflict appears to have occurred between the U and the LNDLR. As state tensions mounted in 1925, Mexican Catholics formed the LNDLR as a broad coalition of associations whose aim was first the legal defense of the faith, and later the active support of rebellion. The LNDLR was known simply as "la Liga" (the League) for short. Testimonies gleaned from former members of the U, and even its enemies among the Catholic movement, shed light on the ruptures within Mexican Catholic activism. One of these was a priest, Jesús Enrique Ochoa, better known by his alias "Spectator."[26] According to Ochoa, the rupture between the LNDLR and the U resulted in an organizational break within an affiliated society, the Feminine Brigades of St. Joan of Arc, as well as among Cristero rebels.[27] Ochoa also reveals how in some cases the U was able to maintain local control but also had control among leaders of the LNDLR itself. Intrigues between the two organizations provoked difficulties and tensions between Catholics and distracted them from their mutual enemy: the forces of the regular federal army.

Despite being an enemy of the U, Ochoa argued that the organization was very effective. Along with others, he assumed the organization did not have authorization from Rome.[28] Ochoa also insisted on the fact that both Leopoldo Torres Lara (Bishop of Tacámbaro) and Francisco Orozco y Jiménez (Archbishop of Guadalajara) actively opposed the U. The prelates thus shared the point of view of Jorge José Caruana, then apostolic delegate in Mexico, who thought the U represented a threat to peaceful Catholic resistance in México.[29]

Another case of fissure within Catholic ranks over the activities of

25. Ibid.

26. Jesús Enrique Ochoa, *Los cristeros del volcán de Colima: Escenas de la lucha por la libertad religiosa en México 1926–1929, tomo II* (Mexico City: Editorial Jus, 1961).

27. Fernando Manuel González, *Matar y morir por Cristo Rey* (Austin: University of Texas Press, 2001), 31–39; 137–144.

28. Yves Solis, "Religión y política en secretos," in *La cuestión social, N. 3–4, Catolicismo social y bicentenario,* Año 18, VII–XII (Mexico City: IMDOSOC, 2010).

29. Lauro López Beltrán, *La persecución religiosa en México: Carranza, Obregón, Calles, Portes Gil* (Mexico City: Editorial Tradición, 1987), 552–62.

the U comes from the memoir of Jesús Degollado Guízar, a Cristero general.[30] He describes his recruitment to the U and how he maintained control of the organization's activities in Mexico's central-western region (Jalisco, Colima, Michoacán, and Nayarit). In this capacity, he played a double role, the one as a commissioned leader of military operations of the forces and the other as a member of the secret Catholic organization. As with Jesús Enrique Ochoa, Guízar, through his text, displays the tensions with la Liga and how these tensions hindered the development and organization of the military zones controlled by the Cristeros. Both, however, lacked deeper knowledge about the association, likely because, at most, they were only members of the third grade.

Even as internal division within Catholic ranks increased, the U likewise had to deal with the anticlerical state, which became increasingly suspicious of clandestine Catholic activism. Some affiliates of the U were also being investigated by the police and state secret service.[31] Leaders of the U eventually decided to change the way they reported information about their members, even renaming its commissions. As state surveillance increased, the U became more cautious in order to keep its correspondence secret. Moreover, intensified scrutiny from the Mexican government occasioned a temporary truce of sorts with rival Catholic associations. In one document, a member of the U named Urbano Reyes expressly asked associates of the U, the Union Popular, and the Liga Católica Popular (Popular Catholic League) to help the LNDLR and set rivalries aside.[32]

TRANSNATIONAL SOURCES AND UNANSWERED QUESTIONS

After the 1929 peace accords ended the Cristero Rebellion, the U continued to operate into the early 1930s. New clandestine associations emerged, however, such as Las Legiones and La Base, that would eventually supplant the U. These associations laid the foundation for Sinarquismo, a conservative, ultra-rightist movement founded by Salvador Abascal, the son of Adalberto Abascal, a founding member of the U.

30. Degollado Guízar, *Memorias de Jesús Degollado Guízar*.
31. AHAM, Mariano Cañedo File, Base Luis María Martínez, Carpeta 79, Instituciones II, Letra U y V, Caja 24, Exp. 7.
32. Ibid.

In Salvador Abascal's memoirs, *Mis recuerdos. Sinarquismo y Colonia María Auxiliadora,* he refers to a very precise moment in which a member of the Catholic hierarchy told him about the U and the role played by his father in the association. Even many years removed from the functioning of the U, Adalberto remained guarded about the group's secrets. When Salvador went back to his father, questioning him about the U, Adalberto became angry, saying that the bishop had no right to disclose information about the clandestine association.[33] New archival sources have allowed historians to see the relationship between the U and family networks. In particular, there were several other Catholic organizations led by members of the Abascal family. In addition to the Sinarquista movement led by Salvador, Adalberto's son, his grandson, Carlos Abascal, also became a prominent member of another extreme right-wing movement called El Yunque (the Anvil).

The history of the U also allows a fuller understanding of the tensions inherent in global Catholicism. Although the Vatican endeavored to marginalize the movement, Mexico's revolutionary context hindered the implementation of the Holy See's directives. The push-and-pull between the Vatican and Mexican Catholic activism continued into the 1930s, when the Holy See successfully forced the mainstream of Catholic activists to seek peaceful resistance to anticlericalism exclusively. As Mexican Catholic Action was established along international lines after 1929, one former leader of the U seconded this pacific approach: none other than Luis María Martínez, the founder of the clandestine association. The Vatican duly rewarded Martínez for his change in tactics, naming him papal chargé d'affaires for México in the 1930s and finally appointing him archbishop of Mexico in 1937, a position he held until his death in 1956. The case of the U reveals that, even within Mexico's militant Catholic movement, forces outside local and national Catholicism influenced the direction and trajectory of Catholic activism.

The clandestine nature of the U and its operation in Mexico marks a fundamental issue for those who want to better understand Catholic activism during the religious persecution of the 1920s and 1930s. Yet limited knowledge of the U among contemporaries in the period has filtered down to scholarly works on the association.[34] Among scholars

33. Salvador Abascal, *Mis recuerdos: Sinarquismo y Colonia María Auxiliadora* (México City: Tradición, 2003).

34. Félix Báez-Jorge, *Olor de Santidad* (Mexico City: Universidad Veracruzana, 2006), 158–59.

there are principally two different visions about the U. The first is the product of the Mexican government's vision of the U as projected in the Mexican press after President Obregón's assassination in 1928. The Mexico City newspapers, *El Universal* and *Excelsior*, mirrored the government's version of Obregón's assassination, implicating the U in the president's death. Moreover, books and pamphlets written during this time, such as *¿Quienes mataron al General Obregon?* (*Who Killed General Obregon?*) support the government's point of view.[35] It is, however, very interesting to notice that this version of the U uncovers very few authentic connections to the actual organization.

The second vision of the U, promoted by later scholars, developed from a reliance on the memoirs of either former members of the association or Catholic bishops, both of whom produced only a partial view of the organization.[36] The current historiographical confusion surrounding the U obligates further investigation, placing the ASV in dialogue with other sources, including those already published, as well as with public archives. Lack of access to the archives of the founders or promoters of the organization represented, until recently, a problem. However, it is clear that interest in the history of transnational Catholic activism in Mexico has increased in recent years, and therefore it is crucial to revisit the historiography of the U, taking advantage of the opening of the Vatican Secret Archives and the Archives of the Archdiocese of Mexico.

35. *¿Quiénes mataron al General Obregón? Relato histórico de la tragedia de la Bombilla* (Mexico City: Editorial Popular, 1929).

36. Báez-Jorge, *Olor de Santidad*, 158–59; Tavares, *Los católicos y la política en México*, 167–70; 178–83; 236–47; López Beltrán, *La persecución religiosa en México*, 552–62.

CHAPTER 6

The Transnational Life of Sofía del Valle
Family, Nation, and Catholic Internationalism in the Interwar Years

❖ Stephen J. C. Andes

From May 1934 to June 1937, Sofía del Valle traveled the length and breadth of the United States on a mission. Mexican Catholic officials had given del Valle two fundamental tasks. First, del Valle endeavored to sway American Catholic public opinion in favor of her coreligionists in Mexico, to convince American Catholics that their brothers and sisters to the south were suffering a kind of modern-day martyrdom, mercilessly persecuted by a faction of anticlerical leaders who had risen to power in the wake of the 1910 revolution.[1] Second, del Valle's mission was to raise as much money as possible for Mexican Catholic Action (Acción Católica Mexicana), the nascent reorganization of the Catholic social movement, reconstructed along guidelines provided by Rome after the end of a bloody civil war waged by Catholic militants against the Mexican government, the so-called Cristero Rebellion (1926–1929).

Sofía del Valle's mission took the form of a lecture tour; she spoke anywhere and everywhere she was invited, from small impromptu afternoon tea parties, to Catholic girls' schools, to conferences and congresses organized by well-known lay associations—the Catholic Daughters of America, the Knights of Columbus, the International Federation of Catholic Alumnae—to parish congregations, communities of male and female religious, and seminarians. Del Valle even gave talks for

---

1. For a treatment of the campaign in favor of the Mexican church in the United States, see Matthew A. Redinger, *American Catholics and the Mexican Revolution, 1924–1936* (Notre Dame, Ind.: University of Notre Dame Press, 2005).

gatherings of interested Protestants and Jews. She traveled from Washington, D.C., to Seattle and from Toronto to Chicago. She itinerated mainly in the east, however, working back and forth along the Catholic networks of power and money located between New York, Philadelphia, Boston, Baltimore, New Jersey, and Washington, D.C. Del Valle was uniquely suited for her mission. Because she spent her childhood in Mexico, Spain, and Switzerland, she spoke English and French fluently, as well as her native Spanish. She never married, allowing her freedom to travel for long periods, but her home was in Mexico City where she lived with her parents. At forty-five years old, in 1934, she had the maturity, experience, and training to interact with the upper crust of Catholic high society in the United States, with prominent American churchmen, as well as with Vatican officials in her trips to Europe.[2]

Hers was a life in movement, lived in multiple, yet interrelated, networks of varying scale, transposed across an expanding Catholic sacred landscape. For del Valle, the family represented a core identity marker, a movable, yet stable structure within which she found solace, wisdom, and respite. Whether in Mexico, Europe, or the United States, her parents and her siblings provided a grounded base. To her, the Catholic family provided a model for social relations, for the harmony of society. In the dislocations of travel, the idealized Catholic family was extended to a spiritual family embodied in male clerics who became her "spiritual fathers," while she always remained their "daughter in the Lord." The Catholic family, moreover, was a powerful symbol of opposition in the early twentieth century, presenting the devotionalized "Holy Family"—Joseph, Mary, and Jesus—as the authentic pattern for earthly familial bliss in the midst of modern moral decay.[3] Catholic conceptions of gender and class were informed by this model family identity. Sofia del Valle presented herself as a fashion-

2. Two important documentary sources provide the basis for this study. First, is a dossier of correspondence between del Valle and the Apostolic Delegate to Mexico, Archbishop Leopoldo Ruiz y Flores, exiled in San Antonio, Texas. The file covers the period of del Valle's travels in the United States and Europe between 1934–1937, and is located at the Vatican Secret Archives, Archivio Segreto Vaticano (ASV), Arch. Deleg., Stati Uniti, Appendice Messico, fasc. 28, "Sofia del Valle." Second, a recent edited edition of del Valle's memoirs provides information on her early life, supplementary information regarding her fundraising tour, and other anecdotal material. See Manuel Olimón Nolasco, *Sofía del Valle: Una mexicana universal* (Mexico City: Instituto Nacional de las Mujeres, 2009).

3. Barbara Corrado Pope, "A Heroine without Heroics: The Little Flower of Jesus and Her Times," *Church History* 57, no. 1 (March 1988): 53–54.

able, yet intentionally modest woman who acted and spoke in line with a bourgeois social ethic.

Further afield, yet no less deeply embedded in her self-understanding, was del Valle's fierce national loyalties, her conviction to work for the good of God and Mexico; to represent Mexico to the Americans, to the French and Belgian Catholic ladies with whom she contacted, and to fight for the permanence of a Mexican Catholic identity in the postrevolutionary period of state formation (ca. 1920–1940). In all her embrace of the universal forms of Catholicism, del Valle maintained a close association between a national territory (Mexico), a people (Mexicans), and a culture (Mexican culture). According to Vásquez and Marquardt, as a "political form, the nation-state ... was universally expected to be particular and unique."[4] For del Valle, the notion of national uniqueness extended to her vision of Catholicism, carrying with her a devotion to local practices of the faith even as she practiced the common rituals of ultramontane and antimodernist Catholicism. Finally, Sofia del Valle participated in a transnational network of Catholic piety and activism, where Rome operated as a center of a Catholic "Imagined Community," providing a narrative of local/familial, national, and international disorder, a unified field of action in which to play out the discourses of antimodernism.[5]

As Schloesser wrote, beginning in the mid-nineteenth century, "ultramontanist Catholicism both imagined itself and was imagined by others as the antithesis of the dominant 'modern' cultural and intellectual ideologies: Liberalism in politics, Science (i.e., positivism), and historicism in thought, Realism and Naturalism in art. Ultramontanism looked 'beyond the mountains' of the Alps, beyond national churches ... to the pope in Rome for the center of a cosmopolitan 'Roman Catholicism'—transnational identity in the age of nationalism."[6] The multiple networks in which Sofia del Valle moved—family, nation, ultramontane revival—challenge us to envision new narratives of Catholic history in the interwar period, which integrate local, national, and transnational dynamics of Catholic identity formation. As shown

4. Vásquez and Marquardt, *Globalizing the Sacred*, 89.

5. On Rome as an important galvanizing center for Catholic activism in the United States and Latin America, see D'Agostino, *Rome in America*; and Andes, *The Vatican and Catholic Activism in Mexico and Chile*.

6. Stephen Schloesser, *Jazz Age Catholicism: Mystic Modernism in Postwar Paris, 1919–1933* (Toronto: University of Toronto Press, 2005), 5.

in the previous chapters in this volume, particularly those by Robert Curley and Yves Solis, the religious conflict in Mexico was an event that forged new connections between Catholics in Mexico, the United States, and Rome. The transnational life of Sofia del Valle reveals a fluid and overlapping interplay between multiple geographies where Catholic subjectivities found expression.

A CONSERVATIVE CATHOLIC HERITAGE

Sofia del Valle was born in 1891, her family pertaining to an elite social class in Mexico, extremely wealthy compared to the majority, but according to her, Sofia's father endeavored to wield his financial success without aristocratic pretentions or ostentation. Securing a comfortable home for his large family—six daughters and two sons—and educating them were among his chief concerns. Del Valle was the daughter of a Mexican-born French mother named Sofia Goeury Smith. Her father, Francisco del Valle Ballina, was one of the many Spanish immigrants who came from Spain to Mexico during the Porfiriato (1876–1911) to "hacer la América" (make America), the phrase used at the time for those leaving Europe to make their fortune and improve their social status in Latin America. At 32, Francisco married Sofia Goeury and children quickly followed; their second daughter was given the name Sofia del Valle. Del Valle's family heritage placed her on a particular side of Mexican history: conservative, linked to the old regime, organizational Catholics of an antirevolutionary stripe.[7]

EXCURSUS: THÉRÈSE OF LISIEUX AND
THE CATHOLIC FEMALE IDEAL

Like many Catholics of the day, Sofia del Valle was especially devoted to the newly canonized Thérèse of Lisieux, "the Little Flower," who, although living a cloistered life, would inspire worldwide affection and become a model of female piety suited to antimodern and ultramontane Catholic sensibilities. A brief portrait of Thérèse of Lisieux will provide an important context for understanding Sofia del Valle's life and work. Born Thérèse Martin in 1873 to pious parents, she grew up

7. Olimón Nolasco, *Sofia del Valle*, 17–25.

in northern France, where she would spend the vast majority of her short life. Thérèse was the youngest of five living children. Her mother, Zelie Martin, died tragically of breast cancer when Thérèse was only four-and-a-half years old. At thirteen, Thérèse expressed her desire to enter the Carmelite order at Lisieux, following the example of several older siblings. But the rules of the religious order stated that novices had to be sixteen. At fifteen she would take the most important trip of her life, a pilgrimage to Rome, where she accompanied her father and one of her sisters. During an audience with Pope Leo XIII (1878–1903), arranged by her father, Thérèse, in disobedience to an express order by the papal staff to remain quiet during the meeting, fell before the pope, clung to his knees, and did not let go until Leo permitted her to enter the Carmelites early. She got her way, and on returning to France, she joined the religious community at the Lisieux Carmel. She took the name Thérèse de l'Enfant-Jésus et de la Sainte-Face (Thérèse of the Child Jesus and the Holy Face). For the remaining nine years of her life she lived within the cloister, until her premature death of tuberculosis at twenty-four years old in 1897.[8]

Thérèse's brand of spirituality centered on interior prayer, self-abnegation, and daily sacrifice. She rejected the idea of becoming a great saint, instead endeavoring to gain union with God through the ordinary duties and routines of life. And although Thérèse repudiated the notion of being a great saint, saintliness remained her central focus. She likened the status of her soul to that of a daisy or violet in the world of flowers, not comparable to magnificent lilies or roses. If she were not a great soul, just as daisies and violets were not great flowers, she would still seek to give joy to "God's glances when He looks down at His feet."[9] From this reference came her name "the Little Flower," by which millions of Catholics would come to know her. The Little Flower promoted a "little way," a path that recognized "complicated methods

8. The literature on Thérèse of Lisieux is enormous. On the links between Catholic piety and devotion to Thérèse, see, for example, James P. McCartain, "The Sacred Heart of Jesus, Thérèse of Lisieux, and the Transformation of U.S. Catholic Piety, 1865–1940," *U.S. Catholic Historian* 25, no. 2 (Spring 2007): 53–67; Steffan Losel, "Prayer, Pain, and Priestly Privilege: Claude Langlois's New Perspective on Thérèse of Lisieux," *The Journal of Religion* 88, no. 3 (July, 2008): 273–306; Richard D. E. Burton, *Holy Tears, Holy Blood: Women, Catholicism, and the Culture of Suffering in France, 1840–1970* (Ithaca, N.Y.: Cornell University Press, 2004), esp. chapter 2; Pope, "Heroine without Heroics," 46–60.

9. Losel, "Prayer, Pain, and Priestly Privilege," 277–78.

are not for simple souls," and she would write in her autobiography begun just two years before her death, "I am one of those."[10] Her mysticism, then, was not that of ecstatic experience or soaring visions but emphasized holiness as union with God practiced by means of the love with which individuals perform the ordinary tasks of life. Her diary attests to this, highlighting some of the menial tasks in which God could be found, including reading, folding clothes, daydreaming, and observing nature.[11] The little way was about daily self-sacrifices, the lack of spiritual consolation, hiding pain—mental and physical—behind a smile, and reveling in one's smallness, hiddenness, and obscurity. As Barbara Pope describes, "because God watched every act, no matter how small, each act became a kind of drama."[12] Thérèse's spiritual quest "offered a balance against the rational organization which so powerfully shaped late nineteenth- and early twentieth-century piety, allowing a growing number of individuals to transcend the ordered drive of modernity and attain a profoundly personal union with the divine."[13] Thérèse's emphasis on interiority, self-transformation, personal experience, suffering, and innocence provided a powerful antimodernist devotional repertoire mounted against the skepticism, materialism, and rationalism ascendant in modern culture. As Pope goes on to say, Thérèse's little way "described how Catholics could act 'in the world' without being harmed by it."[14]

Thérèse of Lisieux's precipitous rise from obscure nun at her death in 1897 to canonization and acclaim by Catholics worldwide by 1925 can be explained through a combination of savvy marketing and genuine appeal.[15] Thérèse helped bring the world of the contemplative cloister into the realm of popular piety, as Steffan Losel has recently put it.[16] She was the perfect heroine. A young woman who had achieved a living martyrdom in the alienated world of an isolated religious community, she was the innocent, suffering, and miracle-working girl who reflected the Catholic preconciliar disposition of withdrawal inward but whose vibrant intimate relationship with Jesus worked from the inside out, united in Christ's suffering to bring about salvation not only of the individual soul but the family, the nation, and the world as well.[17]

10. McCartain, "The Sacred Heart," 64. 11. Ibid.
12. Pope, "Heroine without Heroics," 59. 13. McCartain, "The Sacred Heart," 56.
14. Pope, "Heroine without Heroics," 59. 15. Ibid., 52.
16. Losel, "Prayer, Pain, and Priestly Privilege," 281–84.
17. Ibid., 274.

We can catch a glimpse of Thérèse reflected in the life of Sofía del Valle. The Little Flower became the patroness of the Mexican Young Women's Catholic Association (Juventud Católica Femenina Mexicana, or JCFM), which Sofía helped establish. Sofía's hardships, small sufferings, and even the monotony of her journeys—all recorded in her correspondence with the apostolic delegate—give us a sense of a spiritual simulacrum reenacted in Sofía's daily search for a union with God and a mission to sanctify the worlds surrounding her. Her letters evoke a deep intimacy with God, whom Sofía constantly referred to as "Diosito" (dear little God); a self-effacing humility; and an evaluation of herself as no one special but still someone through whom God could do great things. Yet Sofía lived out her devotion and activism in the world. As Silvia Arrom and Margaret Chowning have shown, Mexican women were never neatly confined to the traditional spheres of acceptable female piety, the convent, on the one end, and conjugal domesticity, on the other.[18] But revolution in Mexico and total war in Europe, for whatever political reorganizations these processes certainly set in motion, had likewise opened up new possibilities for women.[19] While for Catholic women these possibilities remained bounded by a male-dominated hierarchy, female activism was especially promoted by these same church leaders, who desired to encourage a robust Catholic femininity as a counterbalance to the perceived threat of liberal feminism.[20] Moreover, in Latin America, the mobilization of the laity, and especially women, was in large part a development stemming from the realities of priestly scarcity and the fear of Protestant evangelization, socialist labor, and a supposed deficiency in moral and religious education.[21] Neither

18. Silvia Marina Arrom, The Women of Mexico City, 1790–1857 (Palo Alto, Calif.: Stanford University Press, 1985); and Arrom, "Mexican Laywomen Spearhead a Catholic Revival," 50–77; Margaret Chowning, "The Catholic Church and the Ladies of the Vela Perpetua"; and Chowning, Rebellious Nuns: The Troubled History of a Mexican Convent, 1754–1863 (New York: Oxford University Press, 2006).

19. Leila J. Rupp, Worlds of Women: The Making of an International Women's Movement (Princeton, N.J.: Princeton University Press, 1997); Stephanie Mitchell and Patience A. Schell, eds., The Women's Revolution in Mexico, 1910–1953 (Lanham, Md.: Rowman & Littlefield, 2007); Stephanie J. Smith, Gender and the Mexican Revolution: Yucatán Women and the Realities of Patriarchy (Chapel Hill: University of North Carolina Press, 2009); Jocelyn Olcott, Revolutionary Women in Postrevolutionary Mexico (Durham, N.C.: Duke University Press, 2005); Jocelyn Olcott, Mary Kay Vaughn, and Gabriela Cano, eds., Sex in Revolution: Gender, Politics, and Power in Modern Mexico (Durham, N.C.: Duke University Press, 2006).

20. Losel, "Prayer, Pain, and Priestly Privilege," 280–86.

21. Gertrude M. Yeager, "In the Absence of Priests: Young Women as Apostles to the Poor, Chile 1922–1932," The Americas 64, no. 2 (October 2007): 207–42.

nun nor mother, Sofía del Valle, like many Catholic women in Europe and the Americas, helped shape this public role for female lay activists and, in the process, created remarkably durable organizations which came to dominate the Catholic Action movement.

SOFÍA DEL VALLE AND THE CATHOLIC FAMILY

Sofía del Valle's memories of childhood read like a family romance, taken from the pages of Thérèse of Lisieux's autobiography, *The Story of a Soul*. The family romance genre, popular with early-twentieth-century Catholics, provided an ideal model of paternal provision, maternal sacrifice, a family built on domestic stability, founded in daily devotional practices such as the rosary, quotidian communion, and corporate prayer. The family romance operated as an antimodernist critique of the social disintegration lamented by Catholics in Europe and the Americas, caused, according to them, by the eroding forces associated with contemporary society: urbanization, industrialization, and the growing strength of the secular state.[22] Sofía recalled with fondness the family home, which was one of the first to be built in the Colonia Roma neighborhood of Mexico City, an area of the capital soon to be associated with the urban, Hispanicized Catholic lay elite. A new church, run by the Jesuit order, called La Sagrada Familia (The Holy Family) would be built in Colonia Roma in 1910; in 1912 Jesuit priests administered 45,961 communions in the church.[23] Moreover, the archdiocesan headquarters would come to be located in the borough. One of the early neighbors to the del Valle family was Pedro Lascuráin, a conservative Catholic and the foreign secretary under President Francisco I. Madero (1911–1913), who played an important role in General Victoriano Huerta's coup d'état in 1913.[24] But Sofía did not experience the 1910 revolution and its aftermath firsthand, as Francisco del Valle moved his family to Europe in 1907, when Sofía was sixteen. Yet, the course and process of the revolution left an indelible mark on Sofía; her later work as a Catholic social activist was conceived in response to a society in reconstruction, where Catholics endeavored to forward their own plan for Mexico's future.

22. Ann S. Blum, *Domestic Economies: Family, Work, and Welfare in Mexico City, 1884–1943* (Lincoln: University of Nebraska Press, 2009), 108.

23. José Gutiérrez Casillas, *Jesuitas en México durante el siglo XX* (Mexico City: Editorial Porrúa S.A., 1981), 49.

24. In fact, Lascuráin donated the land on which La Sagrada Familia was built. Ibid.

The Catholic alternative to revolution would emphasize the integrity of the family, from resisting socialist education to promoting protection for a family wage.[25]

In addition to memories of her home life, the intimate atmosphere, and the happy family meals, Sofía recalled the influence of her maternal grandmother, who lived with the family. The example of her grandmother, who spoke Spanish only partially, a product of the French enclave in which she remained after the death of her husband, loomed large in Sofía's early experience with Catholicism. Sofía remembered her fortitude, as well as her sense of humor. "¡Hija sé fuerte!" (Be strong, girl!) she often heard her grandmother say. Yet Sofía's grandmother mixed her exhortations with levity; she always had some joke or funny story to tell the children. It was her grandmother who taught Sofía to pray and to recognize that spiritual realities surrounded life on earth. Prayer was about fostering gratitude according to Sofía's grandmother: "To pray not only asking, as if God were a chest full of stuff available to suit my tastes, but joyously giving thanks for the beauty that surrounded me in the rain, for flowers, for the birds, for the children who sang and played around me and invited me to their games, the joy of a home in peace."[26] Sofía del Valle's memories reflect an idealization of the Catholic family: inward without being insular; ordered, happy, and the foundation for peace in the social world.

Sofía del Valle spent her remaining formative years in Europe, alternating between Villaviciosa, Asturias (Spain), her father's hometown, and Lausanne, Switzerland. In Lausanne Sofía encountered a cosmopolitan world; in school she met students from various parts of Europe; she learned to command French and English and developed friendships with girls from diverse religious traditions, especially Jewish émigrés to the city.[27] Sofía recounted, "We had contact with young people from different European countries and different religions. This helped us to expand our view of life, to understand better what the world is and more than once, to get some good little lesson helpful for

25. Randall S. Hanson, "The Day of Ideals: Catholic Social Action in the Age of the Mexican Revolution, 1867–1929," PhD diss., Indiana University, Bloomington, 1994.

26. Olimón Nolasco, *Sofía del Valle*, 25–25.

27. Sofía del Valle's memories of her relationship with Jewish young women might have been filtered through a post–Vatican II understanding. However, the interwar years were an important period of intellectual change in interfaith relations. See Breanna Moore, "Philosemitism under a Darkening Sky: Judaism in the French Catholic Revival (1900–1945)," *The Catholic Historical Review* 99, no. 2 (April 2013): 262–97.

the future." These lessons came not only through her studies at the
Catholic Institute of Lausanne, which she attended every morning, but
also through her studies at a Jewish school called "Bonne Brise." There
she recalled a friendship with a young Jewish girl who challenged her
character: "Sofía, I want to tell you something that I believe you'll take
with the same rect intention in which I tell you," her friend came to
her one day. "I find that your judgments in general are very quick; you
don't wait to have all the necessary information before airing them. I
recommend this phrase that has helped me in life: *D'abord comprendre
et ensuite juger* [First understand and then judge]."[28] Sofía recalled that
her friend's words affected her deeply. She came to believe that criticism, if not based in real facts, led to actions or modes of thinking that
were unjust. This sense of justice, in herself and in others, would be a
deeply felt ideal throughout Sofía's life.

During her teenage years, Sofía's father played a central role in her
life. She remembered vividly how her father had received an offer of
marriage for Sofía from a distant family relative. At just sixteen, her
father did not believe Sofía ready for an engagement and politely refused the proposal; later he humorously recounted the proposal to his
daughter. Sofía herself was relieved and agreed that marriage was not
on her horizon at the time.[29] In fact, marriage would not be part of
Sofía's future. Outside of this early proposal, Sofía never spoke about
any romantic attachments, neither in her memoir nor in her correspondence. She also never expressed a desire to be a nun, to join a
religious order like her sister Hortensia. In fact, she made sure to distinguish herself from the consecrated life, often taking offense at the
suggestion that she was a nun, as she later traveled alone, as a single
woman past the age when most women had already married. Yet her
independence was bounded by the recognition of her parent's authority, as well as the close relationships she formed with Mexican clergy.
She nodded to the spiritual direction of prominent bishops and priests,
and as her correspondence showed, she always remained "una hija en
el Señor" (a daughter in the Lord).[30]

Seven years were spent in Lausanne, until the outbreak of European war in 1914 disturbed the family's safe, tightly knit cocoon. Travel-

28. Olimón Nolasco, *Sofía del Valle*, 40.
29. Ibid., 34–35.
30. ASV, Arch. Deleg. Stati Uniti, Appendice Messico, fasc. 28, "Sofía del Valle."

ing from Switzerland through France and on to Spain via train offered
another kind of education to Sofía and her siblings. The war wounded
crowded the train cars, many scarred from battle, leaving a deep impression on the del Valle children. Sofía remembered that Providence
helped the family pass safely through France and finally to Asturias.
They remained only briefly in Villaviciosa and soon relocated to Gijón
for the remainder of the war. In Gijón, Sofía and her sister Matilde first
began to work in social Catholic projects, assisting the wives of fish-
erman in religious education and providing fiestas for young people,
giving them healthy pastimes, as she described in her memoir. She
worked closely with a Jesuit in Gijón, who provided her with freedom
to develop her ministries with a degree of autonomy.[31]

In 1918 Sofía's father returned to Mexico. Word came that the individual left in charge of his assets had sold them using Zapatista currency, which had become worthless. Francisco del Valle did not feel
it safe for the family to return at that time and instead moved them
to New Orleans. There they remained another four years until 1922.
While in New Orleans, tragedy struck the family. The oldest son, Francisco, was killed in an accident. Other members of the family began
to make their own way as well. A sister married in New Orleans and
started life with her new husband. Another sister, Hortensia, entered
the Assumptionist order in Philadelphia. Matilde, the oldest, stayed in
Spain to take care of Sofía's aged paternal grandmother. Thus, when
the family finally returned to Mexico in 1922, only four siblings made
the journey. Although the family unit had contracted, Sofía recalled
that the return to Mexico brought a sense of stability; Francisco bought
a house outside Mexico City in Tlacopac, then an unincorporated part
of the city, which today has been absorbed into the urban sprawl. The
house was dubbed "Quinta Sofía" after Sofía's mother, her namesake.
A small garden, planted with fruit trees, cactus, and flowers helped
provide a sense of tranquility, an oasis separate from the bustle of the
city and the postrevolutionary political, social, and cultural reconstruction in the capital.[32] It became a point of departure and return for
Sofía, who quickly integrated herself in the Catholic renewal led in part
by the Jesuit Alfredo Méndez Medina, and his team of lay workers at
the Mexican Social Secretariat (Secretariado Social Mexicano, or SSM).

31. Olimón Nolasco, *Sofía del Valle*, 40–47.
32. Ibid., 48–50.

Méndez Medina returned to Mexico from Europe in 1913, trained in social Catholic techniques and a broad vision to organize workers into professional unions with a confessional identity. He joined the Catholic movement already in motion. Four social congresses had convened in the first decade of the twentieth century, seconded by a multitude of smaller conferences called "social weeks," held in various locations around the republic. These events, while mainly intellectual endeavors, helped lay the foundation for numerous lay associations by 1910. Méndez Medina's participation in the Second Workers Diet in 1913 catapulted him to renown within the Catholic activist community. He assisted in founding workers' associations, helped draft social legislation, and convened social study groups. But, as Mexico's democratic aperture under Francisco Madero rapidly closed with the coup d'état led by Victoriano Huerta, Méndez Medina was reassigned to the seminary in San Salvador, El Salvador.[33] By 1920, with a measure of stability returning to Mexico, the bishops named Méndez Medina director of a new institute, the SSM, whose mission would be to provide resources and technical direction to social Catholic projects. The SSM was based on the Belgian social secretariat founded by Father Georges Rutten. A financial committee composed of laymen directed the funds for the savings-and-loan bank established by the SSM, called the Cajas de Ahorros León XIII. This committee included Mexican Catholic businessmen such as Roberto D. Hutchinson, Pedro Lascuráin, Francisco Mijares, José Aguirre Mantecón, and Sofía's father, Francisco del Valle Ballina.[34]

Sofía del Valle straddled social worlds in Mexico. During the morning she worked as a personal assistant, first at La Corona, a petroleum company, and later at the telephone company Ericcson. Her knowledge of Spanish, French, and English allowed her to translate for the company leadership. Sofía's experience and time in Lausanne made her an excellent choice as the personal assistant to the foreign manager of Ericcson, a Swedish company.[35] From 8 a.m. to 1 p.m. she worked in

33. Stephen J. C. Andes, "A Catholic Alternative to Revolution: The Survival of Social Catholicism in Postrevolutionary Mexico," *The Americas* 68, no. 4 (April 2012): 529–62.

34. Olimón Nolasco, *Sofía del Valle*, 54.

35. Susie S. Porter, "De obreras, señoritas y empleadas: Culturas de trabajo en la ciudad de México en la Compañía Ericsson," in *Género en la encrucijada de la historia social y cultural*, ed. Susie S. Porter and María Teresa Fernández Aceves (Mexico City: El Colegio de Michoacán/ CIESAS, forthcoming).

her professional position. In the afternoons, she labored in the SSM as the secretary of feminine works. Her industrial contacts provided through her father gave her entrance to Mexico City's factories and workshops, where she was allowed access to begin organizing female workers. Her mission was to provide religious education and professional skills to the female workers, not to form unions with the power of collective bargaining. Thus, she was allowed to organize workers in El Buen Tono, a cigar maker, and the clothing producers El Nuevo Mundo and La Británica, as well as the perfumer Casa Bourgeois. She made contact with the Professional Employees Union (Unión Profesional de Empleadas), which gathered women working in various workshops, and helped found the Teachers Professional Union (Unión Profesional de Maestras) and the Needleworkers (Obreras de la Aguja). These working women were invited to come to classes taught by Sofia and various other women at the SSM: classes in religion, reading, writing, and the responsibilities of domestic life.[36]

The apostolic work of Sofia del Valle was structured within a gendered social world. Her work at the SSM was officially directed by Father Méndez Medina, and later his successor in 1925, Father Miguel Darío Miranda. Sofia's entrée into professional organizing was enabled through her father's business contacts. As a single woman, her father would take her home at the end of the day, or if this was not possible, a male member of the SSM would accompany her to the electric train that traveled from the city center to her home in Tlacopac. Her family would be advised when she left, and the family's gardener would wait for her at the stop with a lantern, as electric lighting had not yet been installed in the community. Sofia remembered that one time she encountered the gardener asleep on a bench beside the stop, apparently affected by too much pulque. "Ya llegué" (I've arrived), Sofia said tersely, waking up the embarrassed gardener. Dinner would be waiting on her arrival. Saturdays and Sundays were free; Sofia would enjoy the garden, cut flowers, and participate in family devotional life: frequent communion and daily mass was always a part of Sofia's routine. Even as she embarked on greater apostolic endeavors, the family remained the core of her enlarging networks: "I can never sufficiently thank Our Lord for the parents he gave me who allowed me to enjoy an atmo-

36. Olimón Nolasco, *Sofía del Valle*, 55–56.

sphere of peace, tranquility, love, joy and service, as my family and my home were always the great school of my life."[37] Within the boundaries of family, gender, and social class, Sofía endeavored to serve and to participate in the Catholic movement. For her, these boundaries did not represent restrictions on her freedom but firm bases from which to act in the social and cultural worlds outside her safe domestic garden.

SOFÍA DEL VALLE AND MEXICAN CATHOLIC ACTIVISM

With the change in leadership at the SSM in 1925 came a new mission for Sofía del Valle, one that focused her vision on creating a national education project for Catholic women. Miguel Darío Miranda was cut from a different cloth than Méndez Medina. Whereas the latter emphasized action, organizing, and the expansion of confessional unions, Miranda valued study, consolidation, and the establishment of a strong Catholic formation. Miranda's first month at the SSM was spent observing the institution's ministries, speaking with lay activists, and developing an educational strategy. The inertia of the SSM slowed almost immediately however. Miranda envisioned the SSM as a catalyst for Catholic education—forming the Catholic conscience—of priests and lay activists. He saw Sofía as an integral part of that mission. Miranda, after his month of observation, called Sofía for an interview. "What you are doing is very laudable," he said, "but it has one great defect: your function in my opinion is to multiply Sofías."[38] After the meeting, Sofía del Valle's efforts redoubled in the area of female education. Together, Miranda and del Valle founded the Superior Institute of Feminine Culture (Instituto Superior de Cultura Femenina) in June 1926, even as church–state tensions began to boil. Again, Sofía's father would assist his daughter's mission, negotiating with Miranda and the owner of the SSM's headquarters at Motolonía 9 the construction of a second floor with classrooms, a bathroom, and a patio for breaks between courses. Cultura Femenina's mission was to provide young women an advanced education with a Catholic foundation.[39]

37. Ibid., 56.
38. Ibid., 58.
39. Many religious orders dedicated themselves to the training of young girls before the 1910 Revolution, but Cultura Femenina was unique in its focus on the education of Catholic women. See Valentina Torres Septién, *La educacción privada en México (1903–1976)* (Mexico City: El Colegio de México/Universidad Iberoamericana, 1997).

Sofía also helped establish a sister organization, the JCFM, which focused on putting this Catholic formation into practice through social
works.[40] Both organizations would be the major works she devoted her
energies to for the remainder of her life. It was her efforts for these
institutions that would lead her to the United States, Canada, and on
to Europe.

Cultura Femenina faced several immediate obstacles. First, Father
Miranda and Sofía del Valle had to recruit women to enroll in classes,
committing to a course of four years. She recalled that convincing the
parents of young women that their daughters would benefit from studies at the institute was a difficult prospect. At the time, there were few
female institutions of higher learning in Mexico. Women were invited
from various parts of the republic, and one young student moved to
Mexico from Chiapas to begin classes. Another telephone operator
from Sofía's old employer Ericcson had to change her work schedule
to the night shift in order to attend classes in the morning. Numerous
meetings were held with parents of the new students, allaying their
fears that Cultura Femenina would hinder their domestic responsibilities. Moreover, Sofía remembered that one prominent member of
the hierarchy was skeptical of the educational project. In order to win
him over, Miranda and del Valle invited him to the final exams given
at the end of a course of study. The bishop commented, "My question
is whether these wise ladies can cook a good meal."[41] Sofía took this
as a challenge and at the next exam period invited this same prelate.
The young women, in addition to the intellectual aspect of the final
exams, prepared an elaborate meal for those in attendance. The bishop
was convinced, and Sofía remembered that with this the bishop's prejudices against Cultura Femenina had been conquered. She recalled
that her goal was "to demonstrate that there was compatibility between
knowledge and being a good housewife."[42] Although the first class of
Cultura Femenina included a mere eight students, over the next decade approximately five hundred young women would complete the
four-year course of study.

40. Kristina A. Boylan, "The Feminine 'Apostolate in Society' versus the Secular State: The
Unión Femenina Católica Mexicana, 1929–1940," in *Right-Wing Women: From Conservatives
to Extremists around the World*, ed. Paola Bacchetta and Margaret Power (New York: Routledge,
2002), 176–77.
41. Olimón Nolasco, *Sofía del Valle*, 60.
42. Ibid.

If gender prejudices challenged the institute's mission, Mexico's religious conflict only compounded the difficulties in establishing the school. Just a little over a month after the establishment of Cultura Femenina, tensions between church and state came to a head. The so-called Calles Law, enabling legislation enacted by congress setting fines and imprisonment for infractions to the religious articles of the 1917 constitution, came into effect on August 1, 1926. In protest, the ecclesiastical hierarchy had approved an interdict, which went into effect the same day. At issue was the forced registration of priests with secular authorities, mandated by article 130 of the constitution. Throughout Mexico, many priests refused to fulfill the obligation. In many states, priests fled their parishes, many others stayed, but Mexico City became a locus where exiled *curas* congregated. Clandestine masses were given throughout the city. Catholic propaganda efforts continued, and the police began searching for mimeograph machines where antigovernment flyers were being printed. Police inspectors raided the offices of the SSM at Motolonía 9, where a mimeograph machine was used for Cultura Femenina's courses. This was used as justification to close the offices, take the files, and expropriate the funds of the savings-and-loan bank. Miranda; his deputy director, Rafael Dávila Vilchis; Sofía's brother-in-law; and several other men were jailed. The women present, Sofía among them, had their purses and belongings searched, but were not detained. Only Miranda was kept in jail. For three days he was held. Sofía recounted that he was brought out by the police and threatened with execution. A collection of five hundred pesos was raised by Catholics associated with the SSM and Cultura Femenina, and Miranda was finally released.[43]

The forced closure of the Motolonía offices left not only the SSM in a state of disarray but also Cultura Femenina and the JCFM, which headquartered there. Sofía and the young women in both organizations determined to continue, even if it meant, as Sofía remembered, "on the benches of the Alameda."[44] Classes met in private homes; at one time they even gathered in a house adjacent to the Mexican ambassador from the Soviet Union. The women arrived one at a time, never in groups, and someone always remained at the door. A priest from Huajuapam de León, exiled from his parish and resident in Mex-

43. Ibid., 61–62.
44. Ibid., 62–63.

ico City, brought the consecrated Host to the house every morning. He would come disguised differently each day. At 8 a.m. he deposited the Eucharist in a small *sagrario* (tabernacle) manufactured by the women, and he would return at 1 p.m. to celebrate Mass and distribute communion.[45]

EXCURSUS: THE ROMAN MODEL OF CATHOLIC ACTION

After the Cristero Rebellion ended in June 1929, the chief task of the Mexican hierarchy was to implement an international model of Catholic Action. In theory, the movement was defined as the participation of the laity in the apostolic work of the hierarchy.[46] Thus imagined, Catholic activists built through this apostolate a parallel hierarchy of the laity. Just as bishops held the highest rank in the Catholic hierarchy, urban, Hispanicized lay elites held the most power in the Catholic Action movement, at least in terms of the structural formation. International Catholic Action on the Roman model thus emanated from Europe, was received by the national bishops, and duly delegated to middle- and-upper-class Catholics, who took their role seriously and often moved quickly to implement the organization first in the archdiocese, then in the parishes of the capital, and after to the auxiliary dioceses and parishes of the republic. The annual bishops meetings debated how to organize Catholic Action within national contexts, setting up episcopal subcommittees with direct control of the organization, usually designating one or more bishops to be the national assessors of the movement. From there, four main branches were established through a series of directives agreed upon by the bishops: men, women, young men, and young women.[47]

If the Vatican Secretariat of State thought it necessary, the process was assisted by a Pontifical Letter, drafted by the papal bureaucracy, but duly signed by Pius XI (1922–1939). Not all Latin American countries

45. Ibid., 63.

46. John F. Pollard, "Pius XI's Promotion of the Italian Model of Catholic Action in the World-Wide Church," *The Journal of Ecclesiastical History* 63, no. 4 (October 2012): 758–84.

47. The Roman model of Catholic Action became the pattern for the movement in Italy, Spain, and Latin America, while French and Belgian Catholic Action developed more specialized movements of workers based on "milieu." See ASV, Concilio Vaticano II (Conc. Vat. II), Busta 1176, comm. praeparatoria, XXIX–XXXVII, subcommissio I, "Note caratteristiche dell'Azione Cattolica" 15-IX-1961, Mons. Luigi Civardi.

146 ❖ Stephen J. C. Andes

received such a letter, and it was a mark of distinction when it could be solicited or urged by bishops and lay Catholics.[48] The letter provided legitimacy for the work of reorganization of the Catholic movements in Latin America—from a loose confederation of associations to a highly corporatist structure—that naturally needed to take place and was often a strategy at eliminating the multiplicity of ideas about what Catholic Action meant. Of course, the letters were always received and interpreted through the lens of previous organizational attempts. But they lent an important urgency to the work of establishing Catholic Action on a Roman model. The branches of women and young men had operated in most Latin American republics in some form for over two decades. The Roman model meant that the branches would be expanded, encompassing a National Committee, often called a junta, of the presidents of the four main branches. The pattern was also to be established on the diocesan and parish levels. At each level the hierarchy was certainly present, from the National Assessor of Catholic Action on down to the diocesan and parish ecclesiastical assistants. But the activity of establishing diocesan and parish centers for each branch was led by lay Catholics, usually the elite lay Catholics of the capital, who received with their apostolic mandate, a new authority and wide berth for action.[49]

In Mexico, the religious conflict made the process of organizing Catholic Action that much harder. Not only did Romanizing bishops and clerics have to contend with a patchwork of local religious traditions and lay militancy, but also with an anticlerical government.[50] Father Miranda left Mexico for Europe after the closing of the SSM. Europe held the prospect of raising funds for the reestablishment of the Catholic social movement when the church-state conflict abated. Moreover, in Europe, Miranda felt that Sofía del Valle could receive training in Catholic Action methodology and practice. In 1930 she traveled to France, Belgium, and Italy to observe the female branches of Catholic Action and to network with the leaders of the movement. One impor-

48. ASV, Arch. Nunz. Argentina Busta 119, Lettera Autografa di S.S. Papa Pio XI "Vos Argentinae Episcopos," February 4, 1931, circa l'Azione Cattolica.

49. ASV, Arch. Nunz. Argentina, Busta 119, Informe de los trabajos realizados por la Liga de Damas Católicas, December 1931.

50. Andes, *The Vatican and Catholic Activism in Mexico and Chile*, chapter 6; María Luisa Aspe Armella, *La formación social y política de los católicos mexicanos: La Acción Católica Mexicana y la Unión Nacional de Estudiantes Católicos, 1929–1958* (Mexico City: Universidad Iberoamericana, 2008).

tant early contact was Christinne de Hemptine, the daughter of Belgian nobles; her father was a major patron of Catholic Action in the 1930s. Her mother operated a school for Catholic girls. Christinne was elected president of the section of female youth for the International Union of Catholic Women's Leagues (Union Internationale des Ligues Féminines Catholiques), led by Madame Florentine Steenberghe-Engeringh from the Netherlands. Sofía and Christinne quickly developed a friendship, and as the two grew closer, Sofía noticed that there was a contradiction between the noble work carried out by Christinne in organizing and how she presented herself, especially in her manner of dress. Sofía recalled that Christinne "was part of an organization in which any female grooming was attributed to vanity and was therefore avoided." To Sofía, there was no conflict between a social conscience and a women's outward presentation. Sofía and Christinne's mother worked together to persuade Christinne to put a larger investment into her manner of dress, for which a portion of Christinne's salary was put aside to buy clothes and to ensure a more feminine appearance. Social class played a role in this effort. Sofía always held the position that a woman's appearance reflected not only her femininity, which should be modestly highlighted, but also her family and social situation.[51]

Vatican officials viewed the female branches of Catholic Action as the wings of the movement most suited for early organization, and tasked women such as Christinne de Hemptine with a mission to South America. In Mexico, despite the hurdles Sofía del Valle and Miranda had to leap in order to organize the Mexican Catholic Women's Union (Unión Femenina Católica Mexicana) and the JCFM, by the early 1940s these sections had begun to grow considerably.[52] Monsignor Giuseppe Pizzardo commissioned Hemptine to travel to South America to provide technical training to the female branches in Peru, Brazil, Venezuela, Bolivia, and Chile. She acted as a personal envoy for the Roman model of Catholic Action, and the Catholic and national press of these countries reported her journeys in detail.[53]

51. Olimón Nolasco, *Sofía del Valle*, 72–73.
52. Kristina A. Boylan, "Gendering the Faith and Altering the Nation: Mexican Catholic Women's Activism, 1917–1940," in *Sex in Revolution: Gender, Politics, and Power in Modern Mexico*, ed. Jocelyn Olcott, Mary Kay Vaughn, and Gabriela Cano (Durham, N.C.: Duke University Press, 2006), 210.
53. ASV, Affari Ecclesiastici Straordinari (AES), Brasile, IV per., 1932–1937, pos. 513a, fasc. 37, "Compte Rendu succint du travail effectué au Bresil du 26 Juin au 15 Aout 1932." ff. 4r–6r.

SOFÍA DEL VALLE AND TRANSNATIONAL CATHOLICISM

Money for the work of organization became a major priority in the success of Catholic Action, both in Europe as well as Latin America. In Italy, a program was established where members of Catholic Action had to pay for affiliation. The Tessera, as it was called, formally gave full membership rights to the individual, who was then officially affiliated with the parish group. A similar program was begun in Spain, and this model was especially popular in Latin America, with mixed results.[54] It was hard enough to lure lay Catholics into taking ownership of Catholic Action and implementing the Roman hierarchical formulation. Requiring money for membership in a church organization was still more difficult. Thus, Sofía del Valle's mission to the United States to raise money for Mexican Catholic Action was seen as an intermediary step. As the membership rolls increased, and Catholic Action gained a greater number of dues-paying members, it was hoped that international donations would be less essential.[55]

In May 1934 Sofía del Valle arrived in Washington, D.C., where she contacted Father John J. Burke of the National Catholic Welfare Council. To Burke, economic assistance and the technical knowhow of the female Catholic organizations in the United States were the best that could be provided by American Catholics. Sofía embarked on her first visit to Philadelphia, seeking to make contacts and testing the feasibility of the mission, a bit bewildered by whom to speak with and who might provide entrance into American Catholic society. However, she believed her mission was providential: "God willing something will be arranged to facilitate the terribly difficult projects that we have to finish in Mexico and that are so problematic for want of funds."[56]

After her initial trips to destinations such as Pennsylvania, Sofía returned to Washington, D.C. She soon realized in conversation with her contacts that a poor idea of Mexican Catholic Action existed among the Americans with whom she spoke. But a climate of sympathy existed,

---

54. Archivo del Secretariado Social Mexicano (ASSM), "Orden del Dia para la sesión del viernes 22 de diciembre de 1933," Mexico City, December 19, 1933; ASV, Concilio Vaticano II (Conc. Vat. II), Busta 1176, comm. praeparatoria, XXIX–XXXVII, subcommissio I, "La Acción Católica en España" por Alberto Bonet, no date.

55. ASV, Arch. Deleg. Stati Uniti, Appendice Messico, fasc. 28, "Sofía del Valle," Letter from Sofía del Valle to Leopoldo Ruiz y Flores, May 19, 1934, 4rv.

56. ASV, Arch. Deleg. Stati Uniti, Appendice Messico, fasc. 28, "Sofía del Valle," Letter from Sofía del Valle to "Excelencia Reverendisima," Washington, D.C., May 11, 1934. 3r.

which helped alleviate her anxieties as to the success of her mission. By mid-May 1934 she had developed an initial plan of action. She devised a series of lectures, where she would visit the parish and diocesan courts of the Catholic Daughters of America as well as plan a national campaign of speaking at the groups affiliated with the International Federation of Catholic Alumnae. Because classes were currently letting out for the summer vacation, September would be an ideal time to begin the speaking crusade. In the meantime, she tested the waters. The bishop of Newark, Monsignor Walsh, heartily received her, commenting to Sofia that she should "tell the Apostolic Delegate and the Archbishop of Mexico that the Bishop of Newark and his Diocese will do anything in their power to help Catholics in Mexico."[57] But words, although encouraging, needed to be backed up by monetary support, and Sofia made sure to make the possibility of donations a basic part of her speaking tour.

By the summer of 1934, Sofia was wanted back in Mexico and briefly visited Chicago on her way through San Antonio to report to Ruiz y Flores, who had been exiled there in 1932 by the Mexican government. She then went on to Mexico City, where she attended the congress of the JCFM. During her stay, she attended to Cultura Femenina and JCFM leadership, where she was elected treasurer of the Junta Nacional. American Catholic tourists visited, a not-unusual event, as female Catholic activists came and went during the 1930s. To Sofia, the situation worsened daily, and she confided in a letter to Ruiz that God was in control and that her mission was being placed in his hands.[58]

In September 1934, Sofia returned to the United States to begin her lecture tour. Sofia spoke about persecution in Mexico, the experiences she herself had witnessed in Mexico City, and the story of Cultura Femenina and the JCFM, as well as the general conditions of the religious situation in Mexico. These lectures were then a platform for the creation of "Mission Crusade Groups," smaller gatherings where pledges for donations would be made, and then later collected by a designated woman in charge. The donations were then to flow either to Miranda or to the apostolic delegate, Ruiz y Flores. In practice, the donations often came directly to del Valle. After a few months a bank

57. ASV, Arch. Deleg. Stati Uniti, Appendice Messico, fasc. 28, "Sofia del Valle," Letter from Sofia del Valle to Leopoldo Ruiz y Flores, Philadelphia, July 4, 1934, 5rv.

58. ASV, Arch. Deleg. Stati Uniti, Appendice Messico, fasc. 28, "Sofia del Valle," Letter from Sofia del Valle to Leopoldo Ruiz y Flores, Mexico City, July 27, 1934, 7r.

account was established at the National City Bank of New York, in both Miranda's name and hers.[59] The work of informing American Catholic public opinion was indeed the stated mission; raising money for Cultura Femenina, the JCFM, and the reconstructed SSM was the immediate goal.

During the fall of 1934, Sofia sojourned mainly in the Eastern United States. In Washington, D.C., she had further contacts with Father Burke, the Jesuit Wilfred Parsons, and the staff of the National Catholic Welfare Conference. She traveled to New York; Newark, New Jersey; Baltimore; and Philadelphia, there giving conferences and feeling her way through, still hesitant as to whether anything would come of the mission. Matters became complicated in the fall of 1934 because several letters sent to and from Ruiz y Flores, Miranda, and Sofia were intercepted by the Mexican consulate in the United States. These named a certain "Sofia," who was supposed to be an emissary of the Mexican church, negotiating with American officials. The letters were published in El Nacional, a Mexico City daily. The editorial that accompanied the published letters questioned the identity of this "mysterious Sofia."[60] In the United States the publicity made Sofia appear to be double-dealing: was she on a lecture tour, or a political mission seeking U.S. intervention in Mexico? For some time, Sofia had to work to prove that her mission had been misinterpreted by the Mexican press; not only did she have to overcome the problems of making contacts in the United States but now also had to work to dissipate the reticence of American church officials who did not want to get involved in political affairs. Wilfred Parsons, always the conspiracy theorist, recommended she never travel alone, and that she provide pseudonyms when she spoke. Thus, she went by Mary del Val in Canada and Rose Queen and Victoria Smith in the United States.[61] She received correspondence under these names, as well as distancing herself from the controversy surrounding the "mysterious Sofia," who had been branded an agent of the Mexican church in the United States.

Sofia also ventured to Canada and Detroit in the fall of 1934. She gave conferences to francophone audiences as well as English speaking Catholics in Toronto and Ottawa. In Detroit, she made contact with

59. ASV, Arch. Deleg. Stati Uniti, Appendice Messico, fasc. 28, "Sofia del Valle," Letter from Sofia to Ruiz y Flores, April 3, 1935, 35rv.

60. Olimón Nolasco, Sofia del Valle, 81–96.

61. Ibid., 70.

Father Coughlin, of the famous radio program *Hour of the Little Flower*, devoted to St. Thérèse of Lisieux. She made sure to receive approval for the radio interview with Ruiz y Flores, worried that Coughlin intended to speak about politics; her desire, she wrote, was simply to explain the experiences of Mexican Catholics at the time.[62] By the end of 1934, Sofía was utterly exhausted. In Philadelphia she was able to find some rest with the Mothers of the Assumption, where her sister was a nun. The convent would be a refuge for her throughout her time in the United States. Her schedule was grueling. In one twenty-four-hour period in late 1934, she traveled from New York to Baltimore to give a lecture at 2 p.m., then on to Newark, New Jersey, that same day to give a talk at 8:30 p.m. that evening. By 10:30 p.m. she was back on the train for a return trip to Baltimore, arriving at 2:10 a.m. in order to give a lecture there at 10 a.m. and another later that afternoon. Del Valle spent the next day in bed with a headache but still managed to draft a list of questions she had been asked during her talks, which she would later work through with the help of Father Miranda in order to construct the best possible answers for future lectures.[63] The monotony of her schedule bothered her; she had no time to reflect, to maintain her interior spiritual vitality: "I have been so occupied with my lectures and with all the interviews that so many people have wanted with me ... that there are times that I do not notice the days passing. I live almost automatically and I do not have time to reflect on all that is happening and the consequences of so many hardships, but I can only put myself in God's hands."[64] During the first half of 1935, in addition to lectures within her East Coast nexus (Philadelphia, New York, Baltimore, Washington, D.C.) she made a trip to the Midwest, Chicago, St. Paul, Milwaukee, Great Falls (Montana), and St. Louis, as well as to the West, in Seattle at the National Conference for the Catholic Alumnae, and was invited to speak in British Columbia, Canada, and Portland, Oregon.

A profound interior piety strengthened her resolve, aided by daily mass and communion. Moreover, Sofía del Valle expressed her strong

62. ASV, Arch. Deleg. Stati Uniti, Appendice Messico, fasc. 28, "Sofia del Valle," Letter from Sofía del Valle to Leopoldo Ruiz y Flores, Toronto, November 8, 1934, 13rv.
63. ASV, Arch. Deleg. Stati Uniti, Appendice Messico, fasc. 28, "Sofia del Valle," Letter from Sofía del Valle to Leopoldo Ruiz y Flores, New York, November 29, 1934, 15rv.
64. ASV, Arch. Deleg. Stati Uniti, Appendice Messico, fasc. 28, "Sofia del Valle," Letter from Sofía del Valle to Leopoldo Ruiz y Flores, New York, November 29, 1934, 15v.

belief in Providence, which provided a narrative of her role in God's global plan. God brought to her those individuals who could help her carry out her mission. The mission to the United States would only be a success with the help of sympathetic, well-connected Catholics and with spiritual aid. She wrote to Ruiz y Flores: "Once again, I ask [Your Excellency] to keep me in your prayers ... especially that Our Lord concedes through the special intercession of Sta. Teresita [Thérèse of Lisieux] that this effort might be as successful as we have hoped, as I feel a great responsibility on me with all the efforts and sacrifices that [Your Excellency] and Father Miranda have made to facilitate these trips and I would like to see your sacrifices amply compensated with the fruit of my meager efforts abundantly blessed by God."[65] In every conversation she believed that perhaps Providence had arranged the meeting; the circumstances were not mere happenstance. She set about to work for the good of the Catholic faith and the interests of Mexico and trusted that an unseen hand was guiding her movements, her words, and her lectures. She understood her limitations: a single woman in a country that was not her own, with limited resources, both financial and social, and fighting the preconceptions and prejudices of Americans toward women and Mexicans. But she felt herself to be an instrument of Providence nonetheless—a tool—and Providence was using her to carry out an important work.

Del Valle perceived Providence to be working in bringing to her the right people who could assist in her mission. In Boston, she befriended Elizabeth Ward Loughran, a woman with numerous connections within the city's Catholic community. When Loughran heard Sofía speak about Mexico she immediately offered to connect her to individuals of influence: the rector of the city's seminary, Jesuits at Boston College, and with several prominent priests in the vicinity. Del Valle wrote that when "I arrived in Boston to prepare the terrain there I met, or better said Providence took care of putting me before a young woman who would serve as my 'Guardian Angel' there." Throughout Sofia's time in the United States, Loughran would remain a trusted friend, constant encourager, and a key contact who helped introduce her to Boston's Catholic elite.[66]

65. ASV, Arch. Deleg. Stati Uniti, Appendice Messico, fasc. 28, "Sofía del Valle," Letter from Sofía del Valle to Leopoldo Ruiz y Flores, on board the Sunshine Special, September 30, 1934, 10r.

66. Thomas H. O'Connor, *Boston Catholics: A History of the Church and Its People* (Boston: Northeastern University Press, 1998), 193–236.

Providence also assisted Del Valle in convincing individuals to help her cause. In Chicago, she met a priest who had studied Mexican history but who now had invested in a newfound interest in Japanese history. She could not figure out why this was the case, considering the important work that needed to be done on Mexico, to dispel the many inaccuracies constantly articulated in the international press and by the Mexican State. "With God's favor," she wrote, "I took measures to reconquer his will [tome medidas para la reconquista de esa voluntad] and after several visits and long conversations, I was able to ascertain that his interest had again returned toward Mexico."[67] Sofía planned to put him into contact with Miranda in New York, but when she found out that, unknown to her, Miranda had already arranged a meeting with the priest, she wrote that Providence had taken care of arranging the opportunity. Del Valle felt herself to be a modern Esther, called to such a time as this; her mission, like that of her biblical model, would be to help save a people from destruction through her humble acceptance of God's mission.

In addition to her interior piety and sense of Catholic mission, Sofía del Valle consciously presented herself within an ideal model of female activism. Sofía always remained conscious of appearances. How she presented herself mattered. Her dress and her relations with ecclesiastical authorities, especially men, were intentionally constructed. On her way to Washington, D.C., in September 1934, she stayed a few nights at the Convent of the Incarnate Word in San Antonio, Texas, where Ruiz y Flores lived and ran the apostolic delegation. On the morning of her departure, she went to Mass and received communion, as was her daily custom, and as the Mass went long she had to hurry to leave in order to catch her train. Onboard, she wrote Ruiz y Flores about several business matters, which she had not remembered to tell him in their face-to-face meetings. However, she made sure to extend her apologies for her quick departure, not wanting the sisters of the convent of the Incarnate Word to think she had simply left *a la francesa*, or without regard to propriety and decorum.[68]

The connection between gender, social class, and outward appear-

67. ASV, Arch. Deleg. Stati Uniti, Appendice Messico, fasc. 28, "Sofia del Valle," Letter from Sofía del Valle to Leopoldo Ruiz y Flores, New York, January 15, 1935, 20rv.

68. ASV, Arch. Deleg. Stati Uniti, Appendice Messico, fasc. 28, "Sofia del Valle," Letter from Sofía del Valle to Leopoldo Ruiz y Flores, a bordo del Sunshine Special, September 30, 1934, 10r.

ance was also influenced by Catholic sensibilities of modesty. When Sofia first arrived in the United States, she had an important interview with the bishop of Newark, Monsignor Walsh. At the time she was staying in New York and simply traveled by train the night before the meeting without luggage or a change of clothes. In the morning, she was invited to Mass by the woman with whom she was staying. Before walking the short distance, a torrential rain caused Sofia to ask the woman to call a taxi. The woman decided that a taxi would be unnecessary; they managed to make it to Mass, but in the process, Sofia's wool skirt was soaked. As it dried, the ankle-length suit contracted above her knees, which she felt would cause a great scandal if she had to present herself that way to the bishop. Sofia and several women spent the next hour trying to stretch the skirt—ironing it out—but to no avail. Sofia arrived at the meeting embarrassed at her situation and immediately apologized to Bishop Walsh. The prelate replied humorously, "[T]hese are trials that the Lord permits. Do not worry."[69]

Sofia del Valle's activism evidenced a clear class element. She began her career as a social activist by forming professional associations of working women. Once in the United States, her preoccupation with working women continued. During her already daunting schedule, del Valle gave classes in New York City to Latin American immigrants on the principles and practice of Catholic Action.[70] This group was made up of women living in New York who came from around the Spanish-speaking world: the Caribbean (e.g., Puerto Rico), as well as Central and South America. Sofia modeled the group on the JCFM, giving it the name of the Iberoamerican Young Women's Association. It was parish-based, and an American priest was assigned its first ecclesiastical assistant.[71] Sofia's class status translated into a class paternalism: she believed that she had the responsibility to educate, train, and "lift" working women of a lower-class status through moral instruction. Catholic class distinctions were not hers alone but came imbedded in the Roman model of Catholic Action, which taught that a committed elite, often urban and of a higher social status, would disseminate the Catholic social doctrine to their co-religionists across the social spectrum. The apostolate, or mission, of the hierarchy, was first imparted

69. Olimón Nolasco, *Sofía del Valle*, 69.

70. ASV, Arch. Deleg. Stati Uniti, Appendice Messico, fasc. 28, "Sofia del Valle," Letter from Sofia del Valle to Leopoldo Ruiz y Flores, New York, December 10, 1936, 77rv.

71. Olimón Nolasco, *Sofía del Valle*, 97, 100, 112.

to an elite laity in every sense of the word: educated, most often urban, of financial means, and "whiter," who shared in a cosmopolitan culture and who idealized French, Spanish, Belgian, Italian, and German, Catholic piety and practice. As an elite Catholic woman, del Valle felt called to educate young working women, imparting to them the apostolic mission she had received from the male hierarchy. The Catholic feminine ideal contained a distinct class dimension.

Throughout her time in the United States, recognition made Sofía feel uncomfortable, and revealed the importance of modesty within the Catholic female ideal. In Springfield, Massachusetts, she received a medal from a local Catholic college, given "to the woman who has accomplished some outstanding work." The award was given out at a graduation ceremony, held for the girls of the college. Before diplomas were handed out, three speeches were given by young women on Mexico: "The Church and Spanish Mexico," "The Church and Republican Mexico," and "The Church in Mexico To-day." Then, the local bishop spoke at length on Sofía and her work. Sofía wrote, "I do not understand how these gentleman have taken notice of me." Yet, she put herself in the hands of God and accepted the honor in name of Mexican Catholic women, although she wrote, "I wanted to disappear under my chair."[72] The young women of the college offered her a precious bouquet of flowers, and afterward they had a reception in her honor. While maintaining modesty was important to del Valle, her mission in defense of Mexico also became a mission to embody an ideal Catholic femininity.

Bishops took special note of Sofía's model womanhood. In Boston in July 1936 she spoke in one of the "morning salons" that were celebrated in the parks of the great summer residences of some of the wealthy Catholics in the city. The cardinal archbishop of Boston heard about the event and sent her a note wishing her success. Then through a female friend of the cardinal, Sofía was contacted for a private audience. The visit took place over tea, and the cardinal lavished Sofía with praise, telling her how happy and satisfied he was that Sofía was speaking in his diocese and that she represented "a model of womanhood that he wanted to be spread in his Archdiocese."[73]

72. ASV, Arch. Deleg. Stati Uniti, Appendice Messico, fasc. 28, "Sofía del Valle," Letter from Sofía del Valle to Leopoldo Ruiz y Flores, Baltimore, June 25, 1935, 47r.
73. ASV, Arch. Deleg. Stati Uniti, Appendice Messico, fasc. 28, "Sofía del Valle," Letter from Sofía del Valle to Leopoldo Ruiz y Flores, Philadelphia, August 25, 1936, 71r.

Although often extolled as a model of the ideal Catholic woman, Sofía del Valle was no bland wallflower. She expressed her opinions but always with tact and prudence, even when they conflicted with the ideas of bishops, priests, and laymen. In an early meeting with Father Burke, the influential priest frankly stated that Sofía's mission to raise public opinion among American Catholics would certainly benefit the Mexican church, especially if the enthusiasm she encouraged resulted in financial assistance for Mexican Catholic Action. However, Burke continued, he believed that the Mexican government could not care less about American Catholic public opinion; on this point Sofía sharply disagreed and made sure to express her contrary point of view. Sofía constantly contended with the prejudices of American Catholics toward their Mexican co-religionists. In Boston, John E. Swift, a judge and the future supreme knight of the Knights of Columbus, invited Sofía to a tea, where she made her presentation about the Mexican religious conflict. A question-and-answer period followed, and to Sofía's shock Swift pointedly asked, "Miss del Valle, do you think that the Mexican people would ever take into consideration their annexation to the U.S.A.?" Sofía replied without missing a beat: "They would never give a minute's thought to that idea. They know very well the way you have treated your Indians."[74] In a letter to Ruiz y Flores about the incident, Sofía recounted that Swift had nothing to say after that. Yet, she wrote, the question had put her in a difficult position, her answer had to be given "with a lot of diplomacy [and] without offending even while saying something that would be truthful and definite."[75] She felt the answer, perhaps a bit forthright but within the boundaries of tactful conversation, had been inspired by the Holy Spirit. The interchange was disheartening nonetheless. She wrote Ruiz y Flores: "But just imagine [Your Excellency] these ideas among those that might want to help us. You can see that they do not know our problems accept through their eyes of 'satisfied Americans.'"[76] Sofía del Valle found herself in a gendered world, where her ability to speak articulately, pointedly, and even a bit sharply, helped not only to overcome inherent condescension toward women but as a representative of Mexican Catholics, to also battle racial and national biases she encountered in the United States.

74. ASV, Arch. Deleg. Stati Uniti, Appendice Messico, fasc. 28, "Sofía del Valle," Letter from Sofía del Valle to Leopoldo Ruiz y Flores, Chicago, March 7, 1936, 65r.
75. Ibid.
76. Ibid.

Sofia's gendered performance also came under critique from American women. Again, in Boston she was invited to speak to a meeting of the Junior League, a philanthropic organization composed of the wealthy elite of the city. Sofia took care, as usual, to make sure her physical presentation was just as pristine as her speech. Her hair, dress, shoes, purse—everything was fashionable and neatly ordered. During her lecture, she noticed that many in the crowd were more interested in how she looked than what she said, "I knew that God would help me and that my mother, the Virgin of Guadalupe, would give me victory in the challenge. After the conference, we were offered a tea and I had the pleasure of being congratulated by various participants both for my English and for my attire. Some of the women told me: 'We never thought that a Mexican could present so well.'"[77] In another incident she was asked whether the clothes she wore were made in Mexico or if when she was in her country she wore feathers. She replied that the clothes were indeed made in Mexico and the only feathers she wore were in her hats.[78] National and racial stereotypes came in a gendered package, requiring Sofia to overcome prejudices against Mexico, and with it notions of Mexico's perceived racial "otherness," through a performance of ideal Catholic femininity: being well dressed, fashionable, and articulate and having self-effacing humor. For example, after one lecture, a member of the audience asked if she was a nun. Sofia replied in reference to her well-put-together outfit, "Do I look like a nun?" The audience laughed uproariously, and any tension in the question-and-answer session dissipated.

Sofia's work on behalf of Cultura Femenina and Catholic Action in Mexico did not go unnoticed among Europe's Catholic female elite. Her friendship with Christinne de Hemptine, who remained president of the youth branch of the Union Internationale des Ligues Féminines Catholiques, provided an important contact with the leadership of the European Catholic women's movement. Sofia affiliated Cultura Femenina and the JCFM with the Union Internationale. She had attended the 1930 congress with de Hemptine and was invited to speak at the 1937 meeting in Belgium. The leader of the Union Internationale, Madame Steenbergh-Engeringh, presented her as the representative of Latin America at the congress: "It appears that *Diosito* has wanted to

77. Olimón Nolasco, *Sofía del Valle*, 101.
78. Ibid., 103.

use me as a mouthpiece for Latin America, as I had many opportunities to intervene in the discussions that helped bring a clearer understanding of our mentality and our problems."[79] She attended the
sessions for young women, as well as the ones dedicated to Catholic
Ladies. There, she was given an opportunity to give her point of view
from a Latin American perspective. In all, approximately twenty-two
countries were represented.

After the conference, Madame Steenbergh-Engeringh tasked Sofia
with a mission to Rome. En route she gave several lectures in Paris
and then traveled to the Eternal City. There she met with Giuseppe Pizzardo, Pius XI's point man for the Roman model of Catholic Action.[80]
About the meeting she wrote Ruiz y Flores that Pizzardo

surprised me with his attention and cordiality and I had a conversation with
him for close to three hours. In it, we touched on various points, especially
on Mexico, naturally, and I believe that I was able to shed some light with respect to our situation and especially regarding the constructive work of Catholic Action. He told me things that I will tell [Your Excellency] when we meet, he
asked me for my impressions on things [in the United States], and we left in
the best of terms, asking me to write to him every so often providing him information regarding various issues that I hope to indicate to [Your Excellency].[81]

The next day she had tea with the sisters of Mrs. Macauley, widow of
Nicholas Brady, an American Catholic who had been involved in negotiations to give money to the Cristero cause during 1927. She spoke
at a gathering of aristocratic Catholic women about Mexico. After further meetings with Francesco Borgongini-Duca, another Vatican official, she wrote that she was able to "bathe myself in the atmosphere of
Rome and renew myself internally in the Catacombs and in the magnificent Basilicas, especially in St. Peter's."[82]

Although del Valle's fund-raising tour was less successful than
hoped, she was able to raise a not-inconsequential sum. The exact figures are hard to calculate, as the documentary evidence is incomplete.

79. ASV, Arch. Deleg. Stati Uniti, Appendice Messico, fasc. 28, "Sofia del Valle," Letter
from Sofia del Valle to Leopoldo Ruiz y Flores, Rome, April 14, [1937], 104r.
80. Robert A. Ventresca, *Soldier of Christ: The Life of Pope Pius XII* (Cambridge, Mass.: Harvard University Press, 2013), 66–67; Pollard, "Pius XI's Promotion," 759.
81. ASV, Arch. Deleg. Stati Uniti, Appendice Messico, fasc. 28, "Sofia del Valle," Letter
from Sofia del Valle to Leopoldo Ruiz y Flores, New York, May 12, 1937, 81r.
82. ASV, Arch. Deleg. Stati Uniti, Appendice Messico, fasc. 28, "Sofia del Valle," Letter
from Sofia del Valle to Leopoldo Ruiz y Flores, New York, May 12, 1937, 81r.

Before April 1935, the date when a bank account was opened in New York City, the donations sent back to Mexico were spotty at best. Sofía did not always provide a detailed accounting of the money sent during this earlier period, as well as the fact that much of the money collected went toward her travel expenses, as well as to her own family. It had been decided that the sum of $100 a month would be sent to her family, because she remained an important part of her parents' income during this period. From April to June 1935 Sofía's lectures raised $1,393.37, and $420 from these funds went to the SSM, the JCFM, and Cultura Femenina. Between January 1936 to June 1937 she raised another $6,728.52, of which $3,186.70 was sent to Mexico, divided between her family (a little more than half, $1,605.80) while the rest was provided to Cultura Femenina and Mexican Catholic Action ($1,580.90). Of the other remaining money, $2,687.65 was used for expenses. Thus, from April 1935 to June 1937, she raised a rough sum of $2,000 for Catholic organizations. It does seem that she was able to collect more than this amount, as many of her letters report receiving additional donations. However, it is not possible to say with any accuracy exactly how much, because these additional funds were allocated between expenses, money to her family, and funds sent directly to Mexican Catholic ministries.[83]

Sofía del Valle's work on behalf of Mexico continued even after her fundraising tour in the United States. As the conflict between church and state in Mexico abated in the late 1930s, Sofía not only continued organizing for Catholic Action but also endeavored to put into practice the goals of social Catholicism in the areas of education, social service, and in working for the betterment of women generally. During the presidencies of Manuel Ávila Camacho (1940–1946) and Miguel Alemán (1946–1952), she helped lead and organize some 150 female associations of different stripes. These included not only Catholic groups, but also Jewish community associations and also the influential Comité de Servicio Cultural y Social, A.C. (Committee for Social and Cultural Service), founded by Aurora Arrayales. Under American president Dwight D. Eisenhower, she received a prestigious award given to the woman who had done the most to further inter-American relations by the organization Women of America United for Peace.

83. ASV, Arch. Deleg. Stati Uniti, Appendice Messico, fasc. 28, "Sofía del Valle," Letter from Sofía del Valle to Leopoldo Ruiz y Flores, New York, June 19, 1937, 84r–86r.

Moreover, under John F. Kennedy's Alliance for Progress, Sofía del Valle was elected treasurer of the Mexican committee. At the time of her
death in 1982, Sofía was recognized as an important model and precursor of the contemporary women's movements in Mexico, including the Union Fomentadora de Cultura de la Mujer (Union Promoting
Women's Culture) and the Instituto Nacional de las Mujeres (National
Institute of Women).[84]

CONCLUSION

The interaction between religion and globalization provide some useful tools for understanding the various landscapes of Sofía del Valle's
life. According to one recent definition of *globalization*, it is a process
that "refers to the expansion and intensification of social relations
and consciousness across world-time and world-space."[85] As scholars
have noted, "defined thus, globalization is not a new phenomenon, for
there have been many examples of wide-ranging translocal dynamics
throughout history."[86] New technology and a new concern for international issues after the First World War assisted in accelerating the
time-space compression of the Catholic world in the interwar years.
Vatican Radio was established with the help of Guglielmo Marconi
himself, and Pius XI made his first broadcast in 1931. Transatlantic
travel and communication reached new levels of sophistication, which
the Catholic Church took advantage of in religious tourism to the great
religious sights of Europe and the Holy Land. In 1934 Cardinal Eugenio Pacelli, later Pope Pius XII (1939–1958), was able to travel in a
matter of days to Argentina for the International Eucharistic Congress.
As Daniel Gorman argues, the 1920s saw the rise of international civil
society, embodied in new supranational governmental bodies, such as
the League of Nations, as well as in the strengthening of what Akire
Iriye has called "cultural Internationalism": nongovernmental socialist, economic, and progressive networks, which sought to link national
projects of suffrage, social legislation, and solidarity to an interna-
tionalist ethic.[87] Similar networks also expanded in the arenas of civil

84. Olimón Nolasco, *Sofía del Valle*, 138.
85. Manfred B. Steger, *Globalization: A Brief Insight* (New York: Sterling, 2010).
86. Vásquez and Marquardt, *Globalizing the Sacred*, 35.
87. Daniel Gorman, *The Emergence of International Society in the 1920s* (Cambridge: Cam-

rights, transatlantic literary movements, and the first wave of the international women's movements (ca. 1888–1945). The life of Sofía del Valle, while certainly exceptional in many respects, provides a glimpse into an expanding Catholic international society emerging in the interwar years, where Catholics, especially women, operated in new transnational spaces but that also came to bring definition to more conventional ones: those of the family and the nation.[88]

---

bridge University Press, 2012); Akira Iriye, *Cultural Internationalism and World Order* (Baltimore: Johns Hopkins University Press, 1997); Rupp, *Worlds of Women*; Daniel T. Rodgers, *Atlantic Crossings: Social Politics in a Progressive Age* (Cambridge, Mass.: Harvard University Press, 1998).

88. For the role of Catholic women in building networks of charity and social assistance in Mexico in the nineteenth century, see Silvia Marina Arrom, "Las Señoras de la Caridad: Pioneras olvidadas de la asistencia social en México, 1863–1910," *Historia Mexicana* 57, no. 2 (October–December 2007): 445–90. On the development of female Eucharistic piety and political activism, see Chowning, "The Catholic Church and the Ladies of the Vela Perpetua," 197–237.

PART III ❖ FIGHTING FOR THE SOUL OF THE UNIVERSITY

CHAPTER 7

A "Third Way" in Christ

The Project of the Corporation of Mexican
Students (CEM) in Cold War Mexico

❖ Jaime M. Pensado

The 1950s saw the rise of a new generation of leftist, conservative, and
Catholic students in Latin America that began calling for a unique
form of hemispheric solidarity. Their efforts reflected concerns about
momentous contemporary events that had a profound impact at their
universities, like the anticolonial war in Algeria, the rise of military
dictatorships in Guatemala, and the "iron fist" following the Hungarian insurrection. But these students also harkened back to the "arielis-
ta" language that characterized the first two decades of the twentieth
century.[1] Asserting their ideological positions during the incipient cold
war, they participated throughout the 1950s in multiple international
conferences to further their cause.

One of the most contentious of these student conferences took
place at the seventh meeting of the International Student Conference
in Ibadan, Nigeria, in September of 1957, where various views were
hotly debated. A group of European students, claiming to represent
the position of the International Union of Socialist Youth, gathered
to support a critical view towards the National Liberation Front–led

Research for this project was made possible by the generous support from the Institute for
Scholarship in the Liberal Arts (ISLA) and the Kellogg Institute for International Studies at the
University of Notre Dame.

1. The antipositivist novel *Ariel*, by José Enrique Rodó, had a profound impact across Latin
American universities during the first three decades of the twentieth century. Published in
Uruguay in 1900, it celebrated youth as a "heroic idea." Concerned with the expansion of the
U.S. presence in Latin America, Rodó specifically called upon university students to assume
more active roles as "missionaries" in defense of the "Hispanic Continent."

movement seeking Algeria's independence from France. A more militant group arriving from various Latin American countries protested
against the violent repression of Cuban and Nicaraguan students by
the authoritarian Batista and Somoza governments. They asked their
African and Asian counterparts to join them in defeating the economic and political forces of colonialism and argued against the region's
economic subordination at the hands of antidemocratic, imperialist
nations. A third group from Sudan, as well as the rising Pan-African
movement that had generated great enthusiasm at the conference,
rebuffed Latin American efforts at international solidarity, rejecting
them as romantic expressions of adventurism. They called all students
instead to engage in a Marxist revolution in their respective countries
of origin in support of the growing bloc behind the Iron Curtain. Sit-
ting uneasily among these various groups was a chapter of Mexico's
National Confederation of Students, the Corporation of Mexican Students (Corporación de Estudiantes Mexicanos, or CEM), which represented the Catholic position. They took advantage of this opportunity
to launch their "Third Way," a dual critique of what they called the
"equally detrimental" systems of capitalism and communism. Since its
creation a decade earlier, the CEM had insisted that only a third position, rooted in the social teachings of the Catholic Church, would radi-
cally improve the lives of those residing in what eventually would be
termed the "Developing World."[2]

In this chapter, I examine the alternative position endorsed by the
CEM in cold war Mexico prior to the 1960s. While much of the literature on Catholicism in Mexico focuses on the church–state conflict of
the 1910–1940s period (including the four previous chapters in this
volume), Catholic activisms in the decades after 1950 have been far
less studied. Yet they were also important: the 1950s, writes historian
Soledad Loaeza, "marked the apogee of Mexican Catholicism." As the

2. *Nigeria '57: The Story of the Seventh International Student Conference* (An Information
Bulletin Special Supplement, 1957); *Luchas estudiantiles en América del Sur* (Informe de la Del-
egación de la Conferencia de Estudiantes, 1957); *Hispano-Americano* 34, no. 863 (1958): 25; "La
UIE, brazo del comunismo internacional para el control de los estudiantes," in *Reforma Universitaria: Periódico de la Confederación Nacional de Estudiantes*, September 15, 1958; "Los estudiantes detras de la cortina de hierro escogen la libertad," *Reforma Universitaria*, September 30,
1958; "Los estudiantes cubanos obtienen la victoria contra el dictador Batista," *Reforma Universitaria*, January 15, 1959; "Crónica estudiantil: Panorama universitario latinoamericano," *Corporación*, no. 48 (December 1959); and Samuel Blixen, *Sendic* (Montevideo: Ediciones Trilce,
2005), 43.

cold war intensified during these years and Mexico solidified its collaboration with the United States, the Catholic Church strengthened
its relationship with the Institutionalized Revolutionary Party (Partido
Revolucionario Institucional, or PRI). In this context and, with the
support of new lay organizations, the church was able to substantially
restore the social and political influence it had known before the Mexican Revolution. Moreover, the Vatican's anticommunist propaganda
fueled a new wave of Catholic militancy in Mexico, which coincided
with the PRI's own repression of communists. An enhanced moral authority translated into conservative representatives of the middle class
being transformed into key political players. Besides taking moralizing
campaigns in defense of Mexico's traditional values and "appropriate
forms" of consumption into the public, for example, women played a
crucial role in convincing other women to exercise their civic rights at
the local and national polls.[3]

The resurgence of both the Catholic Church and the conservative
right that came to characterize the political sphere in the 1950s extended to Mexico's most important university—the National Autonomous
University of Mexico (Universidad Nacional Autónoma de México, or
UNAM). Following passage of the university's Organic Law in 1945,
student representatives lost a space in which to discuss academic policies and participate in the appointment of professors and directors. As
a direct result, they were forced to aggressively compete with a new
generation of leaders for the control of the UNAM's most important
student organizations, the University Student Federation (Federación
de Estudiantes Universitarios, or FEU) and the National Confederation
of Students (Confederación Nacional de Estudiantes, or CNE).[4] Eventually Catholic students—who had been at the forefront of student activism in the past—lost the leadership of these organizations, initially

3. Soledad Loaeza, "Mexico in the Fifties: Women and Church in Holy Alliance," *Women's Studies Quarterly* 33, no. 3/4 (2005): 144. See also Emilio Coral García, "The Mexico City Middle Class, 1940–1970: Between Tradition, the State and the United States," PhD diss., Georgetown University, 2011); Julio Moreno, *Yankee Don't Go Home! Mexican Nationalism, American Business Culture, and the Shaping of Modern Mexico, 1920–1950* (Chapel Hill: University of North Carolina Press, 2003), 220–28; and Anne Rubenstein, *Bad Language, Naked Ladies, and Other Threats to the Nation: A Political History of Comic Books in Mexico* (Durham, N.C.: Duke University Press, 1998), 75–103.

4. The FEU and the CNE were founded in the 1920s. Student leaders belonging to these organizations served as brokers between the university community and the emerging corporat-ist state.

to the centrist students and intermediaries sponsored by the government in the 1950s, and later to the new independent leaders associated with the moderate and radical elements of the New Left in the 1960s.[5]

In the new environment of cooptation, provocation, boss politics, and state-sponsored violence that emerged with the institutionalization of the revolution during the postwar period, the defense of Mexico's youth became a central battle cry of the Catholic Church and a priority for the CEM. Religious authorities and representative leaders of this student organization grew increasingly concerned with the gradual loss of economic power, academic freedom, and political autonomy that followed the Organic Law of 1945. In the emerging environment of the cold war, moreover, the leadership of the CEM cautioned against several evils. It warned that, in the absence of moral support and direction, combined with the "rampant consumerism" of their time, Mexican youth could be led astray by "foreign ideologies." Initially, these were represented by Protestantism, Freemasonry, and by what leading voices of the CEM saw as the "new faces" of liberalism, including secularization, materialist positivism, and existentialism. Nevertheless, following the massive labor and student uprisings that exploded in various parts of the nation during the mid-to-late 1950s, the CEM simultaneously grew increasingly apprehensive towards ultraconservative politics, *rebeldismo sin causa* (rebellion without a cause), and especially communism.[6] In their condemnation of the left, however, unlike what is frequently assumed in the literature, *cemistas* (CEM members) did not create a unified "reactionary" movement that unilaterally opposed all of the different aspects of the Mexican Revolution.[7] Rather,

---

5. See, among others, Gabriela Contreras Pérez, *Los grupos católicos en la Universidad Autónoma de México (1933–1944)* (Mexico City: National Autonomous University of Mexico, 2001); Raúl Domínguez, "El perfil político de las organizaciones estudiantiles durante la década de 1950," in *Los estudiantes: Trabajos de historia y sociología*, ed. Renate Marsiske (Mexico City: National Autonomous University of Mexico, 1998): 261–90; and Jaime M. Pensado, *Rebel Mexico: Student Unrest and Authoritarian Political Culture during the Long Sixties* (Palo Alto, Calif.: Stanford University Press, 2013).

6. For two recent and contrasting case studies emphasizing the impact of the labor uprising on the Catholic Church, see Laura Pérez Rosales, "La revista Señal, la cuestion social y el enemigo comunista en México a mediados del siglo XX," *La Cuestion Social: Documentos, ensayos, comentarios y reseñas de libros acerca de lo social* 20, no. 4 (2012): 378–97; and Jaime M. Pensado, "El Movimiento Estudiantil Profesional (MEP): una mirada a la radicalización de la juventud católica mexicana durante la Guerra Fría," *Mexican Studies/Estudios Mexicanos* 31, no. 1 (Winter 2015): 156–92.

7. "Cemistas" is used throughout the chapter in reference to both male and female members

like their predecessors of the 1930s, the *unecos* (members of the National Union of Catholic Students, or UNEC), they shared many of the same concerns that were articulated by the left. In seeking an alternative position to both capitalism and communism, its representative voices contended not only that the revolution was "dead" by the 1950s, as a group of renowned leftist intellectuals had famously proclaimed, but also that its institutions had been transformed into instruments of control and cooptation for the benefit of a few powerful *caciques* (strongmen) and government-sponsored *pistoleros* (thugs).[8]

But instead of looking back for answers to the most progressive elements of the Constitution of 1917, as the emerging new voices of Mexico's moderate New Left did, cemistas found inspiration for their movement in the famous papal encyclicals of an earlier era, as well as in key documents written on higher education and university reform in Latin America by iconic figures who had defended the pedagogical principles of the Catholic tradition.[9]

CATHOLIC STUDENT ACTIVISM IN LATIN AMERICA
AND THE EXPANSION OF THE CEM

The CEM was founded in 1947 with the support of the Mexican Episcopate and the guidance of the Jesuit priest David Mayagoitia.[10] Two

---

of the CEM. The reader should keep in mind, however, that the overwhelming majority of young people who participated in this Catholic organization were male students.

8. In the rich history of student activism in Mexico, it is frequently (and misguidedly) assumed that all Catholic organizations blindly opposed the ideals of the revolution. The CEM, as will be argued in this chapter, rather took issue with those individuals who benefitted, economically and politically, from the corruption of the revolution. In this sense, cemistas indirectly agreed with influential voices of the left, such as Cosío Villegas, Octavio Paz, Carlos Fuentes, Oscar Lewis, and Pablo González Casanova (among others).

9. On the moderate politics of Mexico's incipient New Left, see Pensado, *Rebel Mexico*, 147–80.

10. In 1934 David Mayagoitia earned his doctoral degree in theology from St. Mary's College in Kansas. Three years later, he was ordained as a Jesuit priest. He returned to his native Mexico in 1943 and taught at El Colegio Patria, a small private college in the nation's capital. A year later, he became a full-time professor of philosophy at UNAM, where he collaborated in the creation of the influential Centro Cultural Universitario—the same institution that served as the foundation for the Universidad Iberoamericana (UI) in 1953. See José Rubén Sanabria and Mauricio Beuchot, *Historia de la filosofía cristiana en México* (Mexico City: Universidad Iberoamericana, 1994), 214–16; and Unión Femenina de Estudiantes Católicas (UFEC), *David Mayagoitia, S.J.: Apóstol intelectual* (Mexico City: UFEC, 2001). On the foundation of the CEM, see "Vida de la Corporación de Estudiantes Mexicanos," *Corporación*, no. 1 (March 1950); José

years later, hoping to bring international attention to its efforts, it played a leading role in hosting the first Pax Romana conference in Latin America.[11] As historian Ana María Bidegain has argued, two parallel currents shaped Catholic student activism across the Spanish-speaking hemisphere following World War II. One, along the lines of Pax Romana, was more politically conservative. More "oriented toward a former Catholic elite," it rapidly established representative federations in nearly all Latin American countries, and following the Second Vatican Council, it would play an important role in articulating the teachings of liberation theology. The other, led by the International Catholic Student Youth (Juventud Estudiantil Católica Internacional, or JECI), was more open politically to progressive forms of nationalism and populism. It particularly reached out for an open dialogue with those promoting Aprismo in Peru, Peronismo in Argentina, and Christian Democracy in Chile and Venezuela. The two currents were critical of imperialism and—influenced by Jacques Maritain, Emmanuel Mounier, and Luis-Joseph Lebret, among other prominent Catholic social thinkers of the era—they called for the creation of an "international bridge of solidarity."[12] This line of solidarity would help overcome the most pressing problems shared by all Latin American countries at the time, namely, widespread poverty, massive illiteracy, corruption, the lack of strong democratic structures, the violation of the autonomy of their universities, and U.S. expansion in the Americas.[13]

In this global context, cemistas acknowledged that an increasing population of Marxist students had also become genuinely concerned with the same issues. Nevertheless, in agreement with the early representatives of Pax Romana, they too dismissed the possibility of engaging in a productive dialogue with them. Cemistas criticized the nascent and isolated voices of the church that had begun calling for a

Audifred, "Estructuración, organización y formación de la Corporación de Estudiantes Mexicanos," *Corporación*, no. 39 (December 1957); David Mayagoitia, "Notas sobre la fundación de la Corporación de Estudiantes Mexicanos," *Corporación*, no. 46 (July 1958); and Archivo Histórico del Arzobispado de México (AHAM), Vol. 74, Exp. 32, Octavio Márquez, Archbishop of Puebla, "Comisión Episcopal para el Apostolado de los Seclares," October 5, 1961.

11. *III Asamblea Interamericana del MIEC de Pax Romana. Abril de 1949. Memoria* (Mexico City: Ediciones de la ACM, 1949).

12. Bidegain, "From Catholic Action to Liberation Theology."

13. Ibid.; "Problemas de América Latina," in *Reforma Universitaria*, November 15, 1958; and Carlos Horacio Urán and Ana María Bidegain de Urán, *El movimiento estudiantil latinoamericano, entre la reforma y la revolución, bosquejo histórico-político* (Montevideo: Comunidad del Sur, 1970).

pragmatic relationship with the left. Instead, cemistas argued that only a more "intimate contact" with the working class and the *campesinos* (peasants), in general, and a more direct involvement in politics, in particular, would allow its members to grasp a better understanding of the common roots that had led to the underdevelopment of the Latin American hemisphere.[14]

In agreement with growing and increasingly progressive voices of both Pax Romana and the JECI, moreover, the CEM called for the creation of a "new church"—one that maintained its rigid hierarchical structure, but simultaneously possessed a more open view toward the modern world. Making specific references to the papal encyclicals *Immortale Dei* (1885) and *Rerum novarum* (1891), in general, and the teachings of David Mayagoitia, in particular, they asked their members to reach out to devoted Catholic teachers and, with their support, exercise their civic rights by engaging more aggressively in student elections.[15] Collectively, cemistas hoped to create new corporatist organizations at their schools capable of regaining control of the student body and advocating a better understanding of the needs of those in subordinate economic and political positions.[16] The leadership of the CEM lamented that Mexico's Catholic youth lacked a basic understanding of the social and spiritual teachings of Christ. These youth had fallen through the cracks of a secular educational system that had disastrously supported a liberal concept of progress. The term *progress* became an institutionalized catchphrase that had been monopolized by the state, they lamented, one that only offered vague and empty solutions to the social and economic problems of the nation.[17] Furthermore, CEM leaders (and their supporters) contended that the *priísta* government

14. See, among others, "Vida de la CEM," *Corporación*, (March 1950); "La piramide invertida o que es el comunismo," *Corporación*, (March–April 1951); and Archivo Histórico de la Acción Católica, Biblioteca "Francisco Xavier Clavigero" de la Universidad Iberoamericana (AHAC), Vol. 10.62, David Mayagoitia, "Informe sobre las actividades de la CEM durante el presente año de 1959," October 14, 1959.

15. Of particular importance was David Mayagoitia's *Ideario* (1951). Eventually, cemistas were also influenced by Jaime Castiello and Julio J. Vértiz, who, respectively, wrote, among other influential books, *Una psicología humanista de la educación* (Mexico City: Jus, 1947) and *Su mensaje a la juventud* (Mexico City: CEM, 1959).

16. Isaac Guzmán, "El estudiante universitario y los problemas sociales," *Corporación* (July 1950); Grupo de la Facultad de Derecho de la UNAM, "Crisis de la revolución," *Corporación* (July 1950); "El deber cívico," *Corporación* (December 1951); and Jorge Demetriades, "El corporativista y su misión de jefe," *Corporación* (March 1958).

17. Ibid.; and "Participación estudiantil en el gobierno universitario," *Corporación* (May 1950).

had corrupted the same principles of the revolution that it claimed to defend while, at the same time, it had deliberately erased the historical role Catholics had played at the vanguard of social justice, democracy, and liberty.[18]

By highlighting the crucial role young Catholic students had played since the beginning of the twentieth century in supporting university autonomy, welfare for the needy, and international solidarity, historical citation became a frequent tool for the CEM. It often referred to a wide range of popular meetings organized by religious students in the past for inspiration. For example, the CEM celebrated the "heroic" role young Catholic leaders, such as Alejandro Gómez Arias and Baltasar Dromundo, had played during the 1929 student movement. Cemistas frequently noted in their writings that these students, besides achieving freedom for the academy and gaining representational power at their schools, had also mobilized an important voice that successfully exposed the "tyrannical" government of Plutarco Calles.[19] In a similar fashion, they made repeated celebratory references to the Ibero-American Congress of Catholic Students, organized by the UNEC in 1931. Cemistas stressed that the Congress had given birth to one of Latin America's most successful Catholic organizations in promoting social action and global solidarity, the Ibero-American Confederation of Catholic Students (Confederación Iberoamericana de Estudiantes Católicos, or CIDEC) in Peru. The CEM suggested cemistas should aim at achieving the same goals.[20]

While more progressive Catholic organizations such as the Professional Student Movement (Movimiento Estudiantil Profesional, or MEP) increasingly questioned the conservative politics of the Mexican church, the CEM by contrast portrayed the student uprisings of the 1950s at the National Polytechnic Institute (Instituto Politécnico Nacional, or IPN),

18. See, for example, Luis Calderón Vega, "Reflexiones universitarias," *Corporación* (March-April 1951); and "En torno a la autonomía de la UNA," *Corporación* (May 1954).

19. Ibid. See also Luis Calderón Vega's "Gente de Casa" columns, in *Reforma Universitaria*, September 15 and 30, 1958. On the student movement, see Renate Marsiske, *El movimiento estudiantil de 1929 y la autonomía de la Universidad Nacional de México* (Mexico City: National Autonomous University of Mexico, 1981); and Manuel Gómez Morín, *La lucha por la libertad de cátedra* (Mexico City: National Autonomous University of Mexico, 1996).

20. Luis Calderón Vega, "Cuba 88," *Corporación*, no. 37 (October 1957); "Editorial, Diez años de servicio," *Corporación*, no. 39 (December 1957); and AHAM, Vol. 188, Exp. 51, David Mayagoitia to Miguel Miranda y Gómez, "Situación actual de las universidades oficiales mexicanas," June 10, 1964.

the universities of Michoacán and Guadalajara, and the normal schools, as "chaotic acts of sabotage."[21] Occupied school buildings, street barricades, Molotov cocktails, and an unprecedented language of "hate" disguised with "Marxist catch phrases," had only brought "terror" to Mexico, some cemistas insisted.[22] Others, stressing their growing concern over a new generation of *revoltosos* (troublemakers) who "lacked Catholic values" more explicitly contended that "the chaos at our schools will only disappear when we reestablish our moral values … and eliminate, once and for all, the *internal* and *external* forces that had manipulated university students and had stimulated them to engage in violent uprisings and anarchy."[23]

By "internal forces" the CEM was pointing to the politics of *caciquismo* (boss rule) and "paternalism." In agreement with the emerging independent voices of the left, cemistas accused *charros* (government-sponsored intermediaries), pseudo-student leaders, and "thugs-for-hire" of taking advantage of the Organic Law of 1945 to infiltrate the university's most important student organizations.[24] They concluded that only a new reform movement that openly embraced the social and humanistic teachings of the church would put an end to the "politicking" that had proliferated inside UNAM. In particular, the CEM called its members to exercise their voting rights, progressively take over the presidencies of the different student organizations, and, ultimately, replace government-sponsored leaders and intermediaries with young honest men committed to strengthening the autonomy of their schools and embodying the "justice, love and hope" of Christ.[25]

21. While the CEM remained loyal to the hierarchical structure of the church throughout the 1950s and 1960s, other organizations such as the Movimiento Estudiantil Profesional (MEP) grew increasingly critical of it—to the extent that in the 1960s, mepistas (MEP members) began to create independent chapters that, over the years, gave rise to the founding leaders of Mexico's most influential urban guerrilla uprising, the Liga Comunista 23 de Septiembre. See Pensado, "El Movimiento Estudiantil Profesional (MEP)."

22. CEM, "Diez años de servicio," *Corporación* (March 1958); and "Avance comunista en las filas estudiantiles," *Corporación* (May 1959). See similar sentiments expressed by the National Confederation of Students (CNE) in "El movimiento estudiantil en el DF contra el alza de tarifas de los autobuses de servicio urbano" and Horacio Guajardo, "Este Orden," *Reforma Universitaria*, August 31, 1958; and "Nuevos choques estudiantiles en la Ciudad de Guadalajara," *Reforma Universitaria*, November 15, 1958.

23. Editorial: Anarquía universitaria," *Corporación* (July–August 1960); emphasis added.

24. Ibid.; "Faltan más maestros que los estudiantes," *Reforma Universitaria*, September 30, 1958; and Ignacio de la Concha, "En torno a los problemas de la Universidad," *Reforma Universitaria*, September 30, 1958.

25. Ibid. See also José Audiffred, "La Conferencia Nacional de Estudiantes," *Corporación*

By "external forces" threatening Mexico's Catholic identity, the cemistas were referring to the wider influences of positivism, existentialism, Marxism, and ultraconservative politics. A long history of Positivism and liberalism, they contended, had created an unparalleled culture
of "selfishness" in Mexico. Liberalism, introduced during the nineteenth
century and reappropriated by the revolutionary state during the last
four decades, had allegedly given birth to a generation of young Mexicans who cared more about individual notions of prosperity, political
ambition, and economic profit than the collective needs of the nation.[26]
They also argued that existentialist philosophy had made its way to Mexican schools via the "idealist" theories of Immanuel Kant, and through
the translated works of Heidegger and Sartre. These had further contributed to the unprecedented selfishness that, they insisted, "had sunk
our students into a sterile state of anguish." This "egoism" was manifested in several ways. It was demonstrated in the cult of personality that
many student leaders had acquired as representative leaders of the new
student organizations. Cemistas also noted the fascination that many
young people had expressed in their imitation of the "infamous" *rebeldes
sin causa* (rebels without a cause).[27]

Finally, the CEM simultaneously warned its members of the dangers of falling prey to the polarizing ideologies of the incipient cold
war. The new ultraconservative movements led inside the schools by
Jorge Siegrist from the Mexican Nationalist Party (Partido Nacionalista
Mexicano), among others, they lamented, had brought an unparalleled
level of violence to schools. What the school needed was a new generation of spiritual leaders who spoke against the violent elements of opportunistic intermediaries affiliated with the government, the militant
leaders of the radical left, and the reactionary figures of the conservative right. As conscious Catholics, they insisted, it was their obligation not only to reject the "false expressions of humanism" but also to

(December 1951); and "La acción cívica estudiantil: Ponencia presentada por la CEM en el XX
Congreso de la CNE," *Corporación* (May 1953).

26. "Editorial: Una conciencia universitaria vigorosamente católica," *Corporación* (Sep-
tember-October 1950); and Mayagoitia, "Informe sobre las actividades de la CEM durante el
presente año de 1959."

27. AHAC, Vol. 10.62, David Mayagoitia to Miguel Miranda y Gómez, "Situación actual
de las universidades"; and David Mayagoitia, "Memorándum sobre un sondeo respecto del at-
eísmo en el medio universitario (maestros y alumnos), profesional, y de investigación," August
1967. See also Antonio Díaz Soto y Gama, "Navidad y los rebeldes sin causa," *Reforma Universitaria*, December 15, 1958.

counterbalance the rising cult of materialism with a humanistic and spiritual understanding of Christ.[28]

To achieve their long-term goals in defense of Mexico's Catholic values, cemistas sent their messages across the nation and proposed a series of logistical plans. Under the leadership of its first five presidents, the CEM witnessed a significant growth of its base.[29] It rose from a handful of young students representing small and isolated chapters in Tampico, Orizaba, and Mexico City, in 1947, to a broader national base composed of hundreds of young men. These represented more than thirty-seven chapters expanding across Mexico, in the late 1950s. From Tijuana to Campeche, the CEM called its members to embrace a new university consciousness based on the social teachings of Christ and the values of the Catholic Church, namely, sacrifice, morality, integrity, and commitment to the poor. "One cannot fight for Christ," they argued, "unless one truly understands and remains loyal to His message." As represented in the CEM's new logo, "For Christ, the University" and further detailed in their 1951 *Ideario* (*Principles*), their goal was to bring this message to the classrooms and, in so doing, transform the university from a political institution serving the needs of a few opportunistic leaders into a true representative body of the people.[30]

With these goals in mind, cemistas inaugurated new cultural, educational, and political events, including athletic, oratory and literary competitions, workshops, and conferences. In these spaces and, in collaboration with their female *compañeras* (colleagues) from the Union of Female Catholic Students (Unión Femenina de Estudiantes Católicas, or UFEC), they promoted unity among Catholic students, hitherto divided in isolated organizations. In collaboration with the youth wings of Mexican Catholic Action (Acción Católica Mexicana), moreover, they organized religious conferences during weekends and led spiritual retreats during summer vacations. In their respective schools they promoted "appropriate" films endorsed by the Vatican, discussed

28. These sentiments were also shared by the CNE. See, for example, "La vida del estudiante de medicina en el DF," *Reforma Universitaria*, November 15, 1958; "Primera reunión regional de dirigentes estudiantiles de la zona norte del país, realizada por la CNE," *Reforma Universitaria*, December 15, 1958; "Dirigir, enseñar, profesar," *Reforma Universitaria*, January 15, 1959; and "Educación de la voluntad," *Reforma Universitaria*, March 31, 1959.

29. The first and most active presidents of the CEM included Gabriel de Alba 1947–1950, José Audifred 1950–1953, José Manuel Covarrubias 1953–1956, Jorge Bermeo 1956–1957, and Joaquin López Campuzano 1957–1960.

30. Vida de la Corporación de Estudiantes Mexicanos," *Corporación*, no. 1 (March 1950).

the various cinematic movements that had emerged at the time, and celebrated annual parades on the second week of December to the hill of Tepeyac (the site of the appearance of the Virgin of Guadalupe).[31]

As its membership grew, the organization's philosophy, approach, and tactics grew in sophistication. In workshops and educational retreats, CEM members developed a comprehensive teaching of the social commitments of the Catholic Church, learned about the idiosyncrasies of the Mexican political system, and discovered their role as young and socially committed activists. Here, they became acquainted with nonviolent methods and theoretical concepts utilized by student activists in other countries. They also learned to distinguish between "legitimate" political grievances and "misguided" and/or "empty" promises that many leaders articulated during student elections. Cemistas asked their fellow members to create new student organizations composed of representative corporatist bodies (of teachers and students) and collectively infiltrate the Sociedades de Alumnos (Societies of Students) and the University Council (Consejo Universitario).[32] They pressured their schools to replace "mediocre teachers" with humanists who understood the "Western values of Christianity" and reminded their *compañeros* (colleagues) of their goal to socialize the university professions. Future doctors, lawyers, and engineers would need to care more about the collective needs of the nation and less about individual profit. After all, they argued in an elitist (even paternalistic) voice, "As [privileged] young students, we have inherited the most noble mission of leading our *pueblo* [people]."[33] In this effort, and hoping to compete with the new social programs created by the PRI's National Institute of Mexican Youth (Instituto Nacional de la Juventud Mexicana) cemistas also opened new medical clinics and Student Support Houses (Casas Estudiantiles de Asistencia) that offered scholarships and subsidized medical help, meals, and shelter to those students who needed them.[34]

31. "Peregrinación al Tepeyac," *Corporación* (August–October 1952); José Manuel Covarrubias, "Informe de la CEM en el medio universitario," *Corporación* (March 1958); and Javier Padilla de Alba, "Desarrollo nacional de la CEM," *Corporación* (March 1958).

32. "Editorial: Participación estudiantil en el gobierno universitario," *Corporación* (May 1950); Mayagoitia, "Notas sobre la fundación"; "Misión de la universidad frente al movimiento intelectual actual," *Corporación*, no. 48 (December 1959); and Diego H. Zavala, "Responsabilidad del profesional católico en la vida de los universitarios mexicanos," *Corporación* (March 1960).

33. "Realización de la vocación social del estudiante católico universitario," *Corporación* (January–February 1961).

34. Adrian García Cortes, "Vida del estudiante universitario: Casa, vestido, sentido," *Cor-*

As discussed earlier, like those in the organizations of the left, ce-mistas also brought greater attention to their movement by participating in multiple international conferences. Besides hosting the International Congress of Pax Romana in 1947 and sending a representative chapter to the Nigerian conference a decade later, they also played a leading role in organizing the First National Conference of Catholic Culture in 1953 in Guadalajara. Further, with the help of the UFEC, they sent leading representatives to the World Congress of Marian Congregations in New-ark, New Jersey, in 1959. At UNAM, they provided a forum for other Lat-in American Catholic students to travel to Mexico, offered scholarships to its members to organize trips abroad, and reached out to influential individuals for their financial and political support.[35] These included leading conservative intellectuals José Vasconcelos, Mariano Azuela, and Antonio Díaz Soto Y Gama,[36] as well as key figures affiliated with the National Action Party (Partido Acción Nacional, or PAN), including Luis Calderón Vega (leading founder of the party and father of future presi-dent of Mexico, Felipe Calderón Hinojosa), Horacio Guajardo (former president of the UNEC, frequent contributor to *Reforma Universitaria*, and a leading voice of Mexico's Christian Democratic movement), and Carlos Septién García (influential journalist and founder of the PAN's *La Nación*).

With growing support from leading national figures, the CEM pub-lished and distributed thousands of key documents that articulated the ideology of its members and played a crucial role at schools and fac-tories in exposing the "dangers" of importing "foreign" ideologies to Mexico. Of particular importance was the distribution of tens of thou-sands of reproductions of Pope Pius XII's *Definámonos! ¿Católicos o Comunistas?* (*Let's Define Ourselves! Are We Catholics or Communists?*,

poración (July 1950); CEM, "Instituto Nacional de la Juventud Mexicana," March 3, 1957; CEM, "Informe sobre actividades de la Corporación de Estudiantes Mexicanos durante el presente año de 1959; and "Realización de la vocación social del estudiante católico universitario," *Cor-poración* (January–February 1961).

35. Antonio Obregón Padilla, "IX asamblea nacional de la CEM," *Corporación* (March 1958); and Mayagoitia, "Informe sobre las actividades de la CEM durante el presente año de 1959."

36. Vasconcelos, Azuela, and Díaz Soto Y Gama were all key intellectuals of the Mexican Revolution who moved to the conservative opposition in the 1930s and 1940s. See, among others, Luis Barrón, "Conservadores liberales: Luis Cabrera y José Vasconcelos, reaccionarios y tránsfugas de la Revlución," in *Conservadurismo y derechas en la historia de México: Tomo II*, ed. Erika Pani (Mexico City: Fondo de Cultura Económica, 2009): 435–66; and Jeffrey Kent Lucas, *The Rightward Drift of Mexico's Former Revolutionaries: The Case of Antonio Dias Soto Y Gama* (Lewiston, N.Y.: Edwin Mellen Press, 2010).

1951), which further influenced the "Third Way" championed by the CEM in the 1950s; David Mayagoitia's *Ideario* (*Principles*, 1951), which laid out the goals of the CEM; and Mayagoitia's *El Deber Cívico* (*Our Civic Duties*, 1952), which called on cemistas to play a more direct role in student politics. With their help, moreover, they created new student newspapers, including *Jaiba*, *El Boletín de la Corporación*, *El Generalito*, and *Corporación*. Of these, *Corporación* represented the most important and widely read journal published for and by young Catholic students during the 1950s.[37] Its purpose, as stated in its inaugural editorial page, was to provide Mexican solutions "con sentido Cristiano" (based in Christianity) to the nation's most detrimental problems. The logo of *Corporación*—"By Students for Students"—further emphasized the commitment of the CEM and its journal to defend the autonomy of the university, strengthen the corporatist relationship between students and teachers, and expose the university community to Christ.

Corporación, as envisioned by its principal leader David Mayagoitia, provided students with easy access to the main tenets and national political alternatives suggested by "the Third Way."[38] Students could buy the journal at their schools every other month for the mere sum of seventy-five cents. In this publication readers were reintroduced to the Cristero Rebellion and became familiar with the oppositional voices of Mexico's Catholic right, as evident in the writings of José Vasconcelos, Luis Calderón Vega, Manuel Gómez Morín, and Carlos Septién García. They learned about what the creators of its pages saw as the effects associated with decades of secularization of the nation's schools. This included the rise of a materialist culture, the lack of common interest across different sectors of society in solving social problems, and a lack of civic responsibility among students. Readers were provided with empirical findings highlighting the increasing alienation of the world's youth—as emphasized in the new phenomenon of "rebeldismo sin causa." They were warned of the dangers of flirting with communism

37. *Señal* and *Juventud* were also important Catholic magazines widely read by students throughout the 1950s.

38. As previously noted, in 1947 David Mayagoitia successfully received the support from the Episcopate to create the CEM, the Unión Femenina de Estudiantes Católicas (UFEC), and the Unión Nacional de Profesionistas (UNP—where young cemistas continued their movement after graduation). Three years later, he reached out to the influential journalist Carlos Septién García, and in collaboration with Horacio Guajardo, the young panista and ardent promoter of the Christian Democratic movement in Mexico, they launched the first issue of *Corporación* in March 1950.

and were asked to reject the ultraconservative reactions endorsed by a few opportunistic leaders. Using language reminiscent of their leftist counterparts, readers were asked to reject the "paternalistic" behavior of "cacique-like" leaders representing the interests of those in power.[39] In this sense, the CEM used *Corporación* to create a critical space and forum of discussion for those opposing the "oligarchical" and "corrupt" structure of the PRI. "After fifty years of its revolution," a 1959 article noted, echoing the pages of the PAN's *La Nación*, "Mexico has forty percent illiteracy while millions of malnourished rural people continue to live in extreme poverty."[40] The CEM insisted that, although the radicalism of the Cuban Revolution seemed to offer an attractive alternative, such a route would only bring further anarchy to Mexico.[41]

Corporación also played an important role in introducing its readers to a broad range of global issues and events. It demonstrated great interest in informing its readership about developing a better relationship with Pax Romana. Consistent with its expressed view of the Cuban Revolution as extremist, the pages of the journal also commented on the Hungarian insurrection of 1956, the Festival of the Communist Youth in Prague and Budapest, the reformist movements in Latin America, the anticolonial movements in Africa, and the racial problems in the United States. As a vehicle for propagandizing an alternative view, the journal functioned not only to keep its readers informed but also to convey the message that extremism was creating an increasingly polarized world, one that desperately needed humane, and particularly Christian, solutions to world crises.[42]

In sum, for cemistas, to be a young Catholic student in the 1950s meant to embody the principles of Christ. For many, this strictly translated into a more conscious commitment on their part to help ameliorate the lives of the poor and guide the politically disenfranchised. For others, what mattered most was defending Mexico's presumed Catholic identity from what they saw as the multiple foreign ideologies that had sprung from liberalism and Marxism since the nineteenth century. Yet for others their love for God was simultaneously evident in

39. See, among others, "El deber cívico," *Corporación* (December 1951).
40. "Crisis de la Revolución," *Corporación* (February 1959).
41. "La tragedia de Cuba," *Corporación* (November–December 1961).
42. See, for example, "La acción cívica estudiantil," *Corporación* (May 1952); "Panorama universitario latinoamericano," *Corporación* (December 1959); and "El estudiante iberoamericano frente al comunismo," *Corporación* (March–April 1962).

their articulation of a louder voice of political opposition. In the growing context of the cold war this materialized into a poignant critique of
the corruption of the PRI, but not necessarily of the corporatist politics
of the government or its "revolutionary" projects for the poor. After
all, many believed that welfare for the needy could only be achieved
from above in the form of charity, virtuous political commitment, and
a robust educational system. What Mexico needed urgently, they contended, was the empowerment of young Catholic leaders in key positions of power at the university, capable of balancing the extremisms of
socialism and capitalism, guaranteeing academic freedom, protecting
the autonomy of their universities, containing rampant consumerism,
and eliminating the evils of caciquismo. "We must unequivocally affirm," they noted as self-described apostles of the truth, morality, and
social justice, "[o]ur commitment is with Christ. As leaders [of the
CEM], it is He whom we must follow. It is He who has chosen and sent
us here."[43]

CONCLUSION

Among the numerous memoirs, plays, novels, essays, books, and academic articles written about student activism in Mexico over the last
forty years, few have avoided the tendency to reduce this rich history
to a single event—the 1968 movement. They have tended to minimize
the importance of earlier student revolts and to prioritize the perspectives of leftist male leaders. Of particular interest here is the caricature
of the right and the Catholic movement during the period as monolithic, isolated, and/or merely reactionary. In comparison to the French,
Italian, German, Canadian, and U.S. cases, historical studies illustrat-
ing the complexity of Catholic student activism in Mexico remain surprisingly few in number.[44] Among these, most have focused on actors
and events in decades other than the 1950s.

Some have shed light on the young Catholic actors immediately im-
pacted by the anticlerical movement sweeping across parts of Mexico

43. "Nuestro compromiso es con Cristo y a El tendremos que rendirle cuentas de nuestros
actos como jefes [de la CEM], pues El es quien nos designa y El es quien nos envía."
44. See, among other comparative examples, Mark Edward Ruff, *The Wayward Flock: Catholic Youth in Postwar West Germany* (Chapel Hill: University of North Carolina Press, 2005);
and Nancy Christie et al., eds., *The Sixties and Beyond: Dechristianization in North America and
Western Europe, 1945–2000* (Toronto: University of Toronto Press, 2013).

during the Cristero Rebellion or on students who grew increasingly militant during the 1960s. In terms of studies of student organizations, some historians have written excellent case studies on the importance of the UNEC and the Mexican Catholic Youth Association during the first four decades of the twentieth century.[45] Jumping to the turbulent 1960s, about which the majority of the literature has focused, studies have centered on the influence of a broad range of iconic events surrounding the rise of Catholic militancy, including the Cuban Revolution, the Second Vatican Council, Liberation theology, and the Medellín conference.[46] With the exception of a few recent articles, little has been written on the interim years that has breached these two important periods.[47] This era has been generally described by historians as the peak of the "golden years" of Mexico's political stability, economic prosperity, and national unity.[48]

45. Contreras Pérez, Los grupos católicos en la Universidad Autónoma de México (1933–1944); María Luisa Aspe Armella, La formación social y política de los católicos mexicanos; David Espinosa, "Student Politics, National Politics: Mexico's National Student Union, 1926–1943," The Americas, 62, no. 4 (April 2006), 533–62; and Bernardo Barranco V., "La Iberoamericanidad de la Unión Nacional de Estudiantes Católicos (UNEC) en los años treinta," in Cultura e identidad nacional, ed. Roberto Blamcarte (Mexico City: Fondo de Cultura Económica, 1994), 188–232.

46. See, among others, María Gracia Castillo Ramírez, "Jóvenes católicos de izquierda revolucionaria (1965–1975)," in Violencia y sociedad: Un hito en la historia de las izquierdas en América Latina, ed. Verónica Okión and Miguel Urrego (Morelia: IIH-UMSNH/El Colegio de Michoacán, 2010), 111–40; Alfonso Yáñez Delgado, La manipulación de la fe: Fúas contra Carolinos en la Universidad Poblana (Puebla, Mexico: Benemérita Universidad Autónoma de Puebla, 1996); Edgar González Ruiz, MURO, Memorias y Testimonios, 1961–2002 (Puebla, Mexico: Benemérita Universidad Autónoma de Puebla, 2004); Fernando Manuel González, "Algunos grupos radicales de izquierda y derecha con influencia católica en México, 1965–1975, Historía y Grafía, no. 29 (2007): 57–93; Mónica Naymich López Macedonio, "Historia de una colaboración anticomunista transnacional: Los Tecos de la Universidad Autónoma de Guadalajara y el gobierno de Chiang Kai-Shek a principios de los años setenta," Contemporánea: Historia y Problemas del Siglo XX 1, no. 1 (2010): 133–58; María Martha Pacheco, "Cristianismo sí, comunismo no: anticomunismo eclesiástico en México," in La Iglesia contra México, ed. Octavio Rodríguez Araujo (Mexico City: Orfila, 2010): 259–90; and Jaime M. Pensado, "'To Assault with the Truth': The Revitalization of Conservative Militancy in Mexico during the 1960s," The Americas 70, no. 3 (January 2014): 489–521.

47. Some recent exceptions include: Loaeza, "Mexico in the Fifties; Soledad Loaeza, "La Democracia Cristiana y la modernizacón de Acción Nacional, 1957–1965, Historía y Grafía, no. 14 (2000): 147–82; Valentina Torres Septién and Leonor Magaña, "Belleza reflejada: El ideal de la belleza femenina en el discurso de la Iglesia, 1920–1970," Historía y Grafía, no. 19 (2002): 55–87; Martha Santillán, "Discurso de redomesticación femenina durante los procesos modernizadores en México, 1946–1958," Historía y Grafía, no. 31 (2008): 103–32; and Pérez Rosales, "La revista Señal."

48. See, among many other examples, the collection of chapters in Gilbert M. Joseph, Anne Rubenstein, and Eric Zolov, eds., Fragments of a Golden Age: The Politics of Culture in Mexico since 1940 (Durham, N.C.: Duke University Press, 2001).

The history of the CEM and its multifaceted conservative movement inside the nation's most important universities questions this narrative. It provides us with a glimpse of a student population that saw the decade of the 1950s as a crucial moment in Mexico's history— "ripe," as some cemistas emphasized, for the creation of an alternative Catholic movement that equally opposed the extremism of both capitalism and socialism. The CEM was fundamentally a corporatist student organization whose solutions to Mexico's problems endorsed an elitist and hierarchical relationship with those who had been excluded from Mexico's economic "miracle." Under the stringent leadership of the influential Jesuit priest David Mayagoitia, cemistas formulated an innovative concept of political activism and promoted unity among Catholic students. In the name of Christ, they began to conceive of themselves as active agents of social justice and defenders of the church. Looking back for inspiration to those who participated in the autonomist movement of 1929, as well as to those who formed UNEC in the 1930s, they argued for a holistic, that is, "Catholic," understanding of the social, political, and economic problems that the overwhelming majority of Mexicans faced during this period. This mission required a more aggressive participation by cemistas in student politics, religious ceremonies, and social programs. In addition to bringing back the "autonomy" of the university, they would spark changes needed to renovate the teachings of the church, "depoliticize" their schools, "humanize" the professions, and ultimately transform Mexico into a more prosperous and independent nation.

The CEM provided an important nexus and forum at the UNAM for various Catholic student organizations. It successfully infiltrated dozens of Sociedades de Alumnos and became particularly influential among the leadership of the National Confederation of Students. These not only remained committed to defending the autonomy of the university but also, like the efforts of the left, spoke against and frequently exposed the corruption of those student organizations that received the support from the government. In the process, the CEM created a new generation of leaders who, after graduation, continued their "mission" as members of the National Union of Professional Alumni (Unión Nacional de Profesionistas), persuaded others to exercise their civic duties at the student polls, and encouraged new members to develop a more intimate relationship with the nation's poor. As *profesionistas* (professional alumni), older cemistas continued to participate in key national and international conferences and, with the support of David Mayagoitia, collectively and/or individually used their experience to further strengthen the University Cultural Center (Centro Cultural Universitario)—a crucial institution in Mexico's university history that played an important role in the creation of the Mexico's most important Catholic University, the Universidad Iberoamericana.[49] Eventually, many would flock to the far right and join the multiple battles that took place across the continent in "defense" of Christianity.[50]

By contrast, the most progressive elements of this generation would influence the shaping of a "Catholic anticapitalism" that would give rise to a Latin American New Left during the global sixties.[51] The CEM, as evident in its continuous publication of *Corporación*, would not be immune to such change. By 1964, when the journal had sold more than eighty thousand copies over sixty-four issues, cemista leadership, similar to that of Pax Romana, began endorsing a more progressive attitude towards politics. The social teachings of *Rerum novarum* remained relevant, but so were key papal encyclicals that would radicalize growing sectors of the church throughout the 1960s, including *Mater et magistra* (1961) and *Pacem in terris* (1963).[52] This transition, evident in nearly all Latin American countries by the mid-1960s, was strengthened following the 1968 student massacre. A moribund CEM core remained committed to its principles following the violent events that unfolded at the Plaza of Tlatelolco, but its members seemed to have demanded more progressive solutions.[53] This change in attitude became evident in the new name used to replace their magazine—*Rumbo*—that is, "direction" or "course." Such a "course" paralleled the direction that many young Catholic organizations embraced. The change affected not only the few isolated chapters that remained loyal to the CEM in the late

49. UFEC, *David Mayagoitia, S.J.*
50. Pensado, "'To Assault with the Truth.'"
51. On similar organizations in Central America, see Joaquín Chávez, "Catholic Action, the Second Vatican Council, and the Emergence of the New Left in El Salvador (1950–1975)," *The Americas* 70, no. 3 (January 2014): 459–87; and Deborah Levenson-Estrada, *Trade Unionist against Terror: Guatemala City, 1954–1985* (Chapel Hill, N.C.: University of North Carolina Press, 1994).
52. See, among others, "Teilhard de Chardin," *Corporación* (July–August 1965); and "La CEM a la luz del concilio," *Corporación* (January-February 1967).
53. AHAM, Vol. 187, Exp. 20, Equipo de reflexión, "Conflicto estudiantil y reflexión Cristiana," 1968.

1960s but also other institutions that David Mayagoitia helped to create, namely, the Universidad Iberoamericana and its journal, *Comunidad*. In the same year that David Mayagoitia passed away, 1969, *Rumbo* began to adopt a more lenient attitude towards the left and, in agreement with the pages of *Comunidad* as well as those of *Liberación* and *Contacto* (among others), became an important forum for analyzing social problems and promoting an open dialogue between Christians and non-Christians. Jacques Maritain, Emmanuel Mounier, and Louis Lebret remained important references in its pages, but so did Martin Luther King, Paulo Freire, Camilo Torres, Ernesto Cardenal, Gustavo Gutiérrez, Roger Garaudy, and Herbert Marcuse.[54]

The history of the CEM sheds light on a rich chapter of Catholic activism in Latin American universities prior to the Second Vatican Council. The 1950s, as understood by these two different organizations, represented a key moment not only for evangelization but also in defense of the autonomy of their respective schools, on one hand, and the opening of a more conscious commitment to social action, on the other. As "university apostles," Catholic students across the Americas expressed a broader concern with the social question and the world around them; and in the process, they grew increasingly politicized, discovered alternative visions to the social order, and questioned the growing contradictions of the cold war era.

54. See, among others, David Mayagoitia, "Hace veinticinco años," *Rumbo* (March–April 1968); Jorge Rendón Alarcón, "Martin Luther King," *Rumbo* (May–June 1968); and Francisco Riñon G., "Unas palabras para el diálogo marxista cristiano," *Rumbo* (March–April 1971).

CHAPTER 8

Catholic Campuses, Secularizing Struggles
Student Activism and Catholic Universities in Brazil, 1950–1968

❖ Colin M. Snider

When university students in Brazil's Catholic University Youth (Juventude Universitária Católica, or JUC) movement tried to define their mission in 1956, they proclaimed that, while social issues were important, the organization's focus would continue to be "evangelization," even while also addressing social inequalities. These efforts at evangelization alongside social reform among university youth in Brazil in the late 1950s and early 1960s preceded similar official changes in the Catholic Church with Vatican II (1962–1965) and the Bishops' Conference in Medellín in 1968. By the end of 1966, Catholic activism faced a very different context. The church abolished the JUC even while Catholic students mobilized on campuses throughout Brazil, and evangelization had all but disappeared from student activists' agenda. Even as the Brazilian church itself turned increasingly toward issues of social justice and human rights in the context of liberation theology and a military dictatorship in Brazil, "political action" became the primary focus of Catholic students throughout the country.[1]

Far from being planned or inevitable, these changes reveal the fluid and complex nature of activism among Catholic students in Brazil. As the country shifted from the democratic nationalism of the 1950s through increasing cold-war polarization in the early 1960s and into a right-wing military dictatorship after 1964, Catholic students' politics

---

1. Luiz Alberto Gomes de Souza, *A JUC, os estudantes católicos e a política* (Petrópolis: Editora Vozes, 1984), 105, 122.

also transformed, both shaping and shaped by the institutional and political contexts in which they occurred. As these political transformations transpired, the lines between religious and secular activism further blurred. Simultaneously, Brazil's university system, and especially Catholic universities, began to increase rapidly in number. As they did so, students from elite backgrounds acquired the means to network and spread their own social and spiritual activism. Between 1950 and 1970, Catholic student activism endured a turbulent period, moving from evangelization of the 1950s to a mixture of religious and secular issues in the 1960s, ultimately focusing on worldly issues over the spiritual after the military coup of April 1, 1964. As a result, the period from 1950 to 1970 saw a dual transformation in Catholic activism: the expansion of Brazilian Catholic universities provided new institutional mechanisms through which increasingly left-leaning student movements could further expand and radicalize. This transformation, combined with intensifying cold-war politics at the national and international levels and eventual establishment of a military dictatorship in 1964, led to a Catholic student activism that blurred religious and political activism, eventually favoring the latter over the former among student activists.

ORIGINS OF CATHOLIC STUDENT ACTIVISM IN BRAZIL

Although Catholic students would be among the most active in the 1960s and 1970s, activism among Catholic students had much more humble, subdued origins. The ability to mobilize on Catholic campuses prior to the mid-1950s was virtually nonexistent; there were only four Catholic universities in the early 1950s, and none had been around for more than fifteen years.[2] Instead, Catholic student activism in the 1950s operated most visibly via the JUC. A lay organization that initially submitted to the hierarchical authority of the clergy, the JUC had its roots in the Catholic Action movement in the 1930s, when Rio de Janeiro's Cardinal Sebastião Leme—discussed earlier in the essay by Dain Borges in this volume—began to reassert the church's presence in politics.[3] Within this vision, local chapters of the JUC formed in sev-

2. Instituto Brasileiro de Geografia e Estatística (IGBE), *Anuário estatístico do Brasil IGBE*, vol. 16, (1955): "Distribuição dos cursos, segundo o caráter dos estabelecimentos—1955." The four Catholic universities of Brazil prior to 1952 were in Rio de Janeiro (1940), São Paulo (1946), Rio Grande do Sul (1948), and Pernambuco (1951).

3. Kenneth P. Serbin, *Secret Dialogues: Church-State Relations, Torture, and Social Justice in*

eral Brazilian cities, focusing on providing Christian guidance and education to university students who represented the country's elite and growing, but small, middle classes.[4] Yet this activism was doubly limited: on one hand, there were roughly sixty thousand Brazilians enrolled in universities in a country of nearly sixty million people in 1954;[5] on the other hand, it reflected the church's definition of "faith as an inward process of having close personal contact with Jesus Christ in a devotional sense."[6]

Acknowledging the need for greater coordination between the varying chapters scattered throughout the country, the JUC unified and became a national organization in 1950. This restructuring allowed the organization to coordinate nationally, giving the JUC a greater presence in politics at both the national and local levels. Yet in the first years of the 1950s, the JUC continued to function primarily in the religious arena, emphasizing messages and religious gatherings that fit within "traditional Christianity."[7] Under the guidance of Romeu Dale, a Dominican friar who supervised the JUC from 1949 to 1961, the members of the JUC were primarily middle- and upper-class students who made up Brazil's university population at the time. In the first half of the 1950s, the organization focused almost singularly on proselytizing and educating students in the Catholic faith, regularly sponsoring masses, pilgrimages, and other religious events, such as a welcoming mass and reception for students to Rio de Janeiro's University of the Federal District or a collective Easter celebration for all of Rio's university students. Such events fit within the JUC's original religious role as a lay organization designed to strengthen the church's presence and authority among generally privileged university youth. The JUC's national leadership itself emphasized its successes as a religious organization, with its frequent masses and pilgrimages as "proof of the

---

Authoritarian Brazil (Pittsburgh, Penn.: University of Pittsburgh Press, 2000), 24; Souza, *A JUC, os estudantes católicos e a política,* 60.

4. Even in 1949, the total number of students enrolled in higher education throughout the entire country numbered only 38,003 in a country where illiteracy rates were still above 50 percent. IGBE, *Anuário estatístico do Brasil,* vol. 17 (1956): "Especificação Segundo Algumas Modalidades de Ensino."

5. IGBE, *Anuário estatística do Brasil,* vol. 17 (1956): "Educação," Table IV.A, "Principais Resultados, segundo as categorias do ensino—1940/54."

6. Mainwaring, *The Catholic Church and Politics in Brazil, 1916–1985,* 28.

7. See, for example, *Jornal do Brasil,* May 25, 1950, 8. See also Souza, *A JUC, os estudantes católicos e a política,* 100.

unity of the university class."[8] In this regard, the JUC's religious focus and its efforts to spread the Catholic faith among university students fit within part of the broader "pinnacle of neo-Christendom" that defined the church's strength in Brazil in the 1950s.[9]

However, within just a few years of forming at the national level, the JUC also began to consider more worldly social problems facing Brazil, even while using a Christian framework to understand society. In 1951 the JUC's leadership rejected a proposal that the organization include a focus on "the university in the social question." Just two years later, however, the JUC's national leadership made an about-face, placing the university's role in the broader social matrix within the JUC's broader national agenda.[10] The following year, the JUC sponsored conferences on "Reaction, Revolution, Social Reform" and on "the university student and the social question."[11] In this transition, more progressive, if not yet leftist, students were beginning to assert their presence in student politics. In 1950 conservative students had taken power of the National Student Union (União Nacional dos Estudantes, or UNE). Although the conservative students controlled UNE from 1950 to 1956, progressive students remained active, and in the JUC, they found an early outlet to reconsider and reposition their own views of religion and society. Such ideas of reform were not isolated from religious matters; rather, the JUC's leaders placed the secular issue of universities and society within a broader religious discourse that examined the role "of the University before God."[12] While not a radical rupture with its primarily religious focus, the JUC's activism began to consider more secular issues, including matters of class privilege and student participation in university governance, as part of a broader transformation of student politics in the 1950s.[13]

Throughout the remainder of the 1950s, secular issues existed alongside and were even secondary to religious issues for Catholic activists involved with the JUC. As the JUC's national platform put it in

8. *Jornal do Brasil*, May 24, 1958, 7.

9. Serbin, *Secret Dialogues*, 26.

10. Souza, *A JUC, os estudantes católicos e a política*, 113–14.

11. *Jornal do Brasil*, March 22, 1954, 8; Souza, *A A JUC, os estudantes católicos e a política*, 116.

12. Souza, *A JUC, os estudantes católicos e a política*, 113–14.

13. Ibid., 122. For more on student politics in Brazil in the 1950s, see Victoria Langland, *Speaking of Flowers: Student Movements and the Making and Remembering of 1968 in Military Brazil* (Durham, N.C.: Duke University Press, 2013), chapter 2.

1956, the organization's broader mission remained "the same mission of the Church: EVANGELIZATION."[14] At the same time, students on campuses also began to reevaluate the role of universities in society itself, reconsidering the elite nature of higher education in Brazil.[15] This coexistence of evangelization with the growing focus on secular issues revolving around Brazil's universities and society more generally marked the JUC's "first attempt to situate the University in the broader picture and to discover its roots in the past."[16] The JUC began to move beyond an inward focus that emphasized individual faith to consider broader social issues, even while it held on to the explicitly Christian focus that had characterized the JUC's discourse since the 1930s.

SHIFTING GOALS

Although Catholic activists in the JUC were beginning to express a broader concern with the world around them, their social concerns initially hinged on the institution most immediately present in university students' lives: the university itself. This emphasis on university education in the JUC and among those who attended its conferences was part of a gradual shift that reflected a broader transformation in Brazilian education and student politics. After years of focusing on national issues such as involvement in World War II, the end of Vargas's Estado Novo, and the struggle to nationalize oil,[17] by the late 1950s university students were focusing increasingly on the need to reform higher education. In 1956 José Batista de Oliveira Júnior won election as the president of UNE, marking a return of progressive students to UNE leadership after six years of conservative leadership. His victory was due in no small part to the broad support he received from the JUC's members, many of whom were also involved with UNE.[18] The JUC, the or-

14. Souza, *A JUC, os estudantes católicos e a política*, 123.

15. Even in 1961, only 107,318 students, less than 0.2 percent of the population, were enrolled in universities and colleges in Brazil. IGBE, *Anuário estatística do Brasil*, vol. 24 (1963): "Situação Cultural," Table II.B.2, "Matrículas e Conclusões de Curso."

16. Souza, *A JUC, os estudantes católicos e a política*, 132.

17. Maria Paula Araújo, *Memórias Estudantis: Da Fundação da UNE aos Nossos Dias* (Rio de Janeiro: Ediouro Publicações S.A., 2007), 47–51, 63–68; see also Shawn C. Smallman, *Fear and Memory in the Brazilian Army and Society, 1889–1954* (Chapel Hill: University of North Carolina Press, 2002), chapter 4.

18. Araújo, *Memórias Estudantis*, 78–81.

ganization that had become a home to left-leaning students in the early 1950s, had in turn helped the progressive student sector return to national leadership in UNE. With more progressive students now leading both the JUC and UNE in 1957, the student union sponsored the First National Seminar of Educational Reform in Rio de Janeiro, marking the first time that university reform had become an explicit objective in national student politics.[19] Paralleling this transition, by 1957 the issue of "university life" had also become a "permanent theme" in the JUC's planning and programs.[20] In 1959 the JUC institutionally committed itself to "political action as part of its evangelical commitment"[21] for the first time. Although the evangelical commitment remained, worldly issues had now inextricably become a part of that commitment, something that was completely absent at the beginning of the decade.

As this shift took place within Brazil's student population, Catholic philosophers such as Jacques Maritain and Emanuel Mounier increasingly gained credence among the JUC members, who adopted Maritain's and Mounier's ideas of a "Christian ideal," criticizing how materialist capitalism created real issues of social inequality and prompted the need for Christian socialist alternatives.[22] The embrace was due in no small part to Catholic university students' increasing blending of the political, social, and religious. It was no longer enough to focus on evangelization; as Vatican II would suggest in the early 1960s, it was time to turn Catholic principles to questions of social and economic inequalities at home. Yet reform was not enough; a more radical social and cultural transformation was needed, one that reflected the growing radicalism of the politics of the left in the late 1950s. With the Cuban Revolution in only its first year, in 1960 Catholic students published a document, "Some Directives of a Christian Historical Ideal for the Brazilian People," that, mirroring the language of some Cuban revolutionaries, proclaimed capitalism was "a monstrous structure" that "deserves the condemnation of the Christian conscience."[23] The criti-

19. Arquivo Público do Estado do Rio de Janeiro (APERJ), Livros Apreendidos pelas Polícias Política, L514, *Luta Atual pela Reforma Universitária*, 13.
20. Souza, *A JUC, os estudantes católicos e a política*, 89.
21. Mainwaring, *The Catholic Church and Politics in Brazil, 1916–1985*, 62.
22. For example, see Jacques Maritain, *Integral Humanism: Temporal and Spiritual Problems of a New Christendom*, trans. Joseph W. Evans (New York: Charles Scribner's Sons, 1968), especially 127–32 and 190–95.
23. Cited in Luiz Gonzaga de Souza Lima, *Evolução Política dos Católicas e da Igreja no Brasil* (Petrópolis: Editora Vozes, 1979), 87–89.

cisms of capitalism and the call for a socialist "historical ideal" quite clearly mirrored Jacques Maritain's own vision of a "historical ideal" for Catholics in the twentieth century, even while they perhaps saw international models in the ideals of the Cuban Revolution.[24]

Yet this discursive transformation of Catholic student politics did not occur simply because of a radicalizing politics. Rather, radicalization and an increasingly worldly political concern occurred in the context of expansion of the Catholic university system. By the early 1960s, the number of Catholic universities had rapidly increased from four to eleven.[25] These new university spaces were effectively "blank slates" where Catholic students concerned with social issues could gather and debate social and political issues that produced new understandings of social relations between students and the rest of society. This expansion of Catholic higher education in Brazil also extended the JUC's own reach, as new campuses in cities meant new urban spaces where the JUC could operate. Thus, even as the JUC's politics transformed, so too did its presence in Brazilian cities: where the JUC had only thirteen active chapters in 1950, by 1960, that number was fifty-two.[26] In the process, more and more students who identified as Catholic could and did get caught up in the left-leaning politics of the JUC and UNE.

Secular social and political issues continued to creep into the JUC's activism as the 1960s dawned. In 1960 the JUC hosted a Congress to commemorate its tenth anniversary. In accordance with past practices across the previous decade, the Congress held masses and study groups for students. Yet it also held conference panels on issues pertaining to "The University and Society" that dealt with themes such as "the university student and the worker," "the university student and the rural milieu," and "university policy."[27] Whereas Catholic student activism in the 1950s had subordinated these issues to "the University before God,"[28] by the early 1960s, social issues stood alone, aided by the expansion of the university system, where the JUC's increasingly

24. Maritain, *Integral Humanism*, 127–32; Coleção Projeto Memória Movimento Estudantil (PMME), Fundação Roberto Marinho, transcript of interview with Sepúlveda Pertence. See also PMME, interview with Daniel Aarão Reis.

25. Between 1955 and the military coup of 1964, another seven Catholic Universities formed in Campinas (1955), Minas Gerais (1958), Paraná (1959), Goiás (1959), Pelotas (1960), Salvador (1961), and Petrópolis (1962).

26. Souza, *A JUC, os estudantes católicos e a política*, 90.

27. *Jornal do Brasil*, June 28, 1960.

28. Souza, *A JUC, os estudantes católicos e a política*, 113–14.

progressive politics could spread among the middle- and upper-class student bodies. The change was not a rupture—New Christendom's belief that the church and its members had important roles to play in politics and society continued—but the role of the university and of university students in broader social and political questions of secular educational reforms were increasingly vital.

In May 1961, with many JUC members present, UNE hosted the First National Seminar on University Reform in Bahia. The meeting marked an important shift in student discourse and the ascendancy of university issues as the main focus of student politics in the 1960s, a fact reflected in the name of the meeting itself: where the 1957 meeting had focused on "educational reform," UNE now had narrowed its focus strictly to "university reform." Yet this was not simply a call for better conditions on campuses; the seminar's findings, reported in the "Declaration of Bahia," expressed a vision of university reform that would be instrumental in addressing social inequalities in Brazil. Critical of the unequal development that defined Brazilian capitalism, the declaration called for greater democracy, agrarian and labor reforms that would give workers greater economic and political rights,[29] and, of course, university reform that would open higher education to all Brazilians. This concern with socioeconomic inequalities and the need to address them presaged the papacy's own focus on poverty, social injustice, and the negative impacts of capitalism that would come to make up an important part of the discourse of the Second Vatican Council (1962–1965). However, in 1961, Brazilian students had already developed such a worldview, even going so far as to demand "a form of socialism that makes possible the fulfillment of man and of humanity,"[30] sharing Maritain's and Mounier's vision of Christian societies that abandoned the materialism of liberal capitalism.[31] That same year, Aldo Arantes, a student at the Pontifical Catholic University of Rio de Janeiro (PUC-RJ), won election as UNE's president. Arantes had been

29. Such concerns were similar to those of groups such as the Christian Democrats of Chile. For more on reform movements under Christian Democrat President Eduardo Frei, see Heidi Tinsman, *Partners in Conflict: The Politics of Gender, Sexuality, and Labor in the Chilean Agrarian Reform, 1950–1973* (Durham, N.C.: Duke University Press, 2002), chapters 3 and 4.

30. UNE, "Declaração da Bahia." Reprinted in Maria de Lourdes de A. Fávero, *A UNE em Tempos de Autoritarismo* (Rio de Janeiro: Editora UFRJ, 1995), x.

31. Maritain, *Integral Humanism*, especially 127–32 and 190–95. See also Haroldo Lima and Aldo Arantes, *História da Ação Popular da JUC ao PCdoB* (São Paulo: Editora Alfa-Omega, 1984), 29.

active on the PUC-RJ campus and had been a leading member of the JUC, revealing how the discursive and organizational activism of the JUC and UNE had increasingly become integrated on Catholic campuses even while blurring the lines between university campuses and Catholic organizations such as the JUC.

In a turn that foreshadowed the post-1964 conflict between students and important parts of the church hierarchy, not all Catholic officials welcomed this new political context. High-ranking members of the Brazilian Catholic Church disapproved of Arantes's election and what they viewed to be the political involvement of the JUC, an ostensibly apolitical organization. Under pressure, Arantes officially left the JUC,[32] but continued to be a member of the new Popular Action (Ação Popular, or AP) movement, a more politicized offshoot from the JUC that operated independently of the church but without abandoning some of its social Christian principles. Indeed, by 1962, the main split between national student politics was between the Leninist Brazilian Communist Party (Partido Comunista Brasileiro, or PCB) and AP, which pushed for social justice but which also provided a progressive alternative for students leery of Marxism.[33] Arantes's election marked a watershed, however, because members of AP would serve as presidents of UNE from 1961 up through UNE's effective, if temporary, extinction in the face of military repression in 1972.[34]

TRANSFORMATIVE ACTIONS AND NEW MOBILIZATIONS

Although the JUC and AP faced growing criticisms both from within the church and from more conservative sectors of society, they continued to push for more radical transformations to Brazil's economy, educational system, and society in order to address the needs of Brazil's poor. Following up on the Declaration of Bahia, in 1962 UNE, with Arantes as its president, hosted a Second National Seminar on University Reform. The *Carta do Paraná* that emerged from the seminar

32. PMME, transcript of interview with Marcelo Cerqueira.

33. For example, see PMME, transcripts of interviews with José Paulo Sepúlveda Pertence, Maria Augusta Carneiro Ribeiro, Franklin Martins, and Vladimir Palmeira.

34. Ultimately, AP abandoned its Catholic roots by the late 1960s, turning to the Maoist Communist Party of Brazil (*Partido Comunista do Brasil*, or PCdoB) in the early 1970s before many of its leaders were killed or arrested. See Lima and Arantes, *História da Ação Popular da JUC ao PCdoB*.

continued to emphasize the university's role in broader social transformations and a path towards a humanist socialism that would address
Brazil's socioeconomic inequalities, even while it laid out a concrete
path to university reform. And in May 1962, Rio de Janeiro's *Última
Hora* published a letter from Áurea de Araújo, a student who clarified
and upheld the JUC's social and cultural visions, and the importance
of university reform to social justice. Condemning the university's
own historical role in perpetuating inequalities by failing to train students to help develop the entire country, Araújo called for a reform
that would allow students to "assume leadership roles in popular demands" and thus complete the university's "social mission."[35] Catholic
university students' background may have been middle or even upper
class, but the combination of the JUC's leftward shift with the growing
Catholic university system provided a means through which students
from socioeconomically privileged positions increasingly turned to
leftist politics that criticized inequalities in Brazil.

Catholic student activism in the early 1960s was not limited to a
handful of vanguardists in UNE or the JUC's leadership, however. The
movement that most directly affected the largest number of Catholic
students in Brazil occurred in June 1962, when one hundred thousand
Brazilian students participated in a nationwide strike at both public
and Catholic universities throughout the country. The *Carta do Paraná*
had declared that Brazilian students would have to be the ones to control the process of reform, and the best way to do this would be from
within the universities themselves. By June 1962, students were demanding that for every two professors on university councils, there be
one student representative. When Brazil's university administrators
proved reluctant to give students such a large voice in governing universities, schools throughout the country went on strike in the "Strike
of One-Third." UNE, with former JUC member Aldo Arantes as president, coordinated with the individual academic directories at public
and Catholic schools throughout the country. By June 5, students at
forty-eight universities across twenty-two states had gone on strike.

The Strike of One-Third in 1962 was a transformative moment in
Catholic student activism in Brazil, marking the first time that campuses served as politicized spaces where students mobilized to make
their social demands heard. The strikes demonstrated that student

35. *Última Hora*, May 7, 1962.

activism was not just limited to the JUC or AP leadership in UNE. Indeed, students on Catholic campuses were particularly effective in mobilizing for change; by mid-June, four of the six universities that had conceded one-third representation to their students were Catholic universities.[36] But success did not lead to an end in student mobilization, as Catholic schools that gained one-third representation still maintained "symbolic adhesion" to the strike in support of their colleagues at other schools.[37] Not all students had participated in the JUC or UNE; however, during the Strike of One-Third, students on Catholic campuses had gone on strike en masse, using the new, expanded Catholic university system to mobilize around social and political issues.

The 1962 strike also marked a turning point in the discursive struggles of Catholic student activists. The issue of university reform at the heart of the 1962 lost any references to broader Christian ideals, and students were noticeably silent on how the strike represented social Christianity or Christian ideals. This was a fight for a secular struggle—student representation on university governing boards—and little else, yet it also mobilized students on all of Brazil's Catholic campuses. The very definition and nature of "Catholic activism" had transformed into a question of students in Catholic spaces mobilizing for secular issues.

This is not to say that the religious worldviews themselves had entirely faded away. Evangelization was no longer a primary concern for Catholic student organizations, but students in the early 1960s continued to employ discourses of social justice that drew on the Gospels and on the theories of Maritain and Mounier. In this way, Catholic students in Brazil foreshadowed and paralleled similar arguments that would define Vatican II and papal encyclicals such as John XXIII's *Pacem in terris*, which institutionally sought to give "voice to the voiceless," to advance the "proper development of life," and to have religion directly engage the modern world in order to counter some of the excesses of capitalism. As late as 1963, Brazilian Catholic students demanded "a radical shift in the social structures of Brazil, so that the people can

36. *Jornal do Brasil*, June 15, 1962. The four Catholic universities that granted one-third representation were the Catholic University of Bahia, the Catholic University of Minas Gerais, the Pontifical Catholic University of Porto Alegre, and the Pontifical Catholic University of São Paulo. The remaining two universities were the University of Santa Maria and the University of Rio Grande do Norte.

37. *Jornal do Brasil*, June 17, 1962. For more on the strike, see also Clemente Rosas, *Praia do Flamengo, 132: Crônica do Movimento Estudantil nos Anos 1961–1962* (Recife: FUNDARPE, 1992).

enjoy a more dignified and more Christian life."[38] Yet when it came time to offer concrete solutions, they set aside more philosophical, Christian aspects of reform and turned to the secular issue that most directly affected their own lives: university reform.

In a great irony, just as the Second Vatican Council was entering its latter phases, cementing a program of greater social justice through religion, Catholic student politics and discourses shed the language of evangelization and reform that had defined the early 1960s. The cause for this transformation was simple: amid growing political polarization, increasing inflation, and the seemingly sudden leftward shift of President João Goulart, the military rose up and overthrew Goulart on April 1, 1964, ushering in a twenty-one-year military dictatorship. Many Brazilians welcomed the military intervention, viewing it as another case of the military "saving" Brazil from instability.[39] Yet this intervention would be different: not only did the military fail to quickly step aside, as it had done in the past; it also relied heavily on repression, stripping citizens of political rights, arbitrarily arresting labor leaders and leftist activists, and even employing torture against groups that the regime believed "threatened" the nation politically and morally.[40]

This new political context transformed Catholic student activism in Brazil. Although many students initially remained quiet or even supported the military regime,[41] a handful of students began to mobilize against it. At the Catholic University of Minas Gerais (UCMG), one of the most active Catholic campuses prior to the coup, students twice protested against the military's overthrow of Goulart within the first two

38. *Jornal do Brasil*, May 8, 1963.

39. See, for example, Daniel Aarão Reis, *Ditadura militar, esquerdas e sociedade*, 3rd ed. (Rio de Janeiro: Jorge Zahar Editor, 2000), and Janaina Martins Cordeiro, *Direitas em Movimento: A Campanha da Mulher pela Democracia e a ditadura no Brasil* (Rio de Janeiro: Editora FGV, 2009). For a general history of the coup, see René Armand Dreifuss, *1964: A Conquista do Estado—Ação Política, Poder e Golpe de Classe*, 6th ed. (Rio de Janeiro: Editora Vozes, 2006); and Elio Gaspari, *A Ditadura Envergonhada* (São Paulo: Editora Schwarcz, 2002). For the idea of a military coup as "salvation," see Steve J. Stern, *Remembering Pinochet's Chile: On the Eve of London, 1998* (Durham, N.C.: Duke University Press, 2004), chapter 1.

40. The regime's use of repression in the early years of the dictatorship has been well documented. See Maria Helena Alves, *State and Opposition in Military Brazil* (Austin: University of Texas Press, 1985); Gaspari, *A Ditadura Escancarada*; and Thomas E. Skidmore, *The Politics of Military Rule in Brazil 1964–1985* (Oxford: Oxford University Press, 1988). For the regime's vision of morality and repression, see Benjamin Cowan, "'Why Hasn't This Teacher Been Shot?' Moral-Sexual Panic, the Repressive Right, and Brazil's National Security State," *Hispanic American Historical Review* 92, no. 3 (August 2012): 403–36.

41. PMME, transcript of interview with Jean Marc Von Der Weid.

months of the new regime.[42] With organizations such as the JUC and even AP lacking any central physical base of operation akin to campuses, university campuses themselves became the new politicized space for Catholic students to protest against the dictatorship. This student anger was not limited to the UCMG; by the end of the year, Catholic student activists' discontent was evident throughout the country. Even prior to the coup, military leaders felt students were responsible for no small amount of the social and political unrest that afflicted Brazil.[43] Seeking to increase the executive branch's authority in a number of areas, including student politics, President Humberto Castelo Branco's minister of education and culture, Flávio Suplicy de Lacerda, issued a law (known as the Lei Suplicy) that replaced UNE and the State Student Unions (Uniões Estaduais de Estudantes, or UEes). In their place, the government created the National Directory of Students (Diretório Nacional dos Estudantes, or DNE) and State Directories of Students (Diretórios Estaduais de Estudantes, or DEes). Unlike UNE, the government would directly control the DNE and the DEes, giving it a greater presence in national student politics and eliminating the autonomy with which UNE had operated.

The student response on campuses both public and private nationwide was swift. Regardless of their political stances, students saw UNE and the UEes as their organization, one that had played an important historical role in Brazil's twentieth century, from the entrance into World War II to the end of Vargas's Estado Novo in 1945 and from the nationalization of oil in the 1950s to the legal succession of Goulart to the presidency after Quadros's 1961 resignation.[44] In replacing UNE with the DNE, the military government created an issue around which Catholic students were suddenly more than willing to mobilize. Throughout 1965 and 1966, responding to the political context under military rule, students at Catholic Universities in São Paulo, Rio de Janeiro, and elsewhere spoke out against the Lei Suplicy. Student elections on the Pontifical Catholic University of São Paulo's (PUC-SP)

42. *Jornal do Brasil*, May 11, 1964; *Jornal do Brasil*, May 30, 1964.
43. Centro de Pesquisa e Documentação de História Contemporânea do Brasil—Fundação Getúlio Vargas (CPDOC-FGV), UCi g 1959.11.03, photos 79 and 168–169, "Reflexões que poderiam auxiliar a concepção estratégica de um eficiente repressão do movimento subversivo que as Correntes de Esquerda preparam no Brasil."
44. Thomas E. Skidmore, *Politics in Brazil 1930–1964: An Experiment in Democracy*, 40th anniversary edition (Oxford: Oxford University Press, 2007), chapter 6.

campus hinged on anti-DNE platforms, with progressive students who opposed the military regime winning the elections.[45] As JUC leaders themselves put it, the Lei Suplicy had helped the JUC get a new sense of purpose, as students of various political stripes had now mobilized against a "common enemy."[46]

Unfortunately, just as more students began to mobilize in the increasingly visible face of military repression, the JUC, which had been a key organ for Catholic student activism since the 1930s, saw its relevance wane, as student movements focused on secular issues became the new vehicle for activism in military Brazil. Even before the coup, the JUC had faced growing criticisms from conservative sectors of the church hierarchy and among the civilian population more generally, due to what many believed to be a clearly political role for an organization that was supposed to be religious and apolitical.[47] Shortly after the 1964 coup, Catholic university alumni had even called on the church to abolish the JUC,[48] something the leadership initially refused to do, albeit not without some debate.[49] The military itself openly labeled the JUC as a "subversive" organization within six months of the 1964 coup,[50] and within a year, it was regularly targeting the organization's members for arrest.[51] Meanwhile, AP, the political arm of the JUC, had all but abandoned its religious emphasis by 1965, when its primary focus fell on "the path of the revolution and the problem of an organizing line" for leftist revolution.[52] The result was that programs for revolutionary action against a military regime replaced concerns with applying Christian principles to daily life, a discourse that had defined the JUC and even AP in the 1950s and early 1960s.

While the JUC attempted to continue mobilizing into mid-1966,[53] criticisms of the JUC from within the church itself were also growing. Certainly, progressive clergy in the hierarchy continued to support the organization, including Dom Candido Padim, the official church leader of the JUC from 1962 to 1965.[54] However, conservative clergy had recently taken control in the National Conference of Brazilian

45. *Jornal do Brasil*, August 18, 1966, and September 1, 1966.
46. *Jornal do Brasil*, August 1, 1965.   47. *Jornal do Brasil*, January 14, 1964.
48. *Jornal do Brasil*, April 15, 1964.   49. *Jornal do Brasil*, April 17, 1964.
50. *Jornal do Brasil*, September 20, 1964.   51. *Jornal do Brasil*, August 14, 1965.
52. Lima and Arantes, *História da Ação Popular da JUC ao PCdoB*, 62.
53. *Jornal do Brasil*, July 28, 1966.
54. *Jornal do Brasil*, April 16, 1964, and February 10, 1965.

Bishops (Conferência Nacional dos Bispos do Brasil, or CNBB), and were unwilling to tolerate political opposition to the regime, even as some progressive clergy continued to defend the JUC specifically and Catholic progressivism more generally.[55] This split illustrated divisions in the Brazilian Catholic hierarchy itself in the wake of the military coup. Nonetheless, with conservative bishops leading the church's institutional authority in Brazil, the JUC's ongoing activism doomed the organization: in November 1966, the National Secretariat of the Apostolate of Laypersons officially dissolved the JUC.[56]

It was in this new politico-religious context that university campuses, which had already become increasingly important sites for Catholic student activism in the early 1960s, gained a new vitality for Catholic activism in the wake of the coup. With the AP's abandonment of Christian principles and the dissolution of the JUC, the growing number of Catholic universities was now the main arena, both discursively and physically, through which Catholic students mobilized. An increasingly socially progressive vision of Catholic activism in the late 1950s and early 1960s merged with a political context of repression after 1964, creating a context in which secular and national politics had dialectically shaped what Catholic student activism meant. Whereas before 1964 students had often used social reforms to create a more Christian, equal society, after the coup, the shift turned toward creating a more democratic, less repressive society, and while Catholic activism would find new outlets in the 1970s, Catholic student organizations ceased to be the main vehicle for religious activist discourse. Even as the Second Vatican Council concluded in 1965, student activism based on secular political issues was ascendant in Brazil.

One of the biggest issues that had emerged on Catholic campuses was the purely financial issue of *anuidades*, or annual fees. Although Brazil's federal university system was to be completely free for those admitted, the Catholic universities, recipients of significant federal funding themselves, still had to turn to private tuition and fees to remain open. The issue of anuidades briefly emerged prior to the coup, when students at both PUC-RJ and PUC-SP expressed concern over

---

55. For the politics of CNBB during the first six years of the dictatorship, as well as internal opposition to the conservative leadership of the CNBB, see Mainwaring, *The Catholic Church and Politics in Brazil*, 47, 81–84.

56. Souza, *A JUC, os estudantes católicos e a política*, 231.

rising costs.[57] After the coup, however, anuidades became a focal point for student protest and demonstrations at Catholic universities in Rio de Janeiro, São Paulo, Minas Gerais, and Pernambuco,[58] with the rector of the Catholic University of Pernambuco even receiving death threats over the matter.[59] Certainly, this was a very real problem for students on Catholic campuses, but it was not necessarily a religious problem; rather, activism based on Christian discourses had transformed into activism based on material struggles.

STUDENT ACTIVISM UNDER MILITARY RULE

The issue of university reform itself also gained a new relevance in the context of military rule. Students had seen universities as the crux of national development and social equality since the 1950s, something with which democratic presidents Juscelino Kubitschek and João Goulart had agreed. The military coup did not mark a rupture in this regard, as the new regime continued to place universities at the center of national development and growth.[60] In its efforts to construct its own university reform, the military regime turned to outside assistance to help diagnose the problems confronting higher education.[61] As part of these efforts, Brazil entered into an agreement with the U.S. Agency for International Development (USAID) to construct a possible path to reform. This agreement, known as the MEC-USAID accords, became one of the most objectionable issues to students, ranking with the Lei Suplicy in its ability to mobilize and unify student leaders and masses.[62] Students at Catholic universities were not immune to this outrage; al-

57. For PUC-RJ, see *Jornal do Brasil*, February 24, 1962; for PUC-SP, see *Jornal do Brasil*, March 7, 1964.

58. For examples, see *Jornal do Brasil* on the following dates: January 21, 1965; June 26, 1966; December 20, 1967; March 14, 1968; March 15, 1968; April 27, 1968; and July 3, 1968.

59. *Jornal do Brasil*, May 8, 1968.

60. Colin M. Snider, "'Education for Development': Educational Reform and Presidential Policies in Democratic and Military Regimes in Brazil," unpublished manuscript.

61. See Luiz Antônio Cunha, *A Universidade Reformanda: O Golpe de 1964 e a Moderniza-ção do Ensino Superior* (Rio de Janeiro: Francisco Alves, 1988). Cunha's work focuses primarily on the regime's efforts to create policy, stopping with the University Reform of 1968 without fully placing university reform within the broader political or social context or considering how its implementation operated. Nonetheless, it is a very valuable resource for understanding the different committees and debates that ultimately shaped the military regime's 1968 reform.

62. For contemporary critiques of MEC-USAID, see Márcio Moreira Alves, *Beabá dos MEC-USAID* (Rio de Janeiro: Edições Gernasa, 1968). For the role of MEC-USAID in student

though the schools themselves were private, federal educational laws and regulations applied to them as well. As a result, students on Catholic campuses in Rio de Janeiro, Campinas, and São Paulo, took to the streets, protesting the "imperialism" of the MEC-USAID accords and rejecting the regime's vision for university reform.[63]

In these protests, students' concerns focused less on ethical or religious issues of social inequality and more on questions of democracy and university reforms. Reflecting the importance of campuses as sites of activism among middle-class Catholic students, secret police operatives appeared on Catholic and public campuses alike to monitor "subversives," leaving Catholic students feeling "distant" from victory and fearful of police presence.[64] As a result, Catholic struggles against the dictatorship politicized further, responding to the politically repressive conditions that students confronted on a daily basis. Likewise, political issues increasingly defined protests on Catholic campuses, be it against anuidades, the MEC-USAID, or even censorship.[65] In March 1968, police repression of a student gathering left a young man named Edson Luís de Lima Souto dead. In response, Catholic students joined thousands of Brazilians nationwide in protest to condemn the murder of the young man; while slogans and banners damned the military regime on Catholic campuses, they said little about the role Christianity would play in transforming Brazil.[66] By 1968, the crises in higher education and the police repression of students both on campuses and in the streets nationwide led to broader opposition to the regime, and esoteric questions of how to create a Christian alternative to capitalism were less pressing than were the very real presence of police violence, arbitrary arrests, and the lack of democracy in Brazil that affected all students on both Catholic and public campuses alike.

The struggles on Catholic campuses had fundamentally transformed

---

mobilization, see Colin M. Snider, "Complicated Campuses: Universities, Middle-Class Politics, and State-Society Relations in Brazil, 1955–1990" PhD diss., University of New Mexico, 2011, chapter 3; and Langland, *Speaking of Flowers*.

63. For Rio de Janeiro, see *Jornal do Brasil*, June 26, 1966, and October 2, 1968; for São Paulo, see *Jornal do Brasil*, September 15, 1965; and for the Catholic University of Campinas, see *Jornal do Brasil*, July 3, 1968.

64. *Jornal do Brasil*, June 26, 1966.

65. *Jornal do Brasil*, September 20, 1966, and January 1, 1967.

66. For example, see *Jornal do Brasil*, March 31, 1968. For more on the meaning of Edson Luís's death and the way students used it to mobilize and construct memory around 1968, see Langland, *Speaking of Flowers*, especially chapters 3 and 4.

under military rule. Catholics continued to be activists, but a sense of a particularly Christianized Catholic activism that had defined student activism in the late 1950s and early 1960s and that had come to be a key part of the post–Vatican II context within the church hierarchy itself no longer defined Catholic student activism by 1968. While religious figures such as Mounier and Maritain had been the intellectual models for Catholic student activists in Brazil in the early 1960s, by the end of the decade, things had changed. Even as the Bishops' Conference in Medellín concluded, in November 1968 students at UCMG overwhelmingly selected Herbert Marcuse as their graduating class's "patron,"[67] revealing just how political the definition of "Catholic activism" had changed in the postcoup context in Brazil.

Unfortunately for the students at UCMG, the selection of Marcuse and the context in which it happened would be short-lived. At the end of November, the regime issued its new University Reform, a policy four years in the making and the first comprehensive higher education program since the 1930s.[68] On Friday, December 13, Costa e Silva's administration issued the Institutional Act No. 5 that ushered in the most repressive period of the regime, a five-year span of even greater repression that saw militants turn to armed struggle or exile, even as student organizations went underground.[69] Among other things, the decree indefinitely closed Congress, escalated the use of torture and state-sponsored murder, and cracked down on what limited democracy remained, in a period that came to be known as the "Years of Lead." With the JUC officially defunct, many student leaders in exile or underground, and the AP having completely abandoned its Catholic roots, campuses remained the one arena for Catholic student activists. Although there were isolated incidents of protest throughout 1969, by 1970, the nature of the new phase of repression had greatly limited mobilization on Catholic campuses.[70]

Yet Catholic student activism did not disappear in the new repressive context. Rather, it adopted new techniques, issues, and mecha-

67. *Jornal do Brasil*, November 27, 1968.
68. For more on the 1930s reform, see Luiz Antônio Cunha, *A Universidade Crítica: O Ensino Superior na República Populista* (Rio de Janeiro: Livraria Francisco Alves Editora, 1982). See also Jerry Dávila, *Diploma of Whiteness: Race and Social Policy in Brazil, 1917–1945* (Durham, N.C.: Duke University Press, 2003), 62–63.
69. For the regime's use of repression during the so-called "years of lead," see Gaspari, *A Ditadura Escancarada.*
70. Langland, *Speaking of Flowers.*

nisms, even while maintaining the secular discursive emphasis that had intensified after the 1964 coup. However, the post-1968 context saw three new conditions that shaped activism in the 1970s. First, not only had the JUC disappeared; lay organizations themselves had also ended up in a "secondary position" in the church's effort to implement religious and social change.[71] Additionally, the new repressive era created a "climate of inconfidence" among students throughout Brazil, imprisoning (and sometimes disappearing) student leaders or forcing them underground or into exile, and rendering national organizations such as UNE virtually extinct by 1972.[72] Finally, the University Reform that had preceded AI-5 by just two weeks had led to a rapidly transforming university campus, adding to the educational instability and creating as many (if not more) problems as it sought to address. Together, these three transformations created a new situation of Catholic activism on campuses, one that lacked the national voice of the 1960s and that focused on the very real, but very secular, issues confronting students on Catholic campuses, rather than the evangelical issues that had defined earlier eras of activism. Throughout the 1970s, students on Catholic campuses would continue to mobilize over issues such as anuidades, the decline of the quality of education in the wake of the 1968 university reform, and the lack of jobs available in a glutted market.[73]

CONCLUSION

An examination of activism among Catholic university students in Brazil between 1950 and 1970 reveals just how dynamic and fluid Catholic activism could be, not just philosophically, but institutionally and politically. The Catholic activism that the JUC embraced in 1950 had humble and traditional roots, focusing merely on evangelizing Brazil's future elites. As left-leaning students reorganized in a period of conservative control of UNE in the early 1950s, organizations such

71. *Jornal do Brasil*, May 31/June 1, 1970.
72. *Jornal do Brasil*, November 4, 1970.
73. For just a handful of examples from numerous instances of such complaints, see *Jornal do Brasil*, May 26, 1970; CPDOC, LSL pi Lopes, L.S. 1971.10.00, "Objetivos de uma política científica e tecnológica—Adequação da Administração Pública à melhoria da qualidade da vida," 73; APERJ, Coleção DOPS, Setor Estudantil, Pasta 42, *Quilombo dos Palmares*, Ano II, no. 3 (March 1976); APERJ, Coleção DOPS, Setor Estudantil, Pasta 42, DPPS-DO-SB-SBE, February 24, 1976; *Jornal do Brasil*, April 29, 1973; *Jornal do Brasil*, June 20, 1977; *Jornal do Brasil*, March 30, 1979; and *Jornal do Brasil*, September 7, 1979.

as the JUC provided an important instrument to spread increasingly progressive ideas. At the same time, the growing number of Catholic universities also allowed progressive politics to proliferate more rapidly among Catholic students from traditionally middle- and upper-class backgrounds. The result was that Catholic activists in the JUC and in Catholic schools in the mid-1950s began to express a greater concern with the social inequalities facing Brazil, albeit while offering solutions such as university reform that would benefit students themselves first.

As the political climate in Brazil further polarized in the wake of the Cuban Revolution, Catholic student activists moved further to the left, in the process shaping national student politics even while simultaneously embracing more secular struggles and maintaining philosophically Christian roots. With the military coup of 1964, the very discourse of Catholic activism took new forms, entering into a dialectic relationship with the military regime that led to discursive structures that turned away from explicitly Christian principles and focused on questions of repression and education. With the decline of lay groups after the abolition of the JUC in 1966, Catholic universities became one of the major arenas for student activism, albeit of a highly secularized nature that focused on failed reforms and the quotidian material and political struggles facing students on Catholic campuses during a period of intense repression. As the case of student activism in Brazil demonstrates, while the Brazilian Catholic hierarchy was adopting issues such as human rights and appealing to the language that emerged from Vatican II and the Medellín conference, such reforms did not apply to all Catholic activists in Brazil. Ultimately, for Brazil's university students in the 1960s and 1970s, national politics would prove to be more influential than papal reforms, and universities, not churches, became the main theater of student activism.

PART IV ❖ DEVELOPMENT OR LIBERATION?

CHAPTER 9

The Antigonish Movement of Canada and Latin America

Catholic Cooperatives, Christian Communities, and Transnational Development in the Great Depression and the Cold War

❖ Catherine C. LeGrand

Throughout Latin America during the late nineteenth and early twentieth centuries, Catholics drew inspiration from political and social movements, as well as philosophical inquiries, from the rest of the Catholic world. Latin American Catholic activists sought to implement these foreign practices while, at the same time, adapting them and improvising changes that would make more sense in the local context. One of the most successful examples of this transnational interchange and adaptation occurred between Latin American Catholic activists and a little known but highly influential social movement in the Catholic Scots-Irish region of eastern Nova Scotia.

Initiated by priest-professors associated with St. Francis Xavier University in the town of Antigonish, Nova Scotia, the Antigonish Movement took form in the 1920s and 1930s. The most well known of the organizers were Moses Coady and Jimmy Tompkins, who, of local origin themselves, sought to address the economic problems of this rural region of subsistence farmers, poor fishermen, and miners. Working

I am deeply grateful to David Meren, Cynthia Milton, Susan Fitzpatrick-Behrens, Gregory Baum, Rhonda Semple, and an anonymous reviewer for stimulating comments, and to Catherine Irving of the Marie Michael Library and Kathleen MacKenzie of the St. Francis Xavier University Archives for their invaluable help in the research for this chapter.

through the university's Extension Department, Fathers Tompkins and Coady encouraged people to form study groups to analyze the causes of their poverty and to devise their own solutions.

By the late 1930s, more than 1,300 study groups existed in Nova Scotia. Study-club members pooled their resources to form credit unions and then cooperative lobster factories, fish plants, cooperative stores, housing co-ops, and so on. Thus, informal, practical, and participatory adult education gave rise to an important cooperative movement. Moses Coady articulated the movement's analysis of the root causes of poverty: the capitalist system had stripped common people of the control of resources and production, while their precarious economic situation was the result of exploitation by merchants and large corporations from Central Canada.

A grassroots movement to promote economic action, the Antigonish Movement aimed to generate an alternative, cooperative economic system in which people would directly control and benefit from the productive process, resulting in economic and political democracy and "a full and abundant life" for all. It emphasized community solidarity, direct participation, local leadership, and self-determination. This was a kind of egalitarian, holistic vision of development to meet basic community needs and, beyond this, to enrich the social and spiritual life of community members by fostering dignity, trust, confidence in collective action, and, ultimately, realization of the potential of all individuals.[1]

Father Moses Coady called for structural change—a fundamental reform initiated from below that would result in a network of community-based institutions created, owned, and operated by the people

---

1. On the Antigonish Movement, see Moses M. Coady, *Masters of Their Own Destiny: The Story of the Antigonish Movement of Adult Education through Economic Cooperation* (New York: Harper & Brothers, 1939); Santo Dodaro and Leonard Pluta, *The Big Picture: The Antigonish Movement of Eastern Nova Scotia* (Montreal: McGill-Queen's University Press, 2012); Gregory Baum, *Catholics and Canadian Socialism: Political Thought in the Thirties and Forties* (Toronto: James Lorimer & Co, 1980), 189–211; James D. Cameron, *For the People: A History of St. Francis Xavier University* (Montreal: McGill-Queen's University Press, 1996); Alexander F. Laidlaw, *The Man from Margaree: Writings and Teachings of M. M. Coady Educator/Reformer/Priest* (Toronto: McClelland & Stewart, 1971); Anne Alexander, *The Antigonish Movement: Moses Coady and Adult Education Today* (Toronto: Thompson Educational Publishing, 1997); and Ian MacPherson, "Patterns in the Maritime Co-operative Movement, 1900–1945," in *One Path to Co-operative Studies: A Selection of Papers and Presentations* (Victoria, B.C.: New Rochdale Press, 2007), 31–52. Many of the archives of the Antigonish Movement have been digitalized as the Coady-Extension Digital Collection, "Masters of their Own Destiny: The Coady Story in Canada and across the World," http://coadyextension.stfx.ca and http://collections.stfx.ca/cdm/landing page/collection/stfx_coady.

themselves. By 1938–1939, participants were optimistic that this vision, which Coady called "the Big Picture," would be realized: twenty-one thousand adults in eastern Canada were involved in study groups and sixty thousand in the credit union movement, which was giving rise to consumer, agrarian, and other cooperatives.[2]

By the mid-1930s, the Antigonish Movement of Nova Scotia had begun to attract wide attention from other parts of Canada and the United States, as well as internationally. Newspaper and magazine articles appeared, the Carnegie Foundation and the U.S. National Catholic Welfare Conference sponsored a lecture tour by Coady through the United States, Popes Pius XI and Pius XII commended the work of the Antigonish Movement, and in 1949 the United Nations invited Father Coady to address a plenary session of the UN Economic and Social Council.[3] People from many countries of the global South wrote to the Extension Department, and scores came to visit, to tour the communities of eastern Nova Scotia, and to learn the Antigonish Movement's strategies and methods.[4] In the 1940s, offshoots of the Movement began in Jamaica, Puerto Rico, the Dominican Republic, and, in the 1950s, in Mexico. This chapter charts the transnational trajectory of the Antigonish Movement in Latin America, revealing its dramatic success in building a large network of Catholic development projects throughout the region before the Second Vatican Council.

RELIGIOUS FOUNDATIONS OF THE ANTIGONISH MOVEMENT

The religious foundations of this movement were rich and complex. The Antigonish Movement drew on many precedents: the principles of

2. Dodaro and Pluta, *The Big Picture*, 46–48 and chapter 3. These authors call the Antigonish Movement an economic movement because it aimed to bring about change by means other than political action. They maintain that successful grassroots economic movements, which seek to respond to local material needs, generally build on social, cultural, moral, and spiritual foundations and aspirations; see esp. 3–18.

3. See Race Matthews, *Jobs of Our Own: Building a Stakeholder Society: Alternatives to the Market and the State* (Sydney: Pluto Press, 1999), 8, 149, 153, 164; and Alexander F. Laidlaw, *The Campus and the Community: The Global Impact of the Antigonish Movement* (Montreal: Harvest House, 1961), 93.

4. In 1940 Coady wrote: "Twenty years have gone by and, without any advertising on our part, people are coming to us from all over the earth to study this program" (StFXUA RG 30-3/22/139). See also Ida Delaney, *By Their Own Hands: A Fieldworker's Account of the Antigonish Movement* (Hantsport, N.S.: Lancelot Press, 1985), chapter 14.

the nineteenth century British Rochdale cooperatives, the Danish folk schools for adult education, Quebec's *caisses populaires* (credit unions), Roy Bergengren's credit union work in the United States, and mutualism, Christian socialism, and the social Catholicism of *Rerum novarum* (1891) and *Quadragesimo anno* (1931). Indeed, theologian Gregory Baum has called the Antigonish Movement "the most original and the most daring response of Canadian Catholics to the social injustices during the Depression."[5]

In addition, the Antigonish Movement drew on the Catholic principle of "subsidiarity" expressed in these papal social encyclicals. Subsidiarity in Catholic social teaching is the principle that, if a small community can govern itself well and solve its own problems, this should be valued, and it should be allowed to do so without unnecessary interference from higher powers. Originating in a vision of the self-regulating social order of medieval times, this is a Catholic principle of decentralization. Australian cooperator Race Matthews finds this vision in the British Distributist current of Catholic social thought, which, as expressed by G. K. Chesterton and Hilaire Belloc in the 1910s and 1920s, called for widespread ownership of the means of production, distribution, and exchange as the foundation for a just social order that would counter the problems of dire poverty and inequality generated by the Industrial Revolution. Matthews sees—both in the political theory of British Distributism, as well as in the visions and realizations of the Antigonish Movement and the Mondragon cooperatives of Spain—a melding of Catholic social teaching and the associative and communitarian strands of socialism that criticized both state centralization and unfettered capitalism.[6]

5. Baum, *Catholics and Canadian Socialism*, 202.
6. See Matthews, *Jobs of Our Own*, who also suggests that aspects of the thought of French theologians Jacques Maritain and Emmanuel Mounier supported this viewpoint. For connections between French and Belgian theologians and Latin America, see Olivier Compagnon, *Jacques Maritain et l'Amérique du Sud: Le modèle malgré lui* (Lille: Presses Universitaires du Septentrion, 2003); Yves Carrier, *Théologie pratique de libération au Chili de Salvador Allende: Guy Boulanger, Jan Caminada et l'équipe Calama, une expérience d'insertion en monde ouvrier* (Paris: L'Harmattan, 2013); and Caroline Sappia and Paul Servais, eds., *Les relations de Louvain avec l'Amérique latine: Entre évangélisation, théologie de la libération et mouvements étudiants* (Louvain-la-neuve: Académie Bruylant, 2006). Other transnational works by European historians of the Catholic Church include Florian Michel, *La pensée catholique en Amérique du Nord: Réseaux intellectuels et échanges culturels entre l'Europe, le Canada et les Etats-Unis (années 1920–1960)* (Paris: Desclée de Brouwer, 2010); Caroline Sappia and Olivier Servais, eds., *Mission et engagement politique après 1945: Afrique, Amérique Latine, Europe* (Paris: Editions Karthala, 2010); Caroline

In many parts of the world, cooperatives, as a form of labor organization, came out of anarchist and socialist initiatives. Yet the emphasis on cooperatives is also an important Catholic thread of social thought and practice that is associated with the Catholic social encyclicals, religious responses to the Great Depression of the 1930s, and the Catholic search for a "third way," neither free-market capitalism nor state socialism.

Despite the theological and religious thought implicit in the Antigonish Movement, those involved in Canada talked little of religion, the sacraments, or conversion. From the beginning, the Antigonish Movement was ecumenical, in that people of any faith could join study groups and cooperatives, and several Protestant ministers were active collaborators. It should be noted, however, that the decades in which the Movement spread internationally (1940s–1960s) were the decades that North American Catholic missionaries were beginning to go to Latin America in large numbers. Whereas Canada had been designated a "mission territory" by the Vatican until the early twentieth century, in the 1920s, the Scarboro Foreign Mission Society in Ontario and many orders in Quebec (as well as the Maryknolls in the United States) took form. In the 1920s and 1930s, most went to China, but in the 1940s as they were expelled from China, they turned toward Latin America.[7]

EARLY LATIN AMERICAN NETWORKS

The story of how the Antigonish Movement went into the Caribbean and Mexico in the 1940s and 1950s demonstrates four variants in the pathways of transmission and the reverberations of an adult educa-

Sappia, "Le Collège pour l'Amérique latine de Louvain et son ancrage au Brésil: Outil d'un projet d'Eglise, 1953–1983," PhD diss., Université catholique de Louvain, 2013; and, on Canada, Maurice Demers, *Connected Struggles: Catholics, Nationalists, and Transnational Relations between Mexico and Quebec, 1917–1945* (Montreal: McGill-Queen's University Press, 2014).

7. See Michael J. O'Hearn, "The Political Transformation of a Religious Order," PhD diss., University of Toronto, 1983; Catherine LeGrand, "L'axe missionnaire catholique entre le Québec et l'Amérique latine: Une exploration préliminaire," *Globe: Revue internationale d'études québécoises* 12, no. 1 (2009), 43–66; Catherine LeGrand, "Les réseaux missionnaires et l'action sociale des Québécois en Amérique latine, 1945–1980," *Etudes d'histoire religieuse* 79, no. 1 (2013), numéro spécial: "Les réseaux catholiques au Québec du XXe siècle"; and Catherine Foisy, "Des Québécois aux frontières: Dialogues et affrontements culturels aux dimensions du monde. Récits missionnaires d'Asie, d'Afrique et d'Amérique latine (1945–1980)," PhD diss., Concordia University, 2012.

212 ❖ Catherine C. LeGrand

tion and cooperative movement born in Canada. In Jamaica, just after
the labor riots of 1938, the United Fruit Company funded a group of
young intellectuals and activists to address problems of social welfare
in the rural areas. Seeking ideas abroad, they sent one person to Europe and another, Ed Burke, to Nova Scotia. There, Burke studied the
Antigonish Movement for eight months and then enthusiastically returned home to start up rural study clubs and cooperatives through an
organization called "Jamaica Welfare."

Meanwhile a Jesuit priest from Boston, John Peter Sullivan, who
taught for decades at St. George College in Kingston, also drew on the
Antigonish model to create the Sodality Credit Union movement. Both
Ed Burke and John Peter Sullivan corresponded for years with Moses
Coady in Antigonish, often requesting that materials written for study
groups in Nova Scotia be sent to them for use in Jamaica. The Jamaica
Welfare movement was one significant element in creating among Ja-
maicans the confidence for self-rule and for breaking with British colonialism. Jamaica Welfare brought experts and activists from the city
into collaboration with black peasants and workers, helping to create a
sense of commonality and the nationalist conviction that the Jamaican
people could solve their own problems.[8] Later, on the occasion of the
fiftieth anniversary of St. Francis Xavier University's Extension Department in 1978, prominent visitors from the global South would say that
the Antigonish Movement's emphasis on the ability of people to mobilize themselves and be self-determining in economic development was
especially important to countries that were approaching or had just at-
tained independence.[9] Jamaica was one of these.

Meanwhile, in 1945, the Universidad de Puerto Rico invited Moses Coady to lecture on cooperatives in its summer session. Because

8. On Jamaica Welfare and its connections to the Antigonish Movement, see Susan
Fitzpatrick-Behrens and Catherine C. LeGrand, "Canadian and U.S. Catholic Promotion of
Co-operatives in Central America and the Caribbean and their Political Implications," paper
presented at "Towards a Global History of Consumer Co-operation" conference, Swedish Labour Institute and Archive, Stockholm, May 2–4, 2012; and StFXUA RG 30-3/8/340, RG 30-
3/15/1249, RG 30-3/8/320, RG 5/11/15454, RG 30-3/2/11744, RG 30-2/1/829.

9. Allan J. MacEachen (deputy prime minister of Canada), "Canadian Approaches to Cooperation: The Antigonish Movement and Canada's International Responsibilities," and Sir
Shridath S. Ramphal (secretary general of the Commonwealth Association), "Human Development: Defining the Problem," in *Human Development through Social Change: Proceedings of St.
Francis Xavier University's International Symposium Commemorating the Fiftieth Anniversary of the
Antigonish Movement, 1928–1978, Antigonish, Nova Scotia, Canada*, ed. Philip Milner (Antigonish, N.S.: Formac Publishing Co., 1979), 13, 23.

he was too busy, Coady asked another priest-professor from St. Francis Xavier University, Joseph A. MacDonald, to go instead. MacDonald taught a two-month course to a select group of mature graduate students from the Land Authority, the Agricultural Extension Service, and other ministries who, it seems, were very taken with the Antigonish approach to community development and soon thereafter started a non-church-related cooperative movement with government support. Father Joe MacDonald returned to Puerto Rico almost yearly from 1945 through the 1950s to work with cooperators there, and in 1963 he was living in San Juan in a retirement home. MacDonald is regarded as the founder of the Puerto Rican cooperative movement that, while it never comprised more than 2 or 3 percent of the island's economy, became a vector by which the ideas of Antigonish spread to other parts of South America, because it sent many leaders to work in other Latin American countries.[10]

Whereas Jamaica Welfare and the Puerto Rican cooperatives had no religious affiliation, the Canadian missionary channel through which the Antigonish Movement was introduced into the Dominican Republic gave rise to a Catholic National Federation of Cooperatives, which functioned for a decade during the dictatorship of General Rafael Leonidas Trujillo. In the late 1930s, due to the acute scarcity of Dominican clergy, the archbishop of the Dominican Republic sought to attract Canadian missionaries. By the early 1940s, one-third of all parish priests in the Dominican Republic were Canadian: Scarboros from Ontario administered thirteen parishes in the south, and Pères Missionnaires du Sacré-Coeur from Quebec City oversaw thirteen parishes in the north.

In the late 1940s, Scarboro missionaries, many of whom were born and raised in Nova Scotia, initiated a cooperative movement in their rural parishes based on the Antigonish model. This garnered the collaboration of the Quebecers in the north, Salesians, and Spanish Jesuits. By 1953 activist Scarboro Harvey "Pablo" Steele founded the Dominican Federation of Cooperatives with more than ten thousand members and funding from the Trujillo government, which was courting the Dominican Catholic Church. According to the U.S. Embassy,

10. See Rev. Joseph A. MacDonald, *Antigonish and Puerto Rico: Implementation of the Social Encyclicals* (Roosevelt: Cooperative League of Puerto Rico, 1962); StFXUA, RG 30-3/8/340 and RG 50-2/3/603; and L. A. Suárez, "Cooperatives in Puerto Rico: History, Problems, Research," *Rural Sociology* 18, no. 3 (September 1953): 226–33.

the Canadian-founded cooperative movement was the only popular movement allowed to exist during Trujillo's time.

By 1958, though, Trujillo turned against Steele and expelled him from the country. Father Steele then raised funds in Chicago to found the Interamerican Cooperative Institute (Instituto Cooperativo Interamericano, or ICI) in Panama City in the 1960s, which became a center for training community leaders from all over Latin America in the management of cooperatives and other approaches to local development. Throughout the 1950s and 1960s, Steele corresponded regularly with St. Francis Xavier University; at one point, he sought formal affiliation for his Institute with the Extension Department in Antigonish, indicating that the Panama Institute was its Latin American equivalent that made accessible the ideas of Antigonish to Spanish speakers. Trujillo nearly destroyed the Dominican cooperative movement in the final years of his rule, but the Dominican Federation of Cooperatives (Federación Dominicana de Cooperativas) revived some in the 1960s and remained associated with the Catholic Church. For this reason it was not eligible for funds from the Dominican or Canadian governments, but Catholic students from Quebec who volunteered in the parishes of the Pères du Sacré-Coeur created a nongovernmental organization (NGO; Plan Nagua) that channeled Canadian government funds to Dominican cooperatives. The Dominican Federation of Cooperatives continues to exist today, as do Plan Nagua and the ICI.[11]

The Mexican connection with the Antigonish Movement began in 1949–1950, when two priests (Carlos Talavera and Manuel Velásquez Hernández, both of whom worked in the Archdiocesan Social Pastoral program of Mexico City) went to Nova Scotia to study the Antigonish Movement. Soon thereafter, they both became central figures in the Mexican Social Secretariat, which, as Stephen Andes vividly describes,

11. On Harvey Steele, the Dominican cooperative movement under Trujillo, and the ICI, see Catherine C. LeGrand, "Canadian Catholic Missionary Priests in the Dominican Republic: Dictatorship, the Co-operative Movement and Cultural Adaptations, 1935–1985," paper presented on the panel "The Other Pan-Americanisms: Comparative and Transnational Studies of Canadian-Latin American Relations," Canadian Historical Association, York University, May 31, 2006; Gary MacEoin, *Agent for Change: The Story of Pablo Steele as Told to Gary MacEoin* (Maryknoll, N.Y.: Orbis Books, 1973); Harvey Steele, *Winds of Change: Social Justice through Co-operatives: Evaluation of Co-operatives in Latin America and the Caribbean* (Truro, N.S.: Cooperative Resources, 1986); Harvey Steele, *Dear Old Rebel: A Priest's Battle for Social Justice* (Lawrencetown Beach, N.S.: Pottersfield Press, 1993); StFXUA, RG20/1/1916, RG 30-2/3/3450, 3454, 3456, 3459, RG30-2/175/895, RG 50-1/1/11011, 11051, RG 50-2/?/293; and www.icipanama.org.

revived social action in the Mexican Catholic Church, building on the earlier ideas of Father Alfredo Méndez Medina, who, in the 1930s, had called for trade unions and cooperatives.[12] Their efforts gave rise to the first credit union, founded in October 1951 in a working-class *barrio* (neighborhood) of Mexico City, and then to a credit union movement that coalesced in the Mexican Confederation of Credit Unions (Confederación Mexicana de Cajas Populares), which by 1963 had 474 affiliated groups with 32,000 members in 25 Mexican states.[13]

By the late 1940s and early 1950s, several hundred foreigners were flocking each year to Antigonish, seeking to study the adult education and cooperative movements. These included Fathers Talavera and Velásquez from Mexico, several priests from Chile, and Brazilian Teresita Teixeira Mendes, who, in the 1950s, founded the Credit Union Federation of Rio de Janeiro, and others.[14] The Antigonish Movement's organizers in the Extension Department of St. Francis Xavier University informally accommodated these people—and many more from Asia and Africa—by starting up social leadership classes and offering additional short courses and field study during this time, when there was as yet no school for foreign students.

According to Santo Dodaro and Leonard Pluta, the unanticipated interest manifested by people from all over the world taxed the human and material resources of the Antigonish Movement. It also pushed the Antigonish Movement to define its philosophy and goals in universalistic terms, whereas it previously had focused solely on regional issues.[15] As early as 1939, Moses Coady indicated his interest in creating a "people's research institute" that would welcome people from all over the world to study "The Antigonish Way," learn from each other, and return home to combat poverty and inequality in their home communities.[16] By the late 1940s, there was more talk of this, and St. Francis Xavier

12. See Stephen J.C. Andes, "A Catholic Alternative to Revolution: The Survival of Social Catholicism in Postrevolutionary Mexico," *The Americas* 68, no. 4 (April 2012): 529–62. On social Catholicism in Mexico and the Mexican Social Secretariat, see also Robert Sean Mackin, "The Movement that Fell from the Sky? Secularization and the Structuring of Progressive Catholicism in Latin America, 1920s–1970s," PhD diss., University of Wisconsin, Madison, 2005.
13. StFXUA RG 50-2/10/140.
14. In "The Cross-Cultural Diffusion of a Social Movement," MS thesis, Cornell University, 1962, Desmond Maurice Connor maintains that between 1946 and 1960, thirty-six students from the Caribbean and thirty from Latin America came to study the Antigonish Movement in Nova Scotia.
15. Dodaro and Pluta, *The Big Picture*, chapter 4.
16. Coady, *Masters of Their Own Destiny*, 164–66; and Cameron, *For the People*, 332–34.

University created a group in Boston called "Friends of Antigonish" to raise money in the United States for an international institute. A letter was sent to Joseph Kennedy, who suggested that his son John serve on the board instead. Although John F. Kennedy apparently attended few board meetings, he was clearly aware of the existence of Antigonish.[17]

THE DEVELOPMENT DECADE

Between 1959 and 1961 a sea change occurred. It had multiple facets, some connected to shifting priorities within the Catholic Church and the U.S. and Canadian governments, and some to a generational shift in the Antigonish Movement. With the Cuban Revolution of 1959, the cold war centered on the East–West rivalry over Latin America and Cuba intensified. At the encouragement of Pope John XXIII, thousands of Catholic clergy from the United States, Canada, and Europe headed to Latin America.[18] At the same time, the U.S. and Canadian governments focused on development: indeed the 1960s was called "the Development Decade" with the implementation of the Alliance for Progress (launched by John F. Kennedy in 1961), and the foundation of U.S. Agency for International Development (USAID), the U.S. Peace Corps, and the Canadian International Development Agency (CIDA).[19]

What was going on in Antigonish, and how did these major events affect relations between the Antigonish Movement and Latin America? By 1960, most of the founders of the Antigonish Movement, including Moses Coady, had died, and socioeconomic and political changes in eastern Canada were undermining the vitality of the movement, whose heyday had been the 1930s, 1940s, and into the 1950s. Whereas cooperatives continued to grow, by the 1950s the study groups were in

17. Peter A. Nearing, *He Loved the Church: The Biography of Bishop John R. MacDonald, Fifth Bishop of Antigonish* (Antigonish, N.S.: Casket Printing and Publishing Co., 1975), 67; and Matthews, *Jobs of Our Own*, 9.

18. In 1960 the pope mandated that one-tenth of clergy in North America and Europe go work in Latin America, an important Catholic part of the world threatened by the spread of Communism, Protestantism and secularism. Pope John XXIII convened the Second Vatican Council in Rome, opening the way to Liberation theology. On the Catholic Church and the cold war, see Piotr H. Kosicki's chapter in *The Routledge Handbook of the Cold War*, ed. Artemy M. Kalinovksy and Craig Daigle (London: Routledge, 2014), 259–71.

19. The Alliance for Progress was a major aid and development program for Latin America, intended to prevent the region from following Cuba into socialist revolution.

decline, an interventionist Canadian government was taking on the welfare functions that local communities had previously provided, and St. Francis Xavier University was stepping back from community involvement. By the 1960s, the Antigonish Movement, underfunded and in disarray, had lost its original vision and had little sense of direction. Instead, the directors of the Extension Department dedicated themselves to social scientific research on "development" projects defined and funded by government agencies.[20]

Precisely in the 1959–1961 period, Moses Coady's dream of an international people's school came to fruition. In 1959 St. Francis Xavier University established the Coady International Institute as the international arm of the Antigonish Movement. To do so, it had received a $200,000 grant from the bishop of Boston, as well as the support of U.S. Monsignor Luigi Ligutti, the International Labour Organization (ILO) and the Food and Agriculture Organization (FAO) of the United Nations.[21] Sociologist and educator Father Frank Smyth, previously head of the Social Action Department of the Canadian Conference of Catholic Bishops, became its first director.

Over the next two decades, more than two thousand students from one hundred countries would study at the Coady Institute in Antigonish; most completed the eight-month diploma course in social leadership and others did the summer certificate course. The students, mostly mature men and women, included Christians, Hindus, Buddhists and atheists; parish priests and nuns from Latin America, Asia, and Africa; North American and European clergy who were headed to the "third world"; and lay community activists from the global South and the North. Together, they studied the vision, history and techniques of the Antigonish Movement, cooperative organization, social leadership, adult education, and community development, and each wrote a thesis that related the Antigonish Movement to his or her home context.[22]

20. See Dodaro and Pluta's *The Big Picture*—the only study of the Antigonish Movement that traces long-term changes in the movement in Atlantic Canada from 1920 to 2000.

21. StFXUA RG 30-3/22/99. The Coady International Institute, located at St. Francis Xavier University in Antigonish, N.S., formally opened in October 1961.

22. See Father G. E. Topshee, "The Coady Now," in *Human Development through Social Change: Proceedings of St. Francis Xavier University's International Symposium Commemorating the Fiftieth Anniversary of the Antigonish Movement, 1928–1978, Antigonish, Nova Scotia, Canada*, ed. Philip Milner (Antigonish, NS: Formac Publishing Co., 1979), 152–56, for the curriculum. From 1960 to 1964, the Coady International Institute trained sixty Latin Americans. For lists of Latin American students in the 1960s and what they did when they went back to their home

After graduates returned home or went to their assigned parishes in the third world, the Coady Institute tried to maintain close contact with them through frequent correspondence, visits by Coady staff, and, by the early 1970s, regional workshops that brought graduates together to share ideas and experiences and to advise the staff on what programs might be further developed in Latin America. Experts on cooperatives from the Coady Institute were much in demand, by governments as well as Catholic bishops in third-world countries.

By the early 1960s, there was a definite Latin American focus to the Coady Institute. Peter Nearing explains how the impulse that finally led to the establishment of the institute stemmed from Pope John XXIII's determination to promote aid and cooperation between the churches of North and South America.[23] In the first years, about half of the students at the Coady Institute were Latin Americans. The language difficulty was addressed by having Scarboro missionary priests who had spent years in the Dominican Republic give language courses and translate correspondence and study materials.

A GROWING FOCUS ON LATIN AMERICA

In the 1960s and 1970s, the intensified interaction of the Antigonish Movement (i.e., the Coady Institute) with Latin America is clear in the institute's records, which include correspondence (including requests for information and materials), reports of study visits and workshops held in Latin America, meetings with former students in their home countries, and the theses the students wrote, which sometimes shed amazing light on social processes in the dioceses or the communities from which they came.

As noted earlier, in the 1960s and 1970s the work of St. Francis Xavier University's Extension Department veered toward a social science–oriented and government-promoted concept of development. But in the Coady Institute, the activist social Catholicism that in Latin America both precedes and leads into the period of Liberation theology kept alive the earlier vision of the Antigonish Movement. This Antigonish-inflected Catholic social activism played out in some areas of Latin America

countries, see StFXUA RG 50-2/3/150, RG 62/1/399–445, RG 30-3/22/197–99, and RG 30-3/22/237. The theses written by Coady graduates are in the MML, Coady International Institute, Antigonish, N.S.

23. Nearing, *He Loved the Church*, 97–100.

through the efforts of Latin American and foreign clergy and lay activists on the ground and through international networks. What is fascinating to explore here is how the Antigonish Movement fed into two related but quite different concepts of "what should be done" in Latin America of the 1960s and 1970s—one associated with "community development" along Alliance for Progress lines and the other with Christian base communities as understood by Liberation theology. From the archives of the Coady Institute, it is possible to explore how the Antigonish Movement took different forms and meanings in different places.

First, I concentrate on the Antigonish Movement and the "development" stream. In the 1940s, there was a concern with community development both internationally and in the United States.[24] Father Coady was invited to speak to the United Nations and also to the U.S. State Department. At the same time, the Canadian government took an early interest in the Antigonish Movement. According to Michel Dupuy, president of the CIDA in 1978:

In the early '50s, the Economic and Technical Assistance Branch of the Department of Trade and Commerce commissioned the Extension Department of St. F.X. to train Canadian experts about to go overseas. At the same time, increasing numbers of developing countries, recognizing the contribution 'The Antigonish Way' could make to their own development processes, sent their young development leaders to St. F.X. for training in credit unions, cooperative and leadership techniques. Many of them were sponsored by the Federal Government through scholarships. This active Federal Government support was largely responsible for the University's decision in 1959 to establish an International Institute … When CIDA's predecessor, the External Aid Office, was formed in 1960, th[e] relationship with Coady continued, as it has over the ten years of CIDA's existence.[25]

24. See Daniel Immerwahr, *Thinking Small: The United States and the Lure of Community Development* (Cambridge: Harvard University Press, 2015); Nicole Sackley, "The Village as Cold War Site: Experts, Development, and the History of Rural Reconstruction," *Journal of Global History* 6, no. 3 (Nov. 2011): 481–504; A. Ricardo López, "Conscripts of Democracy: The Formation of a Professional Middle Class in Bogotá during the 1950s and Early 1960s," in *The Making of the Middle Class: Toward a Transnational History*, ed. A. Ricardo López and Barbara Weinstein (Durham, N.C.: Duke University Press, 2012), 161–195; and Nathan J. Citino, "Modernization and Development," in *The Routledge Handbook of the Cold War*, ed. Artemy M. Kalinovsky and Craig Daigle (London: Routledge, 2014), 118–30.

25. Michel Dupuy, "Canada's Role in Development and CIDA's Relationship with the Coady International Institute," in *Human Development through Social Change: Proceedings of St. Francis Xavier University's International Symposium Commemorating the Fiftieth Anniversary of the*

CIDA viewed the Coady Institute as an NGO. Foreign students at the Coady Institute were funded by Canada's External Aid Office, the Department of Indian and Northern Affairs, the Colombo Plan, the ILO, the UN Education, Scientific and Cultural Organization (UNESCO), the Knights of Columbus, the Canadian Conference of Catholic Bishops, the Anglican Church of Canada, the international development agency of the West German Catholic Church (MISEREOR) and missionary groups from Latin America, Asia, and Africa.[26]

In certain regions, such as the Caribbean West Indies, which became independent nations in the 1960s, the Training Resources Division of CIDA and the Coady Institute collaborated closely in making credit unions and cooperatives an important aspect of a new Caribbean Regional Development Agency. By 1970, 150 graduates of the Coady Institute were working in government ministries and with government-sponsored credit unions and cooperatives in the former British Caribbean, and CIDA funded a Coady staff member to evaluate cooperatives that the Antigonish Movement had had a hand in creating and CIDA was supporting there.[27]

Meanwhile, in Peru, the Canadian ambassador asked in 1960 to put on a "Canada week" for students at the newly reopened Universidad de San Cristóbal de Huamanga in Ayacucho. During the week, he devoted two days to the Antigonish Movement and then pressured Canada's government to fund a professor from Antigonish to give a course there. As the university's new rector argued, the problems of poor farmers in highland Peru were similar to those of the Canadian Maritime provinces in the 1930s.[28]

Concurrently, under the Alliance for Progress in the early 1960s, the U.S. government, through USAID, strongly supported the creation of cooperatives as a way of forging a peaceful revolution of self-help, par-

Antigonish Movement, 1928–1978, Antigonish, Nova Scotia, Canada, ed. Philip Milner (Antigonish, N.S.: Formac Publishing Co., 1979), 134.

26. StFXUA RG 30-3/22/271. Created in 1958, MISEREOR, the German Church equivalent to the Canadian Catholic Organization for Development and Peace, was very involved in Latin America in the 1960s and 1970s. It provided significant funding for Catholic social action and development projects.

27. StFXUA RG 50-2/2/1, 3, 4, 9, 384, 423, 427.

28. This is the Peruvian university that gave birth to the Sendero Luminoso (Shining Path) guerrillas. The Canadian ambassador's correspondence, including his description of the Universidad de San Cristóbal de Huamanga in 1960, is in StFXUA RG50-2/3/326, 327, 337, 345, 346, 348, 360. The Canadian government did not fund the professor.

ticipation, community cohesion, and economic betterment that would win the hearts and minds of poor people away from violent Communist paths to redistribution. The Alliance for Progress tied the concept of economic development to social reform and political democracy.[29] In 1962–1963 the Alliance for Progress promoted the signing of agreements between USAID, Latin American governments, and the Credit Union National Association (CUNA; based in Madison, Wisconsin) to create cooperative departments within Latin American government ministries and cooperative training institutes in the various countries.[30] USAID convened and financed the first Conference of Latin American Credit Unions in Lima (Peru) in 1963, which a representative from Antigonish attended; USAID promoted the formation of a cooperative department within the Dominican government of Juan Bosch, and, in the early 1960s, the U.S. agency paid the Puerto Rican cooperative movement to train Peace Corps volunteers to work with exiled Cuban youth.[31] The United States seems to have viewed cooperatives as a reformist "third way" between state-run communism and laissez-faire capitalism in these years.[32]

29. According to Tony Smith, *America's Mission: The United States and the Worldwide Struggle for Democracy* (Princeton, N.J.: Princeton University Press, 2012), chapter 8, the Alliance for Progress was innovative in American development thought in its wedding of the idea of Wilsonian democracy to a Rooseveltian New Deal of social and economic reform for Latin America. See also James William Park, *Latin American Underdevelopment: A History of Perspectives in the United States, 1870–1965* (Baton Rouge: Louisiana State University Press, 1995), 184–234. Concerned that the Latin American peasantry was ready to explode in Communist revolution (i.e., concerned about the appeal of rural guerrilla groups), the Alliance for Progress pushed for redistribution of land through agrarian reform and drew on the Chilean Christian Democratic Party's idea that the recipients of land would benefit most by forming cooperatives that would produce stable, prosperous, and cohesive rural communities. Manuel Larraín, the bishop of Talca (Chile), who was active in the Chilean agrarian reform and instrumental in forming the Latin American Bishops' Conference (CELAM), corresponded actively with Frank Smyth of the Coady Institute in the 1960s.

30. On CUNA, see Ian Macpherson, *Hands around the Globe: A History of the International Credit Union Movement and the Role and Development of World Council of Credit Unions, Inc.* (Victoria, B.C.: Horsdal & Schubart Publishers and World Council of Credit Unions, 1999).

31. StFXUA RG 50-2/3/603.

32. In the 1930s and after, the Antigonish Movement had been accused of having socialist leanings because of its radical critique of capitalism. The birth of a particular Canadian form of socialism in the prairie provinces during the 1930s (the Cooperative Commonwealth Federation, or CCF; Farmer-Labour-Socialist, which became the New Democratic Party) also advocated economic cooperation, as did the conservative, corporatist government of Quebec in the 1930s. See Baum, *Catholics and Canadian Socialism*; and Gilles Routhier and Axel Maugey, *Eglise du Québec, Eglise de France: Cent ans d'histoire* (Ottawa: Novalis, 2006). Once the cold war began, Moses Coady began to emphasize the anticommunist aspect of the cooperative movement,

EARLY INTERACTIONS WITH LIBERATION THEOLOGY

Whereas, during the cold war, the Canadian and, to a certain extent, the U.S. governments drew on the Antigonish Movement for certain ideas and practices related to community development, in these same years the Antigonish Movement contributed to Christian social movements associated with the rise of Liberation theology in several areas of Latin America. Tracing the Christian social action thread of the Antigonish Movement in Latin America sheds light on how one progressive stream of Catholicism in Canada prior to Vatican II continued and evolved in Latin America as Canadian, U.S. and Latin American Catholic clergy and laypeople sought to put into practice the new theology of liberation.

The study groups of the Antigonish Movement of the 1930s and 1940s had much in common with Paulo Freire's later approach to adult education as *conscientización* (consciousness-raising) and empowerment. Indeed both may have come out of the pedagogical method of Specialized Catholic Action, known as Revisión de vida (See-Judge-Act), begun by Belgian Father Joseph Cardijn and spread into Latin America by Cardijn himself and Belgian, French, and Quebecois missionaries in the 1930s through the 1950s.[33]

Also, in the Antigonish Movement's concern with the economic dimension of social and spiritual life, the creation of strong, participatory communities that would analyze everyday problems and act to improve the lives of the poor, and the promotion of lay leadership and lay action, Moses Coady's vision had much in common with the Christian base communities that began to take form in Latin America in the 1960s and 1970s as Liberation theology in action. Father Coady's

---

which is evident in his later writings (see Dodaro and Pluta, *The Big Picture*; and Laidlaw, *Man from Margaree*).

33. On the progressive initiatives of Specialized Catholic Action as a lay movement and especially the Young Catholic Workers (Juventud Obrera Católica) in Latin America, see Ana Maria Bidegain, "From Catholic Action to Liberation Theology: The Historical Process of the Laity in Latin America in the Twentieth Century," Working paper 48, The Helen Kellogg Institute for International Studies, University of Notre Dame, Notre Dame, Indiana, November 1985, http://Kellogg.nd.edu/publications/workingpapers/WPS/048.pdf; Ana Maria Bidegain, "La organización de movimientos de juventud de Acción Católica en América: Los casos de los obreros y universitarios en Brasil y en Colombia entre 1930–1955," PhD diss., Université Catholique de Louvain, Faculté de Philosophie et Lettres, 1979; and Mackin, "The Movement that Fell from the Sky?"

critique of unbridled capitalism and his insight into economic dependency also resonated with progressive Catholic analyses of the Vatican II period. So there are continuities between certain progressive threads in pre–Vatican II Catholicism and the changes that came with Vatican II and the Medellín Latin American Bishops' Conference of 1968.[34]

In the 1950s, 1960s, and 1970s in some areas of Latin America, clergy who had studied at Antigonish and/or Catholic clergy from Canada and the United States who had spent time at the Coady Institute before going to Latin America created cooperatives on the Antigonish model that fed into innovative social movements pushing for socioeconomic and political transformation. Quite often, areas where such a Catholic cooperative movement had taken root were the same places where Christian base communities and other grassroots popular organizations proliferated in the 1960s and 1970s. These areas included Maranhão in northeast Brazil, the dioceses of Veraguas in Panama and Santiago in the Dominican Republic, Honduras, the western highlands of Guatemala, the dioceses of Riobamba and Ibarra in Ecuador, and Mérida and Barquisimeto in Andean Venezuela. I briefly trace the stories of these areas here. In seeking to distinguish patterns, I pay particular attention to the coincidence of cooperatives on the Antigonish model and the emergence of Christian base communities, as well as the Antigonish connections of a number of progressive Latin American bishops who, sociologist Christian Smith maintains, were crucial to the Liberation theology movement in Latin America.[35] Also, important was the role played by missionaries and the financial support tendered by USAID, as well as by international church organizations such as the German MISEREOR.

---

34. A related subject is the "theology of development" articulated by French priest Luis-Joseph Lebret, who shaped Catholic ideas about development from the 1940s to the 1960s, worked in Brazil and Colombia, and influenced the United Nations' conceptualizations of "community development" in the mid-1950s as well as the Papal Encyclical *Populorum progressio* of 1967 on relations between the first world and the third world. In the late 1950s Father Lebret also talked about "base communities." Founder of the "Economie et Humanisme" group of sociologists and theologians, Lebret influenced the Quebec missionary activist Msgr. Gérard Cambron and others. In addition, it should be noted that Pope John XXIII's encyclical *Mater et magistra* (1961) explicitly advocated the formation of cooperatives.

35. Christian Smith, *The Emergence of Liberation Theology: Radical Religion and Social Movement Theory* (Chicago: The University of Chicago Press, 1991).

Maranhão

Maranhão, part of the northeast of Brazil and the "legal Amazon," was the site of some of the first ecclesial base communities in Brazil, which was the pioneer in Latin America.[36] Yves Carrier's detailed study of the Quebec missionary Gérard Cambron's experience in Brazil from 1958 to 1960 and his collaboration with the progressive bishop and auxiliary bishop of Maranhão, José Delgado and Antonio Fragoso, illuminates how one Canadian missionary was transformed by his experience of Latin America and how cooperatives on the Antigonish model (and the Quebec model as well) informed his thought on how to address poverty and inequality and create vital rural lay Catholic communities. Antigonish priest Peter Nearing served in Maranhão at the same time; the bishop sought to bring other experts in cooperatives from Nova Scotia. In the 1970s, Cambron became an important advisor to Christian base communities throughout Brazil: Dom Fragoso called him "the father of the base communities."[37] As will be seen, tracing Cambron's subsequent missionary trajectory through Honduras and Mexico in the 1960s helps to make sense of multiple links between Antigonish and diverse progressive threads in Latin American Catholicism at the time.

Honduras

In Honduras, Quebec missionary priests (the Société des Missions Etrangères, or p.m.é., the Quebec equivalent of the Maryknolls in the United States) administered the whole bishopric of Choluteca (1955–

36. See Latin American Documentation (LADOC), *Basic Christian Communities*, Keyhole Series No. 14 (Washington, D.C.: Latin American Documentation, United States Catholic Conference [USCC], 1976); Madeleine Cousineau Adriance, *Promised Land: Base Christian Communities and the Struggle for the Amazon* (Albany: State University of New York Press, 1995).

37. Yves Carrier, *Lettre du Brésil: L'évolution de la perspective missionnaire. Relecture de l'expérience de Msgr. Gérard Cambron* (Louvain-la-Neuve: Academia Bruylant, 2008). Because of the development policies of the Brazilian military government, Maranhão in the 1960s and 1970s was rent by social conflict over land; this was a place where Canadian priests and nuns tended to embrace social commitment and Liberation theology. Father Victor Asselin (d. August 2013), for example, a Quebec diocesan priest, spent more than thirty years there; he became deeply involved in land and housing struggles, co-founded (with Dom Pedro Casaldáliga and Dom Thomas Balduino) the Pastoral Land Commission of the National Conference of Brazilian Bishops, and wrote an important book on land-grabbing in the Brazilian Northeast and Amazon: *Gralagem, corrupçao e violencia em terras do Carajas* (Petrópolis: Vozes de Petrópolis, 1982; 2nd ed., 2009).

present), and the Conference of Canadian Bishops in 1960 established and ran the Seminario Mayor N. S. de Suyapa in Tegucigalpa to train priests from throughout Central America. Father Gérard Cambron was called from Brazil to head the seminary. As rector from 1960 to 1965, he wrote to the Coady Institute about his ideas on development (by stimulating the emergence of local lay leaders from peasant and poor urban communities). In the early 1960s, responding in part to a request from Cambron, the diocese of Antigonish sent several local priests, who had studied cooperative methods at the Coady Institute, to Honduras to develop co-ops all over the country. In the late 1960s and early 1970s, Honduras gave rise to a dynamic Christian rural social movement that spearheaded the most important Central American peasant land-reclamation movement of the twentieth century. Quebec priests of the Société des Missions Etrangères strongly supported this movement; as a result, the Honduran Congress threatened them with expulsion. The Quebec priests also spearheaded the formation of Christian base communities, animated by lay Delegados de la Palabra de Dios (Delegates of the Word of God) and of adult education by radio on the Colombian model of Radio Sutatenza.[38]

Father Alexander MacKinnon, one of the socially involved Antigonish clergymen who spent ten years as a Catholic missionary in Honduras, became the main staff member at the Coady International Institute in charge of the Latin American program from the 1970s to the early 1990s. His identification and social engagement with Central and South America, as well as his fluency in Spanish, were essential to maintaining the ties with Latin American cooperative movements during these decades. So, although the Antigonish Movement in Latin America was not a missionary program in that it was not a "faith-based" organization and did not try to spread the Catholic religion or formal church institutions, missionary knowledge and informal social

---

38. See Fred Burrill and Catherine C. LeGrand, "Progressive Catholicism at Home and Abroad: The 'Double Solidarité' of Quebec Missionaries in Honduras, 1955–1975," in *Within and Without the Nation: Canadian History as Transnational History*, ed. Karen Dubinsky, Adele Perry, and Henry Yu (Toronto: University of Toronto Press, forthcoming); and Rev. John H. MacEachen, *A Chosen Few: Voluntarios* (Sydney, N.S.: City Printers, Ltd., 1987), on the secular priests from the diocese of Antigonish in Honduras. For Msgr. Cambron's initiatives at the seminary in Tegucigalpa in the early 1960s and his correspondence with the director of the Coady Institute, see StFXUA RG 50-2/9/43, 102, 106, 199. In the early 1960s, the head of the Honduran government's Department of Cooperatives was Marcial Solis, who had studied in Puerto Rico under Father Joe A. MacDonald.

and communication networks played an essential role in the Antigonish Movement's taking root in specific regions of Latin America.[39]

Mexico

In Mexico, the Catholic Church as a whole was not known to be particularly progressive, but the Mexican Social Secretariat and the credit
union movement remained vital in the 1960s and 1970s. In the early
1960s, Father Carlos Talavera was corresponding regularly with the director of the Coady International Institute; indeed, in the first years
of the institute, teachers there relied on Spanish-language pamphlets
and training booklets from the Mexican Federation of Credit Unions to
train students from Latin America.[40] A detailed account from 1963 by
a visitor to Mexico from the Coady Institute indicated that the federation was now autonomous but in close contact with the social secretariat of the Mexican Catholic Church, and Carlos Talavera remained
an important adviser.[41] Father Manuel Velásquez participated in the
Medellín Bishops' Conference of 1968 and the Mexican Social Secretariat subsequently espoused the conclusions of 1968; it was admon-
ished by the church hierarchy in the 1980s, Stephen Andes suggests,
for its "horizontal and immanentist vision" and for "placing too much
emphasis on social and economic ministries at the expense of spiritual
concerns."[42] The credit union movement initiated by Fathers Talavera and Velásquez remained strong throughout the 1980s and 1990s.
In 1987 the confederación invited the Coady Institute to co-sponsor
a workshop in the city of Puebla on "The Antigonish Movement" in

39. The key role that Father Alexander McKinnon played in stimulating and maintaining
ties between the Coady International Institute and Latin America is evidenced in the scores of
weeklong workshops and consultations in Latin America with former Coady students and other
cooperative leaders that he carried out in more than ten countries over a twenty-year period.
From the evidence of the detailed reports he wrote up on every workshop and consultation, he
seems to have been constantly traveling back and forth between Nova Scotia and Latin America.
40. See StFXUA, RG 50-2/10/132, 152–53.
41. StFXUA RG 50-2/10/137–45, "Mexico," report on a visit, September 25–October 1,
1963. On the Mexican cooperative movement in the early 1960s, see also Antonio Rodríguez
Rosa, *La Revolución sin sangre: El Cooperativismo* (Mexico City: B. Costa-Amic Editor, 1964). A
Mexican advertisement for this book, which surveys cooperative movements all over the world,
said: "Este libro es considerado por la Confederación Nacional de Cooperativos de la República
Mexicana como la Biblia del Cooperativismo y fijador del gran movimiento mundial." StFXUA
RG 50-2/10/80.
42. Andes, "A Catholic Alternative to Revolution," 559.

order to convey to younger field workers and educational directors the origins and values of the credit union movement, which emphasized member education and solidarity and which at this time had more than 210,000 members in nearly 190 *cajas populares*.[43]

The connections of Antigonish to progressive Catholicism in Latin America in the 1960s also had an educational dimension: the archives at St. Francis Xavier University contain the correspondence of Father Ivan Illich with the director of the Coady Institute, at the time that Illich was trying to create the Center of Intercultural Formation (later CIDOC) in Cuernavaca, Mexico. The two men perceived an affinity between their projects, as evidenced in their informal and mutually supportive exchange of letters. Illich sent Father Smyth the full prospectus for his center, and Smyth told an acquaintance that clergy and lay volunteers from Antigonish who went to CIDOC for language and intercultural training before heading to Latin America received an especially warm welcome. A visitor from the Coady Institute to CIDOC in 1963 noted,

I found much in common with our ideas ... it might be a good idea for a group of Institutes like ourselves and themselves to collaborate in producing a handbook for the lay person or priest going to do work in a foreign country. This would not merely state what was to be done, but would be backed up by Theological reasoning as well.... Cuernavaca is to have a group of priests and laymen who will do research into the problems that are facing the church in Latin America, and concern themselves with producing a philosophy of action to bring about a solution ...[44]

While he was rector of the Seminary in Honduras, Monsignor Gérard Cambron collaborated with Ivan Illich in conceptualizing and setting up CIDOC, and he taught there now and again until 1965 when he headed back to Brazil to set up the Intercultural Formation Center (Centro de Formacão Intercultural, or CENFI) in Petrópolis, near Rio de Janeiro, that in collaboration with Ivan Illich would fulfill a similar role to CIDOC in preparing foreign missionaries planning to serve in Brazil.[45] Monsignor Cambron headed CENFI for five years and then

43. Kevin LeMorvan, ed., "The Antigonish Movement," report on a workshop co-sponsored by the Coady International Institute and the Confederación Mexicana de Cajas Populares (Puebla, Mexico, August 31–September 6, 1987, MML, Coady International Institute, Antigonish, N.S.).

44. StFXUA RG 50-2/10/145. For other letters from Illich, see RG 50-2/10/21, 45, 47.

45. Carrier, *Lettre du Brésil*, 319–26. G. Cambron headed CENFI from 1965 to 1969.

returned to working with base communities, setting up a coordinating body to allow Christian base communities throughout Brazil to communicate and learn from one another's experiences.

Panama

Panama is known as one of the early areas in which the practices of Liberation theology were worked out in Central America—in the San Miguelito barrio in Panama City through the innovations of clergy from Chicago who had ministered to Mexican immigrants there, and in the rural area of Veraguas where Héctor Gallego, a young priest who arrived from Colombia in 1967, built a Catholic popular movement of producer and consumer cooperatives and Bible study groups that antagonized the local landowning elite. Kidnapped and murdered in 1971, Gallego is renowned in Central America as the first martyr of the Liberation theology period.[46]

The seeds of the Christian social movement of Veraguas associated with Father Gallego were sown in the early 1960s when several priests from Panama studied at the Coady Institute: two (Alejandro Vásquez Pinto and Osvaldo Rodríguez) established the first cooperatives in Veraguas, while a third (Oscar Monteza) became head of the Panamanian government's recently founded Department of Cooperatives, connected to the agrarian reform initiative there stimulated by the Alliance for Progress. Father Marcos G. McGrath, who in 1964 was appointed the first bishop of the newly created Diocese of Santiago de Veraguas and later brought Héctor Gallego from Colombia, strongly encouraged social action. He established the social action center Juan XXIII in 1963 with funding from MISEREOR and USAID, where cooperative leaders were formed, invited Harvey Steele to teach a course and, in 1966, sent two schoolteachers from Veraguas to study in Nova Scotia at the Coady Institute.[47]

According to Penny Lernoux, through cooperatives, peasants began

46. See Leo Mahon, with Nancy Davis, *Fire under My Feet: A Memoir of God's Power in Panama* (Maryknoll, N.Y.: Orbis Books, 2007); Maria López Vigil, ¡*Héctor Gallego Está Vivo!* (Panama: Pastoral Social-Caritas Editores, 1996); and Ezer Vierba, "The Committee's Report: Punishment, Power and Subject in 20th-Century Panama" (PhD diss., Yale University, 2013), chapter 6.

47. For a Coady Institute report on a meeting with Bishop McGrath in 1963 and McGrath's correspondence with the Coady Institute in 1966, see StFXUA, RG50-2/9/456, and RG50-2/9/226 and 228.

to think critically about their situation, lay leaders emerged, and people participated more actively in community affairs as they began to think that, through their own efforts, they could change things.[48] In 1976 the United States Catholic Conference (USCC) described the Christian cooperatives and peasant communities of Veraguas as among the earliest ecclesial base communities in Latin America. Of the cooperatives, Father Gallego said, "We are trying to stress the communitarian aspect of work—basically we are forming a community.... Our chief accomplishments are to break with the class that has dominated ... and to create a new sense of confidence and communitarian spirit."[49]

Indeed, in 1968 peasants of Veraguas for the first time refused to vote for the *cacique* (local boss), and consumer cooperatives threatened the economic interests of local landlords and middlemen. The disappearance of Father Gallego in 1971 created a national crisis for the president of Panama, General Omar Torrijos, and the Panamanian Catholic Church, but it did not end the movement. The Veraguas peasant cooperatives continue vital today.[50] Some see them as a solidary, sustainable alternative to the contemporary economic development model centered on foreign mining investment.

Dominican Republic

As in Panama, in the Dominican Republic too, areas where Antigonish-inspired cooperatives were strong gave rise to the first Christian base communities. In the northern parishes run by the Quebec Pères du Sacré-Coeur, a Canadian-initiated cooperative movement had spread in the 1940s and 1950s, as described earlier. In 1967 the bishop of Santiago Roque Adames, supported by the Quebecois priests, created the first Dominican ecclesial base communities in this region, headed by lay leaders known as *presidentes de asamblea* (assembly presidents), which were a model for other countries.[51]

48. See Penny Lernoux, *Cry of the People: The Struggle for Human Rights in Latin America—The Catholic Church in Conflict with U.S. Policy* (New York: Penguin Books, 1982), 123–34, on Veraguas.

49. LADOC "Keyhole" Series, No. 14 "Hector Gallego: Martyr for Justice. Five Vignettes of Him and his Work" in *Basic Christian Communities* (Washington, D.C.: USCC—Latin America Documentation, 1976), 45–56.

50. See the website of Fundación Héctor Gallego/Desde Tierras de Veraguas, www.fundacióngallego.wordpress.com.

51. On Dominican "presidentes de asamblea," see Roque Adames, "San Juan de las Matas

Guatemala

For an understanding of the church-promoted cooperative movement in the western indigenous highlands, Susan Fitzpatrick-Behren's chapter in this volume, and her forthcoming book, are key. Here, I merely wish to indicate that close connections existed between Antigonish and the Christian social movement that took root among Mayan peasants in Guatemala in the 1960s and 1970s. Between 1962 and 1964, a committed Spanish missionary from Galicia and several socially minded Guatemalan laypeople studied at the Coady Institute, as did some U.S. Maryknoll nuns and priests over the years. The theses that the young Spaniard and Guatemalans wrote in Spanish, deposited in this small town in Nova Scotia, shed compelling light on the ideas, practices, and organizations of an important Christian social movement in its infancy as Guatemalans began to take an active role.

Theses from the Coady Institute's "Social Leadership" program authored by Luis Gurriarán López, the Spanish parish priest of Sta. Cruz del Quiché (1963) and by Oscar Humberto Enríquez Guerra of Quetzaltenango (1964) are particularly substantive and passionate. An important promoter of the cooperative movement in Guatemala, Gurriarán sent community activists from Sololá and northern Quiché to study at Antigonish in the late 1960s and 1970s, while Enríquez Guerra founded and for many years directed the cooperative training center (Centro de Adiestramiento de Promotores Sociales, or CAPS) at the Catholic Universidad Rafael Landivar in Guatemala City. Both Gurriarán López and Enríquez Guerra remained in close touch with the Coady Institute, and Enríquez returned to Antigonish to teach once or twice in the summer program. In association with CAPS, Father Alex MacKinnon flew down from Antigonish to give workshops on cooperatives to catechists and local community leaders from all over the country during the 1970s and the 1980s, the years of violence.[52] Fitzpatrick-

---

in the Dominican Republic," in LADOC "Keyhole" Series, no. 14, *Basic Christian Communities* (Washington, D.C.: USCC-Latin America Documentation, 1976), 24–26; and Yves Labbé, *El clero y las vocaciones sacerdotales en la República Dominicana* (Santo Domingo: Amigo del Hogar, 1976), 191–204. A detailed study of a cooperative in this area of the country is Kenneth Evan Sharpe, *Peasant Politics: Struggle in a Dominican Village* (Baltimore: Johns Hopkins University Press, 1977).

52. See "Index of Seminars, Short Courses, and Workshops Conducted in Latin America 1976–1991," MML, Coady International Institute.

Behrens's forthcoming book dealing with the Guatemalan Catholic cooperative movement shows how it became increasingly important economically, radical, and independent of the government over time and how, in the 1980s, the Guatemalan military particularly targeted local co-op leaders as subversives.[53]

Ecuador

Like Guatemala, Ecuador is a country with a large rural indigenous population. At the same time that USAID and the Ecuadorian government were creating an official, government-sponsored credit union and cooperative program,[54] the bishops of Riobamba and Ibarra and a number of activist local priests with a Coady staff member as adviser, plunged into cooperatives as a church-sponsored social program. In Ecuador the 1960s was a period of important agrarian reform and rural development initiatives spearheaded by the Alliance for Progress and Plan Andino, the Ecuadorian government, and the Catholic Church through the initiative of a few progressive bishops, the most well known of whom was Leonidas Proaño Villalba of Riobamba, who later became a significant figure in the Liberation theology movement.[55] When the Ecuadorian government passed its agrarian reform law, bishops in the provinces of Chimborazo (diocese of Riobamba), Azuay, Imbabura (diocese of Ibarra), and Pinchincha carried out their

53. On Guatemala, see Susan Fitzpatrick-Behren's chapter in this book, as well as Fitzpatrick-Behrens and LeGrand, "Canadian and U.S. Catholic Promotion of Co-operatives in Central America and the Caribbean." In the Independent Study Collection of MML, there are ten theses written by Guatemalans and by Spanish and North American missionaries who were headed to Guatemala in the 1960s and 1970s. These include Gurriarán's thesis titled "Horizontes de Luz" (DGD1) and Enriquez Guerra's titled "Templo de Sagradas Enseñanzas de los Justos Ideales Cristianas" (DGD4), both of which connect the ideals of the Antigonish Movement to descriptions of conditions in their home communities and projects for social change.

54. See Gonzalo Hallo, "Educational Program for Cooperativo de Ahorro y Crédito S. Francisco Ltd.: From Ambato-Ecuador," Diploma Program, Coady International Institute, 1990, MML, DE8. This thesis, by an Ecuadorian student, provides an excellent history of the Ecuadorian cooperative and credit union movement, with particular emphasis on the impact of the Alliance for Progress.

55. See Lernoux, *Cry of the People*, 137–53; Francisco Enríquez Bermeo, ed., *Leonidas Proaño, obispo de los pobres* (Quito: Editorial El Conejo, 1989); Luis Maria Gavilanes del Castillo, *Monseñor Leonidas Proaño y su misión profético-liberadora en la iglesia de América latina* (Quito: Fondo Ecuatoriano Populorum Progressio, 1992); and Leonidas Proaño, *Creo en el hombre y en la comunidad: Autobiografía* (Quito: Editora Nacional, 1989). Proaño is known as a pioneer of indigenous theology in Latin America.

own land distribution, subdividing more than forty thousand acres of church-owned haciendas and encouraging peasant land recipients to form cooperatives. In 1961–1962 MISEREOR funded five Ecuadorians to study at the Coady International Institute: these included the diocesan pastoral secretaries of Riobamba and Ambato, the program director of the newly formed church Center for Study and Social Action (Centro de Estudios y Acción Social, or CEAS) in Riobamba,[56] the director of cooperatives of the diocese of Carchi, and the director of education of the Savings and Loan Cooperative Federation (Federación de Cooperativas de Ahorro y Crédito, or FECOAC), an organization created in 1962 by the church and supported by the Alliance for Progress (Punto IV), CUNA International, and the Peace Corps to bring together credit unions promoted by CARITAS-Ecuador and Catholic Relief Services.[57]

Meanwhile in May 1961 Kevin LeMorvan, a young British layman who had studied at St. Francis Xavier University, was sponsored by CARITAS Ecuador and Catholic Relief Services to go to Ecuador to write instructional booklets and offer courses on cooperatives, especially in the northern diocese of Ibarra where a peasant training institute had just been created, and also in Quito. In 1961–1962, in his letters back to the Coady Institute, LeMorvan spoke positively of cooperatives as a brake on communism and of the possibilities of obtaining funding from the Alliance for Progress and the ILO to underwrite the Ecuadorian cooperative movement.[58]

Characteristic of the 1960s in Ecuador, enthusiasm for cooperatives was especially strong in the Sierra, whereas on the coast church was less influential and labor unions more important. However, cooperatives met some resistance from indigenous beneficiaries of land reform, and around 1970 CEAS in Riobamba moved on to other approaches, specifically Freirian-type popular education. Bishop Proaño began to promote radio school broadcasts in Quechua on the Colombian Radio Sutatenza model, lay catechists, and Christian base

---

56. In 1960 the ILO suggested that Bishop Proaño contact the Belgian sociologist Rudolf Reszohazy, a professor at Université Catholique de Louvain, who wanted to work in social action and development in Latin America. Together with local students from Reszohazy's class on social doctrine in the diocese, Bishop Proaño and Reszohazy founded CEAS in 1960, and it is still active today. On the history and present activities of CEAS, see http://CEAS-ecuador.weebly.com.

57. StFXUA RG 62/1/395-97 and 412–15.

58. See StFXUA, RG50-2/3/229, 236, 240, 249, and 255.

communities. Anthropologist Barry Lyons describes an emphasis on forming indigenous community leaders and promoting community authority and indigenous solidarity.[59] Yet Giuseppina Da Ros indicates that in the 1970s progressive Ecuadorian bishops emphasized the formation of cooperatives, and in her field study of Catholic social experiments around 1980, Penny Lernoux says she found 120 cooperatives in the diocese of Riobamba; she writes that cooperatives are one manifestation of *organizaciones de base,* one form of community organization, popular action, and the education of people.[60]

Venezuela

Finally we come to Venezuela, where, like Guatemala, a major cooperative movement took form, spearheaded by graduates of St. Francis Xavier University. In 1958 a Venezuelan priest from Falcón state, José Elias Thielen, went to study at Antigonish and was enthused by what he saw. Father Thielen launched the first Catholic cooperative pilot project in Paraguaná peninsula (Falcón) in 1960 and then, in 1963, with financial support from the Venezuelan Ministry of Agriculture and Livestock and the Ministry of Labor, established an Extension Department and Center for Cooperative Studies on the Antigonish model in the faculty of economics at Universidad de los Andes in Mérida.[61] Kevin LeMorvan became assistant director in 1963, and continued working in Mérida for more than twenty years. Thielen translated Moses Coady's seminal book *Masters of their Own Destiny* into Spanish; published in Argentina in 1964, it was distributed in Venezuela.[62]

59. Barry J. Lyons, *Remembering the Hacienda: Religion, Authority and Social Change in Highland Ecuador* (Austin: University of Texas Press, 2006).

60. Lernoux, *Cry of the People,* 150–51; Giuseppina Da Ros, "El movimiento cooperativo en el Ecuador: Visión histórica, situación actual y perspectivas," *CIRIEC-España, Revista de Economía Pública, Social y Cooperativa,* no. 57 (April 2007): 249–84. Da Ros is an economist-researcher at the Centro de Estudios Cooperativos de la Pontificia Universidad Católica del Ecuador (CEC-PUCE), established in 1981 with support from MISEREOR.

61. Universidad de los Andes is the largest public university in Andean Venezuela. The Center that Father Thielan created continues to exist: it is now known as CIRIEC-Venezuela (Centro interdisciplinario de investigación, formación y documentación de la economía cooperativa, social y pública) and publishes the journal *CAYAPA: Revista Venezolana de Economía Social* (see www.ciriec.ula.ve). For Thielen's correspondence with the Coady Institute, see StFXUA, RG 50-2/3/410, 402, 404, 419.

62. Father Thielen's translation of Coady's work is titled *Dueños de su propio destino: Una experiencia de educación de masas. Historia del Movimiento de Antigonish, una acción educativa por medio de la cooperación económica* (Buenos Aires: Intercoop Editora Cooperativa Ltda., 1964).

Father Thielen and his collaborators at the Extension Department encouraged people in many *municipios* (counties) of Mérida state to form study groups and cooperatives; his correspondence with Frank Smyth in Antigonish and several theses at the Coady Institute authored by Venezuelan priests who worked with Father Thielen in the early 1960s indicate that the cooperative movement in western Venezuela, supported by the Alliance for Progress, took on momentum quickly.[63] Father Thielen and Kevin LeMorvan maintained close relations with the Coady Institute: in the 1970s and 1980s, LeMorvan, sponsored by the Coady Institute, took short trips from his base in Venezuela throughout Latin America with Father Alex MacKinnon to give workshops on cooperativism, popular adult education, and community development and in the summer of 1971, Thielen returned to the Coady Institute to teach in a seven-week summer social leadership course in Spanish coordinated by LeMorvan.[64]

In 1963–1964 Father José Luis Echeverria and two other young Jesuit priests, associates of Father Thielen, studied for eight months at the Coady Institute; together, they wrote an illuminating thesis on the fledgling Venezuelan cooperative movement and how they intended to apply their understanding of the Antigonish Movement back home.[65] The Venezuelans were particularly taken with the adult education focus of the Antigonish Movement and the idea that universities must "serve the people" in promoting the emergence of local lay leaders in rural communities.

On returning to Venezuela, one of the Jesuits, Ricardo Silguero,

---

Intercoop Editora in Buenos Aires reissued it in 1975 and Politécnica Grancolombiana in Bogotá in 2010.

63. See social leadership theses authored by Venezuelan students at the Coady Institute, 1964–1967 (DV1, 2, 3, 5 and 6, in MML); and Belkis A. Rojas V., "CORANDES desde la perspectiva de una historia de vida," *Cayapa: Revista Venezolana de Economía Social* 1, no. 1 (May 2001): 1–11. According to Rojas V., during the 1960s small cooperatives and networks among them propagated throughout Andean Venezuela, and teachers from the Center for Cooperative Studies gave courses for local leaders in Barinas (H. Chavez's birthplace), Maracaibo, and Caracas. Coady Institute records indicate that twenty-three Venezuelans studied in Antigonish between 1958 and 1964.

64. See Coady International Institute, "Index to Seminars, Short Courses and Workshops Conducted in Latin America, 1976–1991," in MML and the workshop reports, mostly authored by A. McKinnon and/or K. LeMorvan, in StFXUA: http://coadyextension.stfx.ca/people/grads (on Thielen) and *Coady International Institute Newsletter* 4, no. 3 (August 1971): StFXUA RG 30/97/21/778.

65. Social Leadership thesis DV1, MML.

worked with and, in 1972, became director of "Radio Occidente," a radio
station established by the Archdiocese of Mérida in 1961 on the model
of Colombia's Radio Sutatenza—discussed in Mary Roldan's chapter in
this volume—to be the "base of a process of *campesino* [peasant] literacy
and training."[66] Meanwhile Father José Luis Echeverria, with several
other Jesuits, chose in 1964 to settle in Barquisimeto in the state of Lara,
a central place in the Andes with a Jesuit high school and a bishop interested in social action, where they hoped to have an impact that would
radiate out to the six surrounding states. These priests, who called themselves *los sociales* (socially committed) began to form cooperatives in the
barrios of Barquisimeto and then in the countryside. In 1968 they affiliated with the Jesuit Centro Gumilla in Caracas and were henceforth
known as Centro Gumilla-Barquisimeto, an independent Jesuit organization that from 1964 until 2006 was dedicated to creating cooperatives
that encouraged local people to come together to define their own problems and act on them, learning along the way to analyze their social realities, articulate their needs, and take action to improve their economic
situation.[67]

66. See Berta Brito, "'Radio Occidente': Modelo de radiodifusión al servicio del desarrollo,"
in *Comunicación: Estudios venezolanos de comunicación* (Caracas: Centro Gumilla, 1986), http://
gumilla.org/biblioteca/bases/biblo/texto/COM198655_42-46.pdf, and Jeremiah O'Sullivan-
Ryan, Irene Cordova, and Ricardo Gondelles, "Radio occidente," in *Alternativas comunicaciona-
les en Venezuela: Experiencias* (Caracas: Editorial Universidad Católica Andrés Bello, 1989), 203–
19, http://saber.ucab.edu.ve/handle/123456789/31207. While, as Mary Roldán shows, Radio
Sutatenza originated in Colombia in 1947, the spread of this Colombian model of alternative
communication and adult literacy training to other Latin American countries seems mainly to
have occurred in the 1960s through the initiative of priests and bishops devising new forms of
social action promoting local development from below. Church radio stations that attempted to
replicate what Radio Sutatenza had done were set up in the Archdiocese of Mérida (Venezuela)
in 1961, by Quebec missionary priests in Choluteca (Honduras) in the same year, and by Bishop Proaño in Riobamba (Ecuador) in 1962. Brito, writing in the 1980s, mentions the existence
of forty-two such Catholic radio stations in seventeen Latin American countries. The Medellín
Bishops' Conference of 1968 explicitly addressed the issue of media and communications: see
section 16, "Mass Media," in the Second General Conference of Latin American Bishops, *The
Church in the Present-Day Transformation of Latin America in the Light of the Council*, vol. 2, *Conclusions* (Washington, D.C., USCC–Division for Latin America, 1970–1973), 212–17.

67. See Nelson Freitez, "El cooperativismo en el Estado Lara, Venezuela, en los años de
1960: Promoción religiosa y crisis política," *Cayapa. Revista Venezolana de Economía Social*, 7,
no. 13 (Jan.-June 2007), 76–104; the website of Centro Gumilla (http://www.gumilla.org) on
the history of the Jesuit center in Barquisimeto; and Jorge Coque Martínez, "Las cooperativas
en América Latina: Visión histórica general y comentario de algunos países tipo," *CIRIEC-España, revista de economía pública, social y cooperativa*, no. 43, extraordinario (November 2002):
145–72. Centro Gumilla was founded in 1968 as the Centro de Investigación y Acción Social de
la Sociedad de Jesús in Venezuela.

236 ❖ Catherine C. LeGrand

In the early 1960s, the Jiménez Pérez dictatorship was over, Venezuela experienced a political opening and the Democratic Action government, in conjunction with the Alliance for Progress, espoused agrarian reform. Like in Ecuador, the government promoted cooperatives for
recipients of agrarian reform land, but the government program was
bureaucratic and top down. Meanwhile, the state of Lara experienced
heightened social tensions; a guerrilla movement was active there. It
was the Jesuit-promoted cooperatives that took root: they had a mobilizing, participatory, grassroots social vision. Daniel Levine's rich study
Popular Voices in Latin American Catholicism (1992) singles out Barquisimeto as a place where, in the 1970s and 1980s, active, self-determining, participatory Catholic groups and movements took form, relatively
autonomous of the church hierarchy, and he provides concrete insight
into how changes in beliefs (consciousness), practices, and organization
associated with local cooperatives and practical adult education fed into
popular Catholicism that became, in this place, a social movement.[68]
In 1967 the cooperatives of Lara created a federation—CECOSESOLA
(Central Cooperativa de Servicios Sociales de Lara)—that is considered
Venezuela's most successful cooperative among those created before
Hugo Chávez came to power. Today the federation comprises a network
of eighty agricultural, consumer, transport, health care, and funerary
cooperatives and credit unions with two hundred thousand members.
Articles celebrating CECOSESOLA's fortieth anniversary point to Lara's
cooperative movement as having given rise to a culture of cooperation
and participation unique in Venezuela.[69]

CONCLUSION

I have focused here on an important Catholic social action movement
that came out of the Catholic rural and mining region of eastern Nova
Scotia just prior to and during the Great Depression and eventually

68. Daniel H. Levine, *Popular Voices in Latin American Catholicism* (Princeton, N.J.: Princeton University Press, 1992).
69. See CECOSESOLA's website, http://cecosesola.org; "El cooperativismo recoge su me-
jor cosecha en Lara," *Actualidad*, January 2, 2011, http://www.ultimasnoticias.com.ve/noticias/
actualidad; Agencia Bolivariana de Noticias, "Cooperativismo larense construye democracia
participativa desde hace 40 años," March 7, 2006, http://www.aporrea.org/endogeno/n80219
.html; and Michael Fox, "CECOSESOLA: Four Decades of Independent Struggle for a Venezuelan Cooperative," July 11, 2006, http://venezuelanalysis.com/print/1793.

spread across the breadth of Latin America.[70] The Antigonish Movement modeled endogenous, self-determining, holistic, grassroots development through popular education and community self-help. Observers in the 1970s called this human or integral development. The vision was of a Christian social order based on wide distribution of property and the common good—a moral economy promoting justice, equality, local leadership, and respect for the capacity of common people. Critical both of free market capitalism and state-centered socialism, the Antigonish Movement called for structural transformation: it was a kind of utopian vision—partially realized in Nova Scotia in the 1930s and 1940s—of an egalitarian, just economic brotherhood, with leaders who emerged from local study groups to articulate the concerns of their neighbors and were responsible to them.[71] It should be noted that conditions in Nova Scotia in the 1920s and 1930s were, in some ways, similar to Latin America at mid-century: primary producers exploited by middlemen and foreign corporations and rural communities sapped by poverty and out-migration.

In the years after World War II, the U.S. government, the British Colonial Office, the United Nations, and other national and international organizations espoused cooperatives as an aspect of local development and as a possible bulwark against communism.[72] At the same time, large numbers of North American Catholic missionaries began to work in Latin America, and the Antigonish Movement became widely known, its influence spreading in the United States, the Caribbean, and Mexico. How this happened varied from place to place:

70. The Antigonish Movement also had offshoots in India, Sri Lanka, Nepal, the Philippines, Taiwan, Korea, Indonesia (in the early years), Nigeria, Ghana, Kenya, Tanzania, Uganda, and elsewhere. See Milner, ed., *Human Development through Social Change*; and personal communication from Catherine Irving, Marie Michael Library, November 14, 2014.

71. According to Roberto Montesinos, "The faculties of the cooperative form of organization were praised by the hierarchy of the church ... who recognized in cooperativism a way of understanding the economy most in line with the Christian concepts of man and community." See Montesinos, "Dos historias del trabajo," in *Una lectura sociológica de la Venezuela actual*, vol. 4 (Caracas: Konrad Adenauer Stiftung-Universidad Católica Andrés Bello, 2008), 58.

72. See Sheila Gorst, *Co-operative Organization in Tropical Countries: A Study of Co-operative Development in Non-self-governing Territories under United Kingdom Administration, 1945–1955* (Oxford: Basil Blackwell, 1959); Rita Rhodes, *Empire and Co-operation: How the British Empire Used Co-operatives in Its Development Strategies, 1900–1970* (Edinburgh: John Donald, 2012); and Rodrigo Mogrovejo, Alberto Mora, and Philippe Vanhuynegem, eds., *El cooperativismo en América latina: Una diversidad de contribuciones al desarrollo sostenible* (La Paz, Bolivia: Oficina Regional de la Organización International del Trabajo (OIT) para América Latina y el Caribe, 2012), 40.

Catholic and secular networks intermeshed in complex ways. In training development workers and forging connections with Latin American governments and experts, the Canadian and U.S. governments and international organizations drew on the knowledge and extensive contacts of Catholic organizations and missionaries. This was particularly obvious during the 1960s.[73]

The Antigonish Movement and the Coady International Institute were not a Catholic missionary enterprise, yet the close ties of Canadian and other foreign missionaries with Latin America and the years they spent living in rural communities and in close contact with Latin American laypeople and clergy there shaped their worldviews and their ideas about social and economic change. Many who spent time in Central America, Brazil, and some other parts of South America became more radical, including Quebecers who came from a conservative church back home.[74] Various socially minded missionaries (and former missionaries, such as Father Alexander McKinnon) played crucial roles in linking the Antigonish Movement to specific areas of Latin America and providing the linguistic and practical knowhow in adult consciousness-raising education, the training of community leaders and organization of cooperatives to build close, ongoing, interactive relationships with people in Latin America.

The transfer of the Antigonish Movement to Latin America was not imposed by North Americans on the South. Indeed, Latin Americans through their own initiative, or that of church or secular organizations in their countries, came to study what was going on in eastern Nova Scotia before the creation of the Coady Institute, and many more arrived in the 1960s and 1970s. Furthermore, scores of community activists from Central America and later South America studied at the Instituto Cooperativo Interamericano, established by Scarboro Harvey Steele in Panama City to give monolingual Spanish speakers access to the Antigonish approach. Many of the initiators of the Catholic social cooperative movements that were particularly successful—those of Mexico, Guatemala, and Venezuela—were local priests who studied at

---

73. See Macpherson, *Hands around the Globe*, 58, 69–70, 108–09; Ruth Compton Brouwer, "When Missions Became Development: Ironies of 'NGOization' in Mainstream Canadian Churches in the 1960s," *The Canadian Historical Review* 91, no. 4 (December 2010), 661–93; and *Globe: Revue internationale d'études québécoises* 12, no. 1 (2009): special issue on "Missions and Development."

74. LeGrand, "L'axe missionnaire catholique entre le Québec et l'Amérique latine."

and were inspired by Antigonish and then returned home to do grass-roots organizing.

Susan Fitzpatrick-Behrens has argued that Franklin Delano Roosevelt's New Deal was in some ways influenced by Catholic thinking,[75] so, it seems, was John F. Kennedy's Alliance for Progress, which drew on the New Deal and on reformist ideas coming out of Jucelino Kubitschek's Brazil, the Christian Democratic Party of Chile, and perhaps Antigonish (recall that J. F. Kennedy was on the board of the Friends of Antigonish in the 1950s). The Alliance for Progress was for macro planning, yet it also had a strong community development aspect and promoted cooperatives, particularly in areas of agrarian reform. During this time the U.S. and Canadian governments drew on the networks and practice of Catholic organizations and clergy to initiate cooperative programs in collaboration with Latin American ministries, programs that in the end were generally not successful because they were implemented in a bureaucratic, top-down manner.[76] They did not include the mobilizing, grassroots educational dimension characteristic of the Antigonish Movement or of Radio Sutatenza.[77] In contrast cooperatives promoted by progressive bishops and local priests were much more likely to be viable in the long run and even turn into social movements because priest-organizers were known and trusted in their communities and had the education, outside contacts and access to resources to bring social action programs to life.[78] In the early 1960s, clergy and church-initiated organizations—even progressive ones—often welcomed financial support from the Alliance for Progress/USAID and the help of Peace Corps volunteers, and some (e.g., the Mérida

75. See Susan Fitzpatrick-Behrens, "Catholic Good Neighbors: The Maryknoll Mission and Latin America," unpublished paper.

76. In the late 1960s, the United Nations Research Institute for Social Development sponsored a major study of rural cooperatives as "agents of planned change" in Latin America, Africa, and Asia under the direction of Colombian sociologist Orlando Fals Borda. The five case studies of cooperatives in South America shed light on problems with government-promoted cooperatives in areas of land redistribution and also on troubles with Church cooperatives initiated by Catholic Action in two conservative *municipios* (counties) in the Department of Antioquia (Colombia). See R. Puch, S. Rivera, M.T. Findji, C. Fonnseca, A. Barreto, H. Ochoa, and J.M. Rojas, *Estudios de la realidad campesina: Cooperación y cambio. Informes y materiales de campo recogidos en Venezuela, Ecuador y Colombia* (Geneva: UNRISD, 1970); and Orlando Fals Borda, *Cooperatives and Rural Development in Latin America: An Analytic Report* (Geneva: UNRISD, 1971). The UNRISD investigation did not study the Antigonish-inspired cooperatives.

77. See Mary Roldán's chapter in this volume.

78. The Venezuelan Jesuits made this point in their 1964 Coady Institute thesis (MML, DV1).

and Barquisimeto Jesuits in Venezuela) began to train government employees from the Latin American ministries that implemented cooperative projects.

In this chapter, I contrasted government ideas about the utility of cooperatives during the cold war with the social movements that emerged out of progressive Catholicism in some parts of Latin America during the 1960s, the period when Liberation theology was taking form. Yet perhaps these perspectives deserve, rather, to be brought into dialogue with each other around the issue of what "community" and what "development" meant to different groups and people during the 1960s (and 1940s and 1950s), and how these relate to cooperatives.

Cooperatives are an important part of working-class history, yet, in contrast to labor unions, they have been little studied.[79] The Canadian and U.S. governments had development and also strategic (anticommunist) concerns in supporting the formation of credit unions and cooperatives during the cold war and—to an extent—in supporting the expansion of the Antigonish Movement overseas. Yet progressive thinkers within the Catholic Church, both in the so-called developed world and in the global South, were also concerned with development in the 1950s and 1960s; they drew on what the social sciences had to offer; and they wrestled with what "human" or "integral" or "social" development should mean, as opposed to crass economic materialism or consumerism.[80] It is said that Gustavo Gutiérrez had thought of calling his path-breaking book "A Theology of Development," but he instead chose "A Theology of Liberation" because he espoused a humanistic approach that emphasized that the poor must be self-determining and self-reliant; that they themselves must act from the grassroots to solve their problems and church people should accompany them in this. In specific local contexts, within the larger context of the cold war, these various approaches intermeshed and clashed in various ways and took different political and spiritual turns.

In his study of the Quebec missionary Gérard Cambron in Latin

---

79. Marcel van der Linden, *Workers of the World: Essays toward a Global Labor History* (Leiden: Brill, 2008), underlines this point.

80. See Milner, ed., *Human Development through Social Change*; Denis Pelletier, *"Economie et Humanisme": De l'utopie communautaire au combat pour le tiers-monde (1941–1966)* (Paris: Les Editions du Cerf, 1996); and Ludovic Bertina, "The Catholic Doctrine of 'Integral Human Development' and its Influence on the International Development Community," in *International Development Policy: Religion and Development*, ed. Gilles Carbonnier (Basingstoke: Palgrave Macmillan, 2013).

America, Yves Carrier puts forth the idea that the late 1950s and 1960s were a time of transition in some regions of Latin America between a traditional church, in which church institutions and the sacraments were primary, toward the decentralized, lay, base communities that connected spirituality to socioeconomic and political transformation in the here and now. He suggests that an emphasis on cooperatives in Latin America and on missionary engagement with Latin American realities through intercultural training, exemplified by Ivan Illich's CI-DOC in Mexico and CENFI in Brazil, were characteristic of this transitional time.[81] I concur with Carrier; in this chapter, I have endeavored to show how cooperatives in the conception and practice of the Antigonish Movement were embryonic Christian base communities that, in some areas of Latin America, generated a proliferation of activist, grassroots, lay groups and popular initiatives imbued with a temporal spirituality of active citizenship, mutuality, and social justice. Father José Luis Echeverria of *los sociales* of Barquisimeto wrote in 1963 that, whereas the Venezuelan cooperative movement drew its ideas and practices from CUNA International and from Antigonish, the Antigonish Movement was particularly motivating because of its *mística* (spirituality, mystique) and *filosofía social* (social philosophy). By the 1960s, though study groups had died out in Nova Scotia and field stays in local communities were no longer part of the Coady Institute's training, the history of the Antigonish Movement continued to be inspiring. Eastern Nova Scotia and the Antigonish Movement of the 1930s through the 1950s had become a myth, a utopian Catholic vision of lay activism and the good socioeconomic order that informed some early expressions of Liberation theology in Latin America.[82] In some places studied in this chapter where cooperatives were implanted in the 1960s, ecclesial

81. Carrier, *Lettre du Brésil*, 11. On the social sciences, André Corten writes, "Liberation Theology was born in the context (anti-communist) of the development of sociology in Latin America, a development partially tributary to the Alliance for Progress. It was also part of the extension of the JOC (Young Christian Workers) of Msgr. Cardijn present in Latin America since the 1930s." See Corten, "Une mise en réseau de la Théologie de la Libération," in *La modernité religieuse en perspective comparée: Europe latine-Amérique latine*, ed. Jean-Pierre Bastian (Paris: Karthala, 2001), 267.

82. Michael R. Welton, *Little Mosie from the Margaree: A Biography of Moses Michael Coady* (Toronto: Thompson Educational Publishing, 2001) emphasizes the mythical dimensions of the Antigonish Movement. Aldiva Sales Diniz and Bruce Gilbert, "Socialist Values and Cooperation in Brazil's Landless Rural Workers' Movement," *Latin American Perspectives* 40, no. 4 (2013): 19–34, explores the notion of *mística* as a motivating factor in social movements, specifically the Brazilian MST.

base communities proliferated in the 1970s. In other locales described earlier, cooperatives became social movements from which other popular organizations were offshoots.

It is worthwhile to note the number of prominent figures associated with Latin American Liberation theology who had antecedents of ties to the Antigonish Movement. For three progressive bishops who played key roles in organizing the conferences and workshops that produced the practice of Liberation theology, the Antigonish Movement provided one step on their larger trajectories. These bishops were first, Manuel Larraín of Talca, Chile, who played an important role in spearheading the Christian Democratic Party's agrarian reform of the 1960s and who was an intimate of Dom Helder Camara of Brazil: together they conceived of and organized the 1968 Medellín Latin American Bishops' Conference.[83] The others were Marcos McGrath of Panama and Leonidas Proaño of Ecuador. All three sent young people from their countries to study at Antigonish, and Larraín and McGrath corresponded with the Coady Institute in the early 1960s. Other important progressives such as Ivan Illich and Gérard Cambron also maintained close contact with the Coady Institute.

AFTERWORD

In Argentina and most cities of the Southern Cone of Latin America, the first credit unions and cooperatives were formed by European immigrant workers from Spain and Italy who brought with them European socialist and anarchist traditions. But in Mexico, Central America, and the northern and Andean regions of South America, Catholic cooperativism, often connected in some way with the Antigonish Movement of Nova Scotia, was of central importance in the 1940s through the 1970s. As this chapter indicates, many of the organizations formed in this period that began by promoting cooperatives continue to exist today.

In various places, cooperatives morphed into "community development" with an emphasis on endogenous, self-determining human development—the social economy, the sustainable economy that values

83. See Hannah W. Stewart-Gambino, *The Church and Politics in the Chilean Countryside* (Boulder, Colo.: Westview Press, 1992). Bishop Larraín died prematurely in 1966 in an automobile accident.

local communities and refuses to divorce the economic from environmental, social and ethical/spiritual concerns. This approach is evident in Brazil's Landless Rural Worker's Movement (the MST), which has Catholic roots; see, too, the websites of the Instituto Cooperativo Interamericano and the Coady International Institute today.[84]

Sociologist Dario Azzellini suggests that the Catholic community activists from Mérida and Barquisimeto who, in the second half of the twentieth century, "adopted co-operation as a tool for social transformation" provided a precedent for Hugo Chávez's vision of "Socialism for the 21st Century." The Chávez government's stated aim before his death was that of replacing the bourgeois state with a "communal state," to consolidate an economy based on self-administered productive units, promoted by the state. According to Azzellini, "[t]his strategy is oriented by a model of radical endogenous development—sustainable development based on local resources and potentials," which Chávez supporters refer to as the "solidarity-based," "popular" or "communal" economy. From 2004 on, the Chávez government actively promoted the spread of cooperatives through the Ministry for the Popular Economy.[85] As portrayed by Azzellini, Hugo Chávez's objectives resonate with Moses Coady's radical project of social and economic transformation of the 1930s that instead of maximizing individual profits according to capitalistic logic would satisfy individuals' aspirations for full human development by working for the common good of people in communities.

Despite all this, too little attention has been paid by scholars to religion, faith and development.[86] Further research is needed about Catholic

84. www.icipan.org and www.coady.stfx.ca.

85. See Superintendencia Nacional de Cooperativas (SUNACOOP), Ministerio para la Economía Popular, "Informe de la República Bolivariana de Venezuela: Cooperativismo en Venezuela," April 2006; and Dario Azzellini, "From Cooperatives to Enterprises of Direct Social Property in the Venezuelan Process," in *Cooperatives and Socialism: A View from Cuba*, ed. Camila Pineiro Harnecker (New York: Palgrave-Macmillan, 2013), 259–75. Azzellini defines the Venezuelan concept of "popular economy" as "a type of economy that is not principally oriented toward the production of surplus value, but instead toward equality through decent remuneration and collective ownership or management, as well as solidarity among workers and toward communities" (273n1).

86. This seems to be a relatively new area for investigation. See Gilles Carbonnier, ed., *International Development Policy: Religion and Development* (Basingstoke: Palgrave Macmillan, 2013); *Canadian Journal of Development Studies/Revue Canadienne d'études du développement* 34, no. 2 (2013): Special Issue: "Religion and International Development"; Andrea Parras, "CIDA's Secular Fiction and Canadian Faith-Based Organisations," *Canadian Journal of Development*

thought and activist initiatives of the pre–Vatican II period concerning capitalism, socioeconomic organization, and societal transformation; the European, North American, and Latin American contributions to this area of Catholic concern; and the exchanges that occurred.

Studies/Revue canadienne d'études du développement 33, no. 2 (June 2012): 231–49; Peter Ernest Baltutis, "Forging the Link between Faith and Development: The History of the Canadian Catholic Organization for Development and Peace, 1957–1982," PhD diss., St. Michael's College Faculty of Theology, University of Toronto, 2012; and Robert Calderisi, *Earthly Mission: The Catholic Church and World Development* (New Haven, Conn.: Yale University Press, 2013).

CHAPTER 10

Popular Cultural Action, Catholic Transnationalism, and Development in Colombia before Vatican II

❖ Mary Roldán

This chapter examines the history and development of Popular Cultural Action (Acción Cultural Popular, or ACPO), the multipronged project of Christian revitalization, local empowerment, and community-
based development whose radio education network, Radio Sutatenza,
founded by a Colombian parish priest in 1947 to address rural adult
illiteracy, became Latin America's first Catholic radio network and the
model for media-based rural education and community development
programs in twenty-four countries throughout Latin America, Asia,
and Africa. In nearly a half century of existence, ACPO published and
distributed more than six million *cartillas* (illustrated instructional
manuals) for its five-point "Fundamental Integral Education" (EFI)
program, which included Alphabet, Numbers, Health, Economy and
Work, and Practical Spirituality; distributed seventy-six million copies
of the newspaper *El Campesino*; received and answered 1.2 million letters from rural listeners and readers; graduated twenty-three thousand
Colombian and foreign radio auxiliaries and community leaders from
its training institutes; logged 1.4 million hours of educational broadcasting; and pressed 690,000 records.[1] By 1990, when ACPO was
forced to shutter its press and record-cutting studios and sell off its

1. Hernando Bernal Alarcón, "Radio Sutatenza: Un modelo colombiano de industria cultural y educativo," http://www.banrepocultural.org/radiosutatenza/textos/radio-sutatenza-un
-modelo-colombiano-de-industria-cultura-y-educativa.
   Boletín Cultural y Bibliográfico 46, no. 82 (2012): 5–41; Emile G. McAnany, "Radio's Role
in Development: Five Strategies of Use," Institute for Communication Research, Stanford University, 1973, http://pdf.usaid.gov/pdf_docs/PNAAD453.pdf.

radio network and buildings, it had a presence in hundreds of rural parishes stretched across the length and breadth of Colombia, and its broadcasts and educational materials were frequently acknowledged as inspiration for many a professional of rural origin.[2]

ACPO was but one among many other Colombian projects inspired by Leo XIII's *Rerum novarum* (1891) and spearheaded by both laypeople and clergy that emerged in the period before Vatican II to redress long-standing social, economic, and cultural inequalities made more acute in the first half of the twentieth century by the specter of totalitarianism, economic crisis, rural migration, urbanization, and incipient industrialization.[3] This chapter traces the history of ACPO between 1947 and 1962. It grew from modest origins, conducting adult rural literacy work and basic community-centered development in three small, Central Andean settlements supported by local in-kind contributions and a small diocesan subsidy. Gradually, it would expand into a multimedia-based educational juggernaut with transnational influence, partners, and funding lauded by Pope Pius XII in a 1953 Vatican Radio broadcast heard throughout Latin America. By the late 1950s, ACPO was held as the model for Catholic-directed, radio-based rural education and community development.[4]

ACPO's success and eventual influence beyond Colombia's borders was partly the result of Catholic transnational activism occurring in the decades before Vatican II. Efforts to redress the excesses of unrestrained capitalism and to build a community based in papal encyclicals such as *Rerum novarum* or *Quadragesimo anno*, even when they stopped short of advocating the kind of structural, grassroots Christian base community approach embraced by Liberation theology, I suggest, laid the foundations for participatory and transformative forms of social action that emerged after Vatican II. In addition, while the immediate intellectual and religious inspiration for Colombian experiments in community-centered social reform such as cooperatives, credit unions, family compensation funds, and Catholic labor associations

2. For testimonials, see http://es.wikipedia.org/wiki/Acci%C3%B3n_Cultural_Popular; "Radio Sutatenza en la Historia" Entrevista realizada por Gabriel Gómez Mejía, Sub gerente de Radio a Hernando Bernal Alarcón en el Programa *Contexto Publico* emitido 17 agosto 2008.

3. Ana Maria Bidegaín, "De la historia eclesiastica a la historia de las religiones: Breve Presentación sobre la transformación de la investigación sobre la historia de las religiones en las sociedades latinoamericanas." *Historia Crítica*, no. 12, January–June 1996.

4. "Radio Message on the Occasion of the Inauguration of the Catholic Radio Network of Sutatenza," April 11, 1953, www.vatican.va/holy_father/pius_xii/speeches.

generally originated in Europe, it was Franklin Roosevelt's New Deal and the U.S. Catholic Church's experience—particularly its rural ministry between the two World Wars—that most closely resembled the challenges facing a rural Catholic majority in Latin America who suffered from comparable conditions of isolation, dispersion, exclusion, illiteracy and a dearth of contact with Catholic teachings or clergy.[5]

Here I attempt to track and highlight the significant but little recognized influence of the U.S. Catholic Church, especially of Catholic clergy and entities such as the National Catholic Welfare Conference (NCWC), National Catholic Rural Life Conference (NCRLC), and the Catholic bishops' Social Action Department (SAD) long associated with work in the fields of organized labor, rural development, and urban welfare who, beginning in the late 1930s and acting in close partnership with members of the U.S. government and its agencies, spearheaded interactions, exchanges, collaboration, and funding that opened the door to the flow of missionaries and humanitarian assistance that would become typical of South–North connections in the post–Vatican II era. I suggest further that development policies and projects assumed to have been the result of secular government agency often carried the imprint of Catholic social doctrine mediated through collaborations between governments, nongovernmental agencies and the Catholic Church in which the Catholic Church and Catholic organizations played a determinant role. To support my argument, I use materials consulted in the Catholic University of America Archives, the JFK Presidential Library, declassified U.S. State Department documents, and materials from the ACPO archive housed in the Biblioteca Luis Angel Arango in Bogotá.

The chapter begins by examining Radio Sutatenza's beginnings as an experimental adult literacy radio project based in a rural Colombian

5. Edwin Vincent O'Hara and John A. Ryan, *The Church and the Country Community* (New York: Macmillan, 1927), especially 19–22. Translations of this book into Spanish and John A. Ryan's *Justicia Redistributiva* were published in Buenos Aires beginning in the 1940s and cited by Colombian authors such as Carlos Mario Londoño, who served in important government offices such as the Secretaría de Gobierno in Antioquia and as the head of the Banco de la República, Banco Central Hipotecario, and Banco Cafetero. A publicly committed adherent to the tenets of *Rerum novarum*, Londoño was an assiduous advocate of cooperativism and micro-financing, basing his support of Colombia's 1961 Agrarian Reform on his belief that economic development had to prioritize human well-being over profit. See Carlos Mario Londoño, *Economia Agraria Colombiana* (Madrid: Ediciones Rialp, 1965). For a detailed description of the challenges facing a rural ministry in the United States, see David Bovee, *The Church and the Land: The National Catholic Rural Life Conference and American Society, 1923–2007* (Washington, D.C.: The Catholic University of America Press, 2010).

parish in 1947. Next, it explores the reasons why Radio Sutatenza, and its umbrella organization, ACPO, came to be adopted and promoted by Colombian governments on a national scale as the basis for a comprehensive, radio-based, rural education system after 1949. The chapter then situates Radio Sutatenza's evolution and growth first within a national context shaped by escalating, predominantly rural, sectarian violence in Colombia (La Violencia, 1948–1958), and, second, within an international context in which cold-war paranoia galvanized the unprecedented influence of economic and cultural development agencies such as the World Bank and UN Educational, Scientific and Cultural Organization (UNESCO) in shaping domestic economic, educational and social policies. The final section explores how the Catholic Church, especially, the U.S. Catholic Church (acting at times at Rome's behest) mediated access to private donors, government officials, international agencies, foundations, and corporations that benefited Catholic transnational development projects such as Colombia's Radio Sutatenza/ ACPO. ACPO's experience, this chapter concludes, provides a valuable and previously unexplored entry point for studying the significance of Catholic transnational development work and the tensions, possibilities, and perils that characterized this process during the ideologically fraught years of the cold war.

FROM BISCUIT TIN TO MEGAWATT

When Tunja Bishop Crisanto Luque Sánchez—the son of Boyacá peasants who rose to become Bogotá's archbishop in 1950 and Colombia's first native-born cardinal in 1953—named recently ordained Father José Joaquin Salcedo as the auxiliary priest in the town of Sutatenza, Boyacá, in August 1947, the town was known as a place where "homicides were frequent and the townspeople were feared for both their ignorance and passions."[6] A "typical parish" in the Colombian Andes, Sutatenza had a population of about 6,800, of which 97.7 percent of the parishioners lived dispersed over a broken terrain of about 150-square kilometers with a difference in altitude of 2,000 meters between the lowest and highest settlement. Only 2.3 percent of the parish population actually

---

6. José Joaquin Salcedo, "Educación del campesino por la radio," Presentation given at the Primer Congreso Católico Latinoamericano Sobre Problemas de la Vida Rural, Manizales (Colombia: Imprenta Departmental, 1953), 259.

inhabited the *caserio* (hamlet) that constituted the religious and administrative center of community life.[7] The roads were poor or nonexistent and the only way to reach people scattered throughout the parish was by foot or mule. The town offered little in the way of culture or entertainment other than Sunday Mass, the occasional religious procession, and drinking at a local *tienda* (store). Lack of potable water and poor sanitation made diphtheria and typhoid almost endemic, while the tendency to squeeze families into one or two rooms increased the incidence of incest. The severely eroded and exhausted soil organized into tiny plots of subdivided land or *minifundios* (plots under a hectare in size) worked with the same crude implements in use for hundreds of years, barely produced enough for a family to survive.[8]

Father Salcedo would have to overcome distance, isolation, indifference, and distrust to win over his parishioners, revitalize their faith, and encourage them to organize collectively to improve their material well-being. Drawing on his experience as a seminarian doing literacy and catechetical training with young army recruits and prisoners, the priest hit on a plan to "seduce" his congregants into becoming better Christians and neighbors by introducing them to the wonders of cinema and radio. First, he showed filmstrips in the public plaza on an old Pathé movie projector, and then, once he'd piqued his parishioners' curiosity, he asked his brother, an amateur radio enthusiast and Jesuit priest, to build a crude radio transmitter, which he delivered in a "biscuit tin." Placing two borrowed receivers in a couple of village homes, the priest sent a message over the airwaves and had the peasants report back whether they had heard the broadcast. The next month, when Father Salcedo installed a hundred-watt transmitter and asked the town to perform a musical interlude on local instruments that was then broadcast to three receivers placed in different homes throughout the parish, the Escuelas Radiofonicas Sutatenza (Sutatenza Radio Schools) were born.

Like other Colombians of his generation, Father Salcedo came of age during the golden era of radio and film. By the mid-1930s, a multiplicity of independently owned and operated local stations with regionally specific programming that ranged from the Caribbean inflected

7. Camilo Torres Restrepo and Berta Corredor Rodriguez, *Las Escuelas Radiofonicas de Sutatenza, Colombia: Evaluacion sociologica de los resultados*. Oficina Internacional de Investigaciones Sociales de FERES, Friburgo y Bogotá (Madrid: Sucesores de Rivadeneyra S.A., 1961), 11.

8. Ibid., 35.

sounds of Barranquilla's La Voz de Barranquilla to the more Andean
centered musical traditions broadcast over Bogotá's Nueva Granada,
La Voz de Colombia, and the Radioemisora Nacional (the government-
funded station for cultural and official broadcasting) operated in Colombia's principal cities. Politicians broadcast their speeches, read
newspaper editorials, and denounced their enemies over radio. Public
school teachers, municipal employees, university students, and wom-
en lobbying for the right to vote broadcast their points of view on radio slots they rented from commercial stations. Interest groups, rang-
ing from credit-union advocates to those denouncing loan sharks and
price gouging, befriended the independent directors of popular *radio-
periodicos* (radio "newspapers") to ensure their opinions and platforms
reached a broad audience. In urban areas, even the poor had access to
radio because neighborhood associations, *tiendas*, bars, and better-off
neighbors typically "shared" their radio sets and people listened collectively.

The problem was that in 1947 most commercial radio station sig-
nals could not reach a population that was still more than 60 percent
rural. Some educational and cultural broadcasting on the National Radio Station, including rural extension programs sponsored by the Jesuit Universidad Javeriana did exist by the mid-1930s, but intervening
mountain ranges blocked the national radio's weak signal, which barely managed to cover metropolitan Bogotá, much less the surrounding
rural areas. In any case, peasants were typically too poor to afford the
still cumbersome and expensive radio receivers that required either a
reliable source of electricity or expensive batteries to run.[9] Illiterate and
isolated, Sutatenza's poor rural inhabitants could hardly be expected
to magically envision or develop skills with which to build a better life.

In October 1947, less than two months after Father Salcedo initiated what would grow into a multimedia approach to rural adult education, the Colombian government launched a national literacy plan that
envisioned the use of radio and cinematography with the participation
of clergy, women, and students to lead the crusade. In his lengthy ex-
position broadcast over the National Radio airwaves that was retrans-

9. Fals Borda noted that the only radio set in the settlement of Saucio in Cundinamarca
where he did his fieldwork was located on the local landowner's estate. Orlando Fals Borda,
Peasant Society in the Colombian Andes: A Sociological Study of Saucio (Gainesville: University of
Florida Press, 1955), 142.

mitted over commercial stations and then repeated at Sunday Mass by parish priests across the nation, Monsignor Pérez Hernandez revealed both the degree to which Catholic Social teachings permeated official Colombian policy and the reason why ACPO and Radio Sutatenza's rural adult education and community development project would rapidly become Colombia's de facto official rural education purveyor and garner significant official and transnational support.

A dearth of schools and teachers, particularly among Colombia's majority rural population, condemned as much as 70 to 80 percent of the population in departments such as Boyacá (where Sutatenza was located) and more than 50 percent of Bolívar, a coastal region with a large Afro-descendent population, to illiteracy and exclusion. The nation's educational deficit was portrayed as the root cause of much of Colombia's social injustice, while the cost of reaching a highly dispersed and isolated population scattered over a topographically varied and mountainous terrain with few access roads and even poorer transportation strained official efforts to offer Colombia's rural majority redress. This was the reason, Monsignor Pérez Hernandez stressed, why Colombia was sending delegates to UNESCO to request technical assistance in developing its literacy program. Badly distributed land, the absence of sanitation and hygiene, a weak social organization, and a lack of "generosity and collaboration in the face of the educational needs of the poor" were problems that had to be redressed, particularly with regard to indigenous people and the descendants of slaves, if Colombia were ever to aspire to becoming a modern and just nation.[10] All the conditions that Father Salcedo had encountered in Sutatenza, in fact, were typical of rural life in Colombia as a whole, and if these issues were not attended to promptly, Monsignor Pérez Hernandez implied, social revolution might not be far behind.

A 1948 U.S. State Department memorandum confirmed the Colombian cleric's grim reckoning of the state of Colombia's citizenry, noting that "80 per cent of the people can't be taxed because of underconsumption … more than a million children could not go to school in Colombia because there was no money for teachers or buildings …

10. Fonoteca, Radio Nacional de Colombia, CD 10531: "Educación Civica." Monseñor Pérez Hernandez, Plan Nacional de Alfabetizatión, October 11, 1947, part 2A. Discurso. Anders Rudquist, "La Organizacion Campesina y la Izquierda: ANUC en Colombia 1970–1980," *Informes de Investigación*, no. 1 (1983): 2.

[and] 90% of the people of Colombia have never worn shoes."[11] Colombians were also notably unhealthy, a situation that prompted the IBRD to suggest that it was "necessary to promote public health awareness by training the information providers, such as doctors, nurses, and teachers."[12] This was a recommendation that ACPO would later take to heart, training its lay volunteers and radio auxiliaries in the basics of hygiene, health, and nutrition, appointing a doctor to oversee the production of its educational materials on health, sexuality and hygiene, and partnering with organizations such as the Federation of Coffee Growers and the Colombian Ministries of Health and Education and their staffs of visiting nurses, extension agents, and nutritional experts.

Radio and cinematography had first been proffered as solutions to the problem of reaching, teaching, improving and integrating Colombia's marginalized rural population in the early 1930s. Luis López de Mesa, a proponent of *Cultura Aldeana* (village or experience based culture) who served as Minister of Education (1934–1935) during Alfonso López Pumarejo's Revolution on the March government had made mass media technologies the centerpiece of his curriculum overhaul of Colombian public education. Partisan polarization over the passage of land and labor reform legislation, however, scuttled an early plan to install radio receivers in every public school and expand the government's National Radio station's programming to provide educational coverage to rural areas. Ten years later, the Conservative government's ambitious plan to produce its own inexpensive radio sets, distribute them to schools and rural settlements, and make listening to radio instruction compulsory was also derailed, this time as a result of Liberal Party leader Jorge Eliécer Gaitán's assassination in Bogota on April 9, 1948, in the midst of the Ninth Pan-American Conference.

The popular urban uprising that erupted in Bogotá (el Bogotazo) to protest Gaitán's assassination and that spread within hours to oil camps on the Magdalena River and industrial cities such as Cali and Medellín, marked the beginning of more than a decade of rural bloodshed that came to be known as La Violencia (1948–1958), a civil war in which more than two hundred thousand mainly rural Colombians died while another two million fled, leaving behind what little they pos-

---

11. Michele Alacevich, *The Political Economy of the World Bank: The Early Years* (Palo Alto, Calif.: Stanford University Press, 2009), 25.

12. Ibid.

sessed to seek refuge in crowded urban areas where the availability of housing, jobs, food and services was already strained.[13] Shocked by the popular fury that destroyed fifty per cent Bogota's downtown area in less than twenty-four hours and convinced that the Bogotazo was the work of communist agitators, the U.S. delegation to the Pan-American Conference headed by General George Marshall moved to prioritize the application for a technical assistance loan the Colombian government had made in 1947, but which had since languished, overshadowed by the International Bank for Reconstruction and Development's (IBRD) focus on European reconstruction.[14] In 1949, at the invitation of Mariano Ospina Pérez's government, the soon-to-be World Bank conducted its first in-country economic mission in Latin America, an event that altered the course not only of Colombia's subsequent development history but, some economists argue, also set the future template for the next several decades of World Bank–backed development projects around the world.[15]

The tragic events of April 9 had a determinant impact on ACPO and Catholic transnational activism as well. The use of mass media technologies for educational purposes, spearheaded by cadres of trained volunteer instructors and local "animators" who might guide peasant families around radio instruction in the home and disseminate Christian teachings about solidarity, cooperation, and tolerance as well as technical information on farming and hygiene—the promise latent in Father Salcedo's Sutatenza radio school experiment—gained a new urgency and importance as Colombia's already-stressed rural areas became the central sites of national violence. For the next two decades, the responsibility to educate, modernize, and insulate Colombian peasants from the double threats of communist and Protestant "infiltration" would fall increasingly on the shoulders of Radio Sutatenza/ACPO.

13. Mary Roldán, *Blood and Fire: La Violencia in Antioquia, Colombia, 1946–1953* (Durham, N.C.: Duke University Press, 2002).

14. Herbert Braun, *The Assassination of Gaitan: Public Life and Urban Violence in Colombia* (Madison: University of Wisconsin Press, 1985). For the perception within the Colombian Catholic Church that Gaitan's assassination was a result of Communist agitation, see Catholic University Archives, United States Catholic Bishops Conference (USCBC), NCWC/USCC Records, SAD Inter-American Catholic Social Action Confederation, General Files 1947, Correspondence, 10, 5, 57, September 1947, *Inter-American Social Action Bulletin* issued by the NCWC, Washington, D.C. Number 4:4.

15. This is the central and compelling thesis of Alacevich's book *The Political Economy of the World Bank.*

254 ❖ Mary Roldán

FUND-RAISING AMONG CATHOLIC AND SECULAR
DONORS ABROAD

In 1948 Father Salcedo undertook the first two of many subsequent trips to New York City. First, he visited the United Nations, where he made a compelling case for the use of radio in rural education. Not long after, UNESCO acknowledged Colombia's path-breaking use of radio in education, noting in its March 5, 1949, *World Review* that "the national broadcasting system of Colombia has just begun its first series of daily school broadcasts ... [and] there are plans to produce an inexpensive receiving set in order that these broadcasts may reach as many listeners as possible."[16] Attributed to the Colombian Ministry of Education, the daily school broadcasts lauded by UNESCO were largely the work of ACPO, who began a close collaboration with the ministry that would continue well into the 1960s. ACPO would assume much of the responsibility for national rural education programming after 1949.

While in New York Father Salcedo also negotiated a contract with General Electric for a model XT-1/1000-watt transmitter and cultivated contacts with wealthy U.S. donors and corporations. Supportive and well-connected U.S. Catholic Church clergy already familiar not only with members of the Colombian Catholic Church hierarchy but with Colombia's president himself as well, enabled Salcedo on a second trip later that same year (1948) to arrange for the purchase of transmission equipment totaling 25,000 watts. Father Salcedo culminated his successful fund-raising drive with a contract with Philips for the construction of five thousand single-channel radio receivers.[17]

By 1949, ACPO had expanded beyond its original base in Sutatenza, Boyacá, to Tibirita in Cundinamarca, where a 250-watt transmitter was installed under the direction of Father José Ramon Sabogal, the priest who would become "the voice" of Radio Sutatenza's educational programming for the next half-century and Father Salcedo's right-hand man and close confidant. Also, 1949 marked the anniversary of ACPO's incorporation as a legal entity with nonprofit status and the

16. *UNESCO World Review*, March 5, 1949, 3.
17. Torres and Corredor, *Las Escuelas Radiofonicas de Sutatenza, Colombia*, 12; Hernando Bernal Alarcón, "Radio Sutatenza," www.banrepcultural.org/radio-sutatenza/textos/radio-sutatenza-un-modelocolombiano-de-industria-cultural-y-educativa.

organization of its board of directors. Four individuals, all members of the clergy, constituted its members: the bishop of Tunja (the diocese where Sutatenza was based); the national director of Colombia's Catholic Social Action, Vicente Andrade Valderrama, a Jesuit who was also the moral adviser and founder of Colombia's Catholic labor union, the Union de Trabajadores Colombianos (UTC); Father Salcedo; and another priest.

In 1951, at the insistence of the Tunja diocese's new bishop, the Jesuit Angel Maria Ocampo Berrio, ACPO was reorganized and made a diocesan project under the direct supervision of Colombia's Department of Catholic Social Action, a relationship that would persist until disagreements with Colombia's conservative episcopacy in the mid-1970s severed the relationship and ACPO became autonomous. For the next decade, ACPO experienced exponential growth, expanding from its original single 100-watt transmitter, three receivers, and three radio "schools" (really a collection of families gathered in a single home for instruction), to 46 transmitters, 453 receivers, and 430 schools in 1951; 412 transmitters, 11,703 receivers and 6,422 schools in 1954; and 871 transmitters, 42,174 receivers, and 18,146 schools in 1958.[18]

When democracy was restored in Colombia, and Liberal Alberto Lleras Camargo took office as president after five years of military rule in 1958, ACPO offered to put at the impoverished government's disposal the collaboration of 855 parish priests committed to "immediate action." They would be the frontline promoters of "a new mentality and spirit among rural inhabitants," needed to address Colombia's pressing social, economic, and educational problems.[19] With unlimited access to Radio Sutatenza's powerful radio network, the government would be able to offer services to Colombia's "neediest classes," and the Ministries of Education, Agriculture, and Public Health would be able to ensure that educational and information campaigns would reach the "most distant places that would otherwise be difficult to reach in any other way."[20] In 1959 ACPO and the Colombian government signed a formal agreement that included a yearly government subsidy and the right to import necessary materials (paper, ink, equip-

18. Torres and Corredor, *Las Escuelas Radiofonicas de Sutatenza, Colombia*, table 1, 15.

19. AGN, "Memorandum al Señor Presidente de la Republica y Ministros del Despacho, Presentado por Acción Cultural Popular." AGN, Presidencia; Despacho Sr. Presidente; Acción Cultural Popular, Escuela Radiofonica/Correspondencia; Caja 108; Carp: 2; F.5.

20. Ibid., F.7.

ment) on a tax-exempt basis for ACPO's radio station and printing press in return for ACPO's collaboration in the provision of national rural education services.

Over the course of its lifetime, ACPO's principal collaborators and financial support involved a complicated patchwork of Colombian government contracts and subsidies and international development and technical assistance projects, both religious and secular. UNESCO; Truman's Point Four Program for technical assistance; the International Cooperation Agency (ICA); USAID; the Ford and Rockefeller Foundations; wealthy private donors in Colombia and the United States; the U.S. bishops' NCWC; the German bishops' Conference international charitable funds, MISEREOR and Adveniat; and U.S. humanitarian and charitable funds such as CARE (active in Colombia since 1954) and Catholic Relief Services (CRS; active in Colombia by 1960–1961) played seminal roles in bankrolling ACPO's growth and influence.

Given the history of ACPO's growth and development in Colombia, it is worthwhile here to look at the broader global context, in order to answer a lingering question: What made it possible for a priest from a small rural town in Colombia who had never previously traveled abroad and spoke not a word of English to undertake a mission to sell his idea of radio-based rural education to the United Nations and then successfully lobby corporations and donors to underwrite ACPO's expansion into becoming Latin America's first Catholic Radio network and largest educational radio network by 1953?

CATHOLIC SOCIAL DOCTRINE, COLOMBIA, AND CATHOLIC TRANSNATIONALISM BEFORE 1948

The entry into the world of Catholic transnational development assistance was forged in the global crisis caused by the outbreak of World War II in Europe, even before the bombing of Pearl Harbor prompted the United States to formally enter the war as a combatant. The Catholic Church took up the role of ambassador between the United States and the predominantly Catholic countries to the south of its border, where it was imperative to secure the access—or at the very least block access to the Axis countries—of valuable resources and commodities needed for the war effort, and the loyalty of governments where immigrant populations of German, Italian, and Spanish descent might prove sympathetic to European fascism. There was no question of a firm commitment on the U.S. Catholic side to the fight against totalitarianism and the defense of "the American way of life." In 1939 Bishop Ryan of Omaha, a well-known Catholic progressive, embarked on a multicountry tour of South America with Monsignor Maurice S. Sheehy to rally Catholic and national support in Brazil, Argentina, Venezuela, and Chile for the fight against totalitarianism.

In a series of broadcasts that were later published by the Council for Democracy in 1941 with a preface written by Assistant Secretary of State Sumner Welles, the "leadership in the U.S. of the Roman Catholic Church" in working to "strengthen and develop in a mutually advantageous manner" the common ties that bound "the governments of the twenty-one American republics" in the fight against totalitarianism was singled out for praise. Radio interviews with figures such as Dr. Oswaldo Aranha, the foreign minister of Brazil, in conversation with Bishop Ryan and Henry Wallace, secretary of the U.S. Department of Agriculture, and Eugene Meyer of the *Washington Post*, accompanied by broadcasts such as "The Pope Condemns Anti-Semitism" and "Brazilian-U.S. Relations" transmitted over the Columbia Broadcasting System, were intended to reassure listeners that Catholics were committed to "a positive, dynamic faith in democracy" and the need to defend "the American way of life ... from within and without by the menace of totalitarianism."[21]

In 1940, moreover, the U.S. State Department's Division of Cultural Cooperation initiated an exchange program that brought into unprecedented contact lay and religious authorities from Latin America with universities and counterparts in the United States in the fields of labor, social work, technical training, science, agriculture, industry, and medicine. For several years beginning in 1940, all expenses paid, six-month training exchanges were offered to between seventy-five and one hundred Latin American professionals, bringing into contact the individuals who would shape their country's development policies, and in some cases, form the core of an incipient, professional Latin American middle class for years to come. The Division of Cultural Cooperation also sent U.S. technical experts, teachers, scientists, and economists to take up renewable positions as consultants to government agencies, visiting

21. Maurice S. Sheehy, *Selected Broadcasts*, published in cooperation with the Council for Democracy (Silver Spring, Md.: Cornelius Printing, 1941).

professors and resident technical experts at universities, experimental agricultural stations, and health and sanitation institutes. Two of the five agricultural experts from Latin America brought over by the State Department to participate in the six-month training sessions in 1944 were Colombian. One was Ciro Molina Garcés, the secretary of agriculture for the Colombian department of Valle and an original promoter of what would become the world-renowned International Center for Tropical Agriculture (CIAT) founded with the support of the Rockefeller Foundation in Palmira. The other Colombian participant in 1944 was Raúl Varela Martínez, CIAT's director in 1943, a prominent agronomist, and a well-known consultant on agricultural matters for the Colombian government.[22] Before being selected to participate in the six month professional exchange program sponsored by the U.S. Department of State's Division of Cultural Cooperation in 1944, Molina Garcés and Varela Martinez had hosted the visit to Valle of U.S. rural sociologist T. Lynn Smith, who, sponsored by the U.S. Department of State, had been sent to observe and report on Colombian rural conditions in response to a Colombian agricultural mission sent to Washington in 1943 to apply for a fifteen-million-dollar technical assistance loan under the leadership of Miguel López Pumarejo, the brother of Colombian president Alfonso López Pumarejo.

Less than six months after participating in the Division of Cultural Cooperation's professional exchange program, Ciro Molina Garcés was back in Cali collaborating with members of the local Catholic hierarchy and Valle's regional economic elite as they hosted the visit of two U.S. Catholic Bishops (Monsignor Joseph P. Morrison of the archdiocese of Chicago and Archbishop Joseph Schlarman of Peoria) and the executive secretary of the National Catholic Rural Life Conference, Monsignor Luigi Ligutti, who had been invited to Valle as regional development advisers.[23] Both T. Lynn Smith, during his visit a year earlier, and

22. Varela Martinez consulted with Colombia's Ministry of Agriculture from the 1920s through the 1950s on everything from banana to rice cultivation and was an outspoken advocate for the need to expand access to cheap credit, cooperatives, housing, technical assistance, and safeguards to rural food producers in order to avoid shortages and stem unfettered rural to urban migration. See his front-page interview in Colombia's largest circulation daily, *El Tiempo*, October 27, 1943.

23. "Inter-American Notes," *The Americas* 1, no. 2 (October 1944): 237; introductory remarks made by Mons. Joseph P. Morrison during his participation in the Primer Congreso Catolico Latinoamericano Sobre Problemas de la Vida Rural, Manizales, Colombia, January 11–18, 1953 (Manizales: Imprenta Departamental, 1953), 175.

the Catholic prelates in 1945 were asked to make recommendations on the best way to transform Valle's "pyramidal" land-tenure system based on a legacy of slavery and industrialized sugar plantations, into a more socially just, flourishing "agrarian middle class."[24] The prelates and the sociologist, approaching the question from different philosophical traditions—one derived from Catholic social thought that privileged the self-supporting, independent, family farm and small industry as an agrarian ideal and the other derived from a Jeffersonian ideal of the sturdy yeoman or rural "middle-class" farmer, but both committed to defeating communism—arrived at exactly the same recommendation: to favor policies that would limit the worst excesses of social inequality and to make available credit, technical assistance, and education for the development of an "agrarian middle class."[25]

In their study of the World Bank since Bretton Woods, Edward Mason and Robert Asher make the provocative suggestion that "in tracing the evolution of IBRD assistance to member countries in development programming, the historian quickly discovers that all roads lead not to Rome, but to Bogotá."[26] It might be more accurate to suggest that all roads lead to Bogotá via (the Church of) Rome.

Six years before Colombian president Mariano Ospina Pérez invited the newly appointed head of the International Bank for Reconstruction and Development, John McCloy,[27] to take part in the Ninth International Conference of American States scheduled to meet in Bogotá at the end of March 1948, a visit that ultimately led Colombia to become the recipient of a steady stream of development-oriented

24. Mons Joseph P. Morrison, "El Apostolado liturgico en los Estados Unidos," *Primer Congreso Catolico Latinoamericano Sobre Problemas de la Vida Rural*, Manizales, Colombia 11–18 de enero 1953 (Manizales: Imprenta Departamental, 1953), 175.

25. On T. Lynn Smith's vision and participation in Colombian development projects, see Francine Cronshaw, "Exporting Ideology: T. Lynn Smith in Colombia," *NS, Northsouth* 7, no. 13 (1982): 95–1. Morrison, Ligutti, and Ciro Molina Garcés would meet again in person at least once more in 1953, at the January 1953 First Latin American Catholic Conference on the Problems of Rural Life held in Manizales, Colombia.

26. Michele Alacevich, *The Political Economy of the World Bank*, 11.

27. John McCloy would wear many hats over the years, among them assistant secretary of war, director of the OSS (Office of Special Services), first U.S. high commissioner for Germany (1949–1952), president of Chase Manhattan Bank (1953–1958), and head of the Ford Foundation (1958–1965) during the period a congressional inquiry took place into the use of the foundation as a cover for CIA agents. McCloy was also a close business and personal associate of the Rockefellers and a fan of liberal President Alberto Lleras Camargo (first Latin American president of the OAS), writing to laud his actions as president of Colombia from 1958 to 1962. BLAA, Manuscritos, Archivo Alberto Lleras Camargo, Correspondencia.

260 Mary Roldán

loans that would make it the model for subsequent World Bank missions in the so-called third world, members of the U.S. clergy associated with the NCWC and the U.S. Bishops Conference's SAD were
coordinating with representatives from Nelson Rockefeller's Office of
Inter-American Affairs and Dr. Richard Pattee, assistant chief of the
Cultural Relations Division of the U.S. State Department, to organize
an international seminar in social studies to be held in August 1942
in Washington, D.C. The stated purpose of the seminar was to offer
"Latin American and North American lay and secular leaders engaged
in the fields of social, economic, urban and rural labor issues ... an opportunity to exchange ideas, meet U.S. leaders, and become acquainted with U.S. educational social and labor institutions."[28]

The 1942 Inter-American Seminar was paid for by Rockefeller's Office of Inter-American Affairs (OIAA). At the insistence of the OIAA,
however, it was advertised as an initiative independently organized
and financed by the U.S. Bishops Conference's SAD and the NCWC.
The theme was "The Americas and the Crisis of Civilization." "Distinguished authorities" were to speak about technical problems in industry,
agriculture, handicraft production, and social legislation and the future
of "Inter-American economic and governmental relations" in the postwar world, as well as "the crisis which confronts civilization and the importance of the Americas, particularly of Catholics in the Americas, in
helping to resolve the crisis."[29] The keynote address was to be given by
the French Catholic philosopher Jacques Maritain, the individual whose
concept of "integral humanism" would shape UNESCO's "integral education" programs and ACPO's "fundamental integral education" approach (and whose ideas had so strongly influenced the Brazilian Catholic activists discussed by Colin Snider earlier in this volume).[30]

Among the fifteen Latin American religious and lay authorities invited to participate in the 1942 Inter-American Seminar were two Colombian priests, Jesuit Father Felix Restrepo Mejía, the rector of the
(Jesuit) Javeriana University in Bogotá, and Father Felix Henao Botero,
the rector of the Universidad Católica Bolivariana (also Jesuit) in Me-

28. Eugene D. Miller, *A Holy Alliance? The Church and the Left in Costa Rica, 1932–1948*
(New York: M. E. Sharpe, 1996), 165.
29. NCWC/USCC Records SAD *Inter-American Seminars*, Washington, D.C. 1942, Correspondence (April 14, 1942–July 9, 1942), Collection 10, Box 4, June 23, 1942.
30. Jacques Maritain and Charles Journet, *L'education a la croisee du chemins* (Paris: Egloff,
1947).

dellín. Both priests were from Antioquia, both had been educated in Europe where they had witnessed firsthand the application of Catholic social thought in Germany, Spain, and Italy, and both were active in organizations associated with Catholic Social Action. Restrepo Mejía had directed the Catholic Youth Organization (JUCO) in Bogotá, written a book on corporativism, and founded the Women's College within the Javeriana in 1940, while Henao Botero was the founder and director of Colombia's *Catholic Hour* radio program modeled on that of U.S. Catholic radio personality, Monsignor Fulton Sheen, and had authored a book on "the social question."

When the second Inter-American Seminar was held in Havana in late 1946, the Colombian delegate would also be a member of the Jesuit order, considered by some to be Colombia's "only significant repository of expertise in matters of a socio-economic nature" and the most "cosmopolitan" sector of the Colombian clergy with the "greatest access to recent international Catholic thinking."[31] Monsignor Vicente Andrade Valderrama was an expert in Catholic teaching on issues of labor who had firsthand experience with European Catholic workers' movements and was the moral adviser for more than twenty years of Colombia's first Catholic labor confederation, the UTC (an outgrowth primarily of agrarian and manufacturing unions based in Antioquia and their struggle to form cooperatives and credit unions). In 1946 President Mariano Ospina Pérez granted the UTC legal recognition and national status.

Vicente Andrade would also be the first and longest-serving director of the National Colombian Coordination of Catholic Social Action, established in 1944 to pursue a more robust revitalization of the Catholic Church in social matters, including "the formation of Catholic leaders among local workers and peasants … [and] the teaching and diffusion of Catholic social principles."[32] A priest recognized for his "widespread network of contacts"[33] and for his staunch refusal to ally himself or the union he oversaw with any political party, Andrade Valderrama would be a member of ACPO's governing board during many years and, like Father Salcedo, would sit on the board of the Colombian Land Credit

31. Kenneth N. Medhurst, *The Church and Labour in Colombia* (Manchester, England: Manchester University Press, 1984), 63.

32. Ibid., 62.

33. Ibid., 63.

Institute (Instituto de Credito Territorial), the agency that awarded low interest credits for the purchase of rural land.

The key organizers on the Catholic side of the partnership with the OIAA and State Department, such as Father McGowan of the SAD, were clearly interested in hosting the Inter-American Seminar to enable "leaders of Social Action in the Americas" who rarely knew each other to come together to "learn from one another and be helped by one another to plan better their work in their own countries and throughout the hemisphere."[34] But other participants and interested parties in the Inter-American seminars had more material and ideological reasons for wanting to foment hemispheric good will among proponents of Catholic Social Action (whose philosophy advocated reforms inspired in Catholic social teachings but adamantly opposed Marxism and totalitarianism).

Representatives of corporate interests such as the W. R. Grace Company (whose owners were Catholic) or William A. Prendergast, the president of the New York and Honduras Rosario Mining Company, a relative of Walter T. Prendergast, Nelson Rockefeller's assistant director of the science and education division in the OIAA, and a key bridge between SAD and the State Department, made it clear that free markets and the threat of communism were uppermost in their minds. Prendergast wrote McGowan's assistant, Catherine Schaefer, to remind the seminar organizers to drive home to the participants from Latin America that "the most effective way in which to help the Latin American countries develop their national resources, and find markets for them" would be for them to remember "the necessity of energizing their economic position." It was the duty of the United States to help Latin Americans remember where their economic interests lay, lest "these countries . . . look to other Nations for the help they need."[35]

In these early experiments in collaboration between the U.S. Catholic Church and the State Department, the beginnings of a tension that would harden by the late 1940s and 1950s—a tension that Catherine LeGrand refers to in her chapter in this volume as a "sea change"—may already be glimpsed. It was a tension that would only become more

34. NCWC/USCC Records SAD *Inter-American Seminars*, Washington, D.C. 1942, Correspondence (April 14, 1942–July 9, 1942), Collection 10, Box 4, letter dated June 15, 1942.

35. NCWC/USCC Records SAD—*Inter-American Seminars* Washington, D.C., 1942 CORR (July 10–22, 1942), 10, 4; Prendergast to CS, July 22, 1942.

acute as the decade of the 1950s developed, until it would explode by the 1960s in the aftermath of the Cuban Revolution. In its essence, it boiled down to this: Could Catholic social teachings be reconciled with the interests of corporations and governments who provided necessary funding, but whose priorities in Latin America increasingly subordinated reform or socially just development to counter-insurgency and the monopolistic extraction of natural resources and profits? In 1942 this dilemma had not fully flowered, but its seeds were present all the same.

THE NATIONAL CATHOLIC RURAL LIFE CONFERENCE AND COLOMBIA

President Mariano Ospina Pérez, the president in office during the Bogotazo and the first official government backer of the radiophonic schools and ACPO's rural education and development initiatives, had a long and close relationship with Catholic social teachings and the Jesuits of the Javeriana University in Bogotá, where Fathers Felix Restrepo and Vicente Andrade Valderrama were based. As the national director of the Federation of Coffee Growers between 1930 and 1934, Ospina Pérez had exercised a crucial role in the creation of the Colombian credit union, the Caja Agraria (1931), and had rallied support for the adoption of Law 134 of 1931, which recognized and regulated the establishment of cooperatives in Colombia during Liberal president Enrique Olaya Herrera's bipartisan Concentración Nacional government (1930–1934).[36] Bipartisan support for Law 134 revealed the fact that important sectors of both the Conservative and Liberal Parties,

36. Cooperatives were first proposed in the late nineteenth century by General Rafael Uribe, the leader of the Liberal Party, but they were endorsed and popularized in the early 1920s by Father Adan Puerto, a priest attached to the Diocese of Tunja, Boyaca (the same diocese to which Father Salcedo and Sutatenza belonged). Puerto was influenced by *Rerum novarum* and his experience observing the success of Catholic cooperatives in Germany. He spread the idea of cooperation to priests in other parts of Colombia through his writings in the Tunja Diocesan Bulletin. Law 134 of 1931 in turn was based on the 1930 law thesis of Francisco Luis Jimenez, an *antioqueño* lawyer influenced by the teachings of *Rerum novarum*, who would go on to found various important cooperatives including the *Cooperativa de Empleados* and *Vivienda*, head the *Centro de Estudios Cooperativos de Antioquia*, and sponsor the First Colombian Cooperative Congress in 1943. Jimenez would be invited to Washington to participate in Inter-American Seminar exchanges sponsored by the State Department in the 1940s. See Mario Arango Jaramillo, *Manual de cooperativismo y economía solidaria* (Medellín: Editorial Universidad Cooperativa de Colombia, 2005); www.crefam.com.co; Alfonso Mejía Robledo, "Cooperativa de la Vivienda," in *Vidas y Empresas de Antioquia* (Medellin: Imprenta Departamental, 1951), 258–60.

which differed significantly on a number of issues, nonetheless shared a concern with the state of Colombia's rural underdevelopment that was rooted in similar philosophical traditions shaped directly or indirectly by Catholic social doctrine.

A comparison of the content and thrust of Alejandro López's 1931 *Idearum Liberal* and the Conservative Party platforms of 1931 and 1937, where "Christian motivation and the papal doctrines" were explicitly cited as the basis for the party's proposals, reveals both a remarkable coincidence in objectives and the degree to which Catholic social teachings implicitly and explicitly formed the basis of secular and religious development efforts and policies intended to address the urgent "social question" in Colombia, even in instances where any explicit reference to its influence was absent.[37]

Both the Liberal and Conservative programs advocated a strong commitment to the defense and expansion of the rights of small property holders, held up the creation of an agrarian "middle class" as the national ideal,[38] pushed for the breakup and taxation of uncultivated lands, insisted on the need for access to cheap credit and the creation of a social safety net for workers and the poor, recognized labor's right to fair wages and representation, and advocated for the promotion of cooperatives and credit unions. Both parties' platforms also expressed worries about the effects of alcoholism, intrafamiliar violence, and the alarming incidence of seduced and abandoned women.[39]

37. Trained as an engineer at the School of Mines in Medellín under the tutelage of Tulio Ospina Vásquez and Pedro Nel Ospina (Conservative president 1922–1926), Alejandro López was a descendent of a long line of artisans who rose to considerable influence within the Liberal Party and was known for his untiring defense of small property holders, artisanal production, and opposition to development schemes that privileged the colonization of distant regions like the Amazon to solve conflicts of production and land tenure between peasants and *latifundia* in settled areas of the nation. The *Idearum Liberal* was published in Paris during López's fifteen-year sojourn in Europe (1920–1935), where he served as head of the Colombian Legation for Liberal Alfonso López Pumarejo's government. Most of López's time in Europe was spent in England, where he was exposed to the ideas of Catholic distributist G. K. Chesterton. Alejandro López, *Escritos Escogidos* (Bogotá: Biblioteca Basica Colombiana, 1976).

38. Note that this concern with the promotion and protection of an "agrarian middle class" predated by almost fifteen years the recommendations made by T. Lynn Smith in his 1944 U.S. Department of State–sponsored report on rural conditions in Colombia, where the phrase "agrarian middle class" was also explicitly invoked.

39. Alejandro López, "Idearum Liberal" [1931], in *Escritos Escogidos* (Bogota: Biblioteca Basica Colombiana, 1976), 215–24; and Roberto Herrera Soto, ed., *Antología del Pensamiento Conservador en Colombia*, tomo II (Bogotá: Colcultura, Bogotana de Impresos, 1982), 1333–43, for the 1931 platform and 1346–50 for the 1937 "Prospectus of Social Action: Position of the

López's *Idearum Liberal* and the Conservative Party's 1937 "Prospectus of Social Action" echoed almost to a phrase the philosophy and concerns of the National Catholic Rural Life Conference's 1923 founding
principles as laid out in Bishop Edwin Vincent O'Hara's *The Church
and the Country Community* of 1927.[40] Like his Colombian counterparts,
O'Hara modeled his ideas on the example of Catholic European experiments: "The religious social service which the church can render the
farmer can be seen in a glance at Europe. The only effective agency in
binding together the social elements of the countryside is the church.
When the church is not doing it, it is not being done. In a Belgian,
a German, an Italian, or a Spanish rural parish, what social work the
church is doing! Promoting the savings and loan societies, cooperative
buying and selling, education and parish recreation centers, and all on
a religious basis."[41] But unlike Europe, where rural parishes were characterized by dense, village-centered settlements, "rural organization,
caused by long distances and bad roads, [was] altogether lacking," in
the United States. This made the challenges faced by the U.S. Catholic
Church's rural ministry similar to the challenges faced by the Catholic
Church in Latin America (and parish priests such as ACPO's Salcedo).
O'Hara went on to conclude what would often be noted about the Catholic Church's relationship to rural areas in Colombia: "no other social
agency ... can knit together the rural community as can the Catholic
parish."[42] The critical task facing the Catholic Church in rural areas in
both the United States and Latin America therefore consisted of recognizing and working to promote the rural inhabitant's right to "religion, health, education, recreation, fellowship, material well-being. All
of these things come normally to human beings through the agency
of social organization.... Man is a social being, and his ordinary development will depend most largely upon his social relationship.... It
is a matter of observation that the farmer gets less of all these things,
which we have mentioned, from his social environment than does the
city man. Why? Because the ordinary condition for social life is proxim-
ity to our neighbor, and that is the one thing which the farm lacks."[43]

U.S. Catholic outreach to Latin America was inspired in part by

Conservative Party vis a vis Conflicts between Labor and Capital," signed by Esteban Jaramillo,
Francisco de Paula Perez, and Mariano Ospina Pérez, among others.
40. O'Hara and Ryan, *The Church and the Country Community.*
41. Ibid., 21.   42. Ibid.
43. Ibid., 20.

the perception after 1937 that the social and economic crisis in agriculture that had been a central focus of U.S. Catholic activism between the wars had become "international in scope."[44] The close interactions forged between organizations such as the NCRLC and SAD and members of Roosevelt's New Deal around issues of rural development and labor during the Depression uniquely positioned the U.S. Catholic Church to be recognized by the U.S. government during the Second World War as an indispensable partner in its efforts to strengthen relations in Latin America's overwhelmingly Catholic societies. U.S. Catholic transnationalism in Latin America was also given a boost when, at an international Catholic Conference on Rural Problems held in Rome in 1950, Pope Pius XII declared that "it was the Christian duty" of the most developed nations and of the most "privileged groups in all nations" to "help realize the improvements necessary to economic life and social conditions,"[45] reinforcing earlier calls by the Vatican urging members of the episcopal hierarchy and religious orders in the "developed" Catholic world to increase the number of missionaries they sent to the global South.

After participating in the 1942 Inter-American Seminar sponsored by the NCWC and the SAD in Washington, D.C., O'Hara founded the Latin America Institute in March 1943. The organization sponsored radio broadcasts on both continents to "help people understand each other's culture better," paid for the publication of books and articles and their translation into Spanish, Portuguese, and English, conducted exchanges of professors and students, and sponsored trips by U.S. Catholic clerics to tour and speak in Latin America. Monsignor Luigi Ligutti, the director of the NCRLC was the Institute's official "advisor on rural affairs." Father John Friede, a Jesuit specialist in industrial problems, advised on labor issues.[46]

The Latin America Institute operated under the supervision of the episcopal committee of the CCD (Confraternity of the Catholic Doctrine), but soon after its foundation decided it was best to "muster its own income from private sources."[47] Bishop Joseph Schlarman of

44. Bovee, *The Church and the Land*, 100.
45. Congreso Catolico Latino Americano de Vida Rural, *Primer Congreso Catolico Latinoamericano Sobre Problemas de la Vida Rural*, 22.
46. Timothy Dolan, *Some Seed Fell on Good Ground: The Life of Edwin V. O'Hara* (Washington, D.C.: The Catholic University of America Press, 1992), 209–10.
47. Ibid., 210.

Peoria,[48] who had written extensively about Mexico, and Archbishop Michael J. Curley of Boston became critical conduits of private donations in support of the Institute's work. In January 1944, moreover, the Institute began publishing a monthly bulletin that was sent to six thousand people on both continents, although the bulletin was suspended six months later when the journal *America* took over its operation.

By 1945 O'Hara was undertaking long trips through South America, in part motivated by the conviction that Latin American agrarian society "cried out for reform" and that it was the U.S. Catholic Church's responsibility to encourage their Catholic counterparts in Latin America to support rural development policies rooted in Catholic social doctrine both to right injustices and to defeat communism and Protestant challenges. Bishop Edwin O'Hara made three trips to South America starting in Brazil, working his way through Argentina, Chile, Peru, and Colombia and stopping each time in Bogotá, between 1945 and 1953.[49] In 1946 O'Hara met in a private audience at the request of Conservative president-elect Mariano Ospina Pérez and delivered a mini-seminar on cooperatives.

Rerum novarum taught that the church's primordial obligation was to defend and promote the smallholder or family-owned farm and the social practices and agencies necessary—cooperatives, credit unions, specialized rural education, and so on—to further that ideal—tenets reiterated in Pius XI's encyclical, *Quadragesimo anno* of 1931. The promotion of a "middle-class agrarian" (the independent family-owned farm) ideal and the fight against communism became inextricably linked in the thought of Monsignor Luigi Ligutti who succeeded Bishop O'Hara as the NCRLC's executive director in 1937. Inspired by the British Catholic Distributist movement's "three acres and a cow" project,[50] Monsignor Ligutti would be famously quoted in a 1941 *Time* article highlighting the link made by "progressive" sectors of the U.S. Catholic Church

48. Bishop Schlarman would be one of three US Catholic prelates—Bishop Morrison of Chicago and Luigi Ligutti of the NCRLC were the other two—invited to advise the industrial and agricultural powerhouse department of Valle del Cauca in 1945 on the development of an "agrarian middle class" and the establishment of a TVA-inspired, hydroelectric power project to further that goal.

49. Mons. Joseph P. Morrison, "El Apostolado litúrgico en los Estados Unidos," in *Primer Congreso Católico Latinoamericano Sobre Problemas de la Vida Rural* (Manizales, Colombia: Imprenta Departamental, 1953), 175.

50. The "three acres and a cow" phrase was coined in the 1880s by Eli Hamshire of the land reform movement and incorporated into the thinking of Christian humanist and Catholic convert philosopher G. K. Chesterton. See *What's Wrong with the World* (Mineola, N.Y.: Dover Publications, 2007).

between social justice policies and anticommunism, as saying that "the cure for communism is to give a man a cow."[51]

In Colombia the NCRLC's anticommunist "cow" philosophy found an echo in the "Vaca Lechera" (milk cow) program first promoted during Mariano Ospina Pérez's government but expanded and put under the supervision of ACPO during the military government of General Gustavo Rojas Pinilla (1953–1957) as a central element of ACPO's rural education and community development project from the 1950s forward. To facilitate peasant purchases of a cow and improve the rural family's health and material prosperity, peasants could tap the Colombian government's credit-lending agency, the Caja Agraria (1931).[52]

The problem of rural development brought together the Vatican, the Colombian government, and the Colombian Catholic Church hierarchy through the mediation of individuals such as Monsignor Antonio Samoré, who occupied various important posts and became a critical link in Catholic transnational activism, especially in Latin America and in the rural arena. A close confidant of Pope Pius XII, later adviser to Pope Paul VI, staunch anticommunist and anti-Liberation theology conservative who served as the counselor of the apostolic delegation in the United States between 1947 and 1950 and then as Colombia's papal nuncio between 1950 and 1953, Antonio Samoré collaborated extensively with Monsignor Ligutti, the executive secretary of the U.S. NCRLC, who by the 1950s also held influential offices connected to rural development in Rome and became the Vatican's delegate to the Food and Agriculture Organization of the United Nations in 1960. Together, Ligutti as the executive director of the National Catholic Rural Life Conference, and Samoré as the Vatican's papal nuncio in Colombia (1950–1953), organized, financed, and then published the proceedings of a weeklong Catholic seminar on rural-life issues held in Manizales, Colombia, in January 1953.

51. "Catholics for Labor," *Time Magazine* 37, no. 22, 67. Clare Booth Luce, the wife of *Time's* co-founder and owner, had been converted to Catholicism by Bishop Fulton Sheen, the well-known host of the radio program *The Catholic Hour*, sponsored by the National Council of Catholic Men, which was broadcast between 1930–1968 on NBC. Sheen was auxiliary bishop of New York between 1951 and 1965.

52. Archivo General de la Nacion (AGN), Sec: Presidencia; F: Secretaría General/Min Educ; Caja: 278; Carp: 25, folio 5–18, "*Conclusiones del Seminario de Profesores de Cursos Campesinos Para Adultos Efectuado en la Escuela Vocacional Agricola de Ubate (Cund.), Del 25 de Julio al 7 de Agosto de 1953 y Organizado Por El Departamento de Educacion Campesina del Ministerio de Educación Nacional*," August 11, 1953.

The Manizales conference was broadcast live on Colombian commercial radio and the transcripts were published and disseminated with the financial support of the Vatican, U.S. Bishops Conference, and the Ford Foundation. Individuals who played prominent roles in Catholic transnational development work, the foundation of Catholic labor unions and Christian Democratic parties, and the formulation of Latin American rural development policies through the period of Vatican II were present or participated in that seminar, the second international rural-life seminar ever sponsored by the Catholic Church (the first had taken place in Rome in 1950) and the first Catholic-sponsored seminar specifically to discuss Latin American rural issues ever held.[53] In the seminar's final "declaration of principles," the seminar's organizers made explicit that "the land should not be the source of benefits for the privileged few and servile labor for everyone else" and insisted that "the farmer and his family have, before anyone else, the right to the fruits of their labor in order to enjoy a decent standard of living. After that right come the rights of the proprietor who does not directly work the land, and then the rights of the State." The conference participants in their final observations also recommended "discouraging *latifundia* (large landholdings) as anti-democratic and anti-social."[54] Father Jose Joaquin Salcedo, the founder of Radio Sutatenza and the director of ACPO, who addressed the rural conference on the issue of a radiophonic approach to rural education and community development, was singled out for praise, and in the published conference conclusions, "Rural Life and Propaganda (film and radio)" was put on a par with the promotion of credit, housing, indigenous affairs, electrification, and the protection of natural resources, as central elements of Catholic-oriented, rural development policy.[55]

In 1955 Vatican secretary of state Cardinal Dominico Tardini, asked Archbishop Antonio Samoré "to take charge of Latin America," an appointment that led Samoré to orchestrate the first meeting of Latin

---

53. *Primer Congreso Catolico Latinoamericano Sobre Problemas de la Vida Rural*, Manizales, Colombia, 11–18 enero de 1953 (Manizales: Inprenta Departamental, 1953), is an astonishingly rich document and necessary reading for any scholar interested in tracing Catholic transnationalism in rural development in the pre–Vatican II era.

54. "Relaciones del hombre con la tierra (declaración de principios)," *Primer Congreso Catolico Latinoamericano Sobre Problemas de la Vida Rural*, 322.

55. "Texto oficial de las Conclusiones del Congreso: Sumario," *Primer Congreso Catolico Latinoamericano Sobre Problemas de la Vida Rural*, 299.

American and Caribbean Bishops in 1955 in Rio de Janeiro, Brazil.[56] The Conference of Latin American Bishops (CELAM) was founded at the Rio meeting and the Conference's official headquarters were established later that year in Bogotá. During CELAM's 1955 Rio de Janeiro meeting, the Latin American bishops, influenced by the success of Colombia's Radio Sutatenza, officially resolved to make the use of mass media technologies the key to combating illiteracy, revitalizing Christianity, and making real the "social" in Catholic Social doctrine. In addition to making the teaching of Catholic Social doctrine obligatory in schools, seminaries, and universities and explicitly calling on women religious and educated lay people of both sexes to serve as catechists in support of social justice and the defense of the poor, CELAM also explicitly called for "the installation of radio stations equipped with staff that is culturally and technically well prepared to direct and operate these," the training of seminarians in the use of radio, and the development of a "radiophonic apostolate."[57] With the support of the Vatican, CELAM, the U.S. Catholic Church, and U.S. government agencies, ACPO's multimedia-centered, lay-driven approach to rural Christian revitalization and education became the model to be emulated and exported not just to other parts of Latin America but throughout the Catholic developing world.

Samoré and Ligutti would reappear time and again, mediating funds and support for Colombian Catholic Social Action activities including ACPO from the early 1950s through the decade of the 1960s. The International Federation of Catholic Institutions of Social and Socio-Religious Research (Federatión Internationale des Institutions Catholiques de Recherches Sociales et Socio-Religeuses, or FERES) research and study group headed by the Belgian Abbé Francois Houtart, with a Latin American headquarters in Bogotá and oversight of a forty-seven-volume study of all aspects of the church and society in Latin America, assumed by many scholars to have been a precursor to the Liberation theology movement and a product of priest-researchers affiliated with LT, for instance, was cofounded by Monsignor Luigi Ligutti of the U.S.-based NCRLC. After expressing an initial reluctance to actively endorse the sociological inquiries promoted by

56. Tom Quigley, "The Great North-South Embrace: How Collaboration among the Churches of the Americas Began," *America: The National Catholic Review*, December 7, 2009, at www.americamagazine.org/issue/718/article/great-north-south-embrace.

57. http://www.celam.org/conferencias/Documento_Conclusivo_Rio.pdf.

FERES—prompted in part by the fear that the church's shortcomings in Latin America might prove embarrassing—the Vatican also backed the FERES project. FERES's publications were made possible through funds Ligutti raised among wealthy Catholic donors and a consortium arrangement that included the Ford Foundation, the Spanish Bishops Conference, and Fordham University of New York in the United States.[58]

An assessment of the impact of Radio Sutatenza and its "radiophonic" schools in Colombia, coauthored by Camilo Torres, (Colombia's famous "revolutionary priest") and Berta Corredor, was commissioned by FERES in 1959. Published in 1961, the volume on Radio Sutatenza was the second in FERES's "vast socio-religious" project to study the Latin American Catholic church's personnel and structures conducted between 1958 and 1967.[59] Father Torres's study established Radio Sutatenza and ACPO's method and accomplishments as the paradigm for multimedia mass education among rural populations, an assessment that was confirmed when l'Abbé Houtart and twelve researchers met in Bogotá to make advanced mimeographed copies of Torres's ACPO report available for distribution to the bishops of CELAM at their third annual meeting in Buenos Aires in late 1960.[60] In September 1960, moreover, Pope John XXIII had appointed Mons Salcedo to the Vatican's recently established Secretariat of Press and Entertainment in preparation for the Second Vatican Council.[61]

58. Eugene K. Culhane, "The FERES Study of Latin America," *America* 3, no. 13 (September 1964), 345. In this same issue of *America*, Culhane wrote a brief piece titled "Upsurge in Latin America," where he noted that seventy priests and leaders from fifteen countries in Latin America had met in Porto Alegre, Brazil, July 13–30, 1964, at the urging of CELAM to disseminate Vatican II's major themes and apply them "to the conditions in their countries." At the Porto Alegre meeting, Mons. Joseph Gremillion of Catholic Relief Services (CRS), who had observed the operation of priests in slum areas of Colombia as early as 1960–1961, recommended that the system devised in Bogotá "and adopted and adapted since then in a series of other dioceses, for organizing three, six or even twenty adjacent parishes to work in harmony," a system called *Pastoral en Conjunto*, be adopted elsewhere in Latin America (343). Although ACPO was not the same as Pastoral Social, this system, also known in Colombia as the "veredal" system, was already in use by ACPO in the 1950s. See Torres and Corredor, *Las Escuelas Radiofonicas de Sutatenza, Colombia.*
59. Culhane, "The FERES Study of Latin America," 345.
60. FERES had its principal headquarters in Brussels, but its regional office was based in Bogotá, just a few blocks from CELAM's headquarters. It had been founded by the US Bishop and longtime National Catholic Rural Life Conference executive director Monsignor Luigi Ligutti and the Belgian Liberation Theologian L'Abbé Francois Houtart from the Catholic University of Louvain. Camilo Torres, Gustavo Pérez, and a variety of other Colombian and Latin American priests associated with Liberation Theology had studied with Houtart at the University of Louvain. See, Culhane, "The FERES Study of Latin America," 346.
61. ACPO, *Documentos Santa Sede y Roma, Correspondencia Años 1955–1972*, Secretaría de

Throughout the decade of the 1950s, a shared rejection of communism and armed revolution, as well as a commitment to the promotion
of modern technologies (such as the use of mass media and technical
inputs to increase agricultural output), framed by Christian principles
mobilized in the service of community-centered rural development,
brought together individuals in the Catholic Church (Camilo Torres
and Antonio Samoré, for instance) who later came to differ in fundamental ways. The two earliest volumes commissioned and published
by FERES with Ligutti's and Samoré's support, for example, were
those researched and authored by Dom Heldar Camara of Brazil and
the Colombian priest, Camilo Torres, both members of the Catholic
clergy who would eventually embrace Liberation theology and vocally
express their sense of frustration and disappointment with the limits
of transnational social activism beholden to collaborations between
the Vatican, members of the Latin American church hierarchy, secular
elites, and private corporate interests.

In 1961, however, Camilo Torres was far from advocating armed
revolution, the abandonment of the priesthood, or rejecting programs
such as ACPO as ill-disguised efforts to maintain the rural status quo
when the only possible solution to entrenched, long-standing deficits
in rights, land, education, and justice lay in radical structural change.
Indeed, in his message "On Land Reform" issued in anticipation of
the Colombian government's 1961 Land Reform Law, which he delivered in August 1960, Camilo Torres's remarks were timid when
compared to the tenor of the inaugural address given by Mons. Raul
Zambrano Camader at ACPO's *Semana de Estudios Cardenal Spellman*
before high-ranking members of the Colombian episcopacy, prominent experts on land law, and government representatives six months
earlier in January 1960 in Bogotá.[62] Like Zambrano Camader, Torres

Estado, Fondo *"Gestión,"* ACPO Archive, Biblioteca Luis Angel Arango, Bogotá. The ACPO archive, made up of thousands of documents, letters, pamphlets, scripts, and materials related
to ACPO (including films and recordings), was donated to Colombia's main public library
in 2007; however, it is so voluminous that it is still being catalogued and is only available to
researchers on a limited basis. I am grateful to the librarians of the Sala de Libros Raros y
Manuscritos for enabling my research assistant, Susana Romero, and me to consult ACPO's
correspondence with the Colombian episcopacy and the Vatican in July 2014.

62. By mid-1958, a private charitable foundation, the American Foundation for Popular
Cultural Action, Inc., had been established in New York City, with its headquarters later housed
at 30 Rockefeller Center, for the exclusive purpose of raising money for ACPO and ensuring the
adoption of radio education programs modeled on it in other parts of Latin America. Among

called for the promotion of "technical assistance, technical education, credit, loans and cooperatives" to address rural underdevelopment in his "Message," but he stopped short of openly questioning capitalism or suggesting that fundamental structural change was called for in Colombia. In contrast, the auxiliary bishop of Popayán addressed these questions head on. Zambrano Camader not only explicitly criticized both *minifundismo* and *latifundismo* (echoing the 1953 Manizales Rural Life Conference's conclusion that *latifundismo* was antisocial and antidemocratic), he stated, "the development of Colombia demands the reforms of its structures, not only to increase production but to achieve a more equitable distribution. All reforms of this nature should be embraced without timidity or delay, … so that in the shortest time possible all Colombians may obtain equal opportunities for their development … and so that the human rights of all Colombians are made effective." "In capitalist systems," the auxiliary bishop continued, "it isn't viable to think that those enmeshed in the system" would take the lead in reforming a system from which they benefited, and so Zambrano Camader firmly concluded, it was up to the Catholic Church "with absolute independence and transparency of motives" to take the lead in supporting the law's approval and acceptance.[63]

CONCLUSION

The remarkable growth of ACPO, from a small Catholic radio station in a remote outpost of Colombia to a nationwide organization whose development model was emulated in the United States as well as in other parts of Latin America, has much to tell us about Catholic trans-

its board members were prominent and wealthy U.S. Catholics, U.S. government officials, and various corporate interest groups, many of them on friendly terms with Francis Cardinal Spellman, the archbishop of New York. Cardinal Spellman, a close associate of Antonio Samoré, wrote a personal check for $5,000 in November 1959 to Monsignor Salcedo to help defray the costs of ACPO's Semana de Estudios, which brought together rural development specialists, members of the Catholic episcopacy, and Colombian government representatives around the issue of land reform and rural development in Colombia. See ACPO, *Documentos Santa Sede y Roma, Correspondencia Años, 1955–1972*; F. Gestión, letters from Salcedo to Samoré dated August 8, 1958 (regarding the establishment of the American Foundation for Popular Cultural Action, Inc.), and May 16, 1960 (regarding Spellman's generous gift).

    63. John Gerassi, ed., *Revolutionary Priest: The Complete Writings and Messages of Camilo Torres* (New York: Vintage, 1971), 95–97; "Economía Moral," keynote address delivered by Mons. Raúl Zambrano Camader, auxiliary bishop of Popayán, *Semana de Estudios Cardinal Spellman*, January 18, 1960.

274 ❖ Mary Roldán

national activism in Latin America. First of all, it contributes yet more evidence—in addition to that demonstrated in the other chapters in this volume—that transnational Catholic social activism in the region predated Vatican II by several decades and, indeed, had much deeper roots. In Latin America, where Liberation theology emerged as a compelling and powerful progressive force in the 1960s and 1970s, many of the clergy associated with the movement were trained as sociologists (Colombian Jesuit Camilo Torres Restrepo and Peruvian Gustavo Gutierrez, to name just two), perhaps feeding the misperception that a link between social science and theology was exclusively the product of an affinity between Liberation theology and the secular Left. In fact the tendency to ground Catholic social teaching in secular material analysis went back to the encyclicals of Leo XIII in the late nineteenth century, when the church first confronted the threat of the rise of socialism among European workers and felt compelled to enjoin the clergy to master the analytical tools needed to make the clergy more responsive to the challenges facing their flock.

In the Colombian case, the U.S. Catholic Church played an important role as both the partner of the U.S. government and in a crucial nexus for connections with Latin Americans concerned with Catholic social teachings and activism. The case of ACPO, and its remarkable ability to expand, was intimately linked to the connections forged between organizations such as the NCRLC, the NCWC, the SAD, the Vatican, and the Colombian church and government. The close association between contained rural development rooted in notions of an "agrarian middle class" that was committed to democracy but was increasingly linked to—and made subordinated in some cases to—ideological and secular objectives by funders such as the U.S. government or private corporations, however, could distort the essence of Catholic teachings with repercussions for domestic organizations such as ACPO. This complicated relationship between Latin American Catholic organizations and U.S. politics would only become more problematic in the decades to come.

CHAPTER 11

The Maya Catholic Cooperative Spirit of Capitalism in Guatemala
Civil-Religious Collaborations, 1943–1966

❖ Susan Fitzpatrick-Behrens

This chapter explores the development of a Maya cooperative movement in Guatemala from the 1940s through the 1960s. The cooperative movement had powerful economic effects in the country. It enabled Mayas to enter the global market, to bypass ladino intermediaries, and to access new land. These changes contributed to an economic transformation with powerful political implications. Maya cooperative leaders gained knowledge and training that facilitated broader organizing. In 1975 *New York Times* journalist Alan Riding described the "Indian cooperative movement" as the "first authentic rural movement in Guatemala's history, so far involving about 20 percent of the 3.5 million Indian population." Riding attributed the origins of the movement to "Catholic priests in remote mountain villages" who started the first cooperatives.[1]

Cooperatives were the product of a transnational religious encounter that became linked with secular national projects. Although the

I would like to express my gratitude to Stephen J. C. Andes and Julia G. Young for organizing the outstanding conference where this chapter and the others in the volume were first presented. Special thanks to Catherine LeGrand for sharing with me her extensive knowledge of global cooperative development and to Mary Roldán for providing insight into the crucial role of Catholic-U.S. cooperation in the development of Radio Sutatenza in Colombia. Silvia Arrom and Jorun Poettering provided extremely helpful comments on distinct versions of this chapter, for which I am also grateful. A preliminary version of this chapter was presented on a panel organized by Edward Wright-Rios in honor of Eric Van Young at the Conference on Latin American History meeting in 2012.

1. Alan Riding, "Change, Even in Central America," *New York Times*, September 14, 1975.

governments of Guatemala and the United States Agency for International Development (USAID) facilitated cooperative development, they built on a religious base. Catholic missionaries who settled in the country in the 1940s, 1950s, and 1960s established the first important cooperatives, cooperative training centers, and cooperative associations in the country. They also acted as pioneers in cooperative development of colonization zones in the Petén and Ixcán.[2] Secular government agencies followed, grafting their cooperative framework onto a Catholic foundation and relying on it to facilitate expansion while, at the same time, seeking to impose a more capitalist-oriented model of cooperative development.

Catholic missionaries introduced cooperatives not just as developmentalist initiatives to improve Mayas' economic well-being but also as religious institutions meant to build Catholic communities. Cooperatives were economic enterprises, but their purpose was to promote integral development of the "whole community," to facilitate cooperation, to encourage human development and to enhance human dignity. Their origins were in Catholic movements in North America initiated in the 1930s and globalized in the 1950s and 1960s. The Antigonish Movement, whose history Catherine LeGrand examines in this volume, played a defining role in cooperative development in Guatemala. In the 1930s, the U.S. National Catholic Rural Life Conference (NCRLC) embraced the Antigonish model, relied on it at home, and later transferred it to Latin America.[3] Many of the clergy and laity in Guatemala engaged in cooperative development received training at the Coady Institute.[4]

2. H. Santiago Otero Diez, *Padre Guillermo Woods: Parroquias San José Ixcán y Candelaria de los Mártires*, 2nd ed. (Ixcán, Quiché Guatemala: Ediciones San Pablo, 2006); Diocese of Quiché, *El Quiché: El pueblo y su iglesia, 1960–1980* (Santa Cruz del Quiché, Guatemala: La Diócesis, 1994).

3. John La Farge, SJ, "Two Catholic Conventions," *America*, November 9, 1929, 104–06; Edward Skillin Jr., "Antigonish Ten Years After," *Commonweal*, December 18, 1942, 232–33; Bovee, *The Church and the Land*, Lima Methods Conference of the Maryknoll Fathers, *Proceeding of the Lima Methods Conference of the Maryknoll Fathers: Maryknoll House, Lima, Peru, August 23–28, 1954* (Maryknoll, N.Y.: Maryknoll Fathers, 1954), 164–67; John J. Considine, ed., *The Missionary's Role in Socio-Economic Betterment* (New York: Newman Press, 1960), *Memoria del tercer congreso católico de la vida rural: Panama* (Panama: Organización Católica de la Vida Rural, 1955); vii–ix; Roger Vekemans, ed., *La tierra y el hombre: Cuarto congreso católico de la vida rural* (Buenos Aires: Talleres Gráficos del Atlantico, 1958), 429–30; Quinto congreso católico de la vida rural: Caracas, Venezuela (1961), 3–4.

4. Catherine LeGrand has found extensive material about clergy and laity affiliated with

Although the origins of Guatemala's cooperative movement were global, its development was local. Cooperatives succeeded as components of broader Catholic programs that resonated with Maya Catholic practices even as clergy conflicted directly and sometimes violently with *costumbrista*, or traditional Maya Catholic leaders. Anticlerical reforms introduced by Guatemala's Liberal governments in the nineteenth century decimated the Catholic Church. In response to a scarcity of clergy and resources, Mayas developed an autonomous practice of faith emphasizing celebration of saints more than sacraments. Mayas transformed *cofradías* (confraternities), which were introduced by Catholic missionaries during the colonial era to promote worship of saints, into autonomous institutions whose leaders guided community worship of saints and fulfilled communities' major civil and religious role.[5] Catholic cooperatives shared similarities with Maya cofradías, which may have contributed to their success in Maya communities. Like cofradías, cooperatives were governed by a hierarchically ordered structure of leaders whose roles entailed both civil and religious responsibilities. Mayas used cooperatives simultaneously to transcend their communities and to reinforce corporate identity. Finally, cooperatives, like cofradías, provided Maya communities with ways to oversee personal and community wealth.[6]

This chapter offers a preliminary history of the secular and religious forces that contributed to the development of Maya cooperatives in Guatemala during the period from 1943 to 1966. The follow-

cooperative development in Guatemala studying at Antigonish. Among the participants was Father Luis Gurriarán, a Spanish Sacred Heart missionary who played a defining role developing cooperatives in El Quiche and in the Ixcán.

5. The literature on Mesoamerican cofradías is beautifully synthesized and analyzed in John K. Chance and William B. Taylor, "Cofradías and Cargos: An Historical Perspective on the Mesoamerican Civil-Religious Hierarchy," *American Ethnologist* 12, no. 1 (February 1985): 1–26. Anthropologists working in Guatemala's western highlands in the 1970s recognized the ways in which new models of Catholicism and the development of cooperatives was affecting the traditional cofradía and the civil-religious hierarchy. See Douglass Brintnall, *Revolt against the Dead: The Modernization of a Mayan Community in the Highlands of Guatemala* (New York: Gordon and Breach, 1979); Kay B. Warren, *The Symbolism of Subordination: Indian Identity in a Guatemalan Town* (Austin: University of Texas Press, 1978); John M. Watanabe, *Maya Saints and Souls in a Changing World* (Austin: University of Texas Press, 1992); Ricardo Falla, *Quiché Rebelde: Religious Conversion, Politics, and Ethnic Identity in Guatemala* (Austin: University of Texas Press, 2001).

6. David McCreery offers an outstanding analysis of the transformation of cofradías in nineteenth-century Guatemala. See McCreery, *Rural Guatemala: 1760–1940* (Palo Alto, Calif.: Stanford University Press, 1994), 135–37, 183.

ing pages offer an examination of the local community contexts in which some of the first Catholic cooperatives were established and the broader global context of their development. It emphasizes the experience of Maryknoll Catholic missionaries, because they were among the first and the largest Catholic organizations to establish missions and cooperatives in Guatemala's western highlands and because they left extensive records, but it seeks to place Maryknoll's experience into the broader context of Catholic mission programs in Guatemala and Catholic Church and secular government collaboration.

THE OCTOBER REVOLUTION'S COOPERATIVE EXPERIMENT, 1944–1954

In October 1944 democratic forces in Guatemala led by urban middle-class teachers and students, reformist members of the Guardia de Honor military battalion, and a company of cadets from the Escuela Politécnica, led a revolt that overthrew General Jorge Ubico, the military dictator who had controlled the country since 1931.[7] In the aftermath of Ubico's ouster a temporary governing junta composed of "the commander of the Guardia de Honor, Major Francisco Arana; a former commander of the company of cadets, Captain Jacobo Arbenz Guzmán, and a prominent civilian, Jorge Toriello" was formed.[8] The junta's major task was to formulate a new constitution and to oversee the democratic election of a president. The resulting 1945 constitution pledged to "orient the national economy to the benefit of the people; with the goal of assuring each individual a dignified existence and benefiting the collectivity."[9] This was a lofty goal in a country where just two percent of the population controlled 72 percent of the land, and the economy depended almost entirely on export agriculture devoted to coffee and bananas and reliant on an exploited indigenous labor force.[10] Guatemala's first elected president, Juan José Arévalo observed that "[t]here has been in the past a fundamental lack of sympathy for the working man

7. Jim Handy, *Revolution in the Countryside: Rural Conflict and Agrarian Reform in Guatemala, 1944–1954* (Chapel Hill: University of North Carolina Press, 1994), 23.

8. Ibid.

9. Roberto Barillas Izaguirre, *Legislación Cooperativa Guatemalteca* (Guatemala: Departamento de Fomento Cooperativo, 1950), III.

10. Stephen Schlesinger and Stephen Kinzer, *Bitter Fruit: The Story of the American Coup in Guatemala* (Garden City, N.Y.: Doubleday Press, 1982), 38.

and the faintest cry for justice was avoided and punished as if one were trying to eradicate the beginnings of a frightful epidemic."[11]

To work toward achieving the goal of orienting the economy for the benefit of the people, the new constitution abolished vagrancy laws, eliminated literacy as a qualification for voting, and replaced appointed *intendentes* (mayors) with elected mayors. It also pledged the government to form cooperatives. The constitution was followed by Decree Law 146, which established the Department of Co-operative Development (DCD) with initial capital of (Guatemalan Quetzal) Q200,000.00. The government believed that credit cooperatives offered the best way to improve conditions for rural workers.[12] Between 1945 and 1948, seventeen credit cooperatives were formed in Guatemala and twenty-one regional offices of the DCD were established to advise and promote the new groups. In 1949 these twenty-one regional offices were transferred to the Institute for Production Development (Instituto de Fomento de la Producción, or INFOP) and emphasis shifted from credit cooperatives to multiservice agricultural cooperatives.[13] INFOP's mandate was to concentrate on increasing the production of basic foodstuffs through expanding credit. "In its first year of operation, the INFOP gave out Q4,500,000 in loans to over 4,000 people. By 1950, this figure had reached Q7 million per year."[14] In 1949 the government passed Decree Law 643, which provided the complete legal foundation for cooperative development.[15]

President Juan José Arévalo claimed that his ideas were based on those of Franklin D. Roosevelt, who, in Arévalo's view, demonstrated that it was possible to maintain the freedom of a democratic system, while "breath[ing] into it a socialist spirit."[16] Cooperatives, which could

11. Jim Handy, *Gift of the Devil: A History of Guatemala* (Cambridge, Mass.: South End Press, 1984), 106.

12. Co-operative Development: Guatemala, 1969–1970, USAID Project No. 520-15-995-206, 2 (http://dec.usaid.gov/index.cfm); Barillas Izaguirre, *Legislación Cooperativa Guatemalteca*, 11. Although the government viewed cooperatives with enthusiasm, there were few promoters in the country with training in cooperative development. As a result, at least one leader was sent to Quebec to study cooperative development, *Fomento de la Cooperación en Guatemala: Breve Reseña del Movimiento Cooperativo de Quebec* (Guatemala: Publicaciones del Departamento de Fomento Cooperativo, 1948), 11.

13. Co-operative Development: Guatemala, 1969–1970, USAID Project No. 520-15-995-206, 8 (http://dec.usaid.gov/index.cfm).

14. Handy, *Revolution in the Countryside*, 26.

15. Barillas Izaguirre, *Legislación Cooperativa Guatemalteca*, 11.

16. Handy, *Gift of the Devil*, 107.

not be classified either as capitalist or as socialist, appeared ideal vehicles to contribute to achieving this end. As Roberto Barillas Izaguirre, director of the DCD observed, "the cooperative can perform all the actions that an individual merchant performs, but one, which is distinctive, fundamental: a merchant operates in order to get a benefit, which is the profit; a cooperative operates performing similar actions and even the same ones but in order to get another kind of benefit: to service its members."[17] Cooperatives offered a way to create economic actors who prioritized service to community. In addition to providing credit, the government saw cooperatives as a means of transferring state-owned fincas and communal lands under government control to workers.[18]

Historian Jim Handy recounts that while official state publications provided glowing reports about the effectiveness of cooperatives, their development suggested they did not quite fulfill government hopes: "Reports from the inspectors of the national fincas that had been converted into cooperatives stressed the abundant harvest they expected in 1954. The DAN estimated that the coffee crop from the cooperative on the former national finca Concepción would be worth Q600,000, one of the best harvests the finca had ever enjoyed and one that would give each member between Q3,500 and Q4,000. The *Tribuna popular* claimed, 'Never has a peasant dreamed of making this much money.'"[19] Yet, when Juan José Arévalo's successor, President Jacobo Arbenz (who was democratically elected in 1952) successfully passed agrarian reform legislation (Decree 900) it did not include the provision to incorporate expropriated land into cooperatives, although this had been part of the original proposal.[20] In fact, the government found that workers "were unsympathetic to the idea of full-producer cooperatives. Only 9 were established out of the 110 national fincas ... Even in the fincas where cooperatives were established, many workers refused to join, instead demanding land of their own."[21]

Even credit cooperatives appeared only partially successful. Roberto Barillas Izaguirre reported that "three years of experience in this project has shown us that the efforts realized by the department have

17. Barillas Izaguirre, *Legislación Cooperativa Guatemalteca*, 14. CIRMA KGD 1370 A29 1949 A 6.

18. Barillas Izaguirre, *Legislación Cooperativa Guatemalteca*, 60–61.

19. Handy, *Revolution in the Countryside*, 95–96.

20. Ibid., 86.

21. Ibid., 121.

improved in a positive way the economy of many municipalities where there are credit cooperatives, they have enhanced production and local lenders have been displaced providing for a more humane and just system of credit." Nonetheless, he concluded, "it is worth saying that the cooperatives are working acceptably as a *business*, but they leave much to be desired as an *association of people*." He explained in more detail, giving a specific example, that

the need for credit pushed almost all producers of one municipality to orga-nize themselves into a cooperative. Once it was established, each member re-quested a loan that generally was granted, and the percentage of defaults is extremely low. Having obtained the loan, the associate withdrew completely from the social engagement, without any more concern than paying his own amortization and interest, without caring if the others did the same, if the as-sociation encountered difficulties, if it experienced an economic bonanza or a complete failure. He did not attend the general meetings, did not exercise any control over the administration and, in a word, acted like a debtor to the soci-ety, but almost never as a member.[22]

Cooperative development in-and-of-itself thus did not guarantee the cre-ation of a society concerned with service to community rather more than narrowly defined economic interests. Barillas lamented that "[i]gnorance, individualism, distrust, ambition, impatience, indifference, indiscipline, have been the principal negative factors that we have confronted ..."[23]

The government initiated cooperative movement seemed to come to an abrupt end in 1954, when the United States orchestrated the overthrow of the democratically elected president Jacobo Arbenz.[24] In its 1970 report on the development of cooperatives in Guatemala, US-AID reported that "[w]ith the revolution of Colonel Castillo Armas in 1954, cooperatives were branded as communistic, mainly due to their association with the Campesino Federation and labor unions, as well as to the mental confusion of "cooperative" and "commune." Many leaders were jailed or fled the country, and, in effect, the cooperative movement ended."[25]

22. Barillas Izaguirre, *Fomento de la Cooperación en Guatemala*, 101.
23. Barillas Izaguirre, *Legislación Cooperativa Guatemalteca*, 46.
24. There is extensive literature about the U.S.-orchestrated military overthrow of Jacobo Arbenz. See Schlesinger and Kinzer, *Bitter Fruit*; Piero Gleijeses, *Shattered Hope: The Guate-malan Revolution and the United States, 1944–1954* (Princeton, N.J.: Princeton University Press: 1991); and Nick Cullather and Piero Gleijeses, *Secret History: The CIA's Classified Account of Its Operations in Guatemala, 1952–1954* (Palo Alto, Calif.: Stanford University Press, 1999).
25. Department of State, Project Title: Cooperative Development, U.S. Obligation Span:

Yet in fact, the cooperative movement did not end. The legal foundation of cooperatives established during the era of the "democratic spring" also allowed for the creation of independent cooperatives. Article 10 of Decree Law 146 "classified cooperatives in two large groups: those affiliated with the national cooperative system or independents. The affiliated cooperatives were organized in agreement with chapter VI of Decree Law 146. Independent cooperatives were organized by the initiative of their members."[26] At the same time that the government sought to promote cooperative development, so did a small group of foreign Catholic missionaries who settled in the highland department of Huehuetenango in 1943. Clergy introduced cooperatives in tandem with catechetical programs, literacy classes, schools, and medical programs. This confluence of programs designed to provide for the needs of the "whole man" contributed to the long-term success of cooperatives. It may have allowed them to overcome some of the challenges described by Barillas.

Catholic cooperatives survived the overthrow of Arbenz, contributing to the foundation for a new cooperative movement fomented by the USAID, the Alliance for Progress, and the Guatemalan government.[27]

THE CATHOLIC COOPERATIVE ENDEAVOR

The reformist government of Guatemala was not alone in seeking solutions to challenges confronting the poor. Nor was it alone in looking for ways to transcend the polarized political choice between socialist and capitalist development strategies. Segments of the Catholic Church were on a similar quest. The Catholic Church, however, could not be accused of supporting communism. The church had been grappling with economic challenges since 1891, when Pope Leo XIII published the encyclical: *Rerum novarum,* which was followed forty years later by Pope Pius XI's encyclical, *Quadragesimo anno.* These encyclicals criticized exploitation of workers by the wealthy and supported the right of workers to organize while, at the same time, taking a firm

---

Fy66 through Fy76, ACS286-76-069, Box 2 Subj 1970 AGR3 coops and credit, National Archives and Records Administration (NARA), 8.

26. Barillas Izaguirre, *Legislación Cooperativa Guatemalteca,* 63.

27. German and Dutch religious and secular nongovernmental organizations would also contribute to the development of cooperatives, as would other U.S.-based secular NGOs, including the Penny Foundation.

stand against socialism and in favor of private property. Just as the Guatemalan government sought to enhance broader participation in the country's political process, Pope Pius XI sought to increase lay participation in the church by introducing Catholic Action.[28]

The Great Depression led clergy to engage these encyclicals and their experience to seek new responses to the challenge of poverty. Among the most influential of these efforts was that undertaken by Father Moses M. Coady, a priest in Nova Scotia concerned with the economic condition of the region's fishermen. Through the Extension Department of St. Francis Xavier University in eastern Nova Scotia, Coady initiated popular education programs that led to the formation of cooperatives. As Catherine LeGrand's chapter in this volume explains, the influence of Antigonish spread across Canada and gathered rapt attention in Catholic circles in the United States. In his praise of the Antigonish Movement, Edward Skillin Jr. observed in the pages of the U.S. Catholic journal *Commonweal* that "[f]or the past ten years we [Catholics in the United States] have all done a lot of talking about the principles in the social encyclicals.... But what new institutions have we set up to meet the new conditions inimical to man, the family and society resulting from modern capitalism? ... The priests of Antigonish do not talk about it much," he concluded, "but by collaborating with the people in meeting their basic problems of existence they believe they have achieved far more than the most eloquent preaching could do."[29] The NCRLC founded in the United States in 1923 by Edwin Vincent O'Hara, a rural priest active in Catholic Action, turned to Antigonish as a model for the United States.[30] Luigi G. Ligutti, an acolyte of O'Hara who became director of the NCRLC in 1937, sought to bring the Antigonish model to life in the United States by accessing grants from the New Deal's Farm Security Administration to create Granger Homesteads in Iowa.[31] Ligutti and the NCRLC would become central forces in U.S. mission to Latin America.[32]

28. For the impact of Catholic Action in Latin America, see Ana María Bidegain, "From Catholic Action to Liberation Theology," Helen Kellog Institute, Working Paper 48, Nov. 1985.

29. Skillin, "Antigonish Ten Years After," 232–33.

30. Jeffrey Marlett, "Harvesting an Overlooked Freedom: The Anti-Urban Vision of American Catholic Agrarianism, 1920–1950," *U.S. Catholic Historian* 16, no. 4 (1998): 90; David S. Bovee, "Catholic Rural Life Leader: Luigi G. Ligutti," *U.S. Catholic Historian* 8, no. 3 (1989): 144.

31. Ibid., 101–02.

32. Gerald M. Costello, *Mission to Latin America: The Successes and Failures of a Twentieth-Century Crusade* (Maryknoll, N.Y.: Orbis Books, 1979), 28.

Franklin Delano Roosevelt, who provided indirect support for the NCRLC by aiding cooperative development, appeared to many Catholics in the United States as the first U.S. president to embrace Catholic ideals and citizens. Father John A. Ryan, an economist and prominent Catholic leader was said to have gushed, "Never before in our history have the politics of the federal government embodied so much legislation that is of a highly ethical order. Never before have government policies been so deliberately, formally and consciously based upon conceptions and convictions of moral right and social justice."[33] In addition to quietly supporting Catholics (a key voting bloc) at home, Roosevelt also introduced the Good Neighbor Policy, which sought to establish new terms for relations between the United States and Latin America. This foreign policy initiative resonated with U.S. Catholics because it drew the largest Catholic region of the world into a relationship founded on the principle (if not the practice) of equality. Catholics claimed that the Good Neighbor Policy offered them a unique opportunity to serve their country's interests by acting as intermediaries who shared with their southern neighbors a foundation in religious faith. As Edwin Ryan observed in the Jesuit journal *America*, "[t]he numerous efforts toward stimulating friendliness among the nations of America … are worthy of all encouragement; but none of them can hope for lasting success without recognizing in a practical manner that in our community of Faith with Latin Americans we Catholics of the United States possess a means of approach far more effective than any other …"[34]

It was with this background of ideas about means to alleviate rural poverty, on one hand, and cautious ties to the U.S. government, on the other, that representatives of the Catholic Foreign Mission Society of America, known popularly as Maryknoll, sent representatives to Latin America in 1943. Guatemala was among Maryknoll's first mission fields in the region. Because of the scarcity of clergy in the country, Maryknoll missionaries were given the opportunity to select a mission territory. Two priests traveled through the country meeting with clergy and ultimately settling on Huehuetenango, a remote department in Guatemala's western highlands, where three-quarters of

---

33. Cited in James Hennessey, *A History of Catholic America: From Columbus to the Quincentennial, 1492–1992* (Sparkill, N.Y.: Shepherd Press, 1991), 259.

34. Edwin Ryan, "A Catholic Pan-American Society," *America* 45, no. 26 (October 3, 1931): 611.

the population identified as Maya speakers of four distinct languages.[35] The priests chose Huehuetenango because, as they put it, "[it is] the ideal mission territory for ourselves … At present there are only 3 priests in this whole section and all 3 of them … seem to be on the fence, so to speak. One wants to go back to Mexico, where he came from. One is old and sickly and unable to do much of anything and if reports are true, he is away from his parish more than half the time. And the third is said to have kicked over all traces …"[36] When the missionaries received their official assignment to Huehuetenango, two of the three priests in the department were immediately reassigned, and six months later, the elderly priest from Mexico died.[37] Fathers Witte and Allie were left to minister to the needs of a population of approximately 176,000, establishing a people to priest ratio of some 88,000 to 1, making it even worse than the national average of 30,000 to 1.[38]

Despite challenging conditions, the Maryknoll priests confidently asserted that there is "no doubt of the welcome we would find [in Huehuetenango]."[39] In some ways, the clergy were right. Although most communities in Huehuetenango had been without priests for decades or, in some cases, more than half a century, cofradías responsible for maintaining the cult of community patron saints ensured the survival of Catholicism but not in a form sanctioned by the Roman Catholic Church or Maryknoll clergy. Cofradías curtailed priests' roles, limiting them to saying masses for saints' feast-day celebrations—a service for which they paid the priest. The Maryknoll priests later complained bitterly about this arrangement: "[I]t is quite evident the priest has only a minor role if even that. Thru generations of being without a priest they have their own rites which they celebrate in conformity to their no-

35. Adrian Recinos, *Monografía del Departamento de Huehuetenango*, 2nd ed. (Guatemala: Editorial del Ministerio de Educación Pública, 1954), 222.

36. "Account of Trip to the West Coast and the Northwestern Highlands," Maryknoll Priests' Diaries, Guatemala, June 9–26, 1943, 80. Maryknoll Mission Archive (MMA).

37. Leigh A. Fuller, S.J., "Catholic Missionary Work and National Development in Guatemala, 1943–68: The Maryknoll Experience," master's thesis, New York University, 1971, 63. Arthur Allie, M.M., Guatemala Diary, February 1944. Maryknoll Preists' Diaries, Guatemala, MMA.

38. Bruce Calder, *Crecimiento y Cambio de la Iglesia Católica Guatemalteca: 1944–1966* (Guatemala: Seminaro de Integración Social Guatemalteca Editorial Jose de Peneda Ibarra Ministerio de Educación, 1970), 19. Recinos, *Monografía del Departamento de Huehuetenango* indicates that the population of Huehuetenango in 1950 was 198,872 (222).

39. "Account of Trip to the West Coast and the Northwestern Highlands," Maryknoll Priests' Diaries, Guatemala, June 9–26, 1943, MMA.

tions of religion. How closely their mentality approximates that of the Protestants! Away with the priest we are running the show: the priest is a nuisance ..."[40]

Nonetheless, when the first Maryknollers arrived, the fiesta seemed a welcome opportunity to experience local Catholicism and it provided priests with an entry to communities where as outsiders they otherwise would have no place. Father Clarence Witte reported, "As soon as we arrived here [in Huehuetenango], in fact it was awaiting our arrival, there was a request for a priest in one of the outlying villages for the celebration of their festival. And it was my lot to go." Initially Witte seemed to find the fiesta and his place in it quaint and appealing: "Coming to the last peak above the village, where the little church first came into view, there the path was strewn with pine needles, and there was a delegation of the village elders to greet me. Each gave me a handshake of welcome, and each thrust into my arms a bouquet of geraniums and lilies. Then the twelve of them, with heads uncovered, paired off on either side of my horse and escorted me the remaining mile or so into the village." Yet he left the community, weighed down "by the villagers' gift of eighteen chickens and two dozen eggs," and lamenting in a patronizing tone typical of early missionary accounts, "what impressed me most was the appalling religious ignorance of these poor people ... They will never be anything but Catholic, but they are far from being knowing, faithful, and practical Catholics."[41]

This first encounter would later seem benign as the priests came into direct confrontation with what offended both their religious sensibilities and their Catholic sense of social justice. Father Witte described a subsequent fiesta visit undertaken in October 1943 to San Rafael Independencia as "a penance, certainly for some reason known to His greater wisdom, if not to me, the Lord did not see fit to give me a good day. It was a horrible day, a horrible trip over horrible trails, a trip that took me to the most horrible experience of my life ..." Witte decried the fiesta as "nothing less than a drunken orgy. Dancing and drinking and the obscenities that cannot be absent from an excess of this combination filled the days and the nights, and without interruption through day or night the marimbas, a very machination of the devil to the ignorant Indian, continued their calls to more revelry, to more excess, to

40. Arthur Allie, M.M., Huehuetenango Diary, April 1946, MMA.
41. Clarence J. Witte, M.M., First Days in Huehuetenango, August 1943, MMA.

more spending, and to more profit for the disreputable dispensers of the damnable drink."[42] Witte reserved his most uninhibited condemnation for Ladinos and governing officials. "Such excess as I saw is, of course, a disgrace to the Indian. But the Indian is ignorant, and I say that the greater disgrace is on the disreputable Ladinos who sell the filthy stuff, who urge on and beguile the simple minded Indian, who have no shame or compassion and seek only personal profit, who by raising the price when the supply of liquor begins to run low to double and triple the standard and by other such tricks rob the poor Indian of the little he has, theirs I say is the greater sin. But the greatest disgrace of all rests with the government that allows such inhumanity."[43] In fact, during the years preceding the "Guatemalan Spring" income from liquor taxes was the state's second-most important source of revenue after import–export duties.[44]

The October revolution of 1944, which led to the presidential elections of Juan José Arévalo and his successor Jacobo Arbenz, occurred almost a year to the month after Father Witte's experience. At the same time that Maryknoll missionaries in Huehuetenango undertook what would become by 1952 a systematic and sometimes brutal effort to reduce the power of local Maya religious authorities to establish their ideal of doctrinal Catholicism, the national government undertook a parallel effort to reform society with a secular agenda. In his study of the Q'eqchi' coffee-growing department of Alta Verapaz, historian Greg Grandin provides a detailed account of the ways that the governments of Arévalo and Arbenz offered community members political alternatives and ways to displace local authorities.[45]

In the department of Huehuetenango the change in government also offered alternatives that disrupted established political structures linked to cofradías. Maryknoll missionaries consciously and unconsciously became one component of this change. In 1946, Maryknoll Father Alfred Smith, a missionary in San Miguel Acatán, described a visit from a Maya man asking for help to learn Spanish. The priest concluded, in an off-

42. Thoughts and Jottings for October in Soloma, Clarence Witte, M.M., October 1943, MMA.
43. Ibid.
44. McCreery, *Rural Guatemala, 1760–1940*, 177. See also David Carey Jr., *I Ask for Justice: Maya Women, Dictators, and Crime in Guatemala, 1898–1944* (Austin: University of Texas Press, 2013).
45. Greg Grandin, *The Last Colonial Massacre: Latin America in the Cold War* (Chicago: The University of Chicago Press, 2004), 37–45.

hand style typical of U.S. priests' accounts: "I figured that afternoon was as good a time as any to start our classes in alfabetization. The government is very interested in literating the illiterate and I figured it would be a handy contact.... One important aspect of this situation is that at present according to the new constitution a native mayor or alcalde can be elected, as opposed to the appointee of Ubico's regime. We now have an Indian alcalde, but unfortunately there are only a handful of Indians qualified for the job, mainly due to language deficiency." Smith linked his "literacy program" to a religious end by arguing that

the Indian has a fearful inferiority complex and a handful of mixed bloods or ladinos have no trouble keeping them in a subservient position. I figure that this lack of self-respect is an obstacle that prevents their becoming full-fledged Catholics and shall do my best to combat it. There is already a nasty undercurrent of talk to the effect that Sacramental Catholicism is for the ladino alone. This talk is mainly prompted by the sacudenes or native priests whose overlordship is threatened by all this talking of obeying the Commandments, praying with a pure heart, receiving Matrimony and Holy Communion.[46]

Thus, the priests started to offer practical assistance in the form of literacy and health programs at the same time that they undermined religious practices guided by cofradías.

The nature of the resulting conflicts between clergy and cofradías and their unintended political consequences are evident in Brother Felix Fournier's 1949 description of a confrontation between Maryknoll Father Jim Curtin and his Catholic acolytes and leaders of the cofradía and their costumbrista Catholic supporters in Ixtahuacán. When Brother Felix arrived in the community to undertake a photo assignment for Maryknoll's publicity magazine, he was told by the pastor, Father James Curtin, that he might "see some fun [because] some stinkers in town have sent down to the capital for some kind of committee to come up and throw me out of Ixtahuacán." What initially appeared a joke proved quite serious. "Next morning," Brother Felix recounted in a letter home to his parents, "we were up early, but not as early as one of the Indians who was at Fr. Jim's bedroom door in the patio. In a mixture of Indian and amazing Spanish he said the Father wouldn't be able to go to the fiesta, and that furthermore he would be wise to stay inside the convento walls and that even now men had gone up into the

46. Alfred E. Smith, M.M., San Miguel Acatán Diary, August 1946, MMA.

hills to get some more men to stay with him and protect him!" Even taking into account Brother Felix's biases, his description suggested that a cadre composed of local governing officials linked to the leadership of the cofradía were the force behind the threat:

All of the malcontents, the witch doctors against whom Fr. Curtin has been relentless until their livelihood has been greatly reduced, opportunists, and drunks, all had been walled into a group by a politico, a former autocrat in the town, a hard man whose word had been law and who spoke often. A couple of years ago, or less, his party lost out in the elections. Since then he had been trying to get back into power. He had always tried to make trouble for Fr. Curtin, on one occasion recently going so far as to denounce him before the President as a political meddler, and as an innovator who was trying to tear the old customs, sacred things as anyone must know, from the Indians, and who refused to ring the bells of the church.

According to Fournier, Don Umberto's denunciation led to an investigation of the priest's work, but ended with a commendation "for the good job he was doing" by a minister in the National Palace, the departmental governor, and the judge in Ixtahuacán. In fact, it seemed that although Catholic clergy were known for their opposition to the "communist" government of Jacobo Árbenz, some of Maryknoll's programs conformed to the interests of the reformist government.[47] By seeking to change practices of Catholicism, missionaries undermined established political hierarchies inextricably linked with the cofradía system.

The confrontation, according to Brother Felix, came to include some five hundred acolytes supporting Father Curtin, a .22 target rifle, the Guardia de Hacienda, and local Ladinos, it concluded in the late afternoon of the next day when the governor arrived, riding in "at the head of a column of soldiers, thirty, from [Brother Felix's] catechism class ... In five minutes all the heads of the movement were in jail and the men dispersed ... the governor made a very strong speech about the fomenters of trouble and what they could expect, and the whole town cheered."[48] This was neither the first nor the last of the vio-

47. Guatemala's papal nuncio, Genaro Verolino, did not consider Jacobo Arbenz's policies to be a threat to the Catholic Church. He maintained cordial relations with the president, who even agreed to permit additional foreign clergy to enter the country. Guatemala's Archbishop Rossell y Arellano, however, identified the president as a communist and played a central role in motivating support for his removal. Piero Gleijeses, *Shattered Hope*, 210–13.

48. All quotes from Brother Felix Fournier, Letter to Will and Mabel, October 26, 1949, Brother Felix Fournier Letters, MMA.

lent confrontations between Maryknoll clergy and Maya costumbrista Catholic leaders. In 1952, after the people of San Gaspar complained to the minister of government about Father Gerbermann's failure to say Mass for the community, he reported that "the chief reason is that the headmen in San Gaspar are all chimanes (medicine men, or rather witch doctors), who do not want to lose their hold over the people, which they would have if the people had begun to learn the doctrine. So they spread the word that I was a Protestant and subjected those who came to Mass and doctrine to all sorts of abuses, even throwing some of them in jail. On one occasion they beat up a poor woman and left her lying on the hammock stretched across the river for footmen."[49]

Even as conflicts raged, Maryknollers also reported what they viewed as remarkable success in drawing Mayas into the Romanized practice of Catholicism. In 1947 Father Sommer, pastor of Jacaltenango, lamented: "I am afraid this is the first diary I've written this year; there is no time to write diaries, no time to do half the Spiritual work the wonderful Indians drop at your feet . . ."[50] In 1949 Father McClear observed that in San Pedro Soloma "in the last year confessions have gone up from 869 to over 3400 and communions from 2000 to better than 9000. We had 246 communions but already in the three months of this year have had 115."[51] In 1951, Father McGuinness reported that in San Marcos, long considered by Maryknoll an intransigent site filled with costumbrista Catholics violently opposed to Catholic doctrine, "we have to have two Masses every Sunday at San Marcos, and

49. Hugo Gerbermann, M.M., Ixtahuacán Diary, March 1952, MMA. See also Hugo Gerbermann, M.M., Ixtahuacán Diary, January 1952. "The New Year began with a record crowd at the Masses. I celebrated two Masses in Ixtahuacán, then went over to Colotenango, about ten miles away, for a third Mass. Colotenango is one of my larger out-stations. Being the nearest and the easiest to get to, I go there every Friday afternoon and return to Ixtahuacán Saturday noon. Almost every week we see a few new faces among those who come in to learn the doctrine. In spite of the fact that the witch doctors and even the alcalde are trying to keep the people away from the doctrine classes, the number is steadily increasing." For similar conflicts in other departments, see Ricardo Falla, *Quiché Rebelde*, and Douglas E. Brintnall, "Race Relations in the Southeastern Highlands of Mesoamerica," *American Ethnologist* 6, no. 4 (November 1979): 638–52; and Brintnall, *Revolt against the Dead.*
50. Paul Sommer, M.M., Jacaltenango Diary, 1947, MMA.
51. J. E. McClear, M.M., Diary of San Pedro Soloma for September 1949, MMA. Brother Felix Fournier (Letter to Kay, April 24, 1949), speaking of Huehuetenango, observed: "The number of daily and Sunday Communions has doubled since my coming down. A goodish number come to night prayers every evening too. And the convento patio is always full of kids, which is a good sign too."

there are about 180 communions."[52] By 1953, even Ixtahuacán, where Brother Felix, Father Curtin, and their supporters faced a potentially violent confrontation, had accepted many of Maryknoll's practices of Catholicism. Father John Breen reported, "This year I told them [the Chimanes] we would celebrate the feast on the 4th of June along with the rest of the Catholic Church. Of course they objected ..." Yet the priest persisted, insisting that the "all the Catholics in the doctrine, would celebrate the feast on the 4th and the others could do what they wanted later ..." To his surprise and that of the Catholics of the doctrine: "The night before, the Catholics from all the aldeas came in ... It would have been a marvelous day for any priest—there were 180 communions in the morning, about 90% received of those who as yet have the right to receive. The procession was orderly and they sang with fervor and attended the Benedictions with devotion ... There was not one drunk and all agreed it was a wonderful fiesta. The result was that at the end of the month the others didn't have their procession according to the '*costumbre*' [tradition], because they said the people would laugh at them now."[53] By 1953, so many Mayas had embraced Maryknoll Catholicism that there simply were not enough priests to meet existing religious needs, while also working to attract new "converts" to the faith.[54]

It was in this context of dramatic religious and political transformation that Maryknoll introduced two innovations: the catechetical system and the cooperative. In 1953 Maryknoll adopted a model of Catholic Action suggested to them by Monsignor Rafael González, who had used it successfully in Totonicapán. Catholic Action called for the development of a catechetical system whereby clergy would teach Mayas Church–sanctioned Catholic prayer and doctrine, and they, in turn, would be responsible for introducing it to five families in their community in their languages. Each catechist maintained responsibility for his (they were overwhelmingly male) five families.[55] Maryknoll found that the exact model of Catholic Action did not fit the needs of the people in Huehuetenango, so it modified the model to conform

52. Edward J. McGuinness, M.M., Guatemala Diary (Jacaltenango), October 1–15, 1951, MMA.

53. John Breen, M.M., Ixtahuacán Diary, June 1953, MMA.

54. Edward J. McGuinness, M.M., Huehuetenango, Guatemala, Cuilco Diary, December 1953, MMA.

55. Ibid.

to existing structures.[56] But the catechetical system created a cadre of educated, religious leaders who served as intermediaries between their communities and Maryknoll priests. Together these Maya men guided the creation of an alternative Catholic community, whose members came to participate in and support cooperative development. In contrast with the government cooperative model, Catholic cooperatives thus grew from communities bound together through shared practices of Catholicism and a distinct intellectual engagement that contributed to community development.

Also in 1953, Maryknoll Brother Felix Fournier introduced the first cooperative in Huehuetenango. Writing to his family in Brooklyn, Brother Felix reported, "We actually started studying last September, meeting faithfully every week, with each member depositing ten cents, (which is the maximum savings each member can afford.) At this time we have a capital of over a hundred dollars." In May the cooperative applied to the government for recognition, but it did not receive presidential approval until August. Brother Felix lamented this delay because "just at this moment is when there is the greatest need of credit ... The farmers, and nearly all the members are farmers, need cash right now to buy corn, the staff of life, until they can harvest their crops in August and September." To illustrate the desperate need for money, Brother Felix offered his family the example of Gregorio Sonique, who as a member had asked to borrow fifteen dollars. He had to explain to Sonique, "as he pretty well knew anyway," that until the credit union received government recognition, it could not grant loans. When a week later the government still had not granted recognition and the $2.40 Sonique had withdrawn was gone, Brother Felix asked his family rhetorically, "What do you do in a case like that? His only recourse would have been to get money from a finca agent, an advance, that is, on an agreement to work down on the coast for six weeks, or to borrow money from a lender. If he were very lucky he might have gotten it at 5% a month, but since money is scarce and corn is scarce too he would probably have had to agree to 10% a month."[57] In the

56. Lima Methods Conference of the Maryknoll Fathers, *Proceeding of the Lima Methods Conference of the Maryknoll Fathers*, 104–11.

57. A 1951 World Bank report stated that in a study of thirty-seven municipalities in Guatemala, the average interest rate for small loans varied from 3.2 percent per month to 12.6 percent per month. This was equivalent to a yearly rate of interest of an astonishing 94.8 percent. Cited in Gleijesis, *Shattered Hope*, 156.

end, Brother Felix loaned Sonique five dollars with the agreement that he would borrow funds from the credit union to repay him as soon as it received recognition. He did, making Gregorio Soniq the credit union's first loan applicant, who received funds at an interest rate of 1 percent a month. "He pays .15 a month instead of a possible 1.50!" declared Fournier.[58]

In addition to providing crucial economic resources, the credit union also created a leadership structure. Mayas—most of them catechists—formed the board of directors. "Looking at those barefoot men," recounted Brother Felix, "in what are surely much patched clothes, the name Board of Directors seems incongruous, but knowing the men, and this is the beauty of the cooperative movement, they are Directors in every sense. While at the moment they are dealing in a hundred dollars it will not be long before the capital will be in the thousands, and the Board of Directors will be taking it in stride too."[59] In 1954, Brother Felix reported to his family that he was writing to "Monsignor [Luigi] Ligutti, of the Catholic Rural Life Conference, for some dope [information] on the Catholic Rural Life Program in the States and other places."[60] A year later in 1955, Brother Felix traveled "to [the] Catholic congress of rural life and coop workshop with Fr. John Lenahan in Panama."[61] By 1956, Maryknoll had established six credit cooperatives in the department: Malactancito, founded in 1953, had 53 members; Cuilco, founded in 1955, had 92 members; Jacaltenango, founded in 1955, had 148 members; San Ildefonso Ixtahuacán, founded in 1956, had 46 members; Santa Eulalia, founded in 1956, had 58 members; and Soloma, founded in 1956, had 45 members.[62] In 1956 Sacred Heart Missionaries from Spain settled in the department of El Quiché, where they established the first credit cooperative in 1958.[63]

58. Brother Felix Fournier, Letter to Will and Mabel, August 12, 1953. MMA.
59. Brother Felix Fournier Letter to Mabel, Will, and Family, July 1, 1953, MMA.
60. Letter to Kay, December 15, 1954. Letters Brother Felix Fournier, MMA.
61. Brother Felix Fournier, March 28, 1955, MMA.
62. By 1957, the missionaries in Huehuetenango had established 5 credit unions, and also opened 5 primary schools, started 7 education programs teaching basic literacy from 3 to 100 adults, and established 13 medical clinics. Technical Assistance Services sponsored by Maryknoll Fathers in Guatemala (Compiled Spring 1957), Maryknoll Library, Maryknoll, N.Y.
63. Luis Samandú, Hans Siebers, Oscar Sierra, *Guatemala: Retos de la Iglesia Católica en una Sociedad en Crisis* (San José, Costa Rica: Editorial Departamento Ecuménico de Investigaciones DEI, 1990), 76–77; and Diocesis El Quiché, *El Quiché: El Pueblo y su iglesia, 1960–1980* (Guatemala: La Diocesis, 1994), 58.

In 1955 Brother Felix informed his family back home that "Catechists and doctrine classes practically dot the countryside"[64] A 1957 Maryknoll report on technical assistance in the department of Huehuetenango listed 602 lay leaders in training. That number increased exponentially not only in Huehuetenango but also throughout the highlands of Guatemala where Catholic Action was established.[65] By 1958 the number of Maryknoll catechists had increased to one thousand.[66] In 1963 Brother Felix noted in an enthusiastic letter home that "[t]he Church in Guatemala is on its way up. That was the big impression that hit me as I was travelling around from the end of July to the end of September. For one thing, there are now five times as many priests in the country as there were when we first came. And there are more catechists (17,000) in the country than there are soldiers."[67]

A NEW COOPERATIVE ERA IN GUATEMALA

Following the overthrow of Jacobo Arbenz, Maryknoll found it difficult to gain recognition for new cooperatives. Brother Felix reported to his parents in July 1955, "last week I returned from Guatemala City where I had been on vacation for two weeks. While there in the capital I tried to push along the cause of the four credit unions that are awaiting recognition, two of them since January. While everyone in the National Palace was very kind, the results are still indistinguishable."[68] That challenge started to dissipate in 1956, when the Guatemalan government introduced Presidential Decree Number 560, which allowed the superintendence of banks to assume the functions that had corresponded with the Department of Cooperative Development. In the same year, the new Guatemalan Constitution included Article 217 mandating that "the State will promote the development of cooperatives and will provide them with necessary technical aid. All State Banks will facilitate credit necessary for their economic development."[69] In 1959 the U.S.

64. Brother Felix Fournier, Letter to Laura, Frank, Christine, March 28, 1955, MMA.

65. In 1964, 70,000 of the 249,704 residents of El Quiché identified as Catholic Action members. Diócesis El Quiché, *El Quiché.*

66. Leigh A. Fuller, SJ, "Catholic Missionary Work and National Development in Guatemala," 116.

67. Brother Felix Fournier, Letter to Dad, Kay, Gaby and Laura, September 6, 1963, MMA.

68. Fournier Letters, July 16, 1955.

69. Tirso Constantino Escobar Loarca, "Cooperativismo agrario en el occidente de Gua-

government reported that "the cooperative movement in Guatemala has entered a new stage of development, aided by the renewal of GOG [Government of Guatemala] interest in the 'cooperative' idea and indirectly by the passage of time since the disbandment of the communist-led 'cooperatives' of the Arbenz era. It has been assisted by the USAID Mission and by the many independent development groups working in the rural areas of Guatemala."[70] In 1956 the Guatemalan government, at the behest of the United States, passed Decree Law 559, also introduced the idea of colonization to settle the sparsely populated northern regions of Guatemala as an alternative to agrarian reform.[71] Cooperatives and colonization later became inextricably linked projects, which together transformed the lives of thousands of Mayas, but not with the outcomes they anticipated.

The United States interest in promoting cooperatives in Guatemala corresponded with a broader effort prompted by the 1959 Cuban revolution to improve relations with the region. In 1959, U.S. president Dwight D. Eisenhower introduced the "Act of Bogotá," a precursor to John F. Kennedy's Alliance for Progress.[72] The act provided for increased funding for development programs in Latin America. It also seemed to offer a foundation for collaboration between religious and secular leaders in the United States.

In 1960 Maryknoll Father John J. Considine was named director of the National Catholic Welfare Conference's Latin American Bureau.[73] In that year Father Considine published *The Missionary's Role in Socio-Economic Betterment* in which he cited Father George E. Topshee of St. Francis Xavier University, Antigonish who made a powerful plea to the missionary to understand the influence of economic life on man's religion. "[H]e must have a strong conviction of the great importance of the role of the economic side of life in the establishment and *in the maintenance* of Christianity.... The day is coming, I believe, when

temala: Estudio de casos concretos," Tesis Ciencias Jurídicas y Sociales de Universidad de San Carlos, Guatemala, 1974, 39.

70. Ibid., 11.

71. Susanne Jonas and David Tobis, eds. *Guatemala* (New York: North American Congress on Latin America, 1974), 21.

72. L. Ronald Scheman, ed., *The Alliance for Progress: A Retrospective* (New York: Praeger Publishers, 1988); and Jeffrey F. Taffet, *Foreign Aid as Foreign Policy: The Alliance for Progress in Latin America* (New York: Routledge, 2007).

73. Angelyn Dries, OSF, "The Legacy of John J. Considine, M.M," *International Bulletin of Missionary Research* (April 1997), 80–84, especially 82.

the Pope will make it mandatory for Church leaders to take a more realistic view of the role of economics in the establishment and maintenance of Christianity."[74] Moreover, Considine observed that "many Catholic missionaries around the world have coordinated their efforts with international programs, such as those launched by UNESCO and UNICEF, or with programs promoted by the International Cooperation Agency (the ICA) of the United States Department of State."[75] A year later in 1961, Pope John XXIII published the encyclical *Mater et magistra*, which included discussion of the challenges confronting rural communities. In 1962, leaders of Catholic rural organizations from throughout the world met in Rome for the International Meeting of Catholics on Rural Life, to develop "fuller knowledge of the overall state of agriculture and deeper study of the guiding lines set down in the Encyclical."[76] In his address to the meeting, Pope John XXIII stressed Catholic collaboration with established international institutions seeking to address agricultural challenges: "Catholics can and should promote this form of collaboration; and, wherever such associations are already in existence, they should endeavor to permeate them with the Gospel spirit of solidarity and mutual understanding."[77]

In addition to encouraging work by Catholics in solidarity with secular agencies, *Mater et magistra* also encouraged cooperative formation. In his address to the meeting focused on the "Agricultural-Rural Sector in "Mater et Magistra," Rt. Rev. Monsignor Pietro Pavan, noted that the encyclical asserted that

rural workers should feel a sense of solidarity one with another, and should unite to form co-operatives and professional associations, which are both necessary if they are to benefit from scientific and technical progress in methods of production, if they are to contribute effectively towards defending the price of their products, and to attain on equal footing with the economic and professional categories of other sectors of production, which are likewise usually organized. Such organization is, indeed, necessary, in order to have a voice in the political field and in the organs of public administration, for today, isolated voices are hardly ever able to make themselves heard, much less heeded.[78]

74. Considine, ed., *The Missionary's Role in Socio-Economic Betterment*, 23.
75. Ibid., 29.
76. *Rural Life in the Light of "Mater et Magistra,"* Proceedings of the International Meeting of Catholics on Rural Life, Rome, September 3–9, 1962 (Rome: Libreria Editrice Ancora, 1962), foreword.
77. Ibid., 12.   78. Ibid., 50.

The Catholic Church encouraged civil–religious collaboration and identified cooperatives as a central means of addressing what Pope John XXIII identified in the encyclical *Mater et magistra* as the growing challenge of agriculture in modernizing societies.[79]

These religious developments corresponded with a political change in the United States that had important ramifications for Latin America. In 1961, the United States elected John F. Kennedy, its only Catholic president. Among his first presidential acts was the introduction of the Alliance for Progress, which built on the Act of Bogotá, but also consciously replicated components of Franklin Delano Roosevelt's Good Neighbor Policy.[80] Section 601 of the Foreign Assistance Act introduced by Kennedy stated that "it is declared to be policy of the U.S. ... to encourage development and use of cooperatives, credit unions, and savings and loan associations."[81] In February 1961, just a month before Kennedy announced the Alliance for Progress, Maryknoll Father John J. Considine had a letter sent to the new president recounting a conversation he had with Maryknoll's Latin American expert, Father Albert J. Nevins, who sought to convey the following message: "I wish someone could get across to President Kennedy the tremendous good will that exists in Latin America for him. It is almost unbelievable. If he could give some concrete attention to Latin America *now*, he would capitalize on this." He concluded his observation by accenting it with local support, "as the Prime Minister of Peru in Lima said today in a private interview, 'We have not had a friend since Franklin Roosevelt died.'" This correspondence surely reflected Maryknoll's desire not only to support the Catholic president in his endeavors but also to illustrate the role they could play by aiding him in Latin America. Maryknoll, suggested Father Considine, was already well established in the region and had contacts with both high governing officials and local communities.

In fact, the letter seemed a follow-up to correspondence between the director of the NCWC's Latin American Bureau (LAB) and government officials. In November 1960, Harmon Burns Jr. of the NCWC Legal Department contacted Father Considine "to report the results of several talks I have had to date with officers of the Department of

79. John XXIII, *Mater et magistra: Encyclical of Pope John XXIII on Christianity and Social Progress*, May 15, 1961, sections 125–130, http://www.vatican.va/holy_father/john_xxiii/encyclicals/documents/hf_j-xxiii_enc_15051961_mater_en.html.

80. Scheman, ed., *The Alliance for Progress.*

81. USAID Project No. 520-15-995-206.

State and its operating component, the International Cooperation Administration respecting the impending Latin American Aid Program." Burns noted that "serious consideration should be given to establishing reliable lay entities in Latin America which should act as legal conduits, as it were, for channeling grant assistance to church-related institutions. This is advanced with the idea of avoiding the hazard of possible ineligibility of such institutions for direct United States grant aid." In effect, Burns suggested that the NCWC-LAB establish what amounted to "front" organizations to ensure that government aid would not violate the United States separation of church and state. He assured Father Considine that "all gentleman [U.S. officials] contacted have shown a marked appreciation for the need of Christian social adjustment in Latin America. Responsible private initiative is welcomed and will be encouraged. In this cordial climate then, it is important to come forward with specific and well-conceived plans and proposals which can benefit the Church in this area."[82]

Father Considine took Harmon Burns's cue, and quickly relayed the message to James Norris, director of Catholic Relief Services, suggesting that "it would appear that we should make remote plans for the establishment in Latin American countries of properly structured organizations that strive to secure substantial sums for operations in the given individual countries."[83] A year later, in 1961, the Right Reverend Luigi Ligutti, director of the NCRLC and founder of the International Rural Life Conference, also seemed drawn into collaboration. He received a letter from Louis Miniclier, chief of the Community Development Division of the International Cooperation Administration of Washington, D.C., suggesting possible collaboration. The church would benefit USAID because it had ties to local communities that were essential to the success of the Alliance for progress. In the same year, Considine also wrote a "Confidential Memorandum" to J. Peter Grace about "Non-Governmental Loans through the Inter-American Development Bank" in which he described a dinner shared by his assistant and a Salvadoran member of the board of directors of the Inter-American Development Bank during which the "subject of non-governmental loans was discussed as friend to friend." "While the

---

82. "Latin-American Coordination-Government Funds," MFBA/U.S.CMA Box 10, F1, MMA.

83. Letter to James Norris, Catholic Relief Services, from (Rev.) John J. Considine, M.M., November 8, 1960, MFBA/U.S.CMA Box 10, F1, MMA.

subject is delicate," recounted Considine "he and others believe an arrangement possible, acceptable to both United States and Latin American governors of the Bank."[84] The church would benefit USAID because it had ties to local communities who were essential to the success of the Alliance for progress.

At the same time that Catholic leaders in the United States were starting to discuss the potential for coll_____ ment programs, U.S. government offic_____ approach Catholic leaders to discuss po_____ the same year that USAID announced its support for the "new cooperative movement in Guatemala," U.S. ambassador to Guatemala L. D. Mallory met with Guatemala's papal nuncio, Monsignor Ambrogio Marchioni, who had just met with Cardinal Spellman in New York, to discuss church–state cooperation. In 1962 the U.S. State Department called on the Guatemala country team to "develop a full evaluation of the capability of the Catholic Church to play a more significant role in countering Communism and contributing to the future welfare of Guatemala."[85] Other meetings between U.S. government and church officials in Guatemala followed.[86]

As these meetings occurred, the cooperative movement was developing. In November 1963 the leaders of five cooperatives met in Guatemala City with the plan of integrating their cooperatives. The cooperatives included those established in the municipalities of Santa Eulalia, Huehuetenango, and Malacatancito in the Department of Huehuetenango; Cabricán and Huitán in the Department of Quetzaltenango; and the Cooperative of Santa Cruz in zone 6 of Guatemala City.[87] At

84. Confidential Memorandum to J. Peter Grace from John J. Considine, M.M., director, Latin America Bureau, May 5, 1961, NCWC-USCC, 10/186/11, Catholic University Archive.

85. To Mr. Orrick from ARA Mr. Cottreel. Subject: Byroade Survey Mission: Progress Report, Reference your memorandum of Feb. 27, 1963 ... a report on the progress made thus far in implementing the recommendations advanced by the interdepartmental Survey Group (Byroade Group) after its visit to Guatemala in September 1962. Folder POL 1963 NARA RG59, D517 Box 3 Records; Guate 1956–63.

86. Airgram A-418, March 19, 1966, Week 11. "5. Catholic Church Interest in Alliance Effort," RG59, Political and Defense Central Foreign Policy Files, 1964–1966, Box 2249, November, 1970, from American Embassy Guatemala to Secretary of State, Priority, Subject: Church-Related Special Development Projects, RG59, Subject Numeric Files 1970–1973, Box 2337, Folder Pol 15-2 Guatemala, NARA.

87. José Miguel Gaitán Alvarez, "El Movimiento Cooperativista de Guatemala: Desarrollo de la Federación Nacional de Cooperativas de Ahorro y Credito," *Estudios Sociales* 7 (August 1972): 33–62, esp. 39–40.

least five of these cooperatives had been started by Maryknoll clergy. Together the cooperatives created The National Federation of Savings and
Credit Cooperatives of Guatemala (FEACOAD), whose purpose was to
develop ties of union and representation throughout the entire Republic of Guatemala.

A year later, in 1964, USAID established a Credit Union National
Association in Guatemala City to promote cooperative development.
USAID pledged cooperation with FEACOAD and sent three credit
union extension agents to promote further development.[88] USAID/
CUNA established the Federation of Savings and Credit Cooperatives
in 1964 and it received juridical recognition a year later. The new association offered a parallel to and possibly even an umbrella for FEACO-
AD and other cooperative associations whose formation followed.[89] In
the same year, Brother Felix Fournier wrote to his family telling them
about a national conference he attended in Guatemala City focused on
social and economic welfare. He recounted that "the Guatemalan government with the Organization of American States and the Alliance for
Progress undertook to show us national problems ... delicately making
us feel that a collaboration among all the agencies there represented
would go a long way towards solving the problems." He concluded, "[R]
ight now Maryknollers are right in the middle of a good percentage of
the activities suggested during this community development seminar.
They are in basic education, increased farm production, road-building,
preventive medicine and housing design (among others)."[90]

At the same time as these institutional developments were occurring, the number of foreign clergy in Guatemala increased. In fact, in
the aftermath of the overthrow of Jacobo Arbenz, the government of
Castillo Armas actively encouraged foreign clergy to settle in Guatemala.[91] By 1966, of the 1,432 clergy in Guatemala, 1,235 were foreign.[92]
Many had been influenced by the same global Catholic ethos that defined Maryknoll's work in the country; indeed, many had been influ-

88. USAID project no. 520-15-995-206, 12; and Gaitán Alvarez, "El Movimiento Cooperativista de Guatemala," 40.

89. Diego Pulido Aragón, "La Necesidad de Implantar en Guatemala Las Cooperativas de
Comercialización," Tesis, Facultad de Ciencias Económicas, Universidad de Rafael Landívar,
1971, 27.

90. Brother Felix Fournier, June 9, 1964, MMA. Box 29 F6.

91. Richard N. Adams, *Crucifixion by Power: Essays on Guatemalan National Social Structure, 1944–1966* (Austin: University of Texas Press, 1970), 195.

92. Calder, *Crecimiento y Cambio*, 19.

enced by Maryknoll. Virtually all foreign clergy developed catechetical programs and many introduced cooperatives. To facilitate this development they created not only education centers, where Mayas from throughout the western highlands could come together to learn about Catholic doctrine, but also coopcrative development and agricultural innovation. In Huehuetenango, Maryknoll created the Center of Integral Development (Centro de Desarrollo Integral, or CDI),[93] in El Quiché Spanish Sacred Heart missionaries introduced a Casa Central for education, in Alta Verapaz Benedictines established Centro San Benito,[94] in Izabal Centro de Capacitación Campesina de Santo Tomás de Castilla was established. These centers and others together created a national Catholic infrastructure for Maya cooperative development.

Departmental Catholic education centers often became linked to USAID cooperative education centers. In 1966 Guatemala's Archbishop Mario Casariego y Acevedo organized a meeting among Catholic clergy and USAID officials. "Initial informal conversations centered upon projects in the low-cost cooperative housing field, cooperatives and credit unions generally, literacy and leadership training. A joint informal "working group" has been established to discuss the matter further."[95] An in-country training program (CAPS) for social promoters and cooperative leaders supported by USAID was established at the Catholic Universidad Rafael de Landívar. By 1968, CAPS had prepared 350 leaders, many of whom were Maya men with roots in Catholic Cooperative projects in Guatemala's Western Highlands.[96] Father L. J. Twomey of the Catholic University of Loyola in New Orleans, where USAID funded another leadership training program attended by Maya leaders, delivered a series of lectures to clergy working in Guatemala on the role of the

93. Otero Diez, *Padre Guillermo Woods*, 58.

94. Rafael Melgar (Salesian), *Segunda Parte: Los Ultimos Cincuenta Años* (unpublished manuscript, n.d.), 52.

95. AIRGRAM A-418, March 19, 1966, Week No. 11, RG59 Political and Defense Central Foreign Policy Files, 1964–1966, Box 2249. The U.S. government would continue to pay close attention to Catholic initiatives in Guatemala. A 1970 memorandum provides a detailed account of the character and work of each of Guatemala's bishops and the potential for providing them with small amounts of economic support that would benefit U.S. projects (November 1970, Am Embassy Guatemala to Sec State, Priority, Secret Guatemala, Subject: Church-Related Special Development Projects, RG59 Subject Numeric Files 1970–73, Box 2337, Folder Pol 15-2 Guat, NARA).

96. "Compruebase en Zacapa la Eficacia de los Promotores Landivarianos," por el doctor Epaminondas Quintana, August 12, 1968, and "Promotores Sociales Rurales: Labores a que se están dedicando," July 27, 1967, CIRMA "CAPS, Promotores Sociales" Infostelle.

church in economic and social development.[97] The CAPS program at
Landívar was complemented by USAID's establishment in 1968 of The
Agrarian Training School of Cooperatives (La Escuela de Adiestramiento
de Cooperativas [Agrícolas], or EACA) in Chimaltenango, Guatemala,
where clergy in rural departments sent cooperative leaders for training.[98]
Cooperatives became one component of what USAID described in 1969
as "the project known as Rural Community Leadership and Modernization [which] consists of four activities: Credit Union Development/
CUNA, Rural Organization Development/IDF, Training Center for Promotores Sociales (C.A.P.S.)/Landivar University, and the Agricultural
Co-operative School ... its ultimate objective is the development on the
aldea (village) and *municipio* (county) levels of politically-aware, activist
leadership elements combined with strong popular organizations which
together will act as a major force on the Government and vested interests to bring about change and modernization in rural communities."[99]
This "USAID scheme to develop local leadership and popular organizations in the rural areas of Guatemala" was possible in part because of
direct and indirect collaboration with Catholic programs.

The number of cooperatives in Guatemala increased dramatically
because of the confluence of Catholic- and secular USAID-sponsored
cooperative programs. Emphasis on credit cooperatives grew to include
agricultural and consumer cooperatives by the early 1970s. The Federation of Coffee Growers alone increased from two cooperatives with
ninety members and 2,000 quintales of coffee production in 1964–
1965 to thirty-three cooperatives with 3,900 members and 55,000 quintales of coffee production in 1968–1969.[100] By 1970, there were some
270 agricultural cooperatives with more than 14,191 members and a
volume of trade of Q6,105,377.[101]

97. May 28, 1966, A-517, Week 21, "Alliance for Progress: 6. Visit of Father Twomey of
Loyola," RG59 Political and Defense Central Foreign Policy Files, 1964–1966, BOX 2249; Stephen M. Streeter, "Nation-Building in the Land of Eternal Counter-insurgency: Guatemala and
the Contradictions of the Alliance for Progress," *Third World Quarterly* 27, no. 1 (2006): 57–68,
especially 62.

98. USAID Project 520-11-810-187, Rural Community Leadership and Modernization, Agricultural Co-operative School, 1969–1973, 3, http://dec.usaid.gov/index.cfm.

99. USAID Project 520-11-810-187, Rural Community Leadership and Modernization, Agricultural Co-operative School, 1969–1973, 3, http://dec.usaid.gov/index.cfm.

100. *Cooperación: Expresión del Cooperativismo Nacional*, Año II, Guatemala, November–
December 1973, No. 29. Hemeroteca, Biblioteca Nacional, Guatemala.

101. Pulido Aragón, "La Necesidad de Implantar en Guatemala Las Cooperativas de Comercialización," 23.

Cooperatives appeared to Guatemalan governing officials alternatively as a popular force to be coopted or as a threat to be controlled or even eliminated. Alan Riding's 1975 article describing the extraordinary success of the cooperative movement also noted that General Kjell Eugenio Laugerud García, recently brought to power through fraudulent elections, had announced support for cooperatives as a component of his national development plan and a means of garnering popular approval of his government. The vice president, Mario Sandoval Alarcón of the ultraright wing National Liberation Movement (MLN),[102] self-identified as the national party of institutionalized violence, responded by publicly accusing the president of being a communist. Even though cooperatives grew from Catholic programs and were fully integrated into the Guatemalan economic structure, they could not escape fully from the taint of communism that they carried from the Arbenz era. Moreover, cooperatives sought to improve socioeconomic conditions among Mayas and contributed to creating autonomous Maya leaders. By the late 1960s, in Guatemala these goals were sufficient to cause the country's military and elite to identify any movement or individual as communist. The very success of Mayas in the cooperative movement later made them the targets of military repression.

Focusing only on this repression, however, obfuscates the history of cooperative development and the ways in which transnational Catholic actors through direct and indirect association with secular governing officials contributed to cooperative development. This process started during Guatemala's "Democratic Spring" when the 1945 constitution and subsequent government legislation created the foundation for cooperative development. It continued because Catholic cooperatives survived the overthrow of Arbenz and became linked with a new secular government agenda promoted by the United States and accepted by the Guatemalan government. Ironically, the same U.S. assistance that contributed to cooperative development also supported the creation of the police and military forces that later targeted cooperative leaders as "communists." Understanding the thriving cooperative movement that journalist Alan Riding encountered in 1975 requires examination of this long-term historical development and the defining role that a transnational force of Catholic clergy and laity played in it.

---

102. Grandin, *The Last Colonial Massacre*, 89.

Historicizing Catholic Activism in Latin America

❖ Stephen J. C. Andes and Julia G. Young

A flawed teleology exists in the historiography of Catholic activism in Latin America. In this narrative the Catholic Church before the Second Vatican Council was conservative, preservationist, concerned with its institutional interests as opposed to the plight of the poor, and fundamentally antimodern. It was a church in captivity, chained by its own elite-centered interests, ignorant of its call to shepherd the People of God. The history of the church, in essence, was progressing from captivity to liberation: the Second Vatican Council and its Latin American interpretation, the Conference of Latin American Bishops at Medellín in 1968 was the turning point, the crucial pivot toward an embrace of the modern world. If Vatican II provided a much-needed *aggiornamento* (updating) to the age-old traditions of the faith, Medellín was therefore Catholic activism's call to arms in Latin America. The church was no longer to be defined as an ecclesiastical hierarchy but as the journey of the People of God in history. Medellín and subsequent meetings of Latin American bishops at Puebla (1979) would define a new pastoral strategy: *acompañamiento* (walking with) the people in their struggles, their work, their daily lives, and their journey. The worlds of global Catholicism were thus cleaved in two, divided before the council and after: a new dating system by which Catholic activism before Vatican II was likened to the "dark ages" and, after the council, to a rebirth, the Renaissance of Catholic presence in the church and the world.

Indeed, the Renaissance analogy appears apt. Nineteenth-century historians such as Jacob Burckhardt argued that progress in art and letters in Europe between the fourteenth and seventeenth centuries represented a clean break with the past.¹ However, revisionist historians with a penchant for analyses of *longue durée* have, for several generations now, questioned the extent to which profound continuities existed between the European Middle Ages and the early modern era: "the Renaissance was connected to the Middle Ages by a thousand ties," according to Panofsky.² Some scholars have even gone so far as to claim a "twelfth-century Renaissance" in Europe, bringing into question the utility of the conventional Renaissance periodization itself.³ But historians are keen to chop history into discrete segments, and history can be "rent asunder" in any number of ways, so to speak. And so it is with the history of Latin American Catholic activism.

The teleology underpinning the Catholic Church's progress from archaic institution to dynamic defender of the poor is understandably rooted in its theological self-understanding. Liberation theologians themselves were important propagators of the thesis. Gustavo Gutiérrez, one of the intellectual founders of the movement, perceived that the choice before the Latin American church was a stark one: on a plane ride to Switzerland, where he was to deliver a talk called "The Meaning of Development," he changed the title to "Notes on a Theology of Liberation."⁴ Half measures availed nothing, according to Gutiérrez and his fellow young radicals, and the developmentalist path had failed in Latin America. Historian and sociologist Enrique Dussel endeavored to provide an historical interpretation from a liberationist perspective in *A History of the Church in Latin America: Colonialism to Liberation (1492–1979)*. Dussel, perhaps echoing Augustine as much as Marx, presents a history of Latin American Christianity straining toward freedom from the oppression of the past. Epochal shifts and discrete historical periods mark the Latin American church's march toward the end of history and as yet-to-be-realized liberation. His work, and that of the Commission for Latin American Church History, made "liberation" its hermeneutic for reading the region's sacred history and, as with the study of the Renaissance, emphasized rupture over continuity with the past. The post–

1. Jacob Burckhardt, *The Civilization of the Renaissance in Italy*, English ed. (New York: Dover Publications, 2010).

2. Erwin Panofsky, "Renaissance and Renascences," *The Kenyon Review* 6, no. 2 (Spring 1944): 202.

3. R. N. Swanson, *The Twelfth-Century Renaissance* (Manchester, England: Manchester University Press, 1999).

4. Christian Smith, *The Emergence of Liberation Theology: Radical Religion and Social Movement Theory* (Chicago: The University of Chicago Press, 1991), 176–77.

Vatican II period represented the florescence of Catholic activism in Latin America, a new era fundamentally different from the preconciliar variety of Catholic activism.

The chapters in this volume present a different story. Each in its own way emphasizes a history of Catholic activism in Latin America with "a thousand ties" to the pre–Vatican II period. Both progressive and conservative faces of Catholic activism operated in Latin America before Vatican II. Liberation theology, for example, did not spring from a vacuum but developed out of a rich tradition of Catholic social activism emerging in the late nineteenth and early twentieth centuries. Indeed, the liberationist perspective shared many of the same concerns as preconciliar Catholic labor and student activists, especially solidarity with workers, a robust critique of capitalism and an unfettered market, and education and literacy, as well as the project of accurately depicting Latin America's social reality. Historicizing Catholic activism in Latin America helps describe a much longer process of development of Catholic thinking on how to solve society's problems; providing a "Catholic answer" to contemporary social upheaval was one of the main priorities of Catholic activism since the late nineteenth century.

Within this context, Liberation theology emerged as but one of many streams of Catholic thought on how best to confront modernity and its ills. Certainly, Catholic strategies and methods shifted, developed, and grew over time. Early Catholic activists seemed much more concerned with fighting state-led secularization, thereby preserving the faith against both liberal and socialist attacks. Indeed, social and theological conservatism provided a powerful hold over many bishops, priests, and lay Catholics. Throughout Latin America many bishops remained silent or even colluded with military dictatorships in countries such as Argentina. Women and indigenous people suffered violence, discrimination, and death at the hands of Latin American security forces, seconded and prodded by U.S. money, matériel, and the global cold war.

But even before the Second World War, shifting priorities of Catholic activists can be perceived. Mexican women such as Sofía del Valle, even while crusading in the United States against anticlericalism closer to home, brought a retooled vision for the goals of Catholic activism: educating women, organizing female labor, and opening a way for a more pronounced role for women within church ranks. Students in

Mexico and Brazil likewise turned their attention away from secularizing struggles, giving their attention to university reform, developing their thinking on a Catholic "third way" between capitalism and statist solutions, and investing their energies in an emerging civil society, where and when it was open to their participation. Moreover, the chapters by LeGrand, Roldán, and Fitzpatrick-Behrens reveal that Catholic activism was not on an inevitable course leading to Liberation theology, but rather, Catholic developmentalist projects had a life of their own and did not disappear when liberationist activists chose a different trajectory for their strategies. Indeed, the question was not, to many Catholic activists, a zero-sum game—development or liberation?—but often a mutually reinforcing coexistence. Just as Liberation theology took shape and gave momentum to Catholic activism after Vatican II, so, too, did a more incrementalist approach backed by many Catholic development projects. Institutional support, especially from an ascendant progressive hierarchy, proved crucial to both liberationist and developmentalist perspectives.

The transnational focus of this book thus allows us to further reconfigure our periodization of nineteenth- and twentieth-century Catholic activism. The chapters in this volume demonstrate that national and international contexts were routinely transcended as Latin American Catholics—both lay and clerical—sought to discover, articulate, and incorporate ideas from outside their national boundaries into a local context. Furthermore, they sought to export their own practices and ideas, as well as to narrate their own experiences to interested audiences in Rome, the United States, and Europe. These connections meant that Latin American Catholicism was transnational not only in the abstract—for, of course, the church is inherently a global church—but also in concrete, quotidian ways felt by Catholics at all social strata.Viewing Catholic activism as a multifaceted movement in Latin America, rooted in a distinct historical process of development, provides better perspective on conservative reactions after Vatican II. The progressive trajectory of global Catholicism in the 1960s was followed by a retrenchment of conservative church leaders both globally and locally. In this alternative framework, Catholic activists, both lay and clerical, male and female, began clearing new paths for the Catholic Church's mission for several generations before the 1960s. Many of these movements received institutional support and encouragement at the time of the council, which shows the crucial importance of the conciliar era. Yet by the late 1970s, change was afoot: Pope John Paul II (1978–2005) oversaw a revision of many of the most radical implications of Vatican II; in Latin America, Liberation theology came under increasing scrutiny, activists such as Leonardo Boff were silenced, and a generation of conservative bishops was appointed to the region's episcopal offices. Pope Benedict XVI continued these policies. Indeed, the multiple pathways of Catholic activism received new challenges after Vatican II: military dictatorship, cold-war rivalries, homegrown anticommunist violence, revolutionary radicalism, and a conservative turn in the Vatican.

On this latter point, then, the election of Latin America's first pope becomes significant. Pope Francis displays many of the ambiguities inherent in the history of Latin American Catholicism since the nineteenth century: conservative on many social issues, concerned with institutional reform, but acutely aware of the church's mission to the poor, marginalized, and disenfranchised. Pope Francis's apostolic exhortation, *Evangelii gaudium* (2013), emphasized economic inequality as a root of injustice in contemporary society, decrying the "idolatry of money" gripping today's world. Furthermore, Pope Francis has recently taken steps toward a possible reconciliation between the institutional church and the legacy of Liberation theology, inviting liberationist priest Gustavo Gutiérrez to the Vatican and supporting the beatification of Archbishop Óscar Romero.

The chapters in this book, by focusing on the longer story of Catholic activism within Latin America, help to contextualize the complexities of Francis's papacy. They reveal that Catholic activism's story is far from a fated teleology, leading ever onward to progress and liberation. In contrast, the relationship between global Catholicism and Latin American Catholicism continues to uncover a narrative susceptible to fits and starts, progress and reversal. Within Latin America, in the hemisphere as a whole, and throughout the world, both global and local tensions within the Catholic Church will continue to struggle, participate, and, ultimately, create the future of a local church and a global church.

Bibliography

ARCHIVES

Archive of the Archdiocese of Oklahoma City (AAOC)
Archivo del Arzobispado de Santiago (AAS)
Acción Cultural Popular (ACPO)
Archivio Affari Ecclesiastici Straordinari (AES)
Archivo General de la Nacion (AGN)
Archivo Histórico de la Acción Católica (AHAC)
Archivo Histórico del Arzobispado de México (AHAM)
Archives of Loyola University, Chicago, Illinois (ALU)
Archivio della Nunziatura in Brasile (ANC)
Arquivo Público do Estado do Rio de Janeiro (APERJ)
Archivio Segreto Vaticano (ASV)
Biblioteca Luis Ángel Arango (BLAA)
Centro de Investigaciones Regionales de Mesoamérica (CIRMA)
Centro de Pesquisa e Documentação de História Contemporânea do Brasil (CPDOC)
Fonoteca, Radio Nacional de Colombia (FRNC)
Maryknoll Mission Archive (MMA)
Marie Michael Library, Coady International Institute (MMC)
National Archives and Records Administration (NARA)
National Catholic Welfare Conference/United States Catholic Conference, The Catholic University of America Archives (NCWC/USCC)
Projeto Memória Movimiento Estudiantil (PMME)
St. Francis Xavier University Archives (StFXUA)

WORKS CITED

III Asamblea Interamericana del MIEC de Pax Romana. Abril de 1949. Memoria. Mexico City: Ediciones de la ACM, 1949.
Abascal, Salvador. *Mis recuerdos: Sinarquismo y Colonia María Auxiliadora.* Mexico City: Tradición, 2003.
Abreu, Martha. "Pensamento Católico, abolicionismo e festas religiosas no Rio de Janeiro, 1870–1890." In *Escravidão, exclusão e cidadania,* edited by Marco Antonio Villela Pamplona and Eduardo da Silva, 75–105. Rio de Janeiro: Access, 2001.
Actas y Decretos del Concilio Plenario de la América Latina (Edición fácsimil). Vatican City: Libreria Editrice Vaticana, 1999.
Adames, Roque. "San Juan de las Matas in the Dominican Republic." In LADOC "Keyhole" Series, no. 14, *Basic Christian Communities,* 24–26. Washington, D.C.: USCC-Latin America Documentation, 1976.

Adams, Richard N. *Crucifixion by Power: Essays on Guatemalan National Social Structure, 1944–1966.* Austin: University of Texas Press, 1970.

Adriance, Madeleine Cousineau. *Promised Land: Base Christian Communities and the Struggle for the Amazon.* Albany: State University of New York Press, 1995.

Aguiar, Sylvana Maria Brandão de, and Lúcio Renato Mota Lima. "A Fábrica de Tecidos de Camaragibe e sua organização cristã do trabalho (1891–1908)." *Revista de Teologia e Ciências da Religião da UNICAP* 1, no. 1 (December 2012): 160–95.

Aguirre Cristiani, María Gabriela. *¿Una historia compartida? Revolución mexicana y catolicismo social, 1913–1924.* Mexico City: IMDOSOC, Xochimilco, 2009.

Alacevich, Michele. *The Political Economy of the World Bank: The Early Years.* Palo Alto, Calif.: Stanford University Press, 2009.

Alacoque, Margaret Mary. *The Autobiography of St. Margaret Mary.* Rockford, Ill.: Tan Books and Publishers, 1986.

Albuquerque, Antonio Luiz Porto e. *Utopia e crise social no Brasil, 1871–1916: O pensamento de Padre Júlio Maria.* Rio de Janeiro: Fundação Casa de Rui Barbosa, 1994.

Alexander, Anne. *The Antigonish Movement: Moses Coady and Adult Education Today.* Toronto: Thompson Educational Publishing, 1997.

Alvarez, David. *Spies in the Vatican: Espionage and Intrigue from Napoleon to the Holocaust.* Lawrence: University Press of Kansas, 2002.

Alves, Márcio Moreira. *Beabá dos MEC-USAID.* Rio de Janeiro: Edições Gernasa, 1968.

Alves, Maria Helena. *State and Opposition in Military Brazil.* Austin: University of Texas Press, 1985.

Andes, Stephen J. C. "A Catholic Alternative to Revolution: The Survival of Social Catholicism in Postrevolutionary Mexico." *The Americas* 68, no. 4 (April 2012): 529–62.

———. *The Vatican and Catholic Activism in Mexico and Chile: The Politics of Transnational Catholicism, 1920–1940.* Oxford: Oxford University Press, 2014.

Anon. "Intenção geral do mez de setembro: As classes operárias." *Mensageiro do Coração de Jesus* 3, no. 27 (August 1898): 121–27.

Anon. *Obra de la exposición y adoración nocturna del Santísimo Sacramento en la Ciudad de México.* Mexico City: J. M. Lara, 1869 and later.

Anon. "Pelo Brazil." *Vozes de Petropolis*, no. 3 (Julho 1909–Junho 1910): 222.

Anon. "Secção retrospectiva (Continuação): Taubaté." *Boletim Ecclesiástico de São Paulo* 1, no. 10 (Abril 1906): 319–20.

Armella, María Luisa Aspe. *La formación social y política de los católicos mexicanos: La Acción Católica Mexicana y la Unión Nacional de Estudiantes Católicos, 1929–1958.* Mexico City: Universidad Iberoamericana, 2008.

Arango Jaramillo, Mario. *Manual de cooperativismo y economía solidaria.* Medellín: Editorial Universidad Cooperativa de Colombia, 2005.

Araújo, Maria Paula. *Memórias Estudantis: Da Fundação da UNE aos Nossos Dias.* Rio de Janeiro: Ediouro Publicações S.A., 2008.

Arizona Archives Online. "Juan Navarrete y Guerrero Collection." http://www.azar chivesonline.org/xtf/view?docId=ead/uoa/UAMS423.xml;query=;brand=default.

Arrom, Silvia Marina. *The Women of Mexico City, 1790–1857.* Palo Alto, Calif.: Stanford University Press, 1985.

————. "Mexican Laywomen Spearhead a Catholic Revival: The Ladies of Charity, 1863–1910." In *Religious Culture in Modern Mexico*, edited by Martin Austin Nesvig, 50–77. Lanham, Md.: Rowman & Littlefield, 2007.

————. "Las Señoras de la Caridad: Pioneras olvidadas de la asistencia social en México, 1863–1910." *Historia Mexicana* 57, no. 2 (October–December 2007): 445–90.

"A Sociedade de São Vicente de Paulo." www.ssvpbrasil.org.br/?pg=sobre_a_ssvp.

Asselin, Father Victor. *Gralagem, corrupcao e violencia em terras do Carajas.* 2nd edition. Petrópolis: Vozes de Petrópolis, 2009.

Athayde, Johildo Lopes de. "La ville de Salvador au XIXe siécle: Aspects démographiques (D'apres les registres paroissaux)." PhD diss., Université de Paris-X, 1975.

Atkin, Nicholas, and Frank Tallett. *Priests, Prelates, and People: A History of European Catholicism since 1750.* New York: Oxford University Press, 2003.

Aubert, Roger, et al. *The Church in the Industrial Age.* Translated by Peter Becker. New York: Crossroad Publishing Company, 1981.

Auza, Néstor Tomás, recopilador. *Documentos del episcopado argentino, Tomo I: 1889–1909.* Buenos Aires: Conferencia Episcopal Argentina, 1993.

Azevedo, Thales de. *A guerra aos párocos: Episódios anticlericais na Bahia.* Salvador: Empresa Gráfica da Bahia, 1991.

Azzellini, Dario. "From Cooperatives to Enterprises of Direct Social Property in the Venezuelan Process." In *Cooperatives and Socialism: A View from Cuba*, edited by Camila Pineiro Harnecker, 259–75. New York: Palgrave Macmillan, 2013.

Azzi, Riolando. "O Início da Restauração Católica no Brasil: 1920–1930." *Síntese-Revista de Filosofia* 4, no. 10 (1977): 61–89.

————. *O estado leigo e o projeto ultramontano, vol. 4, História do pensamento católico no Brasil.* São Paulo: Paulus, 1994.

Báez-Jorge, Félix. *Olor de Santidad.* Mexico City: Universidad Veracruzana, 2006.

Baltutis, Peter Ernest. "Forging the Link between Faith and Development: The History of the Canadian Catholic Organization for Development and Peace, 1957–1982." PhD diss., St. Michael's College Faculty of Theology, University of Toronto, 2012.

Barata, Alexandre Mansur. *Luzes e sombras: A ação da Maçonaria brasileira (1870–1910).* Campinas: Editora da UNICAMP and Centro da Memória-UNICAMP, 1999.

Barbosa, Rui. "Prefácio." *O Papa e o Concílio: A questão religiosa* [1877]. In *Obras*, volume 1. Rio de Janeiro, Brazil: Ministério de Educação e Cultura, Fundação Casa de Rui Barbosa, 1977.

Barillas Izaguirre, Roberto. *Fomento de la Cooperación en Guatemala: Breve Resena del Movimiento Cooperativo de Quebec.* Guatemala City: Publicaciones del Departamento de Fomento Cooperativo, 1948.

————. *Legislación Cooperativa Guatemalteca (Comentarios al Decreto 643 del Congreso).* Guatemala City: Departamento de Fomento Cooperativo, 1950.

Barman, Roderick J. "The Brazilian Peasantry Reexamined: The Implications of the Quebra-Quilo Revolt, 1874–1875." *Hispanic American Historical Review* 57, no. 3 (1977): 401–24.

Barranco V., Bernardo. "La Iberoamericanidad de la Unión Nacional de Estudiantes

Católicos (UNEC) en los años treinta." In *Cultura e identidad nacional*, edited by Roberto Blamcarte, 188–232. Mexico City: Fondo de Cultura Económica, 1994.

Barrón, Luis. "Conservadores liberales: Luis Cabrera y José Vasconcelos, reaccionarios y tránsfugas de la Revlución." In *Conservadurismo y derechas en la historia de México: Tomo II*, edited by Erika Pani, 435–66. Mexico City: Fondo de Cultura Económica, 2009.

Baum, Gregory. *Catholics and Canadian Socialism: Political Thought in the Thirties and Forties*. Toronto: James Lorimer & Co, 1980.

Bederman, Gail. "'The Women Have Had Charge of the Church Long Enough': The Men and Religion Forward Movement of 1911–1912 and the Masculinization of Middle Class Protestantism." In *A Mighty Baptism: Race, Gender, and the Creation of American Protestantism*, edited by Susan Juster and Lisa MacFarlane, 107–40. Ithaca, N.Y.: Cornell University Press, 1996.

Beltrán, Lauro López. *La persecución religiosa en México: Carranza, Obregón, Calles, Portes Gil*. Mexico City: Editorial Tradición, 1987.

Bermeo, Francisco Enríquez, ed. *Leonidas Proaño, obispo de los pobres*. Quito: Editorial El Conejo, 1989.

Bernal Alarcón, Hernando. "Radio Sutatenza: Un modelo colombiano de industria cultural y educativa." *Boletín Cultural y Bibliográfico* 46, no. 82 (2012): 5–41.

Bertina, Ludovic. "The Catholic Doctrine of 'Integral Human Development' and Its Influence on the International Development Community." In *International Development Policy: Religion and Development*, edited by Gilles Carbonnier, 115–27. Basingstoke: Palgrave Macmillan, 2013.

Betances, Emilio. *The Catholic Church and Power Politics in Latin America: The Dominican Case in Comparative Perspective*. Lanham, Md.: Rowman & Littlefield, 2007.

Bidegaín, Ana María. "La organización de movimientos de juventud de Acción Católica en América: Los casos de los obreros y universitarios en Brasil y en Colombia entre 1930–1955." PhD diss., Université Catholique de Louvain, Faculté de Philosophie et Lettres, 1979.

———. "From Catholic Action to Liberation Theology: The Historical Process of the Laity in Latin America in the Twentieth Century." The Helen Kellogg Institute for International Studies, University of Notre Dame, Working Paper 48, November 1985.

———. "De la historia elesiastica a la historia de las religiones: Breve Presentación sobre la transformación de la investigación sobre la historia de las religiones en las sociedades latinoamericanas." *Historia Crítica*, no. 12 (Enero–Junio 1996): 5–16.

Blaschke, Olaf. "The Unrecognized Piety of Men: Strategies and Success of the Remasculinisation Campaign around 1900." In *Christian Masculinity: Men and Religion in Northern Europe in the Nineteenth and Twentieth Centuries*, edited by Yvonne Maria Werner, 21–45. Leuven: University of Leuven Press, 2011.

Blixen, Samuel. *Sendic*. Montevideo: Ediciones Trilce, 2005.

Blum, Ann S. *Domestic Economies: Family, Work, and Welfare in Mexico City, 1884–1943*. Lincoln: University of Nebraska Press, 2009.

Boletín Eclesiástico del Arzobispado de Santiago de Chile: Tomo XII (1892–1894). Santiago: Imprenta de Emilio Pérez L., 1895.

Boletín Eclesiástico o sea colección de edictos, estatutos i decretos de los prelados del Arzo-bispado de Santiago de Chile. Tomo VI. Santiago: Imprenta de "El Correo," 1880.

Bonner, Jeremy, Christopher D. Denny, and Mary Beth Fraser Connolly, eds. *Empowering the People of God: Catholic Action before and after Vatican II.* New York: Fordham University Press, 2014.

Borges, Dain. "Intellectuals and the Forgetting of Slavery in Brazil, 1888–1933." *Annals of Scholarship* 11, no. 1–2 (1996): 37–60.

———. "Healing and Mischief: Witchcraft in Brazilian Law and Literature, 1890–1922." In *Crime and Punishment in Latin America: Law and Society since Late Colonial Times*, edited by Ricardo D. Salvatore, Carlos Aguirre, and Gilbert M. Joseph, 181–210. Durham, N.C.: Duke University Press, 2001.

Bovee, David S. "Catholic Rural Life Leader: Luigi G. Ligutti." *U.S. Catholic Historian* 8, no. 3 (1989): 143–58.

———. *The Church and the Land: The National Catholic Rural Life Conference and American Society, 1923–2007.* Washington, D.C.: The Catholic University of America Press, 2010.

Boylan, Kristina A. "The Feminine 'Apostolate in Society' versus the Secular State: The Unión Femenina Católica Mexicana, 1929–1940." In *Right-Wing Women: From Conservatives to Extremists around the World*, edited by Paola Bacchetta and Margaret Power, 169–82. New York: Routledge, 2002.

———. "Gendering the Faith and Altering the Nation: Mexican Catholic Women's Activism, 1917–1940." In *Sex in Revolution: Gender, Politics, and Power in Modern Mexico*, edited by Jocelyn Olcott, Mary Kay Vaughn, and Gabriela Cano, 199–222. Durham, N.C.: Duke University Press, 2006.

Braun, Herbert. *The Assassination of Gaitan: Public Life and Urban Violence in Colombia.* Madison: University of Wisconsin Press, 1985.

Brazil. Congreso Agricola. *Edição fac-similar dos anais do Congresso Agrícola, realizado no Rio de Janeiro, em 1878.* Rio de Janeiro: Fundacão Casa de Rui Barbosa, 1988.

Brazil. Directoria Geral de Estatística. *Annuário Estatístico do Brazil (1908–1912), vol. 3, Cultos, Assistencia, Repressão e Instrucção.* Rio de Janeiro: Typographia da Estatistica, 1927.

Brazil. Directoria Geral de Estatistica. *Recenseamento da população do Imperio do Brazil a que se procedeu no dia 1º. de agosto de 1872.* Rio de Janeiro: A Directoria, 1876.

Brazil. Ministério da Agricultura, Indústria e Commercio, Directoria Geral de Estatística. *Recenseamento do Brazil realizado em 1 de setembro de 1920, Volume IV, 5ª parte, População: População do Brazil, por Estados e Municípios, segundo o sexo, a nacionalidade, a idade e as profissões*, Tomo II. Rio de Janeiro: Typographia Da Estatistica, 1930.

Brazil. Ministério do Império. *Relatório, 1867.* Rio de Janeiro: Typographia Nacional, 1868.

Brintnall, Douglas. "Race Relations in the Southeastern Highlands of Mesoamerica." *American Ethnologist* 6, no. 4 (November 1979): 638–52.

———. *Revolt against the Dead: The Modernization of a Mayan Community in the Highlands of Guatemala.* New York: Gordon and Breach, 1979.

Brito, Berta. "'Radio Occidente': Modelo de radiodifusión al servicio del desarrollo." http://gumilla.org/biblioteca/bases/biblio/texto/COM198655_42-46.pdf.

Brouwer, Ruth Compton. "When Missions Became Development: Ironies of 'NGOization' in Mainstream Canadian Churches in the 1960s." *The Canadian Historical Review* 91, no. 4 (December 2010): 661–93.

Brown, Peter. *The Cult of the Saints: Its Rise and Function in Latin Christianity*. The Haskell Lectures on History of Religions. Chicago: The University of Chicago Press, 1982.

Brownmiller, Susan. *Against Our Will: Men, Women and Rape*. London: Secker & Warburg, 1975.

Bruneau, Thomas. *The Political Transformation of the Brazilian Catholic Church*. Cambridge: Cambridge University Press, 1974.

Bruno-Jofré, Rosa. "The Catholic Church in Chile and the Social Question in the 1930s: The Political Pedagogical Discourse of Fernando Vives de Solar, S.J." *The Catholic Historical Review* 99, no. 4 (October 2013): 703–26.

Burckhardt, Jacob. *The Civilization of the Renaissance in Italy*. English edition. New York: Dover Publications, 2010.

Burdick, John. *Looking for God in Brazil: The Progressive Catholic Church in Urban Brazil's Religious Arena*. Berkeley: University of California Press, 1993.

Burdick, Michael A. *For God and the Fatherland: Religion and Politics in Argentina*. Albany: State University of New York Press, 1996.

Burrill, Fred, and Catherine C. LeGrand. "Progressive Catholicism at Home and Abroad: The 'Double Solidarité' of Quebec Missionaries in Honduras, 1955–1975." In *Within and Without the Nation: Canadian History as Transnational History*, edited by Karen Dubinsky, Adele Perry, and Henry Yu. Toronto: University of Toronto Press, 2015.

Burton, Richard D. E. *Holy Tears, Holy Blood: Women, Catholicism, and the Culture of Suffering in France, 1840–1970*. Ithaca, N.Y.: Cornell University Press, 2004.

Butler, Matthew. *Faith and Impiety in Revolutionary Mexico*. New York: Palgrave, 2007.

———. "La coronación del Sagrado Corazón de Jesús en la Arquidiócesis de México, 1914." In *Revolución, cultura, y religión: Nuevas perspectivas regionales, siglo XX*, edited by Yolanda Padilla Rangel, Luciano Ramírez Hurtado, and Francisco Javier Delgado Aguilar, 24–68. Aguascalientes: Universidad Autónoma de Aguascalientes, 2012.

Butsch, Joseph. "Catholics and the Negro." *The Journal of Negro History* 2, no. 4 (October 1917): 393–410.

Calder, Bruce. *Crecimiento y Cambio de la Iglesia Católica Guatemalteca: 1944–1966*. Guatemala City: Seminaro de Integración Social Guatemalteca Editorial Jose de Peneda Ibarra Ministerio de Educación, 1970.

Calderisi, Robert. *Earthly Mission: The Catholic Church and World Development*. New Haven, Conn.: Yale University Press, 2013.

Callahan, C.D.P. Sister Mary Generosa. "Constantineau, Henry A." *Handbook of Texas Online* (http://www.tshaonline.org/handbook/online/articles/fcobl). Published by the Texas State Historical Association.

Cameron, James D. *For the People: A History of St. Francis Xavier University*. Montreal: McGill-Queen's University Press, 1996.

Carbonnier, Gilles, ed. *International Development Policy: Religion and Development*. Basingstoke: Palgrave Macmillan, 2013.

Carey, David, Jr. *I Ask for Justice: Maya Women, Dictators, and Crime in Guatemala, 1898–1944.* Austin: University of Texas Press, 2013.

Carlen, Claudia, ed. *The Papal Encyclicals, 1740–1878.* Volume 1. Ann Arbor, Mich.: The Pierian Press, 1990.

———. *The Papal Encyclicals, 1878–1903.* Volume 2. Ann Arbor, Mich.: The Pierian Press, 1990.

———. *The Papal Encyclicals, 1903–1939.* Volume 3. Ann Arbor, Mich.: The Pierian Press, 1990.

Carrier, Yves. *Lettre du Brésil: L'évolution de la perspective missionnaire: Relecture de l'expérience de Msgr. Gérard Cambron.* Louvain-la-Neuve: Academia Bruylant, 2008.

———. *Théologie pratique de libération au Chili de Salvador Allende: Guy Boulanger, Jan Caminada et l'équipe Calama, une expérience d'insertion en monde ouvrier.* Paris: L'Harmattan, 2013.

Carta pastoral que el Ilmo. i Rmo. Señor Arzobispo de Santiago e Ilmos. Señores obispos sufragáneos de la provincia eclesiástica de Chile, dirijen a los sacerdotes i fieles de sus respectivas diócesis. Santiago: Imprenta del Correo, 1874.

Carvalho, José Murilo de. "A ortodoxia positivista no Brasil: Um bolchevismo de classe média." *Revista Brasileira* 4, no. 8 (1989): 50–56.

Casanova, Mariano. *Pastoral del Illmo. i Rmo. Sr. Arzobispo Dr. D. Mariano Casanova sobre la reforma constitucional.* Santiago: Imprenta Católica de Manuel Infante, 1888.

———. "Carta al clero sobre la escasez de vocaciones al sacerdocio." In *Obras pastorales del Ilmo. y Rmo. Señor Dr. don Mariano Casanova, Arzobispo de Santiago de Chile,* edited by Mariano Casanova, 83–96. Friburgo de Brisgovia, Germany: B. Herder, 1901.

Casillas, José Gutiérrez. *Jesuitas en México durante el siglo XX.* Mexico City: Editorial Porrúa S.A., 1981.

Castiello, Jaime. *Una psicología humanista de la educación.* Mexico City: Jus, 1947.

Castillo Ramírez, María Gracia. "Jóvenes católicos de izquierda revolucionaria (1965–1975)." In *Violencia y sociedad: Un hito en la historia de las izquierdas en América Latina,* edited by Verónica Okión and Miguel Urrego, 111–40. Morelia: IIH-UMSNH/El Colegio de Michoacán, 2010.

Castro, Eduardo Góes de. *Os "quebra-santos": Anticlericalismo e repressão pelo DEOPS-SP.* São Paulo: Humanitas, 2007.

CECOSOLA. "Inicio." http://www.cecosesola.org.

Chadwick, Owen. *A History of the Popes, 1830–1914.* Oxford: Oxford University Press, 2003.

Chakrabarty, Dipesh. *Provincializing Europe: Postcolonial Thought and Historical Difference.* Princeton, N.J.: Princeton University Press, 2000.

Chance, John K., and William B. Taylor. "Cofradías and Cargos: An Historical Perspective on the Mesoamerican Civil-Religious Hierarchy." *American Ethnologist* 12, no. 1 (February 1985): 1–26.

Chávez, Joaquín. "Catholic Action, the Second Vatican Council, and the Emergence of the New Left in El Salvador (1950–1975)." *The Americas* 70, no. 3 (January 2014): 459–87.

Chesnut, R. Andrew. *Born Again in Brazil: The Pentecostal Boom and the Pathogens of Poverty*. New Brunswick, N.J.: Rutgers University Press, 1997.

Chesterton, G. K. *What's Wrong with the World*. New York: Dodd, Mead, and Co., 1910.

Chowning, Margaret. *Rebellious Nuns: The Troubled History of a Mexican Convent, 1752–1863*. New York: Oxford University Press, 2006.

———. "The Catholic Church and the Ladies of the Vela Perpetua: Gender and Devotional Change in Nineteenth-Century Mexico." *Past and Present* 221, no. 1 (2013): 197–237.

Christie, Nancy, et al., eds. *The Sixties and Beyond: Dechristianization in North America and Western Europe, 1945–2000*. Toronto: University of Toronto Press, 2013.

Citino, Nathan J. "Modernization and Development." In *The Routledge Handbook of the Cold War*, edited by Artemy M. Kalinovsky and Craig Daigle, 118–30. London: Routledge, 2014.

Cleary, Edward L. *Crisis and Change: The Church in Latin America Today*. Maryknoll, N.Y.: Orbis Books, 1985.

Coady, Moses M. *Masters of Their Own Destiny: The Story of the Antigonish Movement of Adult Education through Economic Cooperation*. New York: Harper & Brothers, 1939.

———. *Dueños de su propio destino: Una experiencia de educación de masas. Historia del Movimiento de Antigonish, una acción educativa por medio de la cooperación económica*. Translated by J. E. Thielen. Buenos Aires: Intercoop Editora Cooperativa Ltda., 1964.

Cobb, L. Stephanie. *Dying To Be Men: Gender and Language in Early Christian Martyr Texts*. New York: Columbia University Press, 2008.

Cohen, Thomas. *The Fire of Tongues: Antonio Vieira and the Missionary Church in Brazil and Portugal*. Palo Alto, Calif.: Stanford University Press, 1998.

Colonnese, Louis M. *The Church in the Present-Day Transformation of Latin America in the Light of the Council*. Volume 2, *Conclusions*. Washington, D.C.: USCC–Division for Latin America, 1970–73.

Compagnon, Olivier. *Jacques Maritain et l'Amérique du Sud: Le modèle malgré lui*. Lille: Presses Universitaires du Septentrion, 2003.

Confederação Catholica de São Paulo. *Annaes Catholicos: Publicação Mensal sob os Auspicios da Confederação Catholica de São Paulo* 1, no. 1 (March 1917): 6–18.

Congreso católico uruguayo celebrado en Montevideo en los días 28, 29 y 30 abril de 1889. Montevideo: Imprenta de "El Telégrafo Marítimo," 1889.

Connor, Desmond Maurice. "The Cross-Cultural Diffusion of a Social Movement." Master's thesis, Cornell University, 1962.

Considine, John J., ed. *The Missionary's Role in Socio-Economic Betterment*. New York: Newman Press, 1960.

Coppa, Frank J. *The Modern Papacy since 1789*. Longman History of the Papacy, edited by A. D. Wright. London: Longman, 1998.

Coque Martínez, Jorge. "Las cooperativas en América Latina: Visión histórica general y comentario de algunos países tipo." *CIRIEC-España, revista de economía pública, social y cooperativa*, no. 43, extraordinario (November 2002): 145–72.

Cordeiro, Janaina Martins. *Direitas em Movimento: A Campanha da Mulher pela Democracia e a ditadura no Brasil*. Rio de Janeiro: Editora FGV, 2009.

Correa, Eduardo J. *El Partido Católico Nacional y sus directores: Explicación de su fracaso y deslinde de responsabilidades*. Mexico City: Fondo de Cultura Económica, 1991.

Correia, Manoel Francisco, ed. *Consultas: Conselho de Estado sobre negócios ecclesiásticos, compiladas por ordem de S. Ex. O Sr. Ministro do Império*, 3 vols. Rio de Janeiro: Typographia Nacional, 1869.

Corten, André. "Une mise en réseau de la Théologie de la Libération." In *La modernité religieuse en perspective comparée: Europe latine-Amérique latine*, edited by Jean-Pierre Bastian, 267–86. Paris: Karthala, 2001.

Costello, Gerald M. *Mission to Latin America: The Successes and Failures of a Twentieth-Century Crusade*. Maryknoll, N.Y.: Orbis Books, 1979.

Cowan, Benjamin. "'Why Hasn't This Teacher Been Shot?' Moral-Sexual Panic, the Repressive Right, and Brazil's National Security State." *Hispanic American Historical Review* 92, no. 3 (August 2012): 403–36.

Cronshaw, Francine. "Exporting Ideology: T. Lynn Smith in Colombia." *NS, North-south* 7, no. 13 (1982): 95–109.

Culhane, Eugene K. "The FERES Study of Latin America." *America* 111, no. 13 (September 1964): 345–47.

———. "Upsurge in Latin America." *America* 111, no. 13 (September 1964): 343–44.

Cullather, Nick, and Piero Gleijeses. *Secret History: The CIA's Classified Account of Its Operations in Guatemala, 1952–1954*. Palo Alto, Calif.: Stanford University Press, 1999.

Cunha, Luiz Antônio. *A Universidade Crítica: O Ensino Superior na República Populista*. Rio de Janeiro: Livraria Francisco Alves Editora, 1982.

———. *A Universidade Reformanda: O Golpe de 1964 e a Modernização do Ensino Superior*. Rio de Janeiro: Francisco Alves, 1988.

Curley, Robert. "Political Catholicism in Revolutionary Mexico." Working Paper 349. Hellen Kellogg Institute, Notre Dame, 2008.

D'Agostino, Peter. *Rome in America: Transnational Catholic Ideology from the Risorgimento to Fascism*. Chapel Hill: University of North Carolina Press, 2003.

da Fonseca, Luiz Anselmo. *A escravidão, o clero, e a abolição*. Bahia: Imprensa Economica, 1887.

Da Ros, Giuseppina. "El movimiento cooperativo en el Ecuador: Visión histórica, situación actual y perspectivas." *CIRIEC-Espana, Revista de Economía Pública, Social y Cooperativa*, no. 57 (April 2007): 249–84.

Dargaud, Joseph. *The Eucharist in the Life of St. Margaret Mary*. Kenosha, Wisc.: Prow/ Franciscan Marytown Press, 1979.

David Mayagoitia, S.J.: Apóstol intellectual. Mexico City: UFEC, 2001.

Dávila, Jerry. *Diploma of Whiteness: Race and Social Policy in Brazil, 1917–1945*. Durham, N.C.: Duke University Press, 2003.

Davis, William B. *Experiences and Observations of an American Consular Officer during the Mexican Revolutions*. Whitefish, Mont.: Kessinger Publishing, LLC, 1920.

de A. Fávero, Maria de Lourdes. *A UNE em Tempos de Autoritarismo*. Rio de Janeiro: Editora UFRJ, 1995.

de Aquino, Maurício. "Modernidade republicana e diocesanização do catolicismo no Brasil: As relações entre Estado e Igreja na Primeira República (1889–1930)." *Revista Brasileira de História* 32, no. 63 (2012): 143–70.

de Groot, C. F. G. *Brazilian Catholicism and the Ultramontane Reform, 1850–1930*. Amsterdam: CEDLA, 1996.

de Menezes, Carlos Alberto. *Ação social católica no Brasil: Corporativismo e sindicalismo*, edited by Padre Ferdinand Azevedo, S.J. São Paulo: CEPEHIB and Edições Loyola, 1986.

de Souza Lima, Luiz Gonzaga. *Evolução Política dos Católicas e da Igreja no Brasil*. Petrópolis: Editora Vozes, 1979.

Delaney, Ida. *By Their Own Hands: A Fieldworker's Account of the Antigonish Movement*. Hantsport, N.S.: Lancelot Press, 1985.

Della Cava, Ralph. "Brazilian Messianism and National Institutions: A Reappraisal of Canudos and Joaseiro." *Hispanic American Historical Review* 48, no. 3 (August 1968): 402–20.

———. *Miracle at Joaseiro*. New York: Columbia University Press, 1970.

———. "Catholicism and Society in Twentieth-Century Brazil." *Latin American Research Review* 11, no. 2 (1976): 7–50.

Demers, Maurice. *Connected Struggles: Catholics, Nationalists, and Transnational Relations between Mexico and Quebec, 1917–1945*. Montreal: McGill-Queen's University Press, 2014.

Dennis, James S., Harlan P. Beach, and Charles H. Fahs, eds. *World Atlas of Christian Missions*. New York: Student Volunteer Movement for Foreign Missions, 1911.

Diacon, Todd. *Stringing Together a Nation: Cândido Mariano da Silva Rondon and the Construction of a Modern Brazil, 1906–1930*. Durham, N.C.: Duke University Press, 2004.

Dinius, Oliver. *Brazil's Steel City: Developmentalism, Strategic Power, and Industrial Relations in Volta Redonda, 1941–1964*. Palo Alto, Calif.: Stanford University Press, 2010.

Diniz, Aldiva Sales, and Bruce Gilbert. "Socialist Values and Cooperation in Brazil's Landless Rural Workers' Movement." *Latin American Perspectives* 40, no. 19 (2013): 19–34.

Diocese of Quiché. *El Quiché: El pueblo y su iglesia, 1960–1980*. Santa Cruz del Quiché, Guatemala: La Diócesis, 1994.

do Santo Rosário, Irmã Maria Regina [Laurita Pessoa Raja Gabaglia]. *O Cardeal Leme (1882–1942)*. Rio de Janeiro J. Olympio, 1962.

Dodaro, Santo, and Leonard Pluta. *The Big Picture: The Antigonish Movement of Eastern Nova Scotia*. Montreal: McGill-Queen's University Press, 2012.

Dolan, Timothy. *Some Seed Fell on Good Ground: The Life of Edwin V. O'Hara*. Washington, D.C.: The Catholic University of America Press, 1992.

Domínguez, Raúl. "El perfil político de las organizaciones estudiantiles durante la década de 1950." In *Los estudiantes: Trabajos de historia y sociología*, edited by Renate Marsiske, 261–90. Mexico City: National Autonomous University of Mexico, 1998.

dos Santos, Edwiges Rosa. *O jornal Imprensa Evangelica: Diferentes fases no contexto brasileiro (1864–1892)*. São Paulo: Universidade Presbiteriana Mackenzie, 2009.

Dreifuss, René Armand. *1964: A Conquista do Estado—Ação Política, Poder e Golpe de Classe*. 6th edition. Rio de Janeiro: Editora Vozes, 2006.

Dries, Angelyn. "The Legacy of John J. Considine, M.M." *International Bulletin of Missionary Research* 21, no. 2 (April 1997): 80–84.

Duffy, Eamon. *Saints and Sinners: A History of the Popes.* New Haven, Conn.: Yale University Press, 1997.

Dupuy, Michel. "Canada's Role in Development and CIDA's Relationship with the Coady International Institute." In *Human Development through Social Change: Proceedings of St. Francis Xavier University's International Symposium Commemorating the Fiftieth Anniversary of the Antigonish Movement, 1928–1978, Antigonish, Nova Scotia, Canada,* edited by Philip Milner. Antigonish, N.S.: Formac Publishing Co., 1979.

Dussel, Enrique. *A History of the Church in Latin America: Colonialism to Liberation (1492–1979).* Grand Rapids, Mich.: Eerdmans, 1981.

Edwards, Lisa M. *Roman Virtues: The Education of Latin American Clergy in Rome, 1858–1962.* New York: Peter Lang, 2011.

Episcopado Brasileiro: Carta pastoral do Episcopado brasileiro ao clero e aos fieis de suas diócesis por occasião do Centenário da Independência, 1922. Rio de Janeiro: Papelaria e Typographia Marques, Araujo e Cia., 1922.

Episcopado Brasileiro: O Episcopado brazileiro ao clero e aos fiéis da Egreja do Brazil. São Paulo: Typografia Salesiana a Vapor do Lyceu do Sagrado Coração, 1890.

Escobar Loarca, Tirso Constantino. "Cooperativismo agrario en el occidente de Guatemala: Estudio de casos concretos." Tesis Ciencias Juridicas y Sociales de Universidad de San Carlos, Guatemala, 1974.

Espinosa, David. "Student Politics, National Politics: Mexico's National Student Union, 1926–1943." *The Americas* 62, no. 4 (April 2006): 533–62.

"Exposición del episcopado de Venezuela al señor Presidente de la República, Dr. J. P. Rojas Paul 26-9-1889." In *Conferencia Episcopal Venezolana, Decretos y reglamentaciones 1889–1984,* with introduction, compilation, and notes by Monseñor Baltazar Porras Cardozo, 7–22. Caracas: Ediciones de la Presidencia de la República, 1986.

Eyzaguirre, José Ignacio Victor. *Los intereses católicos en América.* 2 vols. Paris, France: Librería de Garnier Hermanos, 1859.

Falla, Ricardo. *Quiché Rebelde: Religious Conversion, Politics, and Ethnic Identity in Guatemala.* Austin: University of Texas Press, 2001.

Fallaw, Ben. *Religion and State Formation in Postrevolutionary Mexico.* Durham, N.C.: Duke University Press, 2013.

Fals Borda, Orlando. *Peasant Society in the Colombian Andes: A Sociological Study of Saucio.* Gainesville: University of Florida Press, 1955.

———. *Cooperatives and Rural Development in Latin America: An Analytic Report.* Geneva: UNRISD, 1971.

Feder, Ernest. *The Rape of the Peasantry: Latin America's Landholding System.* Garden City, N.Y.: Doubleday Anchor Books, 1971.

Finchelstein, Federico. *Transatlantic Fascism: Ideology, Violence, and the Sacred in Argentina, 1919–1945.* Durham, N.C.: Duke University Press, 2010.

Finke, Roger, and Patricia Wittberg. "Organizational Revival from Within: Explaining Revivalism and Reform in the Roman Catholic Church." *Journal for the Scientific Study of Religion* 39, no. 2 (June 2000): 154–70.

Fitzpatrick-Behrens, Susan. "Catholic Good Neighbors: The Maryknoll Mission and Latin America." Unpublished paper.

————. *The Maryknoll Catholic Mission in Peru, 1943–1989: Transnational Faith and Transformations*. Notre Dame, Ind.: University of Notre Dame Press, 2011.

Fitzpatrick-Behrens, Susan, and Catherine C. LeGrand. "Canadian and U.S. Catholic Promotion of Co-operatives in Central America and the Caribbean and Their Political Implications." In *A Global History of Consumer Co-operation since 1850: Movements and Businesses*, edited by Mary Hilson, Silke Neunsinger, and Greg Patmore. Submitted to Brill Publishers in Leiden, 2014.

Foisy, Catherine. "Des Québécois aux frontières: Dialogues et affrontements culturels aux dimensions du monde. Récits missionnaires d'Asie, d'Afrique et d'Amérique latine (1945–1980)." PhD diss., Concordia University, 2012.

Fragoso, Hugo. "As Beatas do Pe. Ibiapina: Uma forma de vida religiosa para os sertões do Nordeste." In *Padre Ibiapina e a igreja dos pobres*, ed. Georgette Desrochers and Eduardo Hoonaert, 85–106. São Paulo: Edições Paulinas, 1984.

Freitez, Nelson. "El cooperativismo en el Estado Lara, Venezuela, en los años de 1960: Promoción religiosa y crisis política." *Cayapa: Revista Venezolana de Economía Social* 7, no. 13 (January–June 2007): 76–104.

Freston, Paul. *A carreira de Gilberto Freyre*. São Paulo: Instituto de Estudos Econômicos, Sociais e Políticos de São Paulo, 1987.

Freyre, Gilberto. *Order and Progress: Brazil from Monarchy to Republic*. Berkeley: University of California Press, 1986.

Fuller, Leigh A. "Catholic Missionary Work and National Development in Guatemala, 1943–68: The Maryknoll Experience." Master's thesis, New York University, 1971.

Furey, Francis T. *Life of Leo XIII and History of his Pontificate: From Official and Approved Sources*. New York: Catholic Educational Company, 1903.

Gaffey, James P. *Francis Clement Kelley and the American Catholic Dream*. Vol. 2. Bensenville, Ill.: The Heritage Foundation, 1980.

Gaitán Alvarez, José Miguel. "El Movimiento Cooperativista de Guatemala: Desarrollo de la Federación Nacoinal de Cooperativas de Ahorro y Credito." *Estudios Sociales* 7 (August 1972): 33–62.

Gallo Lozano, Fernando A., comp. *Compilación de leyes de reforma*. Guadalajara: Congreso del Estado de Jalisco, 1973.

García, Emilio Coral. "The Mexico City Middle Class, 1940–1970: Between Tradition, the State and the United States." PhD diss., Georgetown University, 2011.

Gaspari, Elio. *A Ditadura Escancarada*. São Paulo: Editora Schwarcz, 2002.

Gavilanes del Castillo, Luis Maria. *Monseñor Leonidas Proaño y su misión profético-liberadora en la iglesia de América latina*. Quito: Fondo Ecuatoriano Populorum Progressio, 1992.

Gerassi, John, ed. *Revolutionary Priest: The Complete Writings and Messages of Camilo Torres*. New York: Vintage, 1971.

Gilbert, Joseph M., Anne Rubenstein, and Eric Zolov, eds. *Fragments of a Golden Age: The Politics of Culture in Mexico since 1940*. Durham, N.C.: Duke University Press, 2001.

Gill, Anthony. *Rendering unto Caesar: The Catholic Church and the State in Latin America*. Chicago: The University of Chicago Press, 1998.

Giumbelli, Emerson. *O cuidado dos mortos: Uma história da condenação e legitimação do espiritismo.* Rio de Janeiro: Ministério da Justicia, Arquivo Nacional, 1997.

Gleijeses, Piero. *Shattered Hope: The Guatemalan Revolution and the United States, 1944–1954.* Princeton, N.J.: Princeton University Press, 1991.

Gómez, Máximo Pacheco. *La separación de la Iglesia y el Estado en Chile y la diplomacia vaticana.* Santiago: Editorial Andrés Bello, 2004.

Gómez Morín, Manuel. *La lucha por la libertad de cátedra.* Mexico City: National Autonomous University of Mexico, 1996.

González Ruiz, Edgar. *MURO, Memorias y Testimonios, 1961–2002.* Puebla, Mexico: Benemérita Universidad Autónoma de Puebla, 2004.

González, Fernando Manuel. *Matar y morir por Cristo Rey.* Austin: University of Texas Press, 2001.

———. "Algunos grupos radicales de izquierda y derecha con influencia católica en México, 1965–1975." *Historía y Grafía,* no. 29 (2007): 57–93.

Gorman, Daniel. *The Emergence of International Society in the 1920s.* Cambridge: Cambridge University Press, 2012.

Gorst, Sheila. *Co-operative Organization in Tropical Countries: A Study of Co-operative Development in Non-self-governing Territories under United Kingdom Administration, 1945–1955.* Oxford: Basil Blackwell, 1959.

Graham, Richard. *Britain and the Onset of Modernization in Brazil 1850–1914.* Cambridge: Cambridge University Press, 1972.

Grandin, Greg. *The Last Colonial Massacre: Latin America in the Cold War.* Chicago: The University of Chicago Press, 2004.

Guízar, Jesús Degollado. *Memorias de Jesús Degollado Guízar: Último general en jefe del ejército cristero.* Mexico City: Editorial Jus, 1957.

Hallo, Gonzalo. "Educational Program for Cooperativo de Ahorro y Crédito S. Francisco Ltd.: From Ambato-Ecuador." Coady International Institute: Diploma Program, 1990.

Handy, Jim. *Gift of the Devil: A History of Guatemala.* Cambridge, Mass.: South End Press, 1984.

———. *Revolution in the Countryside: Rural Conflict and Agrarian Reform in Guatemala, 1944–1954.* Chapel Hill: University of North Carolina Press, 1994.

Hanson, Randall S. "The Day of Ideals: Catholic Social Action in the Age of the Mexican Revolution, 1867–1929." PhD diss., Indiana University, Bloomington, 1994.

Harrison, Carol E. "Zouave Stories: Gender, Catholic Spirituality, and French Responses to the Roman Question." *The Journal of Modern History* 79 (2007): 274–305.

Hastings, Derek. "Fears of a Feminized Church: Catholicism, Clerical Celibacy, and the Crisis of Masculinity in Wilhelmine Germany." *European History Quarterly* 38, no. 1 (2008): 34–65.

Hauck, João Fagundes. "Esboço histórico." In *A igreja e o povo,* edited by Julio Maria, 9–33. São Paulo: Loyola/CEPEHIB, 1983.

Hennessey, James. *A History of Catholic America: From Columbus to the Quincentennial, 1492–1992.* Sparkill, N.Y.: Shepherd Press, 1991.

Herrera Soto, Roberto, ed. *Antología del Pensamiento Conservador en Colombia.* Vol. 2. Bogotá: Colcultura, Bogotana de Impresos, 1982.

Hess, David J. *Spirits and Scientists: Ideology, Spiritism and Brazilian Culture*. College Station: Penn State Press, 2010.

Horacio Urán, Carlos, and Ana María Bidegain de Urán. *El movimiento estudiantil latinoamericano, entre la reforma y la revolución, bosquejo histórico-político*. Montevideo: Comunidad del Sur, 1970.

Immerwahr, Daniel. *Thinking Small: The United States and the Lure of Community Development*. Cambridge, Mass.: Harvard University Press, 2015.

Instituto Brasileiro de Geografia e Estatística (IGBE), *Anuário estatístico do Brasil IGBE*, vol. 16, (1955): "Distribuição dos cursos, segundo o caráter dos estabelecimentos—1955."

"Inter-American Notes." *The Americas* 1, no. 2 (October 1944): 236–239.

Iriye, Akira. *Cultural Internationalism and World Order*. Baltimore: Johns Hopkins University Press, 1997.

Ivereigh, Austen, ed. *The Politics of Religion in an Age of Revival*. London: Institute for the Study of the Americas, 2000.

John XXIII. *Mater et Magistra: Encyclical of Pope John XXIII on Christianity and Social Progress*. May 15, 1961. http://www.vatican.va/holy_father/john_xxiii/encyclicals/documents/hf_j-xxiii_enc_15051961_mater_en.html.

Jonas, Raymond. *France and the Cult of the Sacred Heart: An Epic Tale for Modern Times*. Berkeley: University of California Press, 2000.

Jonas, Susanne, and David Tobis, eds. *Guatemala*. New York: North American Congress on Latin America, 1974.

Kelley, Francis Clement, ed. *The First American Catholic Missionary Congress*. Chicago: J. S. Hyland & Company, 1909.

———. *The Book of Red and Yellow: Being a Story of Blood and a Yellow Streak*. Chicago: The Catholic Church Extension Society of the United States of America, 1915.

———. *The Story of Extension*. Chicago: Extension Press, 1922.

———. *The Great American Catholic Missionary Congresses*. Chicago: J. S. Hyland & Company, n.d.

Keogh, Dermot, ed. *Church and Politics in Latin America*. New York: St. Martin's Press, 1990.

Klaiber, Jeffrey L. "The Catholic Lay Movement in Peru: 1867–1959." *The Americas* 40, no. 2 (October 1983): 149–70.

———. *The Catholic Church in Peru, 1821–1985: A Social History*. Washington, D.C.: The Catholic University of America Press, 1992.

Knight, Alan. *The Mexican Revolution, Volume 2: Counter-revolution and Reconstruction*. Lincoln: University of Nebraska Press, 1990.

Koselleck, Reinhart. *Futures Past: On the Semantics of Historical Time*. Translated and with an introduction by Keith Tribe. New York: Columbia University Press, 2004.

Kosicki, Piotr H. "The Catholic Church and the Cold War." In *The Routledge Handbook of the Cold War*, edited by Artemy M. Kalinovksy and Craig Daigle, 259–71. London: Routledge, 2014.

La asamblea católica de Valparaíso. Santiago: Imprenta de "El Independiente," 1877.

Labbé, Yves. *El clero y las vocaciones sacerdotales en la República Dominicana*. Santo Domingo: Amigo del Hogar, 1976.

Laidlaw, Alexander F. *The Campus and the Community: The Global Impact of the Anti-gonish Movement.* Montreal: Harvest House, 1961.

———. *The Man from Margaree: Writings and Teachings of M. M. Coady Educator/ Reformer/Priest.* Toronto: McClelland & Stewart, 1971.

Langland, Victoria. *Speaking of Flowers: Student Movements and the Making and Re-membering of 1968 in Military Brazil.* Durham, N.C.: Duke University Press, 2013.

Lara, Lucas Guillermo Castillo. *Apuntes para una historia documental de la iglesia venezolana en Archivo Secreto Vaticano.* Caracas: Academia Nacional de Historia, 2000.

Latin American Documentation (LADOC). *Basic Christian Communities.* Washing-ton, D.C.: Latin American Documentation—United States Catholic Conference (USCC), 1976.

LeGrand, Catherine. "Canadian Catholic Missionary Priests in the Dominican Repub-lic: Dictatorship, the Co-operative Movement and Cultural Adaptations, 1935–1985." Paper presented on the panel "The Other Pan-Americanisms: Compara-tive and Transnational Studies of Canadian-Latin American Relations." Canadian Historical Association, York University, May 31, 2006.

———. "L'axe missionnaire catholique entre le Québec et l'Amérique latine: Une exploration préliminaire." *Globe: Revue internationale d'études québécoises* 12, no. 1 (2009): 43–66.

———. "Les réseaux missionnaires et l'action sociale des Québécois en Amérique latine, 1945–1980." *Etudes d'histoire religieuse* 79, no. 1 (Spring 2013): 93–115.

LeMorvan, Kevin, ed. "The Antigonish Movement." Report on Workshop co-sponsored by the Coady International Institute and the Confederación Mexicana de Cajas Populares. Puebla, Mexico, August 31–September 6, 1987. The Marie Michael Library, Coady International Institute, Antigonish, N.S.

Lernoux, Penny. *Cry of the People: The Struggle for Human Rights in Latin America— The Catholic Church in Conflict with U.S. Policy.* New York: Penguin Books, 1982.

Levenson-Estrada, Deborah. *Trade Unionist against Terror: Guatemala City, 1954–1985.* Chapel Hill: University of North Carolina Press, 1994.

Levine, Daniel H. *Popular Voices in Latin American Catholicism.* Princeton, N.J.: Princeton University Press, 1992.

Levine, Robert M. *Vale of Tears: Revisiting the Canudos Massacre in Northeastern Brazil, 1893–1897.* Berkeley: University of California Press, 1992.

Lima Methods Conference of the Maryknoll Fathers. *Proceeding of the Lima Methods Conference of the Maryknoll Fathers: Maryknoll House, Lima, Peru, August 23–28, 1954.* Maryknoll, N.Y.: Maryknoll Fathers, 1954.

Lima, Haroldo, and Aldo Arantes. *História da Ação Popular da JUC ao PCdoB.* São Paulo: Editora Alfa-Omega, 1984.

Loaeza, Soledad. "La Democracia Cristiana y la modernizacón de Acción Nacional, 1957–1965." *Historia y Grafía*, no. 14 (2000): 147–82.

———. "Mexico in the Fifties: Women and Church in Holy Alliance." *Women's Stud-ies Quarterly* 33, no. 3/4 (2005): 138–60.

Londoño, Carlos Mario. *Economía Agraria Colombiana.* Madrid: Ediciones Rialp, 1965.

Londoño-Vega, Patricia. *Religion, Society, and Culture in Colombia: Antioquia and Me-dellín, 1850–1930.* Oxford: Oxford University Press, 2002.

López, A. Ricardo. "Conscripts of Democracy: The Formation of a Professional Middle Class in Bogotá during the 1950s and Early 1960s." In *The Making of the Middle Class: Toward a Transnational History*, edited by A. Ricardo López and Barbara Weinstein, 161–95. Durham, N.C.: Duke University Press, 2012.

López, Alejandro. *Escritos Escogidos*. Bogotá: Biblioteca Basica Colombiana, 1976.

———. "Idearum Liberal" [1931]. In *Escritos Escogidos*, 215–24. Bogota: Biblioteca Basica Colombiana, 1976.

López Macedonio, Mónica Naymich. "Historia de una colaboración anticomunista transnacional: Los Tecos de la Universidad Autónoma de Guadalajara y el gobierno de Chiang Kai-Shek a principios de los años setenta." *Contemporánea: Historia y Problemas del Siglo XX* I, no. 1 (2010): 133–58.

López Vigil, Maria. *¡Héctor Gallego Está Vivo!* Panama: Pastoral Social-Caritas Editores, 1996.

Losel, Steffan. "Prayer, Pain, and Priestly Privilege: Claude Langlois's New Perspective on Thérèse of Lisieux." *The Journal of Religion* 88, no. 3 (July 2008): 273–306.

Lucas, Jeffrey Kent. *The Rightward Drift of Mexico's Former Revolutionaries: The Case of Antonio Díaz Soto Y Gama*. Lewistown, N.Y.: Edwin Mellen Press, 2010.

Lynch, John. "The Catholic Church in Latin America, 1830–1930." In *The Cambridge History of Latin America, Vol. IV, c. 1870–1930*, edited by Leslie Bethell, 527–95. Cambridge: Cambridge University Press, 1986.

———. *New Worlds: A Religious History of Latin America*. New Haven, Conn.: Yale University Press, 2012.

Lyons, Barry J. *Remembering the Hacienda: Religion, Authority and Social Change in Highland Ecuador*. Austin: University of Texas Press, 2006.

MacDonald, Rev. Joseph A. *Antigonish and Puerto Rico: Implementation of the Social Encyclicals*. Roosevelt: Cooperative League of Puerto Rico, 1962.

MacEachen, Allan J. "Canadian Approaches to Co-operation: The Antigonish Movement and Canada's International Responsibilities." In *Human Development through Social Change: Proceedings of St. Francis Xavier University's International Symposium Commemorating the Fiftieth Anniversary of the Antigonish Movement, 1928–1978, Antigonish, Nova Scotia, Canada*, edited by Philip Milner, 13–15. Antigonish, N.S.: Formac Publishing Co., 1979.

MacEachen, Rev. John H. *A Chosen Few: Voluntarios*. Sydney, N.S.: City Printers, Ltd., 1987.

MacEoin, Gary. *Agent for Change: The Story of Pablo Steele as Told to Gary MacEoin*. Maryknoll, N.Y.: Orbis Books, 1973.

Mackin, Robert Sean. "The Movement That Fell from the Sky? Secularization and the Structuring of Progressive Catholicism in Latin America, 1920s–1970s." PhD diss., University of Wisconsin, Madison, 2005.

MacPherson, Ian. *Hands around the Globe: A History of the International Credit Union Movement and the Role and Development of World Council of Credit Unions, Inc.* Victoria, B.C.: Horsdal & Schubart Publishers and World Council of Credit Unions, 1999.

———. "Patterns in the Maritime Co-operative Movement, 1900–1945." In *One Path to Co-operative Studies: A Selection of Papers and Presentations*, edited by Ian MacPherson, 31–52. Victoria, B.C.: New Rochdale Press, 2007.

Mahon, Leo, and Nancy Davis. *Fire under My Feet: A Memoir of God's Power in Panama*. Maryknoll, N.Y.: Orbis Books, 2007.

Mainwaring, Scott. *The Catholic Church and Politics in Brazil, 1916–1985*. Palo Alto, Calif.: Stanford University Press, 1986.

Mainwaring, Scott, and Timothy Scully, eds. *Christian Democracy in Latin America: Electoral Competition and Regime Conflicts*. Palo Alto, Calif.: Stanford University Press, 2003.

Marchi, Euclides. "Igreja e povo: Católicos? Os olhares do Padre Júlio Maria e de Dom Sebastião Leme da Silveira Cintra sobre a catolicidade do brasileiro na passagem do século XIX para o XX." *História Questões & Debates* 55, no. 2 (July–December 2011): 83–110.

Maria, Júlio. "Memoria: A religião. Ordens religiosas. Instituições pias e beneficentes no Brasil." In *Associacão do Quarto Centenário do Descobrimento do Brasil, Livro do Centenário (1500–1900)*, vol. 1. Rio de Janeiro: Imprensa Oficial, 1900.

———. *A igreja e o povo*. Edited by João Fagundes Hauck. São Paulo: Edições Loyola and CEPEHIB, 1983.

Maritain, Jacques, and Charles Journet. *L'education a la croisee du chemins*. Paris: Egloff, 1947.

Maritain, Jacques. *Integral Humanism: Temporal and Spiritual Problems of a New Christendom*. Translated by Joseph W. Evans. New York: Charles Scribner's Sons, 1968.

Marlett, Jeffrey. "Harvesting an Overlooked Freedom: The Anti-Urban Vision of American Catholic Agrarianism, 1920–1950." *U.S. Catholic Historian* 16, no. 4 (1998): 88–108.

Marsiske, Renate. *El movimiento estudiantil de 1929 y la autonomía de la Universidad Nacional de México*. Mexico City: National Autonomous University of Mexico, 1981.

Matthews, Race. *Jobs of Our Own: Building a Stakeholder Society: Alternatives to the Market and the State*. Sydney: Pluto Press, 1999.

Mattoso, Kátia. *Bahia século XIX: Uma província no império*. Rio de Janeiro: Nova Frontiera, 1992.

McAnany, Emile G. "Radio's Role in Development: Five Strategies of Use." Institute for Communication Research, Stanford University, 1973. http://pdf.usaid.gov/pdf_docs/PNAAD453.pdf.

McCartain, James P. "The Sacred Heart of Jesus, Thérèse of Lisieux, and the Transformation of U.S. Catholic Piety, 1865–1940." *U.S. Catholic Historian* 25, no. 2 (Spring 2007): 53–67.

McCreery, David. *Rural Guatemala: 1760–1940*. Palo Alto, Calif.: Stanford University Press, 1994.

McDannell, Colleen. "'True Men As We Need Them': Catholicism and the Irish-American Male." *American Studies* 27, no. 2 (1986): 19–36.

McEachen, R. A. "Our Five Million Immigrants." In *The First American Catholic Missionary Congress*, edited by Francis C. Kelley, 272–78. Chicago: J. S. Hyland & Company, 1909.

Mecham, J. Lloyd. *Church and State in Latin America: A History of Politicoeclesiastical Relations*. Chapel Hill: University of North Carolina Press, 1966.

Medhurst, Kenneth N. *The Church and Labour in Colombia*. Manchester, England: Manchester University Press, 1984.

Mejía Robledo, Alfonso. "Cooperativa de la Vivienda." In *Vidas y Empresas de Antio-quia*, 258–60. Medellin: Imprenta Departamental, 1951.

Melgar, Rafael. *Segunda Parte: Los Ultimos Cincuenta Años*. Unpublished manuscript, n.d.

Memoria de la Asamblea Eucarística celebrada en la ciudad de Puebla el 26 de octubre de 1930, a convocatoria del Consejo Supremo de la Adoración Nocturna Mexicana. Mexico City: Imprenta de J.I. Muñoz, 1930.

Memoria del tercer congreso católico de la vida rural: Panama. Panama: Organización Católica de la Vida Rural, 1955.

Meyer, Jean. *La crisitada: Vol. 2, el conflicto entre la iglesia y el estado 1926–1929*. Mexico City: Siglo XXI, 1989.

Michel, Florian. *La pensée catholique en Amérique du Nord: Réseaux intellectuels et échanges culturels entre l'Europe, le Canada et les Etats-Unis (années 1920–1960)*. Paris: Desclée de Brouwer, 2010.

Miller, Eugene D. *A Holy Alliance? The Church and the Left in Costa Rica, 1932–1948*. New York: M.E. Sharpe, 1996.

Milner, Philip, ed. *Human Development through Social Change: Proceedings of St. Francis Xavier University's International Symposium Commemorating the Fiftieth Anniversary of the Antigonish Movement, 1928–1978*. Antigonish, N.S.: Formac Publishing Co., 1979.

Misner, Paul. *Social Catholicism in Europe: From the Onset of Industrialization to the First World War*. New York: Crossroad Publishing Company, 1991.

Mitchell, Stephanie, and Patience A. Schell, eds. *The Women's Revolution in Mexico, 1910–1953*. Lanham, Md.: Rowman & Littlefield, 2007.

Mogrovejo, Rodrigo, Alberto Mora, and Philippe Vanhuynegem, eds. *El cooperativismo en América latina: Una diversidad de contribuciones al desarrollo sostenible*. La Paz, Bolivia: Oficina Regional de la Organización International del Trabajo (OIT) para América Latina y el Caribe, 2012.

Monte Marciano, João Evangelista. *Relatório apresentado, em 1895, pelo Reverendo Frei João Evangelista de Monte Marciano, ao Arcebispado da Bahia sobre Antonio "Conselheiro" e seu sequito no Arraial de Canudos*. No Publisher, 1895.

Montesinos, Roberto. "Dos historias del trabajo." In *Una lectura sociológica de la Venezuela actual*, vol. 4, 47–62. Caracas: Konrad Adenauer Stiftung-Universidad Católica Andrés Bello, 2008.

Moore, Breanna. "Philosemitism under a Darkening Sky: Judaism in the French Catholic Revival (1900–1945)." *The Catholic Historical Review* 99, no. 2 (April 2013): 262–97.

Moreno Chávez, José Alberto. *Devociones políticas: Cultura católica y politización en la Arquidiócesis de México, 1880–1920*. Mexico City: El Colegio de México, 2013.

Moreno, Julio. *Yankee Don't Go Home! Mexican Nationalism, American Business Culture, and the Shaping of Modern Mexico, 1920–1950*. Chapel Hill: University of North Carolina Press, 2003.

Morrison, Joseph P. "El Apostolado litúrgico en los Estados Unidos." In *Primer Congreso Católico Latinoamericano Sobre Problemas de la Vida Rural*. Manizales, Colombia: Imprenta Departamental, 1953.

Muldoon, P. J. "Immigration and the Immigrants in the United States." In *The Great American Catholic Missionary Congresses*, edited by Frances C. Kelley, 132–47. Chicago: J. S. Hyland & Company, 1909.

Munari, Tiberio. *Derramaron su sangre para Cristo: Los siervos de Dios Anacleto González Flores, Jorge Vargas González, Ramón Vargas González, Luis Padilla Gómez, Ezequiel Huerta Gutiérrez, Salvador Huerta Gutiérrez, Luis Magaña Servín, Miguel Gómez Loza*. Guadalajara: Ediciones Xaverianas, 1998.

———. *Ramón Sáinz Orozco, primer presidente de la Adoración Nocturna en Arandas, sacrificado en 1937*. Guadalajara: Ediciones Xaverianas, 2007.

Muñoz, Edgar Solano. "La participación del clero costarricense en las campañas políticas de 1889 y 1894." *Diálogos, Revista Electrónica de Historia* 11, no. 2 (September 2010/February 2011): 1–21.

Muñoz, Francisco Puy. *Luis de Trelles: Un laico testigo de la fe*. Madrid: CEU Ediciones, 2009.

Nachman, Robert G. "Positivism, Modernization, and the Middle Class in Brazil." *Hispanic American Historical Review* 57, no. 1 (1977): 1–23.

Nagle, Robin. *Claiming the Virgin: The Broken Promise of Liberation Theology in Brazil*. London: Routledge, 1997.

Nearing, Peter A. *He Loved the Church: The Biography of Bishop John R. MacDonald, Fifth Bishop of Antigonish*. Antigonish, N.S.: Casket Printing and Publishing Co., 1975.

Needell, Jeffrey. *A Tropical Belle Epoque: Elite Culture and Society in Turn-of-the-Century Rio de Janeiro*. Cambridge: Cambridge University Press, 1987.

Novaes, Sylvia Caiuby. *The Play of Mirrors: The Representation of Self Mirrored in the Other*. Austin: University of Texas Press, 1997.

Nugent, Joseph. "The Sword and the Prayerbook: Ideals of Authentic Irish Manliness." *Victorian Studies* 50, no. 4 (2008): 587–613.

O'Connor, Thomas H. *Boston Catholics: A History of the Church and Its People*. Boston: Northeastern University Press, 1998.

O'Dogherty, Laura. "Restaurarlo Todo en Cristo: La Unión de Damas Católicas Mejicanas, 1920–1926." *Estudios de Historia Moderna y Contemporánea de México* 14 (1991): 129–58.

O'Dogherty Madrazo, Laura. *De urnas y sotanas: El Partido Católico Nacional en Jalisco*. Mexico City: Conaculta, 2001.

O'Hara, Edwin Vincent, and John A. Ryan. *The Church and the Country Community*. New York: Macmillan, 1927.

O'Hearn, Michael J. "The Political Transformation of a Religious Order." PhD diss., University of Toronto, 1983.

Ochoa, Jesús Enrique. *Los cristeros del volcán de Colima: Escenas de la lucha por la libertad religiosa en México 1926–1929, tomo II*. Mexico City: Editorial Jus, 1961.

Ochs, Stephen J. *Desegregating the Altar: The Josephites and the Struggle for Black Priests, 1871–1960*. Baton Rouge: Louisiana State University Press, 1993.

Ogilvie, Mary H. "Gallagher, Nicholas Aloysius." *Handbook of Texas Online*, http://www.tshaonline.org/handbook/online/articles/fga07. Published by the Texas State Historical Association.

330 ❖ Bibliography

Olcott, Jocelyn, Mary Kay Vaughn, and Gabriela Cano, eds. *Sex in Revolution: Gender, Politics, and Power in Modern Mexico.* Durham, N.C.: Duke University Press, 2006.

Olcott, Jocelyn. *Revolutionary Women in Postrevolutionary Mexico.* Durham, N.C.: Duke University Press, 2005.

Olimón Nolasco, Manuel. *Sofía del Valle: Una mexicana universal.* Mexico City: Instituto Nacional de las Mujeres, 2009.

Otero Diez, H. Santiago. *Padre Guillermo Woods: Parroquias San José Ixcán y Candelaria de los Mártires.* Second edition. Ixcán, Quiché Guatemala: Ediciones San Pablo, 2006.

Owensby, Brian. *Intimate Ironies: Modernity and the Making of Middle-Class Lives in Brazil.* Palo Alto, Calif.: Stanford University Press, 1999.

Pacheco, María Martha. "Cristianismo sí, comunismo no: anticomunismo eclesiástico en México." In *La Iglesia contra México,* edited by Octavio Rodríguez Araujo, 259–90. Mexico City: Orfila, 2010.

Palacios y Olivares, Guillermo de Jesus. "Revoltas camponesas no Brasil escravista: A 'Guerra dos Maribondos' (Pernambuco, 1851–1852)." *Almanack Braziliense* 3 (2006): 9–39.

Palomar y Vizcarra, Miguel. *La comunión de los hombres: La Eucaristía es un sacramento esencialmente viril.* Mexico City: Editorial Ara, 1963.

Pang, Eul-Soo. "The Changing Roles of Priests in the Politics of Northeast Brazil, 1889–1964." *The Americas* 30, no. 3 (1974): 341–72.

Panofsky, Erwin. "Renaissance and Renascences." *The Kenyon Review* 6, no. 2 (Spring 1944): 201–36.

Park, James William. *Latin American Underdevelopment: A History of Perspectives in the United States, 1870–1965.* Baton Rouge: Louisiana State University Press, 1995.

Parras, Andrea. "CIDA's Secular Fiction and Canadian Faith-Based Organisations." *Canadian Journal of Development Studies/Revue canadienne d'études du développement* 33, no. 2 (June 2012): 231–49.

Pasture, Patrick, Jan Art, and Thomas Buerman, eds. *Gender and Christianity in Modern Europe: Beyond the Feminization Thesis.* Leuven: University of Leuven Press, 2012.

Pasture, Patrick. "Beyond the Feminization Thesis: Gendering the History of Christianity in the Nineteenth and Twentieth Centuries." In *Gender and Christianity in Modern Europe: Beyond the Feminization Thesis,* edited by Patrick Pasture, Jan Art, and Thomas Buerman, 7–33. Leuven: University of Leuven Press, 2012.

Pelletier, Denis. *"Economie et Humanisme": De l'utopie communautaire au combat pour le tiers-monde (1941–1966).* Paris: Les Editions du Cerf, 1996.

Pensado, Jaime M. *Rebel Mexico: Student Unrest and Authoritarian Political Culture during the Long Sixties.* Palo Alto, Calif.: Stanford University Press, 2013.

———. "'To Assault with the Truth': The Revitalization of Conservative Militancy in Mexico during the 1960s." *The Americas* 70, no. 3 (January 2014): 489–521.

———. "El Movimiento Estudiantil Profesional (MEP): Una mirada histórica a la radicalización de la juventud católica mexicana durante la guerra fría." *Mexican Studies/Estudios Mexicanos* 31, no. 1 (Winter 2015).

Penyak, Lee M., and Walter J. Petry, eds. *Religion and Society in Latin America: Interpretive Essays from Conquest to Present.* Maryknoll, N.Y.: Orbis Books, 2009.

Pereira, Nilo. "A encíclica Rerum Novarum em Pernambuco." *Ciência & Trópico* 19, no. 2 (Julho–Dezembro 1991): 287–94.

Pérez, Gabriela Contreras. *Los grupos católicos en la Universidad Autónoma de México (1933–1944).* Mexico City: National Autonomous University of Mexico, 2001.

Pérez Rosales, Laura. "La revista Señal, la cuestion social t el enemigo comunista en México a mediados del siglo XX." *La Cuestion Social: Documentos, ensayos, comentarios y reseñas de libros acerca de lo social* 20, no. 4 (2012): 378–97.

Piedade, Lélis. "Diário de um frade." In *Histórico e relatório do Comitê Patriótico da Bahia, 1897–1901,* edited by Antonio Olavo, 240–57. Salvador: Portfolium Editora, 2002.

Pius XI. "Ad un pellegrinaggio messicano: La preghiera per i persecutori." In *Discorsi di Pio XI,* volume II, edited by Domenico Bertetto, 556–57. Vatican City: Libreria Editrice Vaticana, 1985.

Pollard, John F. *Money and the Rise of the Modern Papacy: Financing the Vatican, 1850–1950.* Cambridge: Cambridge University Press, 2008.

———. "Pius XI's Promotion of the Italian Model of Catholic Action in the World-Wide Church." *The Journal of Ecclesiastical History* 63, no. 4 (October 2012): 758–84.

Pope, Barbara Corrado. "A Heroine without Heroics: The Little Flower of Jesus and Her Times." *Church History* 57, no.1 (March 1988): 46–60.

Porter, Susie S. "De obreras, señoritas y empleadas: Culturas de trabajo en la ciudad de México en la Compañía Ericsson." In *Género en la encrucijada de la historia social y cultural,* eds. Susie S. Porter and María Teresa Fernández Aceves. Mexico City: El Colegio de Michoacán/CIESAS, forthcoming.

Poulat, Émile. *Intégrisme et catholicisme intégral: Un réseau secret international antimoderniste: La Sapinière, 1909–1921.* Paris: Casterman, 1969.

Primera carta pastoral que el Excmo. y Rdmo. Sr. Leonidas E. Proaño, Obispo de Bolívar, dirige al Vble. Clero y fieles de la Diócesis. Trata del Seminario. Quito and Guayaquil: Editorial Colón, 1954.

Primer Congreso Católico Latinoamericano Sobre Problemas de la Vida Rural, Manizales, Colombia, January 11–18, 1953. Manizales: Imprenta Departamental, 1953.

Proaño, Leonidas. *Creo en el hombre y en la comunidad: Autobiografia.* Quito: Editora Nacional, 1989.

Puch, Ramon, S. Rivera, M.T. Findji, C. Fonnseca, A. Barreto, H. Ochoa, and J.M. Rosa. *Estudios de la realidad campesina: Cooperación y cambio. Informes y materiales de campo recogidos en Venezuela, Ecuador y Colombia.* Geneva: UNRISD, 1970.

Pulido Aragón, Diego. "La Necesidad de Implantar en Guatemala Las Cooperativas de Comercialización." Thesis: Facultad de Ciencias Económicas, Universidad de Rafael Landívar, 1971.

¿Quiénes mataron al General Obregón? Relato histórico de la tragedia de la Bombilla. Mexico City: Editorial Popular, 1929.

Quigley, Tom. "The Great North-South Embrace: How Collaboration among the Churches of the Americas Began." *America: The National Catholic Review,*

December 7, 2009. www.americamagazine.org/issue/718/article/great-north
-south-embrace.

Quirk, Robert E. *The Mexican Revolution and the Catholic Church, 1910–1929.* Bloomington: Indiana University Press, 1973.

"Radio Message on the Occasion of the Inauguration of the Catholic Radio Network of Sutatenza." April 11, 1953. www.vatican.va/holy_father/pius_xii/speeches.

Ramírez, Manuel Ceballos. *El catolicismo social: Un tercero en discordia. Rerum Novarum, la "cuestión social" y la movilización de los católicos mexicanos (1891–1911).* Mexico City: El Colegio de México, 1991.

Ramphal, Shridath S. "Human Development: Defining the Problem." In *Human Development through Social Change: Proceedings of St. Francis Xavier University's International Symposium Commemorating the Fiftieth Anniversary of the Antigonish Movement, 1928–1978, Antigonish, Nova Scotia, Canada,* edited by Philip Milner. Antigonish, N.S.: Formac Publishing Co., 1979.

Rangel, Yolanda Padilla. *Los desterrados: Exiliados católicos de la Revolución Mexicana en Texas, 1914–1919.* Aguascalientes: Universidad Autónoma de Aguascalientes, 2009.

Recinos, Adrián. *Monografía del Departamento de Huehuetenango.* 2nd edition. Guatemala City: Editorial del Ministerio de Educación Pública, 1954.

Redinger, Matthew A. *American Catholics and the Mexican Revolution, 1924–1936.* Notre Dame, Ind.: University of Notre Dame Press, 2005.

Reese, Thomas. *Inside the Vatican: The Politics and Organization of the Catholic Church.* Cambridge, Mass.: Harvard University Press, 1998.

Reis, Daniel Aarão. *Ditadura militar, esquerdas e sociedade.* 3rd edition. Rio de Janeiro: Jorge Zahar Editor, 2000.

Reis, João José. *Death is a Festival: Funeral Rites and Rebellion in Nineteenth-Century Brazil.* Durham, N.C.: Duke University Press, 2003.

Repositorio Institucional de la Universidad Católica Andres Bello. "Radio occidente." *http://saber.ucab.edu.ve/handle/123456789/31207?show=full.*

Rhodes, Rita. *Empire and Co-operation: How the British Empire Used Co-operatives in Its Development Strategies, 1900–1970.* Edinburgh: John Donald, 2012.

Richardson, Kim. *Quebra-Quilos and Peasant Resistance: Peasants, Religion and Politics in Nineteenth-Century Brazil.* Lanham, Md.: University Press of America, 2011.

Ricoeur, Paul. *Memory, History, Forgetting.* Trans. Kathleen Blamey and David Pellauer. Chicago: The University of Chicago Press, 2004.

Ritual de la Adoración Nocturna Mexicana: Segunda parte del reglamento. Mexico City: Imprenta J. I. Muñoz, 1924.

Rius Facius, Antonio. *México Cristero.* Mexico City: Editorial Patria, 1966.

Rodgers, Daniel T. *Atlantic Crossings: Social Politics in a Progressive Age.* Cambridge, Mass.: Harvard University Press, 1998.

Rodríguez Rosa, Antonio. *La Revolución sin sangre: El Cooperativismo.* Mexico City: B. Costa-Amic Editor, 1964.

Rodríguez, Pedro Fernández. *Biografía de un hombre providencial: Monseñor Luis María Martínez.* Mexico City: Editorial Seminario Conciliar de México, 2003.

Rojas V., Belkis A. "CORANDES desde la perspectiva de una historia de vida." *CAYAPA: Revista Venezolana de Economía Social* 1, no. 1 (May 2001): 1–11.

Roldán, Mary. *Blood and Fire: La Violencia in Antioquia, Colombia, 1946–1953*. Durham, N.C.: Duke University Press, 2002.

Rosas, Clemente. *Praia do Flamengo, 132: Crônica do Movimento Estudantil nos Anos 1961–1962*. Recife: FUNDARPE, 1992.

Routhier, Gilles, and Axel Maugey. *Eglise du Québec, Eglise de France: Cent ans d'histoire*. Ottawa: Novalis, 2006.

Rubenstein, Anne. *Bad Language, Naked Ladies, and Other Threats to the Nation: A Political History of Comic Books in Mexico*. Durham, N.C.: Duke University Press, 1998.

Rubin, Miri. *Corpus Christi: The Eucharist in Late Medieval Culture*. Cambridge: Cambridge University Press, 1992.

Rubin, Sergio, and Francesca Ambrogetti. *El papa Francesco: Conversaciones con Jorge Bergoglio*. Barcelona: Ediciones B, S.A., 2013.

Rudolph, Susanne Hoeber. "Introduction: Religion, States, and Transnational Civil Society." In *Transnational Religion and Fading States*, edited by Susanne Hoeber Rudolph and P. Piscatori, 1–24. Boulder, Colo.: Westview Press, 1997.

Rudqvist, Anders. "La Organizacion Campesina y la Izquierda: ANUC en Colombia 1970–1980." *Informes de Investigación*, no. 1 (1983): 1–27.

Ruff, Mark Edward. *The Wayward Flock: Catholic Youth in Postwar West Germany*. Chapel Hill: University of North Carolina Press, 2005.

Rupp, Leila J. *Worlds of Women: The Making of an International Women's Movement*. Princeton, N.J.: Princeton University Press, 1997.

Rural Life in the Light of "Mater et Magistra." Proceedings of the International Meeting of Catholics on Rural Life, Rome, September 3–9, 1962. Rome: Libereria Editrice Ancora, 1962.

Ryan, Edwin. "A Catholic Pan-American Society." *America* 45, no. 26 (October 3, 1931): 611.

Sackley, Nicole. "The Village as Cold War Site: Experts, Development, and the History of Rural Reconstruction." *Journal of Global History* 6, no. 3 (November 2011): 481–504.

Salcedo, José Joaquin. "Educación del campesino por la radio." Presentation given at the Primer Congreso Católico Latinoamericano Sobre Problemas de la Vida Rural. Manizales, Colombia: Imprenta Departamental, 1953.

Samandu, Luis, Hans Siebers, and Oscar Sierra. *Guatemala: Retos de la Iglesia Católica en una Sociedad en Crisis*. San José, Costa Rica: Editorial Departamento Ecuménico de Investigaciones DEI, 1990.

Sanabria, José Rubén, and Mauricio Beuchot. *Historia de la filosofía cristiana en México*. Mexico City: Universidad Iberoamericana, 1994.

Santillán, Martha. "Discurso de redomesticación femenina durante los procesos modernizadores en México, 1946–1958." *Historia y Grafía*, no. 31 (2008): 103–32.

Sappia, Caroline. "Le Collège pour l'Amérique latine de Louvain et son ancrage au Brésil: Outil d'un projet d'Eglise, 1953–1983." PhD diss., Université catholique de Louvain, 2013.

Sappia, Caroline, and Olivier Servais, eds. *Mission et engagement politique après 1945: Afrique, Amérique Latine, Europe*. Paris: Editions Karthala, 2010.

Sappia, Caroline, and Paul Servais, eds. *Les relations de Louvain avec l'Amérique latine: Entre évangelisation, théologie de la libération et mouvements étudiants.* Louvain-la-neuve: Académie Bruylant, 2006.

Sappia, Caroline. "Le Collège pour l'Amérique latine de Louvain et son ancrage au Brésil: Outil d'un projet d'Eglise, 1953–1983." Phd diss., Université catholique de Louvain, 2013.

Schell, Patience. "An Honorable Avocation for Ladies: The Work of the Mexico City Unión de Damas Católicas Mexicanas, 1912–1926." *Journal of Women's History* 10, no. 4 (1999): 78–103.

Scheman, L. Ronald, ed. *The Alliance for Progress: A Retrospective.* New York: Praeger Publishers, 1988.

Schlesinger, Stephen C., and Stephen Kinzer. *Bitter Fruit: The Untold Story of the American Coup in Guatemala.* Garden City, N.Y.: Doubleday, 1982.

Schloesser, Stephen. *Jazz Age Catholicism: Mystic Modernism in Postwar Paris, 1919–1933.* Toronto: University of Toronto Press, 2005.

Schwaller, John Frederick. *The History of the Catholic Church in Latin America: From Conquest to Revolution and Beyond.* New York: New York University Press, 2011.

Scribner, Bob. "Anticlericalism and the Cities." In *Anticlericalism in Late Medieval and Early Modern Europe*, edited by Peter A. Dykema and Heiko A. Oberman, 147–66. Leiden: E.J. Brill, 1993.

Second General Conference of Latin American Bishops. *The Church in the Present-Day Transformation of Latin America in the Light of the Council*, Volume 2, *Conclusions.* Washington, D.C., USCC—Division for Latin America, 1970–1973.

Seigel, Micol. "Beyond Compare: Comparative Method after the Transnational Turn." *Radical History Review* 91 (Winter 2005): 62–90.

Septién, Valentina Torres. *La educación privada en México (1903–1976).* Mexico City: El Colegio de México/Universidad Iberoamericana, 1997.

Septién, Valentina Torres, and Leonor Magaña. "Belleza reflejada: El ideal de la belleza femenina en el discurso de la Iglesia, 1920–1970." *Historia y Grafia*, no. 19 (2002): 55–87.

Serbin, Kenneth P. "State Subsidization of Catholic Institutions in Brazil, 1930–1964." Working Paper 181, Helen Kellogg Institute for International Studies, University of Notre Dame, 1992.

———. *Secret Dialogues: Church-State Relations, Torture, and Social Justice in Authoritarian Brazil.* Pittsburgh, Penn.: University of Pittsburgh Press, 2000.

———. *Needs of the Heart: A Social and Cultural History of Brazil's Clergy and Seminaries.* Notre Dame, Ind.: University of Notre Dame Press, 2006.

Serrano, Sol. *¿Qué hacer con Dios en la República?: Política y secularización en Chile (1845–1885).* Santiago, Chile: Fondo de Cultura Económica, 2008.

Sharpe, Kenneth Evan. *Peasant Politics: Struggle in a Dominican Village.* Baltimore: Johns Hopkins University Press, 1977.

Sheehy, Maurice S. *Selected Broadcasts.* Published in cooperation with the Council for Democracy. Silver Spring, Md.: Cornelius Printing, 1941.

Sigmund, Paul E. *Liberation Theology at the Crossroads: Democracy or Revolution?* Oxford: Oxford University Press, 1990.

Silva, Candido da Costa e. *Os segadores e a messe: O clero oitocentista na Bahia*. Salvador: Secretaria da Cultura e do Turismo and EDUFBA, 2000.

———. "Os segadores: The Continuing Importance of the Latin American Seminary in Rome is Chronicled." In *Como se faz um bispo: Segundo o alto e o baixo clero*, edited by J. D. Vital. Rio de Janeiro: Civilização Brasileira, 2012.

Skidmore, Thomas E. *Politics in Brazil 1930–1964: An Experiment in Democracy*. 40th anniversary edition. Oxford: Oxford University Press, 2007.

———. *The Politics of Military Rule in Brazil 1964–1985*. Oxford: Oxford University Press, 1988.

Smallman, Shawn C. *Fear and Memory in the Brazilian Army and Society, 1889–1954*. Chapel Hill: University of North Carolina Press, 2002.

Smith, Brian H. *The Church and Politics in Chile: Challenges to Modern Catholicism*. Princeton, N.J.: Princeton University Press, 1982.

Smith, Christian. *The Emergence of Liberation Theology: Radical Religion and Social Movement Theory*. Chicago: The University of Chicago Press, 1991.

Smith, Stephanie J. *Gender and the Mexican Revolution: Yucatán Women and the Realities of Patriarchy*. Chapel Hill: University of North Carolina Press, 2009.

Smith, Tony. *America's Mission: The United States and the Worldwide Struggle for Democracy*. Princeton, N.J.: Princeton University Press, 2012.

Snider, Colin M. "'Education for Development': Educational Reform and Presidential Policies in Democratic and Military Regimes in Brazil," unpublished manuscript.

———. "Complicated Campuses: Universities, Middle-Class Politics, and State-Society Relations in Brazil, 1955–1990." PhD diss., University of New Mexico, 2011.

Solis, Yves. "Asociación espiritual o masonería católica: La U." *Istor* 33, no. 9 (Summer 2008): 121–37.

———. "El orígen de la ultraderecha en México: La U." *El Cotidiano* 23, no. 149 (2008): 25–38.

———. "Religión y política en secretos." In *La cuestión social, N. 3–4, Catolicismo social y bicentenario*, Año 18, VII–XII, 346–60. Mexico City: IMDOSOC, 2010.

Souza, Jessie Jane Vieira de. *Círculos Operários: A Igreja Católica e o mundo do trabalho no Brasil*. Rio de Janeiro: Editora UFRJ and FAPERJ, 2002.

Souza, Luiz Alberto Gomes de. *A JUC, os estudantes católicos e a política*. Petrópolis: Editora Vozes, 1984.

Souza, Wlaumir Doniseti de. *Anarquismo, estado e pastoral do imigrante: Das disputas ideológicas pelo imigrante aos limites da ordem: O caso Idalina*. São Paulo: Unesp, 2000.

Spivak, Gayatri Chakravorty. *A Critique of Postcolonial Reason: Towards a History of the Vanishing Present*. Cambridge, Mass.: Harvard University Press, 1999.

Steele, Harvey. *Winds of Change: Social Justice through Co-operatives: Evaluation of Co-operatives in Latin America and the Caribbean*. Truro, N.S.: Cooperative Resources, 1986.

———. *Dear Old Rebel: A Priest's Battle for Social Justice*. Lawrencetown Beach, N.S.: Pottersfield Press, 1993.

Steger, Manfred B. *Globalization: A Brief Insight*. New York: Sterling, 2010.

Stern, Steve J. *Remembering Pinochet's Chile: On the Eve of London, 1998*. Durham, N.C.: Duke University Press, 2004.

Stewart-Gambino, Hannah W. *The Church and Politics in the Chilean Countryside.* Boulder, Colo.: Westview Press, 1992.

Streeter, Stephen M. "Nation-Building in the Land of Eternal Counter-insurgency: Guatemala and the Contradictions of the Alliance for Progress." *Third World Quarterly* 27, no. 1 (2006): 57–68.

Suárez, L. A. "Cooperatives in Puerto Rico: History, Problems, Research." *Rural Sociology* 18, no. 3 (September 1953): 226–33.

Superintendencia Nacional de Cooperativas (SUNACOOP), Ministerio para la Economía Popular (Venezuela). "Informe de la República Bolivariana de Venezuela: Cooperativismo en Venezuela," April 2006.

Swanson, R. N. *The Twelfth-Century Renaissance.* Manchester, England: Manchester University Press, 1999.

Sylvain, Charles. *Vie du R. P. Hermann, en religion Augustin-Marie du T.-S.-Sacrament, Carme Déchaussé.* Paris: Librairie H. Oudin, 1883.

Taffet, Jeffrey F. *Foreign Aid as Foreign Policy: The Alliance for Progress in Latin America.* New York: Routledge, 2007.

Taracena, Alfredo. *Francisco I. Madero: Biografía.* Mexico City: Editorial Porrúa, 1973.

Tavares, Luis Fernando Bernal. *Los católicos y la política en México.* Mexico City: Milestone, 2006.

Taylor, Zachary C. *The Rise and Progress of Baptist Missions in Brazil: An Autobiography.* Unpublished manuscript. Richmond: Foreign Mission Board Archives, n.d. [1916].

Tinsman, Heidi. *Partners in Conflict: The Politics of Gender, Sexuality, and Labor in the Chilean Agrarian Reform, 1950–1973.* Durham, N.C.: Duke University Press, 2002.

Torres Restrepo, Camilo, and Berta Corredor Rodriguez. *Las Escuelas Radiofonicas de Sutatenza, Colombia: Evaluacion sociologica de los resultados.* Oficina Internacional de Investigaciones Sociales de FERES, Friburgo y Bogotá. Madrid: Sucesores de Rivadeneyra S.A., 1961.

The U.S. National Commission for UNESCO. UNESCO World Review. UNESCO Relations Staff Department of State. Release 3-R, March 5, 1949. Washington, D.C.: U.S. National Commission for UNESCO, 1949.

United States Catholic Conference. *Basic Christian Communities.* LADOC Keyhole Series no. 14. Washington, D.C.: U.S. Catholic Conference, 1976.

van der Linden, Marcel. *Workers of the World: Essays Toward a Global Labor History.* Leiden: Brill, 2008.

Van Osselar, Tine. "Christening Masculinity? Catholic Action and Men in Interwar Belgium." *Gender and History* 21, no. 2 (2009): 380–401.

———. "'Heroes of the Heart': Ideal Men in the Sacred Heart Devotion." *Journal of Men, Masculinities, and Spirituality* 3, no. 1 (2009): 22–40.

———. "'From That Moment On, I Was a Man!' Images of the Catholic Male in the Sacred Heart Devotion." In *Gender and Christianity in Modern Europe: Beyond the Feminization Thesis,* edited by Patrick Pasture, Jan Art, and Thomas Buerman, 121–35. Leuven: University of Leuven Press, 2012.

Vásquez, Manuel A., and Marie Friedmann Marquardt. *Globalizing the Sacred: Religion across the Americas.* New Brunswick, N.J.: Rutgers University Press, 2003.

Vekemans, Roger, ed. *La tierra y el hombre: Cuarto congreso católico de la vida rural.* Buenos Aires: Talleres Gráficos del Atlantico, 1958.

Ventresca, Robert A. *Soldier of Christ: The Life of Pope Pius XII.* Cambridge, Mass.: Harvard University Press, 2013.

Verbitsky, Horacio. *El silencio: De Paulo VI a Bergoglio: Las relaciones secretas de la Iglesia con la ESMA.* 3rd edition. Buenos Aires: Editorial Sudamericana, 2005.

Vértiz, Julio J. *Su mensaje a la juventud.* Mexico City: CEM, 1959.

Vieira, David Gueiros. "Protestantism and the Religious Question in Brazil: 1850–1875." PhD diss., American University, 1972.

Vierba, Ezer. "The Committee's Report: Punishment, Power and Subject in Twentieth-Century Panama." PhD diss., Yale University, 2013.

Villegas Moreno, Gloria. "Estado e Iglesia en los tiempos revolucionarios." In *Relaciones Estado-Iglesia: Encuentros y desencuentros,* edited by Patricia Galeana, 183–204. Mexico City: Archivo General de la Nación-Secretaría de Relaciones Exteriores México, 1999.

Vital, J. D. *Como se faz um bispo: Segundo o alto e o baixo clero.* Rio de Janeiro: Civilização Brasileira, 2012.

Warren, Kay B. *The Symbolism of Subordination: Indian Identity in a Guatemalan Town.* Austin: University of Texas Press, 1978.

Watanabe, John M. *Maya Saints and Souls in a Changing World.* Austin: University of Texas Press, 1992.

Welter, Barbara. "The Feminization of American Religion: 1800–1860." In *Clio's Consciousness Raised: New Perspectives on the History of Women,* edited by Mary Hartman and Lois Banner, 137–57. New York: Harper and Row, 1974.

Welton, Michael R. *Little Mosie from the Margaree: A Biography of Moses Michael Coady.* Toronto: Thompson Educational Publishing, 2001.

Werner, Yvonne Maria, ed. *Christian Masculinity: Men and Religion in Northern Europe in the Nineteenth and Twentieth Centuries.* Leuven: University of Leuven Press, 2011.

Wright-Rios, Edward. *Revolutions in Mexican Catholicism: Reform and Revelation in Oaxaca, 1887–1934.* Durham, N.C.: Duke University Press, 2009.

———. "La Madre Matiana: Prophetess and Nation in Mexican Satire." *The Americas* 68, no. 2 (2011): 241–74.

Xidieh, Oswaldo Elias. *Narrativas pias populares.* São Paulo: Instituto de Estudos Brasileiros, 1962.

Yáñez Delgado, Alfonso. *La manipulación de la fe: Fúas contra Carolinos en la Universidad Poblana.* Puebla, Mexico: Benemérita Universidad Autónoma de Puebla, 1996.

Yeager, Gertrude M. "In the Absence of Priests: Young Women as Apostles to the Poor, Chile 1922–1932." *The Americas* 64, no. 2 (October 2007): 207–42.

Zemon Davis, Natalie. *Sociedad y cultura en la Francia moderna.* Barcelona: Ediciones Crítica, 1993.

Contributors

STEPHEN J. C. ANDES is an assistant professor of Latin American history at Louisiana State University. He specializes in the Mexican Catholic Church, as well as in Vatican policy toward Latin America. Andes is the author of *The Vatican and Catholic Activism in Mexico and Chile: The Politics of Transnational Catholicism 1920–1940*.

DAIN BORGES is an associate professor of Latin American history at the University of Chicago. His current research project, Races, Crowds, and Souls in Brazilian Social Thought, 1880–1920, centers on the ways in which Brazilian intellectuals used race sociology and social psychology to understand popular religion and politics. He is the author of *The Family in Bahia, Brazil, 1870–1945*.

MATTHEW BUTLER is an associate professor of modern Mexican history at the University of Texas, Austin. His research examines the religious history of twentieth-century Mexico. He is the author of *Popular Piety and Political Identity in Mexico's Cristero Rebellion: Michoacán, 1927–1929*, and editor of *Faith and Impiety in Revolutionary Mexico*.

ROBERT CURLEY is a professor of history and the chair of the Departamento de Estudios Sociourbanos at the Universidad de Guadalajara. His primary area of research is on public Catholicism in the Mexican revolution. His book *A Plebiscite of Martyrs: Political Catholicism in Revolutionary Mexico, 1900–1926* is forthcoming.

LISA M. EDWARDS is an associate professor of history at the University of Massachusetts, Lowell. Her current research examines the early history of the Chilean Conservative Party. She is the author of *Roman Virtues: The Education of Latin American Clergy in Rome, 1858–1962*.

SUSAN FITZPATRICK-BEHRENS is a professor of history at California State University, Northridge. Her research focuses on transnational religious missionaries and their role in the social, political, and economic development of Peru and Guatemala. She is the author of *The Maryknoll Catholic Mission in Peru, 1943–1989: Transnational Faith and Transformations*; and coeditor with Manuel Vasquez and David Orique of *The Oxford Handbook of Christianity in Latin America* (forthcoming).

CATHERINE C. LEGRAND is an associate professor of history at McGill University. Her research focuses on the agrarian, social, and cultural history of Latin

America in the nineteenth and twentieth centuries and cultural aspects of U.S. and Canadian relations with Latin America. Her books include *Frontier Expansion and Peasant Protest in Colombia, 1850–1936*, and *Close Encounters of Empire: Writing the Cultural History of U.S.-Latin American Relations*, coedited with Gilbert M. Joseph and Ricardo D. Salvatore.

JAIME M. PENSADO is the Carl E. Koch associate professor of history, director of the Mexico Working Group, and fellow of the Kellogg Institute for International Studies and Institute for Latin Studies (ILS) at the University of Notre Dame. He specializes in contemporary Mexican history, student movements, youth culture, and the cold war. He is the author of *Rebel Mexico: Student Unrest and Authoritarian Political Culture during the Long Sixties*.

MARY ROLDÁN is the Dorothy Epstein chair in Latin American history at Hunter College and a faculty appointment in Latin American history at the Graduate Center (CUNY). Her research interests include nineteenth- and twentieth-century Latin American history; the social and political history of Colombia; violence, state formation, regional politics; and radio, media, and urban history. She is the author of *Blood and Fire: La Violencia in Antioquia, Colombia, 1946–1953*.

YVES SOLIS is the academic coordinator at the Prepa Ibero at the Universidad Iberoamericana and a member of Mexico's National System of Researchers, Level I. His research focuses on the history of the Catholic Church in Mexico; the Catholic Church, the state, and civil society in Mexico; and secret Catholic societies, including La "U" in Mexico. He is the editor of the book *El anticlericalismo en Europa y América Latina: Una visión transatlántica*, coedited with Franco Savarino.

COLIN M. SNIDER is an assistant professor in Latin American history at the University of Texas, Tyler. He has written on student movements in Brazil, presidential regimes, educational policy, and Catholic activism in Brazilian universities. He is the author of "'A More Systemic Fight for Reform': University Reform, Student Movements, Society, and the State in Brazil, 1957–1968," in *The Third World in the Global Sixties*, ed. Samantha Christiansen and Zachary Scarlett.

JULIA G. YOUNG is an assistant professor of Latin American history at the Catholic University of America. Her current research focuses on transnational religious movements in twentieth-century Mexico and Latin America. She is the author of *Mexican Exodus: Emigrants, Exiles, and Refugees of the Cristero War*.

Index

Abascal, Adalberto, 124, 127
Abascal, Carlos, 127
Abascal, Salvador, 126–27
abolitionism, 30–32
ACPO. *See* Popular Cultural Action
Adames, Roque (bishop of Santiago), 229
Aeterni patris (Leo XIII), 17
Aguilar, Cándido, 103–4
Aguirre Mantecón, José, 140
Alacoque, Margaret Mary, 60–61
Alarcón, Mario Sandoval, 303
Alliance for Progress: collaboration with church, 239, 298–99; cooperatives, Antigonish Movement, and, 219–21, 228, 239, 282; del Valle and, 160; in Ecuador, 231–32; in Guatemala, 295, 300; innovation in development, 221n29; introduction and implementation of, 216, 297; in Venezuela, 234, 236
Alvarez, David, 117
Álvarez Tostado, Rosario de, 87
Amaro, Joaquín, 103
American Federation of Catholic Societies, 97n13
American Foundation for Popular Cultural Action, 272–73n62
Andes, Stephen J. C., xxiv–xxv, 20, 57, 119, 214, 226
Andrade Valderrama, Vicente, 255, 261, 263
ANM. *See* Mexican Nocturnal Adoration
anticlericalism: in Brazil, 22–23, 30; in Guatemala, 277; in Mexico, 71, 101, 120–21; traditional violence associated with, 103. *See also* Mexican Revolution
Antigonish Movement, xxvii, 207–9,

236–42, 283; in Asia and Africa, 237n70; Christian social action and Liberation theology, 219, 222–36; community development, 218–21; continued impact of, 242–43; the development decade, the Coady Institute and, 216–18; in the Dominican Republic, 229; early Latin American networks, 211–16; in Ecuador, 231–33; in Guatemala, 230–31, 276; in Honduras, 224–26; in Maranhão, Brazil, 224; in Mexico, 226–28; in Panama, 228–29; religious foundations, 209–11; socialist leanings, accusation of, 221n32; in Venezuela, 233–36. *See also* Coady, Moses
AP. *See* Popular Action
Apostolado da Oração, 40–41, 47
Arana, Francisco, 278
Aranha, Oswaldo, 257
Arantes, Aldo, 192–94
Araújo, Áurea de, 194
Arbenz Guzmán, Jacobo, 278, 287, 289, 294
Arévalo, Juan José, 278–80, 287
Argentina, xiin1,12, 16–17
Argüelles, Samuel, 72
Ariel (Rodó), 165n
Arrayales, Aurora, 159
Arrom, Silvia, 135
Asher, Robert, 259
Asselin, Victor, 224n37
Association of Catholic Ladies, xxiv
Azuela, Mariano, 177
Azzellini, Dario, 243

Balduino, Thomas, 224n37
Barbosa, Rui, 30
Barillas Izaguirre, Roberto, 280–82

❖ *Local Church, Global Church: Catholic Activism in Latin America from* Rerum Novarum *to Vatican II* was designed in Scala Pro with Meta Pro display type and composed by Kachergis Book Design of Pittsboro, North Carolina. It was printed on 60-pound Natures Natural and bound by Thomson-Shore of Dexter, Michigan.